SEVEN PILLARS OF WISDOM

SEVEN PILLARS
OF WISDOM

a triumph

T. E. LAWRENCE

VOLUME I

THE REPRINT SOCIETY
LONDON

facing: AUTHOR]

FIRST PUBLISHED 1935

NEW EDITION 1939
PUBLISHED BY THE REPRINT SOCIETY LTD.
BY ARRANGEMENT WITH
JONATHAN CAPE LTD.

PRINTED IN GREAT BRITAIN IN THE CITY OF OXFORD
AT THE ALDEN PRESS
PAPER BY JOHN DICKINSON & CO. LTD.

To S.A.

I loved you, so I drew these tides of men into my hands
    and wrote my will across the sky in stars
To earn you Freedom, the seven pillared worthy house,
    that your eyes might be shining for me
                When we came.

Death seemed my servant on the road, till we were near
    and saw you waiting:
When you smiled, and in sorrowful envy he outran me
    and took you apart:
                Into his quietness.

Love, the way-weary, groped to your body, our brief wage
    ours for the moment
Before earth's soft hand explored your shape, and the blind
    worms grew fat upon
                Your substance.

Men prayed me that I set our work, the inviolate house,
    as a memory of you.
But for fit monument I shattered it, unfinished: and now
The little things creep out to patch themselves hovels
    in the marred shadow
                Of your gift.

Mr. Geoffrey Dawson persuaded All Souls College to give me leisure, in 1919-1920, to write about the Arab Revolt. Sir Herbert Baker let me live and work in his Westminster houses.

The book so written passed in 1921 into proof: where it was fortunate in the friends who criticized it. Particularly it owes its thanks to Mr. and Mrs. Bernard Shaw for countless suggestions of great value and diversity: and for all the present semicolons.

It does not pretend to be impartial. I was fighting for my hand, upon my own midden. Please take it as a personal narrative pieced out of memory. I could not make proper notes: indeed it would have been a breach of my duty to the Arabs if I had picked such flowers while they fought. My superior officers, Wilson, Joyce, Dawnay, Newcombe and Davenport could each tell a like tale. The same is true of Stirling, Young, Lloyd and Maynard: of Buxton and Winterton: of Ross, Stent and Siddons: of Peake, Hornby, Scott-Higgins and Garland: of Wordie, Bennett and MacIndoe: of Bassett, Scott, Goslett, Wood and Gray: of Hinde, Spence and Bright: of Brodie and Pascoe, Gilman and Grisenthwaite, Greenhill, Dowsett and Wade: of Henderson, Leeson, Makins and Nunan.

And there were many other leaders or lonely fighters to whom this self-regardant picture is not fair. It is still less fair, of course, like all war-stories, to the un-named rank and file: who miss their share of credit, as they must do, until they can write the despatches.

T. E. S.

Cranwell, 15.8.26

SYNOPSIS

HALF-WAY through the labour of an index to this book I re-called the practice of my ten years' study of history; and realized I had never used the index* of a book fit to read. Who would insult his *Decline and Fall*, by consulting it just upon a specific point?

I am aware that my achievement as a writer falls short of every conception of the readable: but surely not so far as to make it my duty, like a Stubbs, to save readers the pain of an unnecessary page. The contents seem to me adequately finger-posted by this synopsis.

INTRODUCTION

THE FOUNDATIONS OF ARAB REVOLT

Some Englishmen, of whom Kitchener was chief, believed that a rebellion of Arabs against Turks would enable England, while fighting Germany, simultaneously to defeat her ally Turkey. Their knowledge of the nature and power and country of the Arabic-speaking peoples made them think that the issue of such a rebellion would be happy: and indicated its character and method. So they allowed it to begin, having obtained formal assurances of help for it from the British Government. Yet none the less the rebellion of the Sherif of Mecca came to most as a surprise, and found the Allies unready. It aroused mixed feelings and made strong friends and enemies, amid whose clashing jealousies its affairs began to miscarry.

Chapter 1. — The strained mentality of rebellion (27) which infected me (28) and still, a year afterwards, prevents my judgement (29).

Chapter 2. — Arabia and the Arabs (31) emigrations, immigrations, and the current of tribal movements (33) sessile or nomad (34-35).

Chapter 3. — The uncompromising Semite (36) religious invention (37) his prophets (37) his creeds (38) his fanaticism (40-1).

Chapter 4. — Arab decay (43) nationalism (44) secret societies (45).

Chapter 5. — Sherifs of Mecca (48) the Holy War (49) thoughts of rebellion (50) Feisal and Jemal (51) Enver (52) the revolt (53).

Chapter 6. — The decay of Turkish imperialism (54) a new factor required (56) Clayton's Arab Bureau (56) Mesopotamia (58-60).

Chapter 7. — The McMahon negotiations (61) his difficulties with his colleagues (61) my private difficulties (62-3) an escape (63).

* An index has been added to this edition.

7

BOOK I

MY FIRST VISIT TO ARABIA

I had believed these misfortunes of the Revolt to be due to faulty leadership, or rather to the lack of leadership, Arab and English. So I went down to Arabia to see and consider its great men. The first, the Sherif of Mecca, we knew to be aged. I found Abdulla too clever, Ali too clean, Zeid too cool. Then I rode up-country to Feisal, and found in him the leader with the necessary fire, and yet with reason to give effect to our science. His tribesmen seemed sufficient instrument, and his hills to provide natural advantage. So I returned confidently to Egypt, and told my chiefs how Mecca was defended not by Rabegh, but by Feisal in Jebel Subh.

Chapter 8. — The *Lama* arrives at Jedda (65) Colonel Wilson welcomes Storrs and myself (66) Emir Abdulla (67) Arab government (68) military situation (69) Storrs persuasive (71).

Chapter 9. — Jeddah (72) a dinner party (74) the Turkish band (75).

Chapter 10. — Emir Ali at Rabegh (76) we ride inland (78) the Tehama and a discussion of water-supplies as affecting Arab strategy (80) encounter at a well (81) tricks of a Sherif (82).

Chapter 11. — Hills of Hejaz (84) Bir el Sheikh (85) highlands by night (86) a spy gives us food (87) a watered village (88).

Chapter 12. — Slave economy (90) a ruined village (91) the rebels (91) my first meeting with the Emir Feisal at Hamra (92).

Chapter 13. — Egyptian troops (93) Feisal's story of his first outbreak in Medina (94) his plans for the moment (97) himself (97-99).

Chapter 14. — A political dinner (100) the royal family of Hejaz (100) nationalism among nomads and townsmen (101) religion (103).

Chapter 15. — Playing the reporter (104) the troops and their native way of fighting (105) the situation (106) artillery (107) envoi (108).

Chapter 16. — The ruined road (109) in Wadi Yenbo (110) Yenbo, Boyle, and hats (111) Admiral Wemyss (111-112) Khartoum, where we argue the Arab Revolt with Sir Reginald Wingate (113) a French idea (113) Sir Archibald Murray (114) I am good (115).

BOOK II

FEISAL'S FIRST EXTENSION NORTHWARD

My chiefs were astonished at such favourable news, but promised help, and meanwhile sent me back, much against my will, into Arabia. I reached Feisal's camp on the day the Turks carried the defences of Jebel Subh. By their so doing the entire basis of my confidence in a tribal war was destroyed. We havered for a while by Yenbo, hoping to retrieve the position: but the tribesmen proved to be useless for assault, and we saw that if the Revolt was to endure we must invent a new plan of campaign at once. This was hazardous, as the promised British military experts had not yet arrived. However, we decided that to regain the initiative we must ignore the main body of the enemy, and concentrate far off on his railway flank. The first step towards this was to move our base to Wejh: which we proceeded to do in the grand manner.

Chapter 17. — Clayton sends me back (117) Garland (117) Yenbo (119).

Chapter 18. — Sherif Abd el Kerim's riding manners (120) a surprise on our road (121) Feisal's explanation of his move (122).

Chapter 19. — Feisal's control (125) life at Arab headquarters (126).

Chapter 20. — My new clothes (129) return to Yenbo (130) a defeat (131) treachery, perhaps (132) defending our base (133).

Chapter 21. — Conflicting policies (135) French and English (136) the military situation develops (137) Wilson gambles on it (138).

Chapter 22. — Feisal prepares to move on Wejh (140) troops for his expedition (141) a test raid (142) the Emir Abdulla (143).

Chapter 23. — The army marches (144) naval politics (145) civil v. military (146) evacuation of Yenbo (147-48) my relief (148) Boyle at Um Lejj (148) Wejh plans (148) too forward (149).

Chapter 24. — Feisal's staff (150) the routine of a march (151) Ageyl (152) Newcombe overtakes us (154) the route (155).

Chapter 25. — Our units (157) good news (159) Wadi Hamdh (162).

Chapter 26. — Reinforcements pour in (164) the Navy again (166).

Chapter 27. — Boyle's victory (168) we re-organize Wejh (169).

A*

BOOK III

CONCENTRATING AGAINST THE MEDINA RAILWAY

Our taking Wejh had the wished effect upon the Turks, who abandoned their advance towards Mecca for a passive defence of Medina and its Railway. Our experts made plans for attacking them. The Germans saw the danger of envelopment, and persuaded Enver to order the instant evacuation of Medina. Sir Archibald Murray begged us to put in such a sustained attack as should destroy the retreating enemy. Feisal was soon ready in his part; and I went off to Abdulla to get his co-operation. On the way I fell sick and while lying alone with empty hands was driven to think about the campaign. Thinking convinced me that recent practice had been better than our theory. So on recovery I did little to the Railway, but went back to Wejh with novel ideas. I tried to make the others admit them, and adopt deployment as our ruling principle; and to put preaching even before fighting. They preferred the limited and direct military objective of Medina. So I decided to slip off to Akaba by myself on test of my own theory.

Chapter 28. — Rewards of victory (171) the need of guns (171) Jaafar Pasha takes command (172) Bremond's proposal (172-3).

Chapter 29. — Life at Wejh (175) armoured cars and navy (176-77).

Chapter 30. — The general war (178) political work (178) Feisal's propaganda (179) and the quality of his achievement (180-81).

Chapter 31. — Clayton's bombshell (182) new dispositions (183) journey inland (183) sickness (186) a death for a death (187).

Chapter 32. — In the hills (188) lava and volcanoes grown cold (190) implacable hostility (190) Emir Abdulla's camp (192).

Chapter 33. — Generalizing the military theory of our revolt (193).

Chapter 34. — Recovery (203) projecting a raid (204) a shepherd (205) fresh plans (207) mine-laying (208) a show (209).

Chapter 35. — Shakir's triumph (210) another raid (211) a storm (212) mine-laying (213) the alarm (215) getting away (217).

Chapter 36. — Emir Abdulla, nature and life (219) Shakir (221-22).

Chapter 37. — Starting for Wejh (223) Beduin characters (224).

Chapter 38. — Feisal again (228) Auda abu Tayi (229) the ruling strategy (231) my criticisms (232) the Akaba scheme (233).

BOOK IV

THE EXPEDITION AGAINST AKABA

Sherif Nasir, Auda, and I set off together for Akaba. Hitherto Feisal had been the public leader; but his remaining in Wejh threw the ungrateful load of this northern expedition upon myself. I accepted it and its dishonest implication as our only means of victory. We tricked the Turks and entered Akaba with good fortune.

Chapter 39. – Our start (235) ourselves (235) Sherif Nasir and his great worthiness (237) a hill-garden (238) interlude (239).

Chapter 40. – Arabic speech (240) our assumptions (241) a pause which relieves my weariness (243) two new men (244).

Chapter 41. – Off again (245) Auda as guide (246) night (247) volcanoes, lava, dry mud and sand (248) camel sickness (250).

Chapter 42. – Crossing the railway (251) into the real desert (253) a hot wind (254) the refreshment of nightfall, after (255).

Chapter 43. – A new day (256) camels (258) ostrich and oryx (259).

Chapter 44. – A man missing (260) alone (260) a joke overworked (264) we win across into Sirhan (264) the power of thirst (264).

Chapter 45. – The new wells (265) an alarm (267) we arrive (270).

Chapter 46. –We taste the full measure of Beduin hospitality (271).

Chapter 47. –With the tribes (276) snakes (277) recruits (279).

Chapter 48. – Over-vaulting ambition (280) true objective (281) false starts (282) my dilemma (282-83) a footnote to history (283) unwelcome power (284) the last feast (284) small talk (285-86).

Chapter 49. – On the road (288) dynamite (290) a poor job (291).

Chapter 50. – A diversion to draw the Turks' notice (293) ambush (295) deserters (296) Zaal's power and my self-denial (297).

Chapter 51. – A prisoner (299) the temptation of fresh meat proves fatal to a fat station-master (300) we surfeit ourselves (301).

Chapter 52. – The King's well (302) action (304) calculation (305) many bridges taken and at once blown up (305) check (306).

Chapter 53. – To the rescue (307) hot fighting (308) a gallop (310) camel-charging (311) prisoners (312) exploiting victory (313).

Chapter 54. – After the battle (314) the dead (315) the crest (316) more victory (316) the last barrier (317) divided counsels (318) the enemy capitulate (319) we regain our familiar sea (320).

BOOK V

EXPLOITING THE NEW BASE

Our capture of Akaba closed the Hejaz war, and gave us the task of helping the British invade Syria. The Arabs working from Akaba became virtual right wing of Allenby's army in Sinai. To mark the changed relation Feisal was transferred, with his Army, to Allenby's command. Allenby now became responsible for his operations and equipment. Meanwhile we organized the Akaba area as an unassailable base, from which to hinder the Hejaz Railway.

Chapter 55. — The sense of victory (322) assuring Akaba (323) to Egypt for help (324) the Inland Water Board carries on (325).

Chapter 56. — Lyttleton (326) the permit-police in the canal zone (327) naval help (328) Allenby (330) two schools (330).

Chapter 57. — The organization of Akaba (331) guard-ships (332) transfer of Feisal and all his troops (333) King Hussein agrees to it (333) palliating secret relations with the enemy (334-35).

Chapter 58. — A new situation (336) changing methods (336) the invasion of Syria (337) the varied peoples composing Syria (338).

Chapter 59. — The towns of Syria (341-42) Syrians (343) Syrian politics (344) our strategy (345) tactics (345) our spirit (347).

Chapter 60. — Operations begin (349) air raids distract the enemy (350) electric mining (351) guns and Lewis guns (352).

Chapter 61. — Project of a railway raid (353) points of character (354) tribal politics (356) the Turkish air patrol (357).

Chapter 62. — Rumm, a tribal watering place in the hills (358).

Chapter 63. — Seeking help (362) a bath (364) excursion into the origins of Christianity (364) an inarticulate prophet (366).

Chapter 64. — We march (367) getting together (368) a rich drink by night, and a change of mind (369-70) reconnaissance (370).

Chapter 65. — Modesty (371) mining (372) a Turkish patrol (374).

Chapter 66. — The Turks threaten us (375) a train comes (375) and stops (376) ten minutes (377) booty (378) prisoners (379).

Chapter 67. — Confusions (380) evacuation (381) rescue (382) a clean get-away in heavy order (383) Rumm by night (385).

Chapter 68. — A training raid (386) obligations of command (387) success (388) and its fruit (389) what we were trying at (390).

BOOK VI

THE FAILURE OF THE BRIDGES

By November, 1917, Allenby was ready to open a general attack against the Turks along his whole front. The Arabs should have done the same in their sector: but I was afraid to put everything on a throw, and designed instead the specious operation of cutting the Yarmuk Valley Railway, to throw into disorder the expected Turkish retreat. This half-measure met with its due failure.

Chapter 69. — Allenby takes the stage (392) his staff (392) our proper role (394) my private hesitation and its reasons (395).

Chapter 70. — An unworthy choice (396) Sherif Ali ibn el Hussein (397) Abd el Kadir (398) a questionable adherent (399).

Chapter 71. — New retainers (400) old retainers (401) Lloyd and Wood (402) our caravan gets off, but offers lamely (403).

Chapter 72. — A Sherari finds a job and finds himself (404) a night-march (406) the railway (407) Auda (408) a false alarm (409).

Chapter 73. — Tribal politics (410) our march (411) desert manners which nearly put an end to us (412) willing help (415).

Chapter 74. — On the road (416) Turks and English (417) we get two great volunteers (418) more accidents (419) a scratchy night in tents (420) denouncing a fear (420) calmness (422).

Chapter 75. — Azrak (423) check (424) hiding (426) ready (427).

Chapter 76. — Apprehension (428) a forced march (430) we attain the bridge at last (431) a panic (432) and a failure (433).

Chapter 77. — A new idea (434) mine-laying (435) hunger, drizzle and the cold sap our patience (436) a long moment (437).

Chapter 78. — Distractions, wise and foolish (439) the mine goes off embarrassingly well (440) a rescue (442) we get away (443).

Chapter 79. — Reconditioning Azrak (444) provisions (445) visitors (445-46) our leader (447) Azrak nights (448) a digression (449).

Chapter 80. — A Turkish garrison (450) in detention (451) an argument (452-53) persuasions (453) which go too far (454) the earned wages of rebellion (455) gentling a broken will (456).

Chapter 81. — The rake's progress (457) I want to get away (458) in my own despite (459) riding non-stop right to Akaba (460-61) another break-down (461) I find healing in Jerusalem (462).

BOOK VII

A WINTER CAMPAIGN

After the capture of Jerusalem, Allenby, to relieve his right, assigned us a limited objective. We began well; but when we reached the Dead Sea, bad weather, bad temper and division of purpose blunted our offensive spirit and broke up our force. I had a misunderstanding with Zeid, threw in my hand, and returned to Palestine reporting that we had failed, and asking the favour of other employment. Allenby was in the hopeful midst of a great scheme for the spring. He sent me back at once to Feisal with new powers.

Chapter 82. — Allenby in Jerusalem (464) he puts me to work again (465) an Arab advance (466) Joyce and I joy-ride (466-67) the British staff do not understand our inconclusiveness (469).

Chapter 83. — My price and bodyguard (471) the Nahabi (472) our camels (474) severities of service (475) vain nihilism (477).

Chapter 84. — Extending our front (478) Sherif Nasir's capture of Jurf (479) winter comes down (480) into Tafileh (481).

Chapter 85. — A Turkish counter-attack (483) we run away (484) but later decide to accept battle (485) the battlefield (486-87).

Chapter 86. — Our front line gets vexed (488) a lull of sunshine (489) a triple attack (490) the aftermath (491) the profit (492).

Chapter 87. — Clearing the Dead Sea (493) snow-bound (494) a dash (495) riding under difficulties (496) corrosive cold (497).

Chapter 88. — Comfort at Guweira (500) a convoy of gold (501) in the open (502) the winter Edomite wind (503) by night (503).

Chapter 89. — Exhausted (505) my camel (506) the castle (507) child-breeding (507) snow-drifts (508) a journey's end (510).

Chapter 90. — Our next programme (511) a sudden check (512) return to Palestine (513) a complaint and resignation justified by the discovery that my nerves and tact had failed (514).

Chapter 91. — Again harnessed (515) joint operations impose a new understanding with Feisal and further resources (516-17).

BOOK VIII

ORTHODOXY ARRIVES

In conjunction with Allenby we laid a triple plan to join hands
across Jordan, to capture Maan, and to cut off Medina, in one operation.
This was too proud and neither of us fulfilled his part. So the Arabs
exchanged the care of the placid Medina railway for the greater burden
of investing, in Maan, a Turk force as big as their available Regular
Army. To help in this duty Allenby increased our transport, that we
might have longer range and more mobility. Maan was impregnable
for us, so we concentrated on cutting its northern Railway and divert-
ing the Turkish effort to relieve its garrison from the Amman side.
Clearly no decision lay in such tactics: but the German advance in
Flanders at this moment took from Allenby his British units: and consequently his advantage over the Turks. He notified us that he was
unable to attack. A stalemate, as we were, throughout 1918 was an
intolerable prospect. We schemed to strengthen the Arab Army for
autumn operations near Deraa and in the Beni Sakhr country. If this
drew off one division from the enemy in Palestine it would make
possible a British ancillary attack, one of whose ends would be our
junction in the lower Jordan valley, by Jericho. After a month's
preparation this plan was dropped, because of its risk, and because a
better offered.

Chapter 92. — Staffs (519) sex (520) plans (521) discipline (522).

Chapter 93. — Away with Mirzuk (524) springtime (525) Allenby falls
    back (526) amateur spying (527) death of Farraj (528-29).

Chapter 94. — The Indians (531) capture of Semna (532) attack on
    Maan (533) to Dawnay (534) his success (536) Young (538).

Chapter 95. — An Allenby surprise (539) his reduced strength (540) a
    gift of camels (541) plans to hold on (542) activity (543).

Chapter 96. — Nasir in the lead (545) our biggest demolition (546).

Chapter 97. — Finding reinforcements for an Arab offensive (548)
    Allenby works against time (549) King Hussein refuses (550).

BOOK IX

MANŒUVRING FOR A FINAL STROKE

Allenby, in rapid embodiment of reliefs from Mesopotamia and India, so surpassed hope that he was able to plan an autumn offensive. The near balance of the forces on each side meant that victory would depend on his subtly deceiving the Turks that their entire danger yet lay beyond the Jordan. We might help, by lying quiet for six weeks, feigning a feebleness which should tempt the Turks to attack. The Arabs were then to lead off at the critical moment by cutting the railway communications of Palestine. Such bluff within bluff called for most accurate timing, since the balance would have been wrecked either by a premature Turkish retreat in Palestine, or by their premature attack against the Arabs beyond Jordan. We borrowed from Allenby some Imperial Camel Corps to lend extra colour to our supposed critical situation; their success glorified them and covered us, while preparations for Deraa went on with no more check than an untimely show of pique from King Hussein.

Chapter 98. — Allenby's ambitions (553) to fog the Turks (554) Imperial Camel Corps for our sector (554) a raid against Deraa (556) snatch-programme for the I.C.C. (556) supply problems become complicated (557) smoothing the road (558).

Chapter 99. — Timing the scheme (559) Buxton (559) Nuri Shaalan (561) confirming the Rualla in their faith (562) Feisal preaching (563) the great gulf between him and me (565).

Chapter 100. — Atonement, redemption, dint of consequence (567).

Chapter 101. — Buxton's night attack (570) peace negotiations (571) British promises to France, Sherif, Arab and Jew (572).

Chapter 102. — By car to Azrak (574) troops (577) Buxton (578).

Chapter 103. — My birthday, by good fortune, is peaceful (579).

Chapter 104. — A hostile raid (585) the I.C.C. on the road (586) Buxton becomes mobile, and my men camel-drivers (587-88).

Chapter 105. — Seen (589) renunciation (590) in the lodge of Amruh (591) Azrak (591) with the armoured cars (592-93).

Chapter 106. — King Hussein breaks out again (595) we begin to repair damages (596) stopping little short of forgery (597-98).

BOOK X

THE LIBERATION OF DAMASCUS

Our mobile column of aeroplanes, armoured cars, Arab regulars and Beduin, collected at Azrak to cut the three railways out of Deraa. The southern line we cut near Mafrak; the northern at Arar; the western by Mezerib. We circumnavigated Deraa, and rallied despite air raids, in the desert. Next day Allenby attacked, and in a few hours had scattered the Turkish armies beyond recovery. I flew to Palestine for aeroplane help, and got orders for a second phase of the thrust northward. We moved behind Deraa to hasten its abandonment. General Barrow joined us; in his company we advanced to Kiswe, and there met the Australian Mounted Corps. The united forces entered Damascus unopposed. Some confusion manifested itself in the city. We strove to allay it; Allenby arrived and smoothed out all difficulties. Afterwards he let me go.

Chapter 107. — Winterton (601) at Azrak (602) a rest (603) plans (604) reinforcements (605) concentration (606) first step (607).

Chapter 108. — It starts ill (608) an air fight (609) bombing Deraa (610) a Rolls-Royce operation (611) running repairs (612).

Chapter 109. – The main line is captured (613) Peake and his tulips (614-15) aerial interference (615) Junor takes a hand (616-17).

Chapter 110. — For the Palestine line (618) Mezerib taken (620) our plunder and a great fire by night attract visitors (620-21).

Chapter 111. — A classical project (622) waiting (623) prudence asserts her lovely self (624) doing the round trip (625).

Chapter 112. — Hejaz line (626) a sunset (627) the last bridge (628).

Chapter 113. — Visitors (630) shaking us up (631) shaking them up (632) need for air reinforcement (633) a night muddle (634) Allenby in victory (635) the Royal Air Force chiefs (637).

Chapter 114. — Back to duty (638) resisting importunity (639) an air success (640) the Handley-Page (640) Nuri Shaalan (641).

Chapter 115. — Another bungle (642) the Turks break (643) a new departure (644) an opposition (645) five different minds (645-46).

Chapter 116. — An army again in all men's eyes (647) three enterprises (648) a pause (649) prisoners in handfuls (650).

Chapter 117. — The main retreat (651) its sting (652) Auda takes charge (653) blood thirst (654) the terror by night (656) alone to Deraa (656) Barrow's welcome (658) Feisal (658).

Chapter 118. — Very near the end (659) war as she should be (660) a good recovery by the British (661) military service (662).

Chapter 119. — The occupation of Damascus (664) the burning stores (665) at the Town Hall (666) Auda breaks out upon the Druses (667) General Chauvel takes over chief control (668).

Chapter 120. — Digging in (670) a new administration (671) public order (672) supplies (673) night falls upon us unready (674).

Chapter 121. — Disorder at dawn (675) peace returns (676) the silent hospital (677) prisoners of war (678) tired out (678).

Chapter 122. — A quiet morning (681) two standards of perfection (682) of Allenby (682) and of Feisal (683) escape (683).

EPILOGUE

Why the taking of Damascus ended my efforts in Syria (684)

APPENDIX I

Nominal rolls of armoured cars and Talbot battery (685-86)

APPENDIX II

A diary of place-names and dates (687-89)

PREFACE BY A. W. LAWRENCE

THE seven pillars of wisdom are first mentioned in the Bible, in the Book of Proverbs (ix. 1).

'Wisdom hath builded a house: she hath hewn out her seven pillars'.

The title was originally applied by the author to a book of his about seven cities. He decided not to publish this early book because he considered it immature, but he transferred the title as a memento.

A four-page leaflet entitled SOME NOTES ON THE WRITING OF THE SEVEN PILLARS OF WISDOM BY T. E. SHAW was issued by my brother to those who bought or were presented with copies of the 1926 edition. It contains the following information:

MANUSCRIPTS

Text I

I WROTE Books 2, 3, 4, 5, 6, 7 and 10 in Paris between February and June of 1919. The Introduction was written between Paris and Egypt on my way out to Cairo by Handley-Page in July and August 1919. Afterwards in England I wrote Book 1: and then lost all but the Introduction and drafts of Books 9 and 10 at Reading Station, while changing trains. This was about Christmas, 1919.

Text I, if completed, would have been about 250,000 words, a little less than the privately printed *Seven Pillars* as subscribers received it. My war-time notes, on which it was largely constructed, were destroyed as each section was finished. Only three people read much of it, before I lost it.

Text II

A month or so later I began, in London, to scribble out what I remembered of the first text. The original Introduction was of course still available. The other ten Books I completed in less than three months, by doing many thousand words at a time, in long sittings. Thus Book VI was written entire between sunrise and sunrise. Naturally the style was careless: and so Text II (though it introduced a few new episodes) came to over 400,000 words. I corrected it at intervals throughout 1920, checking it with the files of the *Arab Bulletin*, and with two diaries and some of my surviving field-notes. Though hopelessly bad as a text, it became substantially complete and accurate. All but one page of this text was burned by me in 1922.

Text III

With Text II available on the table, Text III was begun in London, and worked on there, in Jeddah, and in Amman during 1921, and again in London till February 1922. It was composed with great care. This manuscript still exists. It is nearly 330,000 words long.

PRIVATELY PRINTED TEXTS

Oxford 1922

THOUGH the story, as completed in Text III, appeared to me still diffuse and unsatisfactory, yet for security's sake it was set up and printed textually, in sheets, at Oxford in the first quarter of 1922, by care of the *Oxford Times* staff. Since eight copies were required, and the book was very large, printing was preferred to typewriting. Five copies (bound in book form, for the convenience of those former members of the Hejaz Expeditionary Force who undertook to read it critically for me) have not yet (April 1927) been destroyed.

Subscribers' Text 1. xii. 26

This text, as issued to subscribers in December 1926 and January 1927, was a recension of the Oxford sheets of 1922. They were condensed (the single canon of change being literary) during 1923 and 1924 (Royal Tank Corps) and 1925 and 1926 (Royal Air Force) in my spare evenings. Beginners in literature are inclined to fumble with a handful of adjectives round the outline of what they want to describe: but by 1924 I had learnt my first lessons in writing, and was often able to combine two or three of my 1921 phrases into one.

There were four exceptions to the rule of condensation:

i) An incident, of less than a page, was cut out because two seniors of our party thought it unpleasantly unnecessary.

ii) Two characters of Englishmen were modified: one into nothing, because the worm no longer seemed worth treading on: the other into plain praise, because what I had innocently written as complaint was read ambiguously by an authority well able to judge.

iii) One chapter of the Introduction was omitted. My best critic told me it was much inferior to the rest.

iv) Book VIII, intended as a 'flat', to interpose between the comparative excitements of Book VII and the final advance on Damascus, was shortened of an abortive reconnaissance, some 10,000 words long. Several of those who read the Oxford text complained of the inordinate boredom of the 'flat', and upon reflection I agreed with them that it was perhaps too successful.

By thus excising 3 per cent and condensing the rest of the Oxford text a total reduction of 15 per cent was achieved, and the length of the subscribers' text brought down to some 280,000 words. It is swifter and more pungent than the Oxford text; and it would have been improved yet more if I had had leisure to carry the process of revision further.

The *Seven Pillars* was so printed and assembled that nobody but myself knew how many copies were produced. I propose to keep this knowledge to myself. Newspaper statements of 107 copies can be easily disproved, for there were more than 107 subscribers: and in addition I gave away, not perhaps as many copies as I owed, but as many as my bankers could afford, to those who had shared with me in the Arab effort, or in the actual production of the volume.

PUBLISHED TEXTS

New York Text

A PROOF of the subscribers' text was sent to New York, and reprinted there by the George Doran Publishing Company. This was necessary to ensure U.S.A. copyright of the *Seven Pillars*. Ten copies are offered for sale, at a price high enough to prevent their ever being sold.

No further issue of the *Seven Pillars* will be made in my lifetime.

Revolt in the Desert

This abridgement of the *Seven Pillars* contains about 130,000 words. It was made by myself in 1926, with the minimum of necessary adjustment (perhaps three new paragraphs in all) to preserve sense and continuity. Parts of it appeared serially in the *Daily Telegraph* in December 1926. The whole was published in England by Jonathan Cape, and in U.S.A. by Doran in March 1927.

T. E. SHAW

To bring the information up to date, I add that the remaining copies of the Oxford printed Text of 1922 are still in existence, but will not be made public for at least ten years, and then only in a limited edition. *Revolt in the Desert* will not be printed again, at least during the remainder of the legal term of copyright.

The text of the present edition is identical with that of the thirty-guinea edition of 1926, except for the following omissions and alterations. The omissions are necessary to save hurting the feelings of persons still living; they come on pages 61, 62, and 329 where gaps of the same length are left in the present text. The 1926 edition contains no Chapter XI; the chapters have now been renumbered to remove this anomaly. On p. 300 (line 7) the phrase 'halts to breath' has been changed to 'halts to breathe' in agreement with the corresponding passage in the Oxford Text of 1922, 'we let the camels breathe a little'. On p. 398 (line 14) the word 'Humber' has been printed in italics instead of Roman type, to make the sense clearer; in 1926 the names of some other ships were similarly italicized.

The spelling of Arabic names varies greatly in all editions, and I have made no alterations. It should be explained that only three vowels are recognized in Arabic, and that some of the consonants have no equivalents in English. The general practice of orientalists in recent years has been to adopt one of the various sets of conventional signs for the letters and vowel marks of the Arabic alphabet, transliterating Mohamed as Muḥammad, muezzin as mu'edhdhin, and Koran as Qur'an or Kur'an. This method is useful to those who know what it means, but this book follows the old fashion of writing the best phonetic approximations according to ordinary English spelling. The same place-name will be found spelt in several different ways, not only because the sound of many Arabic words can legitimately be represented in English in a variety of ways, but also because the natives of a district often differ as to the pronunciation of any place-name which has not already become famous or fixed by literary usage. (For example a locality near Akaba is called Abu Lissan, Aba el Lissan or Abu Lissal.) A reference by the author to his views on this matter occurs on page 664. I reprint here a series of questions by the publisher and answers by the author concerning the printing of *Revolt in the Desert*.

Q.

I attach a list of queries raised by F. who is reading the proofs. He finds these very clean, but full of inconsistencies in the spelling of proper names, a point which reviewers often take up. Will you annotate it in the margin, so that I can get the proofs straightened?

A.

Annotated: not very helpfully perhaps. Arabic names won't go into English, exactly, for their consonants are not the same as ours, and their vowels, like ours, vary from district to district. There are some 'scientific systems' of transliteration, helpful to people who know enough Arabic not to need helping, but a wash-out for the world. I spell my names anyhow, to show what rot the systems are.

Slip 1. Jeddah and Jidda used impartially throughout. Intentional?

Rather!

Slip 16. Bir Wahei*da*, was Bir Wahei*di*.

Why not? All one place.

Slip 20. Nuri, Emir of the Ruwalla, belongs to the 'chief family of the Rualla'. On Slip 23 'Rualla horse', and Slip 38, 'killed one Rueli'. In all later slips 'Rualla'.

Should have also used Ruwala and Ruala.

Slip 28. The Bisaita is also spelt Biseita.

Good.

Slip 47. Jedha, the she-camel, was Jedhah on Slip 40.

She was a splendid beast.

Slip 53. 'Meleager, the immoral poet'. I have put 'immortal' poet, but the author may mean immoral after all.

Immorality I know. Immortality I cannot judge. As you please: Meleager will not sue us for libel.

Q.	A.
Slip 65. Author is addressed 'Ya Auruns', but on Slip 56 was 'Aurans'.	Also Lurens and Runs: not to mention 'Shaw'. More to follow, if time permits.
Slip 78. Sherif Abd el Mayin of Slip 68 becomes el Main, el Maycin, el Muein, el Mayin, and el Muyein.	Good egg. I call this really ingenious.

The maps for this edition have been drawn by Mr. E. O. McIntosh; they are based in the main on those of 1926.

A. W. LAWRENCE

ILLUSTRATIONS

AUTHOR	Frontispiece	*pastel*	Kennington
FEYSAL	facing p. 92	*oils*	John
EMIR ABDULLA	225	*pastel*	Kennington
AUDA ABU TAYI	256	*pastel*	Kennington
A FORCED LANDING	pp. 310-11	*line*	Kennington
WIND	p. 328	*line*	Kennington
MAP	facing p. 65		

SEVEN PILLARS OF WISDOM

INTRODUCTION

FOUNDATIONS OF REVOLT

Chapters I to VII

SOME *Englishmen, of whom Kitchener was chief, believed that a rebellion of Arabs against Turks would enable England, while fighting Germany, simultaneously to defeat her ally Turkey.*

Their knowledge of the nature and power and country of the Arabic-speaking peoples made them think that the issue of such a rebellion would be happy: and indicated its character and method.

So they allowed it to begin, having obtained for it formal assurances of help from the British Government. Yet none the less the rebellion of the Sherif of Mecca came to most as a surprise, and found the Allies unready. It aroused mixed feelings and made strong friends and strong enemies, amid whose clashing jealousies its affairs began to miscarry.

CHAPTER I

SOME of the evil of my tale may have been inherent in our circumstances. For years we lived anyhow with one another in the naked desert, under the indifferent heaven. By day the hot sun fermented us; and we were dizzied by the beating wind. At night we were stained by dew, and shamed into pettiness by the innumerable silences of stars. We were a self-centred army without parade or gesture, devoted to freedom, the second of man's creeds, a purpose so ravenous that it devoured all our strength, a hope so transcendent that our earlier ambitions faded in its glare.

As time went by our need to fight for the ideal increased to an unquestioning possession, riding with spur and rein over our doubts. Willy-nilly it became a faith. We had sold ourselves into its slavery, manacled ourselves together in its chain-gang, bowed ourselves to serve its holiness with all our good and ill content. The mentality of ordinary human slaves is terrible — they have lost the world — and we had surrendered, not body alone, but soul to the overmastering greed of victory. By our own act we were drained of morality, of volition, of responsibility, like dead leaves in the wind.

The everlasting battle stripped from us care of our own lives or of others'. We had ropes about our necks, and on our heads prices which showed that the enemy intended hideous tortures for us if we were caught. Each day some of us passed; and the living knew themselves just sentient puppets on God's stage: indeed, our taskmaster was merciless, merciless, so long as our bruised feet could stagger forward on the road. The weak envied those tired enough to die; for success looked so remote, and failure a near and certain, if sharp, release from toil. We lived always in the stretch or sag of nerves, either on the crest or in the trough of waves of feeling. This impotency was bitter to us, and made us live only for the seen horizon, reckless what spite we inflicted or endured, since physical sensation showed itself meanly transient. Gusts of cruelty, perversions, lusts ran lightly over the surface without troubling us; for the moral laws which had seemed to hedge about

these silly accidents must be yet fainter words. We had learned that
there were pangs too sharp, griefs too deep, ecstasies too high for our
finite selves to register. When emotion reached this pitch the mind
choked; and memory went white till the circumstances were humdrum
once more.

Such exaltation of thought, while it let adrift the spirit, and gave it
licence in strange airs, lost it the old patient rule over the body. The
body was too coarse to feel the utmost of our sorrows and of our joys.
Therefore, we abandoned it as rubbish: we left it below us to march
forward, a breathing simulacrum, on its own unaided level, subject to
influences from which in normal times our instincts would have
shrunk. The men were young and sturdy; and hot flesh and blood unconsciously claimed a right in them and tormented their bellies with
strange longings. Our privations and dangers fanned this virile heat,
in a climate as racking as can be conceived. We had no shut places to
be alone in, no thick clothes to hide our nature. Man in all things lived
candidly with man.

The Arab was by nature continent; and the use of universal marriage
had nearly abolished irregular courses in his tribes. The public women
of the rare settlements we encountered in our months of wandering
would have been nothing to our numbers, even had their raddled meat
been palatable to a man of healthy parts. In horror of such sordid
commerce our youths began indifferently to slake one another's few
needs in their own clean bodies — a cold convenience that, by comparison, seemed sexless and even pure. Later, some began to justify
this sterile process, and swore that friends quivering together in the
yielding sand with intimate hot limbs in supreme embrace, found
there hidden in the darkness a sensual co-efficient of the mental passion
which was welding our souls and spirits in one flaming effort. Several,
thirsting to punish appetites they could not wholly prevent, took a
savage pride in degrading the body, and offered themselves fiercely in
any habit which promised physical pain or filth.

I was sent to these Arabs as a stranger, unable to think their thoughts
or subscribe their beliefs, but charged by duty to lead them forward
and to develop to the highest any movement of theirs profitable to
England in her war. If I could not assume their character, I could at

least conceal my own, and pass among them without evident friction, neither a discord nor a critic but an unnoticed influence. Since I was their fellow, I will not be their apologist or advocate. To-day in my old garments, I could play the bystander, obedient to the sensibilities of our theatre ... but it is more honest to record that these ideas and actions then passed naturally. What now looks wanton or sadic seemed in the field inevitable, or just unimportant routine.

Blood was always on our hands: we were licensed to it. Wounding and killing seemed ephemeral pains, so very brief and sore was life with us. With the sorrow of living so great, the sorrow of punishment had to be pitiless. We lived for the day and died for it. When there was reason and desire to punish we wrote our lesson with gun or whip immediately in the sullen flesh of the sufferer, and the case was beyond appeal. The desert did not afford the refined slow penalties of courts and gaols.

Of course our rewards and pleasures were as suddenly sweeping as our troubles; but, to me in particular, they bulked less large. Bedouin ways were hard even for those brought up to them, and for strangers terrible: a death in life. When the march or labour ended I had no energy to record sensation, nor while it lasted any leisure to see the spiritual loveliness which sometimes came upon us by the way. In my notes, the cruel rather than the beautiful found place. We no doubt enjoyed more the rare moments of peace and forgetfulness; but I remember more the agony, the terrors, and the mistakes. Our life is not summed up in what I have written (there are things not to be repeated in cold blood for very shame); but what I have written was in and of our life. Pray God that men reading the story will not, for love of the glamour of strangeness, go out to prostitute themselves and their talents in serving another race.

A man who gives himself to be a possession of aliens leads a Yahoo life, having bartered his soul to a brute-master. He is not of them. He may stand against them, persuade himself of a mission, batter and twist them into something which they, of their own accord, would not have been. Then he is exploiting his old environment to press them out of theirs. Or, after my model, he may imitate them so well that they spuriously imitate him back again. Then he is giving away his own environment: pretending to theirs; and pretences are hollow, worthless things. In neither case does he do a thing of himself, nor a thing so clean as to be his own (without thought of conversion), letting them take what action or reaction they please from the silent example.

In my case, the effort for these years to live in the dress of Arabs, and to imitate their mental foundation, quitted me of my English self, and let me look at the West and its conventions with new eyes: they destroyed it all for me. At the same time I could not sincerely take on the Arab skin: it was an affectation only. Easily was a man made an infidel, but hardly might he be converted to another faith. I had dropped one form and not taken on the other, and was become like Mohammed's coffin in our legend, with a resultant feeling of intense loneliness in life, and a contempt, not for other men, but for all they do. Such detachment came at times to a man exhausted by prolonged physical effort and isolation. His body plodded on mechanically, while his reasonable mind left him, and from without looked down critically on him, wondering what that futile lumber did and why. Sometimes these selves would converse in the void; and then madness was very near, as I believe it would be near the man who could see things through the veils at once of two customs, two educations, two environments.

CHAPTER II

A FIRST difficulty of the Arab movement was to say who the Arabs were. Being a manufactured people, their name had been changing in sense slowly year by year. Once it meant an Arabian. There was a country called Arabia; but this was nothing to the point. There was a language called Arabic; and in it lay the test. It was the current tongue of Syria and Palestine, of Mesopotamia, and of the great peninsula called Arabia on the map. Before the Moslem conquest, these areas were inhabited by diverse peoples, speaking languages of the Arabic family. We called them Semitic, but (as with most scientific terms) incorrectly. However, Arabic, Assyrian, Babylonian, Phoenician, Hebrew, Aramaic and Syriac were related tongues; and indications of common influences in the past, or even of a common origin, were strengthened by our knowledge that the appearances and customs of the present Arabic-speaking peoples of Asia, while as varied as a field-full of poppies, had an equal and essential likeness. We might with perfect propriety call them cousins — and cousins certainly, if sadly, aware of their own relationship.

The Arabic-speaking areas of Asia in this sense were a rough parallelogram. The northern side ran from Alexandretta, on the Mediterranean, across Mesopotamia eastward to the Tigris. The south side was the edge of the Indian Ocean, from Aden to Muscat. On the west it was bounded by the Mediterranean, the Suez Canal, and the Red Sea to Aden. On the east by the Tigris, and the Persian Gulf to Muscat. This square of land, as large as India, formed the homeland of our Semites, in which no foreign race had kept a permanent footing, though Egyptians, Hittites, Philistines, Persians, Greeks, Romans, Turks and Franks had variously tried. All had in the end been broken, and their scattered elements drowned in the strong characteristics of the Semitic race. Semites had sometimes pushed outside this area, and themselves been drowned in the outer world. Egypt, Algiers, Morocco, Malta, Sicily, Spain, Cilicia and France absorbed and obliterated Semitic colonies. Only in Tripoli of Africa, and in the everlasting miracle of Jewry, had distant Semites kept some of their identity and force.

The origin of these peoples was an academic question; but for the understanding of their revolt their present social and political differences were important, and could only be grasped by looking at their geography. This continent of theirs fell into certain great regions, whose gross physical diversities imposed varying habits on the dwellers in them. On the west the parallelogram was framed, from Alexandretta to Aden, by a mountain belt, called (in the north) Syria, and thence progressively southward called Palestine, Midian, Hejaz, and lastly Yemen. It had an average height of perhaps three thousand feet, with peaks of ten to twelve thousand feet. It faced west, was well watered with rain and cloud from the sea, and in general was fully peopled.

Another range of inhabited hills, facing the Indian Ocean, was the south edge of the parallelogram. The eastern frontier was at first an alluvial plain called Mesopotamia, but south of Basra a level littoral, called Kuweit, and Hasa, to Gattar. Much of this plain was peopled. These inhabited hills and plains framed a gulf of thirsty desert, in whose heart was an archipelago of watered and populous oases called Kasim and Aridh. In this group of oases lay the true centre of Arabia, the preserve of its native spirit, and its most conscious individuality. The desert lapped it round and kept it pure of contact.

The desert which performed this great function around the oases, and so made the character of Arabia, varied in nature. South of the oases it appeared to be a pathless sea of sand, stretching nearly to the populous escarpment of the Indian Ocean shore, shutting it out from Arabian history, and from all influence on Arabian morals and politics. Hadhramaut, as they called this southern coast, formed part of the history of the Dutch Indies; and its thought swayed Java rather than Arabia. To the west of the oases, between them and the Hejaz hills, was the Nejd desert, an area of gravel and lava, with little sand in it. To the east of these oases, between them and Kuweit, spread a similar expanse of gravel, but with some great stretches of soft sand, making the road difficult. To the north of the oases lay a belt of sand, and then an immense gravel and lava plain, filling up everything between the eastern edge of Syria and the banks of the Euphrates where Mesopotamia began. The practicability of this northern desert for men and motor-cars enabled the Arab revolt to win its ready success.

The hills of the west and the plains of the east were the parts of Arabia always most populous and active. In particular on the west, the mountains of Syria and Palestine, of Hejaz and Yemen, entered time and again into the current of our European life. Ethically, these fertile healthy hills were in Europe, not in Asia, just as the Arabs looked always to the Mediterranean, not to the Indian Ocean, for their cultural sympathies, for their enterprises, and particularly for their expansions since the migration problem was the greatest and most complex force in Arabia, and general to it, however it might vary in the different Arabic districts.

In the north (Syria) the birth rate was low in the cities and the death rate high, because of the insanitary conditions and the hectic life led by the majority. Consequently the surplus peasantry found openings in the towns, and were there swallowed up. In the Lebanon, where sanitation had been improved, a greater exodus of youth took place to America each year, threatening (for the first time since Greek days) to change the outlook of an entire district.

In Yemen the solution was different. There was no foreign trade, and no massed industries to accumulate population in unhealthy places. The towns were just market towns, as clean and simple as ordinary villages. Therefore the population slowly increased; the scale of living was brought down very low; and a congestion of numbers was generally felt. They could not emigrate overseas; for the Sudan was even worse country than Arabia, and the few tribes which did venture across were compelled to modify their manner of life and their Semitic culture profoundly, in order to exist. They could not move northward along the hills; for these were barred by the holy town of Mecca and its port Jidda: an alien belt, continually reinforced by strangers from India and Java and Bokhara and Africa, very strong in vitality, violently hostile to the Semitic consciousness, and maintained despite economics and geography and climate by the artificial factor of a world-religion. The congestion of Yemen, therefore, becoming extreme, found its only relief in the east, by forcing the weaker aggregations of its border down and down the slopes of the hills along the Widian, the half-waste district

B

of the great water-bearing valleys of Bisha, Dawasir, Ranya and Taraba which ran out towards the deserts of Nejd. These weaker clans had continually to exchange good springs and fertile palms for poorer springs and scantier palms, till at last they reached an area where a proper agricultural life became impossible. They then began to eke out their precarious husbandry by breeding sheep and camels, and in time came to depend more and more on these herds for their living.

Finally, under a last impulse from the straining population behind them, the border people (now almost wholly pastoral), were flung out of the furthest crazy oasis into the untrodden wilderness as nomads. This process, to be watched to-day with individual families and tribes to whose marches an exact name and date might be put, must have been going on since the first day of full settlement of Yemen. The Widian below Mecca and Taif are crowded with the memories and place-names of half a hundred tribes which have gone from there, and may be found to-day in Nejd, in Jebel Shammar, in the Hamad, even on the frontiers of Syria and Mesopotamia. There was the source of migration, the factory of nomads, the springing of the gulf-stream of desert wanderers.

For the people of the desert were as little static as the people of the hills. The economic life of the desert was based on the supply of camels, which were best bred on the rigorous upland pastures with their strong nutritive thorns. By this industry the Bedouins lived; and it in turn moulded their life, apportioned the tribal areas, and kept the clans revolving through their rote of spring, summer and winter pasturages, as the herds cropped the scanty growths of each in turn. The camel markets in Syria, Mesopotamia, and Egypt determined the population which the deserts could support, and regulated strictly their standard of living. So the desert likewise over-peopled itself upon occasion; and then there were heavings and thrustings of the crowded tribes as they elbowed themselves by natural courses towards the light. They might not go south towards the inhospitable sand or sea. They could not turn west; for there the steep hills of Hejaz were thickly lined by mountain peoples taking full advantage of their defensiveness. Sometimes they went towards the central oases of Aridh and Kasim, and, if the tribes looking for new homes were strong and vigorous, might succeed in occupying parts of them. If, however, the desert had not this strength, its peoples were pushed gradually north, up between Medina of the Hejaz and Kasim of Nejd, till they found themselves at the fork of two roads. They could strike eastward, by Wadi Rumh or Jebel Shammar, to follow eventually the Batn to Shamiya, where they would become riverine Arabs of the Lower Euphrates; or they could climb, by slow degrees, the ladder of western oases — Henakiya, Kheibar, Teima, Jauf, and the Sirhan — till fate saw them nearing Jebel Druse, in Syria, or watering their herds about Tadmor of the northern desert, on their way to Aleppo or Assyria.

Nor then did the pressure cease: the inexorable trend northward continued. The tribes found themselves driven to the very edge of cultivation in Syria or Mesopotamia. Opportunity and their bellies persuaded them of the advantages of possessing goats, and then of possessing sheep; and lastly they began to sow, if only a little barley for their animals. They were now no longer Bedouin, and began to suffer like the villagers from the ravages of the nomads behind. Insensibly, they made common cause with the peasants already on the soil, and found out that they, too, were peasantry. So we see clans, born in the highlands of Yemen, thrust by stronger clans into the desert, where, unwillingly, they became nomad to keep themselves alive. We see them wandering, every year moving a little further north or a little further east as chance has sent them down one or other of the well-roads of the wilderness, till finally this pressure drives them from the desert again into the sown, with the like unwillingness of their first shrinking experiment in nomad life. This was the circulation which kept vigour in the Semitic body. There were few, if indeed there was a single northern Semite, whose ancestors had not at some dark age passed through the desert. The mark of nomadism, that most deep and biting social discipline, was on each of them in his degree.

IF tribesman and townsman in Arabic-speaking Asia were not different races, but just men in different social and economic stages, a family resemblance might be expected in the working of their minds, and so it was only reasonable that common elements should appear in the product of all these peoples. In the very outset, at the first meeting with them, was found a universal clearness or hardness of belief, almost mathematical in its limitation, and repellent in its unsympathetic form. Semites had no half-tones in their register of vision. They were a people of primary colours, or rather of black and white, who saw the world always in contour. They were a dogmatic people, despising doubt, our modern crown of thorns. They did not understand our metaphysical difficulties, our introspective questionings. They knew only truth and untruth, belief and unbelief, without our hesitating retinue of finer shades.

This people was black and white, not only in vision, but by inmost furnishing: black and white not merely in clarity, but in apposition. Their thoughts were at ease only in extremes. They inhabited superlatives by choice. Sometimes inconsistents seemed to possess them at once in joint sway; but they never compromised: they pursued the logic of several incompatible opinions to absurd ends, without perceiving the incongruity. With cool head and tranquil judgement, imperturbably unconscious of the flight, they oscillated from asymptote to asymptote.*

They were a limited, narrow-minded people, whose inert intellects lay fallow in incurious resignation. Their imaginations were vivid, but not creative. There was so little Arab art in Asia that they could almost be said to have had no art, though their classes were liberal patrons, and had encouraged whatever talents in architecture, or ceramics, or other handicraft their neighbours and helots displayed. Nor did they handle

---

* The metaphor of oscillation 'from asymptote to asymptote' originated in a conversation with a friend who tells me that he mistakenly applied the term 'asymptote' to the branches of the hyperbola. — A.W.L.

great industries: they had no organizations of mind or body. They invented no systems of philosophy, no complex mythologies. They steered their course between the idols of the tribe and of the cave. The least morbid of peoples, they had accepted the gift of life unquestioningly, as axiomatic. To them it was a thing inevitable, entailed on man, a usufruct, beyond control. Suicide was a thing impossible, and death no grief.

They were a people of spasms, of upheavals, of ideas, the race of the individual genius. Their movements were the more shocking by contrast with the quietude of every day, their great men greater by contrast with the humanity of their mob. Their convictions were by instinct, their activities intuitional. Their largest manufacture was of creeds: almost they were monopolists of revealed religions. Three of these efforts had endured among them: two of the three had also borne export (in modified forms) to non-Semitic peoples. Christianity, translated into the diverse spirits of Greek and Latin and Teutonic tongues, had conquered Europe and America. Islam in various transformations was subjecting Africa and parts of Asia. These were Semitic successes. Their failures they kept to themselves. The fringes of their deserts were strewn with broken faiths.

It was significant that this wrack of fallen religions lay about the meeting of the desert and the sown. It pointed to the generation of all these creeds. They were assertions, not arguments; so they required a prophet to set them forth. The Arabs said there had been forty thousand prophets: we had record of at least some hundreds. None of them had been of the wilderness; but their lives were after a pattern. Their birth set them in crowded places. An unintelligible passionate yearning drove them out into the desert. There they lived a greater or lesser time in meditation and physical abandonment; and thence they returned with their imagined message articulate, to preach it to their old, and now doubting, associates. The founders of the three great creeds fulfilled this cycle: their possible coincidence was proved a law by the parallel life-histories of the myriad others, the unfortunate who failed, whom we might judge of no less true profession, but for whom time and disillusion had not heaped up dry souls ready to be set on fire. To the thinkers of the town the impulse into Nitria had ever been irresistible, not probably that they found God dwelling there, but that in its solitude they heard more certainly the living word they brought with them.

The common base of all the Semitic creeds, winners or losers, was the ever present idea of world-worthlessness. Their profound reaction from matter led them to preach bareness, renunciation, poverty; and the atmosphere of this invention stifled the minds of the desert pitilessly. A first knowledge of their sense of the purity of rarefaction was given me in early years, when we had ridden far out over the rolling plains of North Syria to a ruin of the Roman period which the Arabs believed was made by a prince of the border as a desert-palace for his queen. The clay of its building was said to have been kneaded for greater richness, not with water, but with the precious essential oils of flowers. My guides, sniffing the air like dogs, led me from crumbling room to room, saying, 'This is jessamine, this violet, this rose'.

But at last Dahoum drew me: 'Come and smell the very sweetest scent of all', and we went into the main lodging, to the gaping window sockets of its eastern face, and there drank with open mouths of the effortless, empty, eddyless wind of the desert, throbbing past. That slow breath had been born somewhere beyond the distant Euphrates and had dragged its way across many days and nights of dead grass, to its first obstacle, the man-made walls of our broken palace. About them it seemed to fret and linger, murmuring in baby-speech. 'This,' they told me, 'is the best: it has no taste.' My Arabs were turning their backs on perfumes and luxuries to choose the things in which mankind had had no share or part.

The Beduin of the desert, born and grown up in it, had embraced with all his soul this nakedness too harsh for volunteers, for the reason, felt but inarticulate, that there he found himself indubitably free. He lost material ties, comforts, all superfluities and other complications to achieve a personal liberty which haunted starvation and death. He saw no virtue in poverty herself: he enjoyed the little vices and luxuries — coffee, fresh water, women — which he could still preserve. In his life he had air and winds, sun and light, open spaces and a great emptiness. There was no human effort, no fecundity in Nature: just the heaven above and the unspotted earth beneath. There unconsciously he came near God. God was to him not anthropomorphic, not tangible, not moral nor ethical, not concerned with the world or with him, not natural: but the being ἀχρώματος, ἀσχημάτιστος, ἀναφής, thus qualified not by divestiture but by investiture, a comprehending Being, the egg of all activity, with nature and matter just a glass reflecting Him.

The Beduin could not look for God within him: he was too sure that he was within God. He could not conceive anything which was or was not God, Who alone was great; yet there was a homeliness, an every-day-ness of this climatic Arab God, who was their eating and their fighting and their lusting, the commonest of their thoughts, their familiar resource and companion, in a way impossible to those whose God is so wistfully veiled from them by despair of their carnal un-worthiness of Him and by the decorum of formal worship. Arabs felt no incongruity in bringing God into the weaknesses and appetites of their least creditable causes. He was the most familiar of their words; and indeed we lost much eloquence when making Him the shortest and ugliest of our monosyllables.

This creed of the desert seemed inexpressible in words, and indeed in thought. It was easily felt as an influence, and those who went into the desert long enough to forget its open spaces and its emptiness were inevitably thrust upon God as the only refuge and rhythm of being. The Bedawi might be a nominal Sunni, or a nominal Wahabi, or any-thing else in the Semitic compass, and he would take it very lightly, a little in the manner of the watchmen at Zion's gate who drank beer and laughed in Zion because they were Zionists. Each individual nomad had his revealed religion, not oral or traditional or expressed, but instinctive in himself; and so we got all the Semitic creeds with (in character and essence) a stress on the emptiness of the world and the fullness of God; and according to the power and opportunity of the believer was the expression of them.

The desert dweller could not take credit for his belief. He had never been either evangelist or proselyte. He arrived at this intense condensa-tion of himself in God by shutting his eyes to the world, and to all the complex possibilities latent in him which only contact with wealth and temptations could bring forth. He attained a sure trust and a powerful trust, but of how narrow a field! His sterile experience robbed him of compassion and perverted his human kindness to the image of the waste in which he hid. Accordingly he hurt himself, not merely to be free, but to please himself. There followed a delight in pain, a cruelty which was more to him than goods. The desert Arab found no joy like the joy of voluntarily holding back. He found luxury in abnegation, renunciation, self restraint. He made nakedness of the mind as sensuous as nakedness of the body. He saved his own soul, perhaps, and without danger, but in a hard selfishness. His desert was made a spiritual ice-house, in which was preserved intact but unimproved for all ages a vision of the unity of God. To it sometimes the seekers from the outer world could escape for a season and look thence in detachment at the nature of the generation they would convert.

This faith of the desert was impossible in the towns. It was at once too strange, too simple, too impalpable for export and common use. The idea, the ground-belief of all Semitic creeds was waiting there, but it had to be diluted to be made comprehensible to us. The scream of a bat was too shrill for many ears: the desert spirit escaped through our coarser texture. The prophets returned from the desert with their glimpse of God, and through their stained medium (as through a dark glass) showed something of the majesty and brilliance whose full vision would blind, deafen, silence us, serve us as it had served the Beduin, setting him uncouth, a man apart.

The disciples, in the endeavour to strip themselves and their neighbours of all things according to the Master's word, stumbled over human weaknesses and failed. To live, the villager or townsman must fill himself each day with the pleasures of acquisition and accumulation, and by rebound off circumstance become the grossest and most material of men. The shining contempt of life which led others into the barest asceticism drove him to despair. He squandered himself heedlessly, as a spendthrift: ran through his inheritance of flesh in hasty longing for the end. The Jew in the Metropole at Brighton, the miser, the worshipper of Adonis, the lecher in the stews of Damascus were alike signs of the Semitic capacity for enjoyment, and expressions of the same nerve which gave us at the other pole the self-denial of the Essenes, or the early Christians, or the first Khalifas, finding the way to heaven fairest for the poor in spirit. The Semite hovered between lust and self-denial.

Arabs could be swung on an idea as on a cord; for the unpledged allegiance of their minds made them obedient servants. None of them would escape the bond till success had come, and with it responsibility and duty and engagements. Then the idea was gone and the work ended — in ruins. Without a creed they could be taken to the four corners of the world (but not to heaven) by being shown the riches of earth and the pleasures of it; but if on the road, led in this fashion, they met the prophet of an idea, who had nowhere to lay his head and who depended for his food on charity or birds, then they would all leave their wealth for his inspiration. They were incorrigibly children of the idea, feckless and colour-blind, to whom body and spirit were for ever and inevitably opposed. Their mind was strange and dark, full of depressions and exaltations, lacking in rule, but with more of ardour and more fertile in belief than any other in the world. They were a people of starts, for whom the abstract was the strongest motive, the process of infinite courage and variety, and the end nothing. They were as unstable as water, and like water would perhaps finally prevail. Since the dawn of life, in successive waves they had been dashing themselves against the coasts of flesh. Each wave was broken, but, like the sea, wore away ever so little of the granite on which it failed, and some day, ages yet, might roll unchecked over the place where the material world had been, and God would move upon the face of those waters. One such wave (and not the least) I raised and rolled before the breath of an idea, till it reached its crest, and toppled over and fell at Damascus. The wash of that wave, thrown back by the resistance of vested things, will provide the matter of the following wave, when in fullness of time the sea shall be raised once more.

B*

CHAPTER IV

THE first great rush round the Mediterranean had shown the world the power of an excited Arab for a short spell of intense physical activity; but when the effort burned out the lack of endurance and routine in the Semitic mind became as evident. The provinces they had overrun they neglected, out of sheer distaste of system, and had to seek the help of their conquered subjects, or of more vigorous foreigners, to administer their ill-knit and inchoate empires. So, early in the Middle Ages, the Turks found a footing in the Arab States, first as servants, then as helpers, and then as a parasite growth which choked the life out of the old body politic. The last phase was of enmity, when the Hulagus or Timurs sated their blood lust, burning and destroying everything which irked them with a pretension of superiority.

Arab civilizations had been of an abstract nature, moral and intellectual rather than applied; and their lack of public spirit made their excellent private qualities futile. They were fortunate in their epoch: Europe had fallen barbarous; and the memory of Greek and Latin learning was fading from men's minds. By contrast the imitative exercise of the Arabs seemed cultured, their mental activity progressive, their state prosperous. They had performed real service in preserving something of a classical past for a mediæval future.

With the coming of the Turks this happiness became a dream. By stages the Semites of Asia passed under their yoke, and found it a slow death. Their goods were stripped from them; and their spirits shrivelled in the numbing breath of a military Government. Turkish rule was gendarme rule, and Turkish political theory as crude as its practice. The Turks taught the Arabs that the interests of a sect were higher than those of patriotism: that the petty concerns of the province were more than nationality. They led them by subtle dissensions to distrust one another. Even the Arabic language was banished from courts and offices, from the Government service, and from superior schools. Arabs might only serve the State by sacrifice of their racial characteristics. These measures were not accepted quietly. Semitic tenacity showed itself in the many rebellions of Syria, Mesopotamia and Arabia against the grosser forms of Turkish penetration; and resistance was also made to the more insidious attempts at absorption. The Arabs would not give up their rich and flexible tongue for crude Turkish: instead, they filled Turkish with Arabic words, and held to the treasures of their own literature.

They lost their geographical sense, and their racial and political and historical memories; but they clung the more tightly to their language, and erected it almost into a fatherland of its own. The first duty of every Moslem was to study the Koran, the sacred book of Islam, and incidentally the greatest Arab literary monument. The knowledge that this religion was his own, and that only he was perfectly qualified to understand and practise it, gave every Arab a standard by which to judge the banal achievements of the Turk.

Then came the Turkish revolution, the fall of Abdul Hamid, and the supremacy of the Young Turks. The horizon momentarily broadened for the Arabs. The Young-Turk movement was a revolt against the hierarchic conception of Islam and the pan-Islamic theories of the old Sultan, who had aspired, by making himself spiritual director of the Moslem world, to be also (beyond appeal) its director in temporal affairs. These young politicians rebelled and threw him into prison, under the impulse of constitutional theories of a sovereign state. So, at a time when Western Europe was just beginning to climb out of nationality into internationality, and to rumble with wars far removed from problems of race, Western Asia began to climb out of catholicism into nationalist politics, and to dream of wars for self-government and self-sovereignty, instead of for faith or dogma. This tendency had broken out first and most strongly in the Near East, in the little Balkan States, and had sustained them through an almost unparalleled martyrdom to their goal of separation from Turkey. Later there had been nationalist movements in Egypt, in India, in Persia, and finally in Constantinople, where they were fortified and made pointed by the new American ideas in education: ideas which, when released in the old high Oriental atmosphere, made an explosive mixture. The American schools, teaching by the method of inquiry, encouraged scientific detachment and free exchange of views. Quite without intention they taught revolution, since it was impossible for an individual to be modern in Turkey and at the same time loyal, if he had been born of one of the subject races — Greeks, Arabs, Kurds, Armenians or Albanians — over whom the Turks were so long helped to keep dominion.

The Young Turks, in the confidence of their first success, were carried away by the logic of their principles, and as protest against Pan-Islam preached Ottoman brotherhood. The gullible subject races — far more numerous than the Turks themselves — believed that they were called upon to co-operate in building a new East. Rushing to the task (full of Herbert Spencer and Alexander Hamilton) they laid down platforms of sweeping ideas, and hailed the Turks as partners. The Turks, terrified at the forces they had let loose, drew the fires as suddenly as they had stoked them. Turkey made Turkish for the Turks — Yeni-Turan — became the cry. Later on, this policy would turn them towards the rescue of their irredenti — the Turkish populations subject to Russia in Central Asia; but, first of all, they must purge their Empire of such irritating subject races as resisted the ruling stamp. The Arabs, the largest alien component of Turkey, must first be dealt with. Accordingly the Arab deputies were scattered, the Arab societies forbidden, the Arab notables proscribed. Arabic manifestations and the Arabic language were suppressed by Enver Pasha more sternly than by Abdul Hamid before him.

However, the Arabs had tasted freedom: they could not change their ideas as quickly as their conduct; and the stiffer spirits among them were not easily to be put down. They read the Turkish papers, putting 'Arab' for 'Turk' in the patriotic exhortations. Suppression charged them with unhealthy violence. Deprived of constitutional outlets they became revolutionary. The Arab societies went underground, and changed from liberal clubs into conspiracies. The Akhua, the Arab mother society, was publicly dissolved. It was replaced in Mesopotamia by the dangerous Ahad, a very secret brotherhood, limited almost entirely to Arab officers in the Turkish Army, who swore to acquire the military knowledge of their masters, and to turn it against them, in the service of the Arab people, when the moment of rebellion came.

It was a large society, with a sure base in the wild part of Southern Irak, where Sayid Taleb, the young John Wilkes of the Arab movement, held the power in his unprincipled fingers. To it belonged seven out of every ten Mesopotamian-born officers; and their counsel was so well kept that members of it held high command in Turkey to the last. When the crash came, and Allenby rode across Armageddon and Turkey fell, one vice-president of the society was commanding the broken fragments of the Palestine armies on the retreat, and another was directing the Turkish forces across-Jordan in the Amman area. Yet later, after the armistice, great places in the Turkish service were still held by men ready to turn on their masters at a word from their Arab leaders. To most of them the word was never given; for those societies were pro-Arab only, willing to fight for nothing but Arab independence; and they could see no advantage in supporting the Allies rather than the Turks, since they did not believe our assurances that we would leave them free. Indeed, many of them preferred an Arabia united by Turkey in miserable subjection, to an Arabia divided up and slothful under the easier control of several European powers in spheres of influence.

Greater than the Ahad was the Fetah, the society of freedom in Syria. The landowners, the writers, the doctors, the great public servants linked themselves in this society with a common oath, pass-words, signs, a press and a central treasury, to ruin the Turkish Empire. With the noisy facility of the Syrian — an ape-like people having much of the Japanese quickness, but shallow — they speedily built up a formidable organization. They looked outside for help, and expected freedom to come by entreaty, not by sacrifice. They corresponded with Egypt, with the Ahad (whose members, with true Mesopotamian dourness, rather despised them), with the Sherif of Mecca, and with Great Britain: everywhere seeking the ally to serve their turn. They also were deadly secret; and the Government, though it suspected their existence, could find no credible evidence of their leaders or member-ship. It had to hold its hand until it could strike with evidence enough to satisfy the English and French diplomats who acted as modern public opinion in Turkey. The war in 1914 withdrew these agents, and left the Turkish Government free to strike.

Mobilization put all power into the hands of those members —

Enver, Talaat and Jemal — who were at once the most ruthless, the most logical, and the most ambitious of the Young Turks. They set themselves to stamp out all non-Turkish currents in the State, especially Arab and Armenian nationalism. For the first step they found a specious and convenient weapon in the secret papers of a French Consul in Syria, who left behind him in his Consulate copies of correspondence (about Arab freedom) which had passed between him and an Arab club, not connected with the Fetah but made up of the more talkative and less formidable *intelligenzia* of the Syrian coast. The Turks, of course, were delighted; for 'colonial' aggression in North Africa had given the French a black reputation in the Arabic-speaking Moslem world; and it served Jemal well to show his co-religionists that these Arab nationalists were infidel enough to prefer France to Turkey.

In Syria, of course, his disclosures had little novelty; but the members of the society were known and respected, if somewhat academic, persons; and their arrest and condemnation, and the crop of deportations, exiles, and executions to which their trial led, moved the country to its depths, and taught the Arabs of the Fetah that if they did not profit by their lesson the fate of the Armenians would be upon them. The Armenians had been well armed and organized; but their leaders had failed them. They had been disarmed and destroyed piecemeal, the men by massacre, the women and children by being driven and over-driven along the wintry roads into the desert, naked and hungry, the common prey of any passer-by, until death took them. The Young Turks had killed the Armenians, not because they were Christians, but because they were Armenians; and for the same reason they herded Arab Moslems and Arab Christians into the same prison, and hanged them together on the same scaffold. Jemal Pasha united all classes, conditions and creeds in Syria, under pressure of a common misery and peril, and so made a concerted revolt possible.

The Turks suspected the Arab officers and soldiers in the Army, and hoped to use against them the scattering tactics which had served against the Armenians. At first transport difficulties stood in their way; and there came a dangerous concentration of Arab divisions (nearly one third of the original Turkish Army was Arabic speaking) in North

Syria early in 1915. They broke these up when possible, marching them off to Europe, to the Dardanelles, to the Caucasus, or the Canal — anywhere, so long as they were put quickly into the firing-line, or withdrawn far from the sight and help of their compatriots. A Holy War was proclaimed to give the 'Union and Progress' banner something of the traditional sanctity of the Caliph's battle-order in the eyes of the old clerical elements; and the Sherif of Mecca was invited — or rather ordered — to echo the cry.

CHAPTER V

THE position of the Sherif of Mecca had long been anomalous. The title of 'Sherif' implied descent from the prophet Mohammed through his daughter Fatima, and Hassan, her elder son. Authentic Sherifs were inscribed on the family tree — an immense roll preserved at Mecca, in custody of the Emir of Mecca, the elected Sherif of Sherifs, supposed to be the senior and noblest of all. The prophet's family had held temporal rule in Mecca for the last nine hundred years, and counted some two thousand persons.

The old Ottoman Governments regarded this clan of manticratic peers with a mixture of reverence and distrust. Since they were too strong to be destroyed, the Sultan salved his dignity by solemnly confirming their Emir in place. This empty approval acquired dignity by lapse of time, until the new holder began to feel that it added a final seal to his election. At last the Turks found that they needed the Hejaz under their unquestioned sway as part of the stage furniture for their new pan-Islamic notion. The fortuitous opening of the Suez Canal enabled them to garrison the Holy Cities. They projected the Hejaz Railway, and increased Turkish influence among the tribes by money, intrigue, and armed expeditions.

As the Sultan grew stronger there he ventured to assert himself more and more alongside the Sherif, even in Mecca itself, and upon occasion ventured to depose a Sherif too magnificent for his views, and to appoint a successor from a rival family of the clan in hopes of winning the usual advantages from dissension. Finally, Abdul Hamid took away some of the family to Constantinople into honourable captivity. Amongst these was Hussein ibn Ali, the future ruler, who was held a prisoner for nearly eighteen years. He took the opportunity to provide his sons — Ali, Abdulla, Feisal, and Zeid — with the modern education and experience which afterwards enabled them to lead the Arab armies to success.

When Abdul Hamid fell, the less wily Young Turks reversed his policy and sent back Sherif Hussein to Mecca as Emir. He at once set to

work unobtrusively to restore the power of the Emirate, and strengthened himself on the old basis, keeping the while close and friendly touch
with Constantinople through his sons, Abdulla, vice-chairman of the
Turkish House, and Feisal, member for Jidda. They kept him informed
of political opinion in the capital until war broke out, when they
returned in haste to Mecca.

The outbreak of war made trouble in the Hejaz. The pilgrimage
ceased, and with it the revenues and business of the Holy Cities. There
was reason to fear that the Indian food-ships would cease to come (since
the Sherif became technically an enemy subject); and as the province
produced almost no food of its own, it would be precariously dependent
on the goodwill of the Turks, who might starve it by closing the Hejaz
Railway. Hussein had never been entirely at the Turks' mercy before;
and at this unhappy moment they particularly needed his adherence to
their 'Jehad', the Holy War of all Moslems against Christianity.

To become popularly effective this must be endorsed by Mecca; and
if endorsed it might plunge the East in blood. Hussein was honourable,
shrewd, obstinate and deeply pious. He felt that the Holy War was
doctrinally incompatible with an aggressive war, and absurd with a
Christian ally: Germany. So he refused the Turkish demand, and made
at the same time a dignified appeal to the Allies not to starve his province for what was in no way his people's fault. The Turks in reply at
once instituted a partial blockade of the Hejaz by controlling the traffic
on the pilgrim railway. The British left his coast open to specially-
regulated food vessels.

The Turkish demand was, however, not the only one which the
Sherif received. In January 1915, Yisin, head of the Mesopotamian
officers, Ali Riza, head of the Damascus officers, and Abd el Ghani el
Areisi, for the Syrian civilians, sent down to him a concrete proposal for a military mutiny in Syria against the Turks. The oppressed
people of Mesopotamia and Syria, the committees of the Ahad and the
Fetah, were calling out to him as the Father of the Arabs, the Moslem of
Moslems, their greatest prince, their oldest notable, to save them from
the sinister designs of Talaat and Jemal.

Hussein, as politician, as prince, as moslem, as modernist, and as
nationalist, was forced to listen to their appeal. He sent Feysul, his third

son, to Damascus, to discuss their projects as his representative, and to make a report. He sent Ali, his eldest son, to Medina, with orders to raise quietly, on any excuse he pleased, troops from villagers and tribesmen of the Hejaz, and to hold them ready for action if Feisal called. Abdulla, his politic second son, was to sound the British by letter, to learn what would be their attitude towards a possible Arab revolt against Turkey.

Feisal reported in January 1915, that local conditions were good, but that the general war was not going well for their hopes. In Damascus were three divisions of Arab troops ready for rebellion. In Aleppo two other divisions, riddled with Arab nationalism, were sure to join in if the others began. There was only one Turkish division this side of the Taurus, so that it was certain that the rebels would get possession of Syria at the first effort. On the other hand, public opinion was less ready for extreme measures, and the military class quite sure that Germany would win the war and win it soon. If, however, the Allies landed their Australian Expedition (preparing in Egypt) at Alexandretta, and so covered the Syrian flank, then it would be wise and safe to risk a final German victory and the need to make a previous separate peace with the Turks.

Delay followed, as the Allies went to the Dardanelles, and not to Alexandretta. Feisal went after them to get first-hand knowledge of Gallipoli conditions, since a breakdown of Turkey would be the Arab signal. Then followed stagnation through the months of the Dardanelles campaign. In that slaughter-house the remaining Ottoman first-line army was destroyed. The disaster to Turkey of the accumulated losses was so great that Feisal came back to Syria, judging it a possible moment in which to strike, but found that meanwhile the local situation had become unfavourable.

His Syrian supporters were under arrest or in hiding, and their friends being hanged in scores on political charges. He found the well-disposed Arab divisions either exiled to distant fronts, or broken up in drafts and distributed among Turkish units. The Arab peasantry were in the grip of Turkish military service, and Syria prostrate before the merciless Jemal Pasha. His assets had disappeared.

He wrote to his father counselling further delay, till England should be ready and Turkey in extremities. Unfortunately, England was in a deplorable condition. Her forces were falling back shattered from the Dardanelles. The slow-drawn agony of Kut was in its last stage; and the Senussi rising, coincident with the entry of Bulgaria, threatened her on new flanks.

Feysul's position was hazardous in the extreme. He was at the mercy of the members of the secret society, whose president he had been before the war. He had to live as the guest of Jemal Pasha, in Damascus, rubbing up his military knowledge; for his brother Ali was raising the troops in Hejaz on the pretext that he and Feisal would lead them against the Suez Canal to help the Turks. So Feisal, as a good Ottoman and officer in the Turkish service, had to live at headquarters, and endure acquiescingly the insults and indignities heaped upon his race by the bully Jemal in his cups.

Jemal would send for Feisal and take him to the hanging of his Syrian friends. These victims of justice dared not show that they knew Feisal's real hopes, any more than he dared show his mind by word or look, since disclosure would have condemned his family and perhaps their race to the same fate. Only once did he burst out that these executions would cost Jemal all that he was trying to avoid; and it took the intercessions of his Constantinople friends, chief men in Turkey, to save him from the price of these rash words.

Feisal's correspondence with his father was an adventure in itself. They communicated by means of old retainers of the family, men above suspicion, who went up and down the Hejaz Railway, carrying letters in sword-hilts, in cakes, sewn between the soles of sandals, or in invisible writings on the wrappers of harmless packages. In all of them Feisal reported unfavourable things, and begged his father to postpone action till a wiser time.

Hussein, however, was not a whit cast down by Emir Feisal's discouragements. The Young Turks in his eyes were so many godless transgressors of their creed and their human duty — traitors to the spirit of the time, and to the highest interests of Islam. Though an old man of sixty-five, he was cheerfully determined to wage war against them, relying upon justice to cover the cost. Hussein trusted so much in God that he let his military sense lie fallow, and thought Hejaz able to fight it out with Turkey on a fair field. So he sent Abd el Kader el Abdu to Feisal with a letter that all was now ready for inspection by him in Medina before the troops started for the front. Feisal informed Jemal, and asked leave to go down, but to his dismay, Jemal replied that Enver Pasha, the Generalissimo, was on his way to the province, and that they would visit Medina together and inspect them. Feisal had planned to raise his father's crimson banner as soon as he arrived in Medina, and so to take the Turks unawares; and here he was going to be saddled with two uninvited guests to whom, by the Arab law of hospitality, he could do no harm, and who would probably delay his action so long that the whole secret of the revolt would be in jeopardy!

In the end matters passed off well, though the irony of the review was terrible. Enver, Jemal and Feisal watched the troops wheeling and turning in the dusty plain outside the city gate, rushing up and down in mimic camel-battle, or spurring their horses in the javelin game after immemorial Arab fashion. 'And are all these volunteers for the Holy War?' asked Enver at last, turning to Feisal. 'Yes,' said Feisal. 'Willing to fight to the death against the enemies of the faithful?' 'Yes,' said Feisal again; and then the Arab chiefs came up to be presented, and Sherif Ali ibn el Hussein, of Modhig, drew him aside whispering, 'My Lord, shall we kill them now?' and Feisal said, 'No, they are our guests.'

The Sheikhs protested further; for they believed that so they could finish off the war in two blows. They were determined to force Feisal's hand; and he had to go among them, just out of earshot but in full view, and plead for the lives of the Turkish dictators, who had murdered his best friends on the scaffold. In the end he had to make excuses, take the party back quickly to Medina, picket the banqueting hall with his own slaves, and escort Enver and Jemal back to Damascus to save them from death on the way. He explained this laboured courtesy by the plea that it was the Arab manner to devote everything to guests; but Enver and Jemal, being deeply suspicious of what they had seen, imposed a strict blockade of the Hejaz, and ordered large Turkish reinforcements thither. They wanted to detain Feisal in Damascus; but telegrams came from Medina claiming his immediate return to prevent disorder, and, reluctantly, Jemal let him go on condition that his suite remained behind as hostages.

Feisal found Medina full of Turkish troops, with the staff and head-quarters of the Twelfth Army Corps under Fakhri Pasha, the courage-ous old butcher who had bloodily 'purified' Zeitun and Urfa of Armenians. Clearly the Turks had taken warning, and Feisal's hope of a surprise rush, winning success almost without a shot, had become impossible. However, it was too late for prudence. From Damascus four days later his suite took horse and rode out east into the desert to take refuge with Nuri Shaalan, the Beduin chieftain; and the same day Feisal showed his hand. When he raised the Arab flag, the pan-Islamic supra-national State, for which Abdul Hamid had massacred and worked and died, and the German hope of the co-operation of Islam in the world-plans of the Kaiser, passed into the realm of dreams. By the mere fact of his rebellion the Sherif had closed these two fantastic chapters of history.

Rebellion was the gravest step which political men could take, and the success or failure of the Arab revolt was a gamble too hazardous for prophecy. Yet, for once, fortune favoured the bold player, and the Arab epic tossed up its stormy road from birth through weakness, pain and doubt, to red victory. It was the just end to an adventure which had dared so much, but after the victory there came a slow time of disillusion, and then a night in which the fighting men found that all their hopes had failed them. Now, at last, may there have come to them the white peace of the end, in the knowledge that they achieved a deathless thing, a lucent inspiration to the children of their race.

CHAPTER VI

I HAD been many years going up and down the Semitic East before the war, learning the manners of the villagers and tribesmen and citizens of Syria and Mesopotamia. My poverty had constrained me to mix with the humbler classes, those seldom met by European travellers, and thus my experiences gave me an unusual angle of view, which enabled me to understand and think for the ignorant many as well as for the more enlightened whose rare opinions mattered, not so much for the day, as for the morrow. In addition, I had seen something of the political forces working in the minds of the Middle East, and especially had noted everywhere sure signs of the decay of imperial Turkey.

Turkey was dying of overstrain, of the attempt, with diminished resources, to hold, on traditional terms, the whole Empire bequeathed to it. The sword had been the virtue of the children of Othman, and swords had passed out of fashion nowadays, in favour of deadlier and more scientific weapons. Life was growing too complicated for this child-like people, whose strength had lain in simplicity, and patience, and in their capacity for sacrifice. They were the slowest of the races of Western Asia, little fitted to adapt themselves to new sciences of government and life, still less to invent any new arts for themselves. Their administration had become perforce an affair of files and telegrams, of high finance, eugenics, calculations. Inevitably the old governors, who had governed by force of hand or force of character, illiterate, direct, personal, had to pass away. The rule was transferred to new men, with agility and suppleness to stoop to machinery. The shallow and half-polished committee of the Young Turks were descendants of Greeks, Albanians, Circassians, Bulgars, Armenians, Jews — anything but Seljuks or Ottomans. The commons ceased to feel in tune with their governors, whose culture was Levantine, and whose political theory was French. Turkey was decaying; and only the knife might keep health in her.

Loving the old ways steadily, the Anatolian remained a beast of burden in his village and an uncomplaining soldier abroad, while the subject races of the Empire, who formed nearly seven-tenths of its total population, grew daily in strength and knowledge; for their lack of tradition and responsibility, as well as their lighter and quicker minds, disposed them to accept new ideas. The former natural awe and supremacy of the Turkish name began to fade in the face of wider comparison. This changing balance of Turkey and the subject provinces involved growing garrisons if the old ground was to be retained. Tripoli, Albania, Thrace, Yemen, Hejaz, Syria, Mesopotamia, Kurdistan, Armenia, were all outgoing accounts, burdens on the peasants of Anatolia, yearly devouring a larger draft. The burden fell heaviest on the poor villages, and each year made these poor villages yet more poor.

The conscripts took their fate unquestioning: resignedly, after the custom of Turkish peasantry. They were like sheep, neutrals without vice or virtue. Left alone, they did nothing, or perhaps sat dully on the ground. Ordered to be kind, and without haste they were as good friends and as generous enemies as might be found. Ordered to outrage their fathers or disembowel their mothers, they did it as calmly as they did nothing, or did well. There was about them a hopeless, fever-wasted lack of initiative, which made them the most biddable, most enduring, and least spirited soldiers in the world.

Such men were natural victims of their showy-vicious Levantine officers, to be driven to death or thrown away by neglect without reckoning. Indeed, we found them just kept chopping-blocks of their commanders' viler passions. So cheap did they rate them, that in connection with them they used none of the ordinary precautions. Medical examination of some batches of Turkish prisoners found nearly half of them with unnaturally acquired venereal disease. Pox and its like were not understood in the country; and the infection ran from one to another through the battalion, where the conscripts served for six or seven years, till at the end of their period the survivors, if they came from decent homes, were ashamed to return, and drifted either into the gendarmerie service, or, as broken men, into casual labour about the towns; and so the birth-rate fell. The Turkish peasantry in Anatolia were dying of their military service.

We could see that a new factor was needed in the East, some power or race which would outweigh the Turks in numbers, in output, and in mental activity. No encouragement was given us by history to think that these qualities could be supplied ready-made from Europe. The efforts of European Powers to keep a footing in the Asiatic Levant had been uniformly disastrous, and we disliked no Western people enough to inveigle them into further attempts. Our successor and solution must be local; and fortunately the standard of efficiency required was local also. The competition would be with Turkey; and Turkey was rotten.

Some of us judged that there was latent power enough and to spare in the Arabic peoples (the greatest component of the old Turkish Empire), a prolific Semitic agglomeration, great in religious thought, reasonably industrious, mercantile, politic, yet solvent rather than dominant in character. They had served a term of five hundred years under the Turkish harrow, and had begun to dream of liberty; so when at last England fell out with Turkey, and war was let loose in the East and West at once, we who believed we held an indication of the future set out to bend England's efforts towards fostering the new Arabic world in hither Asia.

We were not many; and nearly all of us rallied round Clayton, the chief of Intelligence, civil and military, in Egypt. Clayton made the perfect leader for such a band of wild men as we were. He was calm, detached, clear-sighted, of unconscious courage in assuming responsibility. He gave an open run to his subordinates. His own views were general, like his knowledge; and he worked by influence rather than by loud direction. It was not easy to descry his influence. He was like water, or permeating oil, creeping silently and insistently through everything. It was not possible to say where Clayton was and was not, and how much really belonged to him. He never visibly led; but his ideas were abreast of those who did: he impressed men by his sobriety, and by a certain quiet and stately moderation of hope. In practical matters he was loose, irregular, untidy, a man with whom independent men could bear.

The first of us was Ronald Storrs, Oriental Secretary of the Residency, the most brilliant Englishman in the Near East, and subtly efficient, despite his diversion of energy in love of music and letters, of sculpture, painting, of whatever was beautiful in the world's fruit. None the less, Storrs sowed what we reaped, and was always first, and the great man among us. His shadow would have covered our work and British policy in the East like a cloak, had he been able to deny himself the world, and to prepare his mind and body with the sternness of an athlete for a great fight.

George Lloyd entered our number. He gave us confidence, and with his knowledge of money, proved a sure guide through the subways of trade and politics, and a prophet upon the future arteries of the Middle East. We would not have done so much so soon without his partnership; but he was a restless soul, avid rather to taste than to exhaust. To him many things were needful; and so he would not stay very long with us. He did not see how much we liked him.

Then there was the imaginative advocate of unconvincing world-movements, Mark Sykes: also a bundle of prejudices, intuitions, half-sciences. His ideas were of the outside; and he lacked patience to test his materials before choosing his style of building. He would take an aspect of the truth, detach it from its circumstances, inflate it, twist and model it, until its old likeness and its new unlikeness together drew a laugh; and laughs were his triumphs. His instincts lay in parody: by choice he was a caricaturist rather than an artist, even in statesmanship. He saw the odd in everything, and missed the even. He would sketch out in a few dashes a new world, all out of scale, but vivid as a vision of some sides of the thing we hoped. His help did us good and harm. For this his last week in Paris tried to atone. He had returned from a period of political duty in Syria, after his awful realization of the true shape of his dreams, to say gallantly, 'I was wrong: here is the truth'. His former friends would not see his new earnestness, and thought him fickle and in error; and very soon he died. It was a tragedy of tragedies, for the Arab sake.

Not a wild man, but *Mentor* to all of us was Hogarth, our father confessor and adviser, who brought us the parallels and lessons of history, and moderation, and courage. To the outsiders he was peacemaker (I was all claws and teeth, and had a devil), and made us favoured and listened to, for his weighty judgement. He had a delicate sense of value, and would present clearly to us the forces hidden behind the lousy rags and festering skins which we knew as Arabs. Hogarth was our referee, and our untiring historian, who gave us his great knowledge and careful wisdom even in the smallest things, because we believed in what we were making. Behind him stood Cornwallis, a man rude to look upon, but apparently forged from one of those incredible metals with a melting-point of thousands of degrees. So he could remain for months hotter than other men's white-heat, and yet look cold and hard. Behind him again were others, Newcombe, Parker, Herbert, Graves, all of the creed, and labouring stoutly after their fashion.

We called ourselves 'Intrusive' as a band; for we meant to break into the accepted halls of English foreign policy, and build a new people in the East, despite the rails laid down for us by our ancestors. Therefore from our hybrid intelligence office in Cairo (a jangling place which for its incessant bells and bustle and running to and fro, was likened by Aubrey Herbert to an oriental railway station) we began to work upon all chiefs, far and near. Sir Henry McMahon, High Commissioner in Egypt, was, of course, our first effort; and his shrewd insight and tried, experienced mind understood our design at once and judged it good. Others, like Wemyss, Neil Malcolm, Wingate, supported us in their pleasure at seeing the war turned constructive. Their advocacy confirmed in Lord Kitchener the favourable impression he had derived years before when Sherif Abdulla appealed to him in Egypt; and so McMahon at last achieved our foundation stone, the understanding with the Sherif of Mecca.

But before this we had had hopes of Mesopotamia. The beginning of the Arab Independence Movement had been there, under the vigorous but unscrupulous impulse of Seyid Taleb, and later of Yasin el Hashimi and the military league. Aziz el Masri, Enver's rival, who was living, much indebted to us, in Egypt, was an idol of the Arab officers. He was approached by Lord Kitchener in the first days of the war, with the hope of winning the Turkish Mesopotamian forces to our side. Unfortunately Britain was bursting then with confidence in an easy and early victory: the smashing of Turkey was called a promenade. So the Indian Government was adverse to any pledges to the Arab nationalists which might limit their ambitions to make the intended Mesopotamian colony play the self-sacrificing role of a Burma for the general good. It broke off negotiations, rejected Aziz, and interned Sayid Taleb, who had placed himself in our hands.

By brute force it marched then into Basra. The enemy troops in Irak were nearly all Arabs in the unenviable predicament of having to fight on behalf of their secular oppressors against a people long envisaged as liberators, but who obstinately refused to play the part. As may be imagined, they fought very badly. Our forces won battle after battle till we came to think an Indian army better than a Turkish army. There followed our rash advance to Ctesiphon, where we met native Turkish troops whose full heart was in the game, and were abruptly checked. We fell back, dazed; and the long misery of Kut began.

Meanwhile, our Government had repented, and, for reasons not unconnected with the fall of Erzerum, sent me to Mesopotamia to see what could be done by indirect means to relieve the beleaguered garrison. The local British had the strongest objection to my coming; and two Generals of them were good enough to explain to me that my mission (which they did not really know) was dishonourable to a soldier (which I was not). As a matter of fact it was too late for action, with Kut just dying; and in consequence I did nothing of what it was in my mind and power to do.

The conditions were ideal for an Arab movement. The people of Nejef and Kerbela, far in the rear of Halil Pasha's army, were in revolt against him. The surviving Arabs in Halil's army were, on his own confession, openly disloyal to Turkey. The tribes of the Hai and Euphrates would have turned our way had they seen signs of grace in the British. Had we published the promises made to the Sherif, or even the proclamation afterwards posted in captured Bagdad, and followed it up, enough local fighting men would have joined us to harry the Turkish line of communication between Bagdad and Kut. A few weeks of that, and the enemy would either have been forced to raise the siege and retire, or have themselves suffered investment, outside Kut, nearly as stringent as the investment of Townshend within it. Time to develop such a scheme could easily have been gained. Had the British headquarters in Mesopotamia obtained from the War Office eight more aeroplanes to increase the daily carriage of food to the garrison of Kut, Townshend's resistance might have been indefinitely prolonged. His defence was Turkishly impregnable; and only blunders within and without forced surrender upon him.

However, as this was not the way of the directing parties there, I returned at once to Egypt; and till the end of the war the British in Mesopotamia remained substantially an alien force invading enemy territory, with the local people passively neutral or sullenly against them, and in consequence had not the freedom of movement and elasticity of Allenby in Syria, who entered the country as a friend, with the local people actively on his side. The factors of numbers, climate and communications favoured us in Mesopotamia more than in Syria; and our higher command was, after the beginning, no less efficient and experienced. But their casualty lists compared with Allenby's, their wood-chopping tactics compared with his rapier-play, showed how formidably an adverse political situation was able to cramp a purely military operation.

CHAPTER VII

OUR check in Mesopotamia was a disappointment to us; but McMahon continued his negotiations with Mecca, and finally brought them to success despite the evacuation of Gallipoli, the surrender of Kut, and the generally unfortunate aspect of the war at the moment. Few people, even of those who knew all the negotiations, had really believed that the Sherif would fight; consequently his eventual rebellion and opening of his coast to our ships and help took us and them by surprise.

We found our difficulties then only beginning. The credit of the new factor was to McMahon and Clayton: professional jealousies immediately raised their heads. Sir Archibald Murray, the General in Egypt, wanted, naturally enough, no competitors, and no competing campaigns in his sphere. He disliked the civil power, which had so long kept the peace between himself and General Maxwell. He could not be entrusted with the Arabian affair; for neither he nor his staff had the ethnological competence needed to deal with so curious a problem. On the other hand, he could make the spectacle of the High Commission running a private war sufficiently ridiculous. His was a very nervous mind, fanciful and essentially competitive.

He found help in his Chief of Staff, General Lynden Bell, a red soldier, with an instinctive shuddering away from politicians, and a conscientiously assumed heartiness.

Two of the General Staff officers followed their leaders full cry; and so the unfortunate McMahon found himself deprived of Army help and reduced to waging his war in Arabia with the assistance of his Foreign Office Attachés.

Some appeared to resent a war which allowed outsiders to thrust into their business. Also their training in suppression, by which alone the daily trivialities of diplomacy were made to look like man's work, had so sunk into them that when the more important thing arrived, they made it trivial. Their feebleness of tone, and niggling dishonesties to one another, angered the military to disgust; and were bad for us, too, since they patently let down the High Commissioner, whose boots the G———s were not good enough to clean.

Wingate, who had complete confidence in his own grasp of the situation in the Middle East, foresaw credit and great profit for the country in the Arab development; but as criticism slowly beat up against McMahon he dissociated himself from him, and London began to hint that better use might be made by an experienced hand of so subtle and involved a skein.

However it was, things in the Hejaz went from bad to worse. No proper liaison was provided for the Arab forces in the field, no military information was given the Sherifs, no tactical advice or strategy was suggested, no attempt made to find out the local conditions and adapt existing Allied resources in material to suit their needs. The French Military Mission (which Clayton's prudence had suggested be sent to Hejaz to soothe our very suspicious allies by taking them behind the scenes and giving them a purpose there), was permitted to carry on an elaborate intrigue against Sherif Hussein in his towns of Jidda and Mecca, and to propose to him and to the British authorities measures that must have ruined his cause in the eyes of all Moslems. Wingate, now in military control of our co-operation with the Sherif, was induced to land some foreign troops at Rabegh, half-way between Medina and Mecca, for the defence of Mecca and to hold up the further advance of the reinvigorated Turks from Medina. McMahon, in the multitude of counsellors, became confused, and gave a handle to Murray to cry out against his inconsistencies. The Arab Revolt became discredited; and Staff Officers in Egypt gleefully prophesied to us its near failure and the stretching of Sherif Hussein's neck on a Turkish scaffold.

My private position was not easy. As Staff Captain under Clayton in Sir Archibald Murray's Intelligence Section, I was charged with the 'distribution' of the Turkish Army and the preparation of maps. By natural inclination I had added to them the invention of the Arab Bulletin, a secret weekly record of Middle-Eastern politics; and of necessity Clayton came more and more to need me in the military wing of the Arab Bureau, the tiny intelligence and war staff for foreign affairs, which he was now organizing for McMahon. Eventually Clayton was driven out of the General Staff; and Colonel Holdich, Murray's intelligence officer at Ismailia, took his place in command of us. His first intention was to retain my services; and, since he clearly did not need me, I interpreted this, not without some friendly evidence, as a method of keeping me away from the Arab affair. I decided that I must escape at once, if ever. A straight request was refused; so I took to stratagems. I became, on the telephone (G.H.Q. were at Ismailia, and I in Cairo) quite intolerable to the Staff on the Canal. I took every opportunity to rub into them their comparative ignorance and in-efficiency in the department of intelligence (not difficult!) and irritated them yet further by literary airs, correcting Shavian split infinitives and tautologies in their reports.

In a few days they were bubbling over on my account, and at last determined to endure me no longer. I took this strategic opportunity to ask for ten days' leave, saying that Storrs was going down to Jidda on business with the Grand Sherif, and that I would like a holiday and joy-ride in the Red Sea with him. They did not love Storrs, and were glad to get rid of me for the moment. So they agreed at once, and began to prepare against my return some official shelf for me. Needless to say, I had no intention of giving them such a chance; for, while very ready to hire my body out on petty service, I hesitated to throw my mind frivolously away. So I went to Clayton and confessed my affairs; and he arranged for the Residency to make telegraphic application to the Foreign Office for my transfer to the Arab Bureau. The Foreign Office would treat directly with the War Office; and the Egypt command would not hear of it, till all was ended.

Storrs and I then marched off together, happily. In the East they swore that by three sides was the decent way across a square; and my trick to escape was in this sense oriental. But I justified myself by my confidence in the final success of the Arab Revolt if properly advised. I had been a mover in its beginning; my hopes lay in it. The fatalistic subordination of a professional soldier (intrigue being unknown in the British army) would have made a proper officer sit down and watch his plan of campaign wrecked by men who thought nothing of it, and to whose spirit it made no appeal. *Non nobis, Domine.*

BOOK I

THE DISCOVERY OF FEISAL

Chapters VIII to XVI

I HAD *believed these misfortunes of the Revolt to be due mainly to faulty leadership, or rather to the lack of leadership, Arab and English. So I went down to Arabia to see and consider its great men. The first, the Sherif of Mecca, we knew to be aged. I found Abdulla too clever. Ali too clean, Zeid too cool.*

Then I rode up-country to Feisal, and found in him the leader with the necessary fire, and yet with reason to give effect to our science. His tribesmen seemed sufficient instrument, and his hills to provide natural advantage. So I returned pleased and confident to Egypt, and told my chiefs how Mecca was defended not by the obstacle of Rabegh, but by the flank-threat of Feisal in Jebel Subh.

NOTE — "J." denotes JEBEL (Mountain)   "W." denotes WADI (Watercourse & Valley)

CHAPTER VIII

WAITING off Suez was the *Lama*, a small converted liner; and in her we left immediately. Such short voyages on warships were delicious interludes for us passengers. On this occasion, however, there was some embarrassment. Our mixed party seemed to disturb the ship's company in their own element. The juniors had turned out of their berths to give us night space, and by day we filled their living rooms with irregular talk. Storrs' intolerant brain seldom stooped to company. But to-day he was more abrupt than usual. He turned twice around the decks, sniffed, 'No one worth talking to', and sat down in one of the two comfortable armchairs, to begin a discussion of Debussy with Aziz el Masri (in the other). Aziz, the Arab-Circassian ex-colonel in the Turkish Army, now general in the Sherifian Army, was on his way to discuss with the Emir of Mecca the equipment and standing of the Arab regulars he was forming at Rabegh. A few minutes later they had left Debussy, and were depreciating Wagner: Aziz in fluent German, and Storrs in German, French and Arabic. The ship's officers found the whole conversation unnecessary.

We had the accustomed calm run to Jidda, in the delightful Red Sea climate, never too hot while the ship was moving. By day we lay in shadow; and for great part of the glorious nights we would tramp up and down the wet decks under the stars in the steaming breath of the southern wind. But when at last we anchored in the outer harbour, off the white town hung between the blazing sky and its reflection in the mirage which swept and rolled over the wide lagoon, then the heat of Arabia came out like a drawn sword and struck us speechless. It was mid-day; and the noon sun in the East, like moonlight, put to sleep the colours. There were only lights and shadows, the white houses and black gaps of streets: in front, the pallid lustre of the haze shimmering upon the inner harbour: behind, the dazzle of league after league of featureless sand, running up to an edge of low hills, faintly suggested in the far away mist of heat.

Just north of Jidda was a second group of black-white buildings, moving up and down like pistons in the mirage, as the ship rolled at anchor and the intermittent wind shifted the heat waves in the air. It looked and felt horrible. We began to regret that the inaccessibility which made the Hejaz militarily a safe theatre of revolt involved bad climate and un-wholesomeness.

However, Colonel Wilson, British representative with the new Arab state, had sent his launch to meet us; and we had to go ashore to learn the reality of the men levitating in that mirage. Half an hour later Ruhi, Consular Oriental assistant, was grinning a delighted welcome to his old patron Storrs, (Ruhi the ingenious, more like a mandrake than a man), while the newly-appointed Syrian police and harbour officers, with a scratch guard of honour, lined the Customs Wharf in salutation of Aziz el Masri. Sherif Abdulla, the second son of the old man of Mecca, was reported just arriving in the town. He it was we had to meet; so our coming was auspiciously timed.

We walked past the white masonry of the still-building water gate, and through the oppressive alley of the food market on our way to the Consulate. In the air, from the men to the dates and back to the meat, squadrons of flies like particles of dust danced up and down the sun-shafts which stabbed into the darkest corners of the booths through torn places in the wood and sackcloth awnings overhead. The atmosphere was like a bath. The scarlet leathers of the armchair on the *Lama's* deck had dyed Storrs' white tunic and trousers as bright as themselves in their damp contact of the last four days, and now the sweat running in his clothes began to shine like varnish through the stain. I was so fascinated watching him that I never noticed the deepened brown of my khaki drill wherever it touched my body. He was wondering if the walk to the Consulate was long enough to wet me a decent, solid, harmonious colour; and I was wondering if all he ever sat on would grow scarlet as himself.

We reached the Consulate too soon for either hope; and there in a shaded room with an open lattice behind him sat Wilson, prepared to welcome the sea breeze, which had lagged these last few days. He received us stiffly, being of the honest, downright Englishmen, to whom Storrs was suspect, if only for his artistic sense: while his contact

with me in Cairo had been a short difference of opinion as to whether
native clothes were an indignity for us. I had called them uncomfortable merely. To him they were wrong. Wilson, however, despite
his personal feelings, was all for the game. He had made preparations
for the coming interview with Abdulla, and was ready to afford every
help he could. Besides, we were his guests; and the splendid hospitality
of the East was near his spirit.

Abdulla, on a white mare, came to us softly with a bevy of richly-
armed slaves on foot about him, through the silent respectful salutes of
the town. He was flushed with his success at Taif, and happy. I was
seeing him for the first time, while Storrs was an old friend, and on the
best of terms; yet, before long, as they spoke together, I began to
suspect him of a constant cheerfulness. His eyes had a confirmed
twinkle; and though only thirty-five, he was putting on flesh. It might
be due to too much laughter. Life seemed very merry for Abdulla.
He was short, strong, fair-skinned, with a carefully trimmed brown
beard, masking his round smooth face and short lips. In manner he
was open, or affected openness, and was charming on acquaintance.
He stood not on ceremony, but jested with all comers in most easy
fashion: yet, when we fell into serious talk, the veil of humour seemed
to fade away. He then chose his words, and argued shrewdly. Of
course, he was in discussion with Storrs, who demanded a high standard
from his opponent.

The Arabs thought Abdulla a far-seeing statesman and an astute
politician. Astute he certainly was, but not greatly enough to convince us always of his sincerity. His ambition was patent. Rumour
made him the brain of his father and of the Arab revolt; but he seemed
too easy for that. His object was, of course, the winning of Arab
independence and the building up of Arab nations, but he meant to
keep the direction of the new states in the family. So he watched us,
and played through us to the British gallery.

On our part, I was playing for effect, watching, criticizing him. The
Sherif's rebellion had been unsatisfactory for the last few months:
(standing still, which, with an irregular war, was the prelude to
disaster): and my suspicion was that its lack was leadership: not intel-
lect, nor judgement, nor political wisdom, but the flame of enthusiasm,

that would set the desert on fire. My visit was mainly to find the yet unknown master-spirit of the affair, and measure his capacity to carry the revolt to the goal I had conceived for it. As our conversation continued, I became more and more sure that Abdulla was too balanced, too cool, too humorous to be a prophet: especially the armed prophet who, if history be true, succeeded in revolutions. His value would come perhaps in the peace after success. During the physical struggle, when singleness of eye and magnetism, devotion and self-sacrifice were needed, Abdulla would be a tool too complex for a simple purpose, though he could not be ignored, even now.

We talked to him first about the state of Jidda, to put him at ease by discussing at this first of our interviews the unnecessary subject of the Sherif's administration. He replied that the war was yet too much with them for civil government. They had inherited the Turkish system in the towns, and were continuing it on a more modest scale. The Turkish Government was often not unkind to strong men, who obtained considerable licence on terms. Consequently, some of the licensees in Hejaz regretted the coming of a native ruler. Particularly in Mecca and Jidda public opinion was against an Arab state. The mass of citizens were foreigners — Egyptians, Indians, Javanese, Africans, and others — quite unable to sympathize with the Arab aspirations, especially as voiced by Beduin; for the Beduin lived on what he could exact from the stranger on his roads, or in his valleys; and he and the townsman bore each other a perpetual grudge.

The Beduins were the only fighting men the Sherif had got; and on their help the revolt depended. He was arming them freely, paying many of them for their service in his forces, feeding their families while they were from home, and hiring from them their transport camels to maintain his armies in the field. Accordingly, the country was prosperous, while the towns went short.

Another grievance in the towns was in the matter of law. The Turkish civil code had been abolished, and a return made to the old religious law, the undiluted Koranic procedure of the Arab Kadi. Abdulla explained to us, with a giggle, that when there was time they would discover in the Koran such opinions and judgements as were required to make it suitable for modern commercial operations, like

banking and exchange. Meanwhile, of course, what townsmen lost by
the abolition of the civil law, the Beduins gained. Sherif Hussein had
silently sanctioned the restoration of the old tribal order. Beduins at
odds with one another pleaded their own cases before the tribal lawman, an office hereditary in one most-respected family, and recognized
by the payment of a goat per household as yearly due. Judgement was
based on custom, by quoting from a great body of remembered prece-
dent. It was delivered publicly without fee. In cases between men of
different tribes, the lawman was selected by mutual consent, or recourse
was had to the lawman of a third tribe. If the case were contentious and
difficult, the judge was supported by a jury of four — two nominated
by plaintiff from the ranks of defendant's family, and two by defendant
from plaintiff's family. Decisions were always unanimous.

We contemplated the vision Abdulla drew for us, with sad thoughts
of the Garden of Eden and all that Eve, now lying in her tomb just
outside the wall, had lost for average humanity; and then Storrs
brought me into the discussion by asking Abdulla to give us his views
on the state of the campaign for my benefit, and for communication to
headquarters in Egypt. Abdulla at once grew serious, and said that he
wanted to urge upon the British their immediate and very personal
concern in the matter, which he tabulated so:—

By our neglect to cut the Hejaz Railway, the Turks had been able
to collect transport and supplies for the reinforcement of Medina.

Feisal had been driven back from the town; and the enemy was
preparing a mobile column of all arms for an advance on Rabegh.

The Arabs in the hills across their road were by our neglect too weak
in supplies, machine guns and artillery to defend them long.

Hussein Mabeirig, chief of the Masruh Harb, had joined the Turks.
If the Medina column advanced, the Harb would join it.

It would only remain for his father to put himself at the head of his
own people of Mecca and to die fighting before the Holy City.

At this moment the telephone rang: the Grand Sherif wanted to
speak to Abdulla. He was told of the point our conversation had
reached, and at once confirmed that he would so act in the extremity.
The Turks would enter Mecca over his dead body. The telephone
rang off; and Abdulla, smiling a little, asked, to prevent such a disaster,

that a British brigade, if possible of Moslem troops, be kept at Suez, with transport to rush it to Rabegh as soon as the Turks debouched from Medina in their attack. What did we think of the proposal?

I replied; first, historically, that Sherif Hussein had asked us not to cut the Hejaz line, since he would need it for his victorious advance into Syria; second, practically, that the dynamite we sent down for demolitions had been returned by him with a note that it was too dangerous for Arab use; third, specifically, that we had had no demands for equipment from Feisal.

With regard to the brigade for Rabegh, it was a complicated question. Shipping was precious; and we could not hold empty transport indefinitely at Suez. We had no Moslem units in our Army. A British brigade was a cumbersome affair, and would take long to embark and disembark. The Rabegh position was large. A brigade would hardly hold it and would be quite unable to detach a force to prevent a Turkish column slipping past it inland. The most they could do would be to defend the beach, under a ship's guns and the ship could do that as well without the troops.

Abdulla replied that ships were insufficient morally, as the Dardanelles fighting had destroyed the old legend of the British Navy and its omnipotence. No Turks could slip past Rabegh; for it was the only water supply in the district, and they must water at its wells. The earmarking of a brigade and transports need be only temporary; for he was taking his victorious Taif troops up the eastern road from Mecca to Medina. As soon as he was in position, he would give orders to Ali and Feisal, who would close in from the south and west, and their combined forces would deliver a grand attack, in which Medina would, please God, be taken. Meanwhile, Aziz el Masri was moulding the volunteers from Mesopotamia and Syria into battalions at Rabegh. When we had added the Arab prisoners of war from India and Egypt, there would be enough to take over the duties momentarily allotted to the British brigade.

I said that I would represent his views to Egypt, but that the British were reluctant to spare troops from the vital defence of Egypt (though he was not to imagine that the Canal was in any danger from the Turks) and, still more, to send Christians to defend the people of the

Holy City against their enemies; as some Moslems in India, who considered the Turkish Government had an imprescriptible right to the Haramein, would misrepresent our motives and action. I thought that I might perhaps urge his opinions more powerfully if I was able to report on the Rabegh question in the light of my own knowledge of the position and local feeling. I would also like to see Feisal, and talk over with him his needs and the prospects of a prolonged defence of his hills by the tribesmen if we strengthened them materially. I would like to ride from Rabegh up the Sultani road towards Medina as far as Feisal's camp.

Storrs then came in and supported me with all his might, urging the vital importance of full and early information from a trained observer for the British Commander-in-Chief in Egypt, and showing that his sending down me, his best qualified and most indispensable staff officer, proved the serious consideration being given to Arabian affairs by Sir Archibald Murray. Abdulla went to the telephone and tried to get his father's consent to my going up country. The Sherif viewed the proposal with grave distrust. Abdulla argued the point, made some advantage, and transferred the mouthpiece to Storrs, who turned all his diplomacy on the old man. Storrs in full blast was a delight to listen to in the mere matter of Arabic speech, and also a lesson to every English-man alive of how to deal with suspicious or unwilling Orientals. It was nearly impossible to resist him for more than a few minutes, and in this case also he had his way. The Sherif asked again for Abdulla, and authorized him to write to Ali, and suggest that if he thought fit, and if conditions were normal, I might be allowed to proceed to Feisal in Jebel Subh; and Abdulla, under Storrs' influence, transformed this guarded message into direct written instructions to Ali to mount me as well and as quickly as possible, and convey me, by sure hand, to Feisal's camp. This being all I wanted, and half what Storrs wanted, we adjourned for lunch.

CHAPTER IX

JEDDAH had pleased us, on our way to the Consulate: so after lunch, when it was a little cooler, or at least when the sun was not so high, we wandered out to see the sights under the guidance of Young, Wilson's assistant, a man who found good in many old things, but little good in things now being made.

It was indeed a remarkable town. The streets were alleys, wood roofed in the main bazaar, but elsewhere open to the sky in the little gap between the tops of the lofty white-walled houses. These were built four or five stories high, of coral rag tied with square beams and decorated by wide bow-windows running from ground to roof in grey wooden panels. There was no glass in Jidda, but a profusion of good lattices, and some very delicate shallow chiselling on the panels of window casings. The doors were heavy two-leaved slabs of teak-wood, deeply carved, often with wickets in them; and they had rich hinges and ring-knockers of hammered iron. There was much moulded or cut plastering, and on the older houses fine stone heads and jambs to the windows looking on the inner courts.

The style of architecture was like crazy Elizabethan half-timber work, in the elaborate Cheshire fashion, but gone gimcrack to an incredible degree. House-fronts were fretted, pierced and pargetted till they looked as though cut out of cardboard for a romantic stage-setting. Every storey jutted, every window leaned one way or other; often the very walls sloped. It was like a dead city, so clean underfoot, and so quiet. Its winding, even streets were floored with damp sand solidified by time and as silent to the tread as any carpet. The lattices and wall-returns deadened all reverberation of voice. There were no carts, nor any streets wide enough for carts, no shod animals, no bustle anywhere. Everything was hushed, strained, even furtive. The doors of houses shut softly as we passed. There were no loud dogs, no crying children: indeed, except in the bazaar, still half asleep, there were few wayfarers of any kind; and the rare people we did meet, all thin, and as it were wasted by disease, with scarred, hairless faces and screwed-up eyes, slipped past us quickly and cautiously, not looking at us. Their skimp, white robes, shaven polls with little skull-caps, red cotton shoulder-shawls, and bare feet were so same as to be almost a uniform.

The atmosphere was oppressive, deadly. There seemed no life in it. It was not burning hot, but held a moisture and sense of great age and exhaustion such as seemed to belong to no other place: not a passion of smells like Smyrna, Naples or Marseilles, but a feeling of long use, of the exhalations of many people, of continued bath-heat and sweat. One would say that for years Jidda had not been swept through by a firm breeze: that its streets kept their air from year's end to year's end, from the day they were built for so long as the houses should endure. There was nothing in the bazaars to buy.

In the evening the telephone rang; and the Sherif called Storrs to the instrument. He asked if we would not like to listen to his band. Storrs, in astonishment, asked What band? and congratulated his holiness on having advanced so far towards urbanity. The Sherif explained that the headquarters of the Hejaz Command under the Turks had had a brass band, which played each night to the Governor General; and when the Governor General was captured by Abdulla at Taif his band was captured with him. The other prisoners were sent to Egypt for internment; but the band was excepted. It was held in Mecca to give music to the victors. Sherif Hussein laid his receiver on the table of his reception hall, and we, called solemnly one by one to the telephone, heard the band in the Palace at Mecca forty-five miles away. Storrs expressed the general gratification; and the Sherif, increasing his bounty replied that the band should be sent down by forced march to Jidda, to play in our courtyard also, 'And,' said he, 'you may then do me the pleasure of ringing me up from your end, that I may share your satisfaction.'

Next day Storrs visited Abdulla in his tent out by Eve's Tomb; and together they inspected the hospital, the barracks, the town offices, and partook of the hospitality of the Mayor and the Governor. In the intervals of duty they talked about money, and the Sherif's title, and his relations with the other Princes of Arabia, and the general course of the war: all the commonplaces that should pass between envoys of two Governments. It was tedious, and for the most part I held myself

c*

excused, as after a conversation in the morning I had made up my mind that Abdulla was not the necessary leader. We had asked him to sketch the genesis of the Arab movement: and his reply illuminated his character. He had begun by a long description of Talaat, the first Turk to speak to him with concern of the restlessness of Hejaz. He wanted it properly subdued, and military service, as elsewhere in the Empire, introduced.

Abdulla, to forestall him, had made a plan of peaceful insurrection for Hejaz, and, after sounding Kitchener without profit, had dated it provisionally for 1915. He had meant to call out the tribes during the feast, and lay hold of the pilgrims. They would have included many of the chief men of Turkey besides leading Moslems of Egypt, India, Java, Eritrea, and Algiers. With these thousands of hostages in his hands he had expected to win the notice of the Great Powers concerned. He thought they would bring pressure on the Porte to secure the release of their nationals. The Porte, powerless to deal with Hejaz militarily, would either have made concessions to the Sherif or have confessed its powerlessness to the foreign States. In the latter event, Abdulla would have approached them direct, ready to meet their demands in return for a guarantee of immunity from Turkey. I did not like his scheme, and was glad when he said with almost a sneer that Feisal in fear had begged his father not to follow it. This sounded good for Feisal, towards whom my hopes of a great leader were now slowly turning.

In the evening Abdulla came to dine with Colonel Wilson. We received him in the courtyard on the house steps. Behind him were his brilliant household servants and slaves, and behind them a pale crew of bearded, emaciated men with woe-begone faces, wearing tatters of military uniform, and carrying tarnished brass instruments of music. Abdulla waved his hand towards them and crowed with delight, 'My Band'. We sat them on benches in the forecourt, and Wilson sent them cigarettes, while we went up to the dining room, where the shuttered balcony was opened right out, hungrily, for a sea breeze. As we sat down, the band, under the guns and swords of Abdulla's retainers, began, each instrument apart, to play heartbroken Turkish airs. Our ears ached with noise: but Abdulla beamed.

Curious the party was. Abdulla himself, Vice-President *in partibus* of the Turkish Chamber and now Foreign Minister of the rebel Arab State; Wilson, Governor of the Red Sea Province of the Sudan, and His Majesty's Minister with the Sherif of Mecca; Storrs, Oriental Secretary successively to Gorst, Kitchener and McMahon in Cairo; Young, Cochrane, and myself, hangers-on of the staff; Sayed Ali, a general in the Egyptian Army, commander of the detachment sent over by the Sirdar to help the first efforts of the Arabs; Aziz el Masri, now Chief of Staff of the Arab regular army, but in old days Enver's rival, leader of the Turkish and Senussi forces against the Italians, chief conspirator of the Arab officers in the Turkish army against the Committee of Union and Progress, a man condemned to death by the Turks for obeying the Treaty of Lausanne, and saved by *The Times* and Lord Kitchener.

We got tired of Turkish music, and asked for German. Aziz stepped out on the balcony and called down to the bandsmen in Turkish to play us something foreign. They struck shakily into 'Deutschland über Alles' just as the Sherif came to his telephone in Mecca to listen to the music of our feast. We asked for more German music; and they played 'Eine feste Burg'. Then in the midst they died away into flabby discords of drums. The parchment had stretched in the damp air of Jidda. They cried for fire; and Wilson's servants and Abdulla's bodyguard brought them piles of straw and packing cases. They warmed the drums, turning them round and round before the blaze, and then broke into what they said was the Hymn of Hate, though no one could recognize a European progression in it all. Sayed Ali turned to Abdulla and said, 'It is a death march'. Abdulla's eyes widened; but Storrs who spoke in quickly to the rescue turned the moment to laughter; and we sent out rewards with the leavings of the feast to the sorrowful musicians, who could take no pleasure in our praises, but begged to be sent home. Next morning I left Jidda by ship for Rabegh.

CHAPTER X

MOORED in Rabegh lay the *Northbrook*, an Indian Marine ship. On board was Colonel Parker, our liaison officer with Sherif Ali, to whom he sent my letter from Abdulla, giving Ali the father's 'orders' to send me at once up to Feisal. Ali was staggered at their tenour, but could not help himself; for his only telegraph to Mecca was by the ship's wireless, and he was ashamed to send personal remonstrances through us. So he made the best of it, and prepared for me his own splendid riding-camel, saddled with his own saddle, and hung with luxurious housings and cushions of Nejd leather-work pieced and inlaid in various colours, with plaited fringes and nets embroidered with metal tissues. As a trustworthy man he chose out Tafas el Raashid, a Hawazim Harb tribesman, with his son, to guide me to Feisal's camp.

He did all this with the better grace for the countenance of Nuri Said, the Bagdadi staff officer, whom I had befriended once in Cairo when he was ill. Nuri was now second in command of the regular force which Aziz el Masri was raising and training here. Another friend at court was Faiz el Ghusein, a secretary. He was a Sulut Sheikh from the Hauran, and a former official of the Turkish Government, who had escaped across Armenia during the war, and had eventually reached Miss Gertrude Bell in Basra. She had sent him on to me with a warm recommendation.

To Ali himself I took a great fancy. He was of middle height, thin and looking already more than his thirty-seven years. He stooped a little. His skin was sallow, his eyes large and deep and brown, his nose thin and rather hooked, his mouth sad and drooping. He had a spare black beard and very delicate hands. His manner was dignified and admirable, but direct; and he struck me as a pleasant gentleman, conscientious, without great force of character, nervous, and rather tired. His physical weakness (he was consumptive) made him subject to quick fits of shaking passion, preceded and followed by long moods of infirm obstinacy. He was bookish, learned in law and religion, and pious almost to fanaticism. He was too conscious of his high heritage to be ambitious; and his nature was too clean to see or suspect interested motives in those about him. Consequently he was much the prey of any constant companion, and too sensitive to advice for a great leader, though his purity of intention and conduct gained him the love of those who came into direct contact with him. If Feisal should turn out to be no prophet, the revolt would make shift well enough with Ali for its head. I thought him more definitely Arab than Abdulla, or than Zeid, his young half-brother, who was helping him at Rabegh, and came down with Ali and Nuri and Aziz to the palm-groves to see me start. Zeid was a shy, white, beardless lad of perhaps nineteen, calm and flippant, no zealot for the revolt. Indeed, his mother was Turkish; and he had been brought up in the harem, so that he could hardly feel great sympathy with an Arab revival; but he did his best this day to be pleasant, and surpassed Ali, perhaps because his feelings were not much outraged at the departure of a Christian into the Holy Province under the auspices of the Emir of Mecca. Zeid, of course, was even less than Abdulla the born leader of my quest. Yet I liked him, and could see that he would be a decided man when he had found himself.

Ali would not let me start till after sunset, lest any of his followers see me leave the camp. He kept my journey a secret even from his slaves, and gave me an Arab cloak and headcloth to wrap round myself and my uniform, that I might present a proper silhouette in the dark upon my camel. I had no food with me; so he instructed Tafas to get something to eat at Bir el Sheikh, the first settlement, some sixty miles out, and charged him most stringently to keep me from questioning and curiosity on the way, and to avoid all camps and encounters. The Masruh Harb, who inhabited Rabegh and district, paid only lip-service to the Sherif. Their real allegiance was to Hussein Mabeirig, the ambitious sheikh of the clan, who was jealous of the Emir of Mecca and had fallen out with him. He was now a fugitive, living in the hills to the East, and was known to be in touch with the Turks. His people were not notably pro-Turkish, but owed him obedience. If he had heard of my departure he might well have ordered a band of them to stop me on my way through his district.

Tafas was a Hazimi, of the Beni Salem branch of Harb, and so not on good terms with the Masruh. This inclined him towards me; and when he had once accepted the charge of escorting me to Feisal, we could trust him. The fidelity of road-companions was most dear to Arab tribesmen. The guide had to answer to a sentimental public with his life for that of his fellow. One Harbi, who promised to take Huber to Medina and broke his word and killed him on the road near Rabegh, when he found out that he was a Christian, was ostracized by public opinion, and, in spite of the religious prejudices in his favour, had ever since lived miserably alone in the hills, cut off from friendly intercourse, and refused permission to marry any daughter of the tribe. So we could depend upon the good will of Tafas and his son, Abdulla; and Ali endeavoured by detailed instructions to ensure that their performance should be as good as their intention.

We marched through the palm-groves which lay like a girdle about the scattered houses of Rabegh village, and then out under the stars along the Tehama, the sandy and featureless strip of desert bordering the western coast of Arabia between sea-beach and littoral hills, for hundreds of monotonous miles. In day-time this low plain was insufferably hot, and its waterless character made it a forbidding road; yet it was inevitable, since the more fruitful hills were too rugged to afford passage north and south for loaded animals.

The cool of the night was pleasant after the day of checks and discussions which had so dragged at Rabegh. Tafas led on without speaking, and the camels went silently over the soft flat sand. My thoughts as we went were how this was the pilgrim road, down which, for uncounted generations, the people of the north had come to visit the Holy City, bearing with them gifts of faith for the shrine; and it seemed that the Arab revolt might be in a sense a return pilgrimage, to take back to the north, to Syria, an ideal for an ideal, a belief in liberty for their past belief in a revelation.

We endured for some hours, without variety except at times when the camels plunged and strained a little and the saddles creaked: indications that the soft plain had merged into beds of drift-sand, dotted with tiny scrub, and therefore uneven going, since the plants collected little mounds about their roots, and the eddies of the sea-winds scooped hollows in the intervening spaces. Camels appeared not sure-footed in the dark, and the starlit sand carried little shadow, so that hummocks and holes were difficult to see. Before midnight we halted, and I rolled myself tighter in my cloak, and chose a hollow of my own size and shape, and slept well in it till nearly dawn.

As soon as he felt the air growing chill with the coming change, Tafas got up, and two minutes later we were swinging forward again. An hour after it grew bright, as we climbed a low neck of lava drowned nearly to the top with blown sand. This joined a small flow near the shore to the main Hejaz lava-field, whose western edge ran up upon our right hand, and caused the coast road to lie where it did. The neck was stony, but brief: on each side the blue lava humped itself into low shoulders, from which, so Tafas said, it was possible to see ships sailing on the sea. Pilgrims had built cairns here by the road. Sometimes they were individual piles, of just three stones set up one above the other: sometimes they were common heaps, to which any disposed passer-by might add his stone — not reasonably nor with known motive, but because others did, and perhaps they knew.

Beyond the ridge the path descended into a broad open place, the Masturah, or plain by which Wadi Fura flowed into the sea. Seaming its surface with innumerable interwoven channels of loose stone, a few inches deep, were the beds of the flood water, on those rare occasions when there was rain in the Tareif and the courses raged like rivers to the sea. The delta here was about six miles wide. Down some part of it water flowed for an hour or two, or even for a day or two, every so many years. Underground there was plenty of moisture, protected by the overlying sand from the sun-heat; and thorn trees and loose scrub profited by it and flourished. Some of the trunks were a foot through: their height might be twenty feet. The trees and bushes stood some-what apart, in clusters, their lower branches cropped by the hungry camels. So they looked cared for, and had a premeditated air, which felt strange in the wilderness, more especially as the Tehama hitherto had been a sober bareness.

Two hours up-stream, so Tafas told me, was the throat where Wadi Fura issued from the last granite hills, and there had been built a little village, Khoreiba, of running water channels and wells and palm-groves, inhabited by a small population of freedmen engaged in date husbandry. This was important. We had not understood that the bed of Wadi Fura served as a direct road from near Medina to the neighbourhood of Rabegh. It lay so far south and east of Feisal's supposed position in the hills that he could hardly be said to cover it. Also Abdulla had not warned us of the existence of Khoreiba, though it materially affected the Rabegh question, by affording the enemy a possible watering-place, safe from our interference, and from the guns of our warships. At Khoreiba the Turks could concentrate a large force to attack our proposed brigade in Rabegh.

In reply to further questions, Tafas disclosed that at Hajar, east of Rabegh in the hills, was yet another supply of water, in the hands of the Masruh, and now the headquarters of Hussein Mabeirig, their Turcophil chief. The Turks could make that their next stage from Khoreiba towards Mecca, leaving Rabegh unmolested and harmless on their flank. This meant that the asked-for British Brigade would be unable to save Mecca from the Turks. For that purpose would be required a force with a front or a radius of action of some twenty miles, in order to deny all three water-supplies to the enemy.

Meanwhile in the early sunlight we lifted our camels to a steady trot across the good going of these shingle-beds among the trees, making for Masturah well, the first stage out from Rabegh on the pilgrim road. There we would water and halt a little. My camel was a delight to me, for I had not been on such an animal before. There were no good camels in Egypt; and those of the Sinai Desert, while hardy and strong, were not taught to pace fair and softly and swiftly, like these rich mounts of the Arabian princes.

Yet her accomplishments were to-day largely wasted, since they were reserved for riders who had the knack and asked for them, and not for me, who expected to be carried, and had no sense of how to ride. It was easy to sit on a camel's back without falling off, but very difficult to understand and get the best out of her so as to do long journeys without fatiguing either rider or beast. Tafas gave me hints as we went: indeed, it was one of the few subjects on which he would speak. His orders to preserve me from contact with the world seemed to have closed even his mouth. A pity, for his dialect interested me.

Quite close to the north bank of the Masturah, we found the well. Beside it were some decayed stone walls which had been a hut, and opposite it some little shelters of branches and palm-leaves, under which a few Beduin were sitting. We did not greet them. Instead, Tafas turned across to the ruinous walls, and dismounted; and I sat in their shade while he and Abdulla watered the animals, and drew a drink for themselves and for me. The well was old, and broad, with a good stone steyning, and a strong coping round the top. It was about twenty feet deep; and for the convenience of travellers without ropes, like ourselves, a square chimney had been contrived in the masonry, with foot and hand holds in the corners, so that a man might descend to the water, and fill his goat-skin.

Idle hands had flung so many stones down the shaft, that half the bottom of the well was choked, and the water not abundant. Abdulla tied his flowing sleeves about his shoulders; tucked his gown under his cartridge belt; and clambered nimbly down and up, bringing each time four or five gallons which he poured for our camels into a stone trough beside the well. They drank about five gallons each, for they had been watered at Rabegh a day back. Then we let them moon about a little, while we sat in peace, breathing the light wind coming off the sea. Abdulla smoked a cigarette as reward for his exertions.

Some Harb came up, driving a large herd of brood camels, and began to water them, having sent one man down the well to fill their large leather bucket, which the others drew up hand over hand with a loud staccato chant. We watched them, without intercourse; for these were Masruh, and we Beni Salem; and while the two clans were now at peace, and might pass through each other's districts, this was only a temporary accommodation to further the Sherif's war against the Turks, and had little depth of goodwill in it.

As we watched, two riders, trotting light and fast on thoroughbred camels, drew towards us from the north. Both were young. One was dressed in rich Cashmere robes and heavy silk embroidered head-cloth. The other was plainer, in white cotton, with a red cotton head-dress. They halted beside the well; and the more splendid one slipped grace-fully to the ground without kneeling his camel, and threw his halter to his companion, saying, carelessly, 'Water them while I go over there and rest'. Then he strolled across and sat down under our wall, after glancing at us with affected unconcern. He offered a cigarette, just rolled and licked, saying, 'Your presence is from Syria?' I parried politely, suggesting that he was from Mecca, to which he likewise made no direct reply. We spoke a little of the war and of the leanness of the Masruh she-camels.

Meanwhile the other rider stood by, vacantly holding the halters, waiting perhaps for the Harb to finish watering their herd before taking his turn. The young lord cried 'What is it, Mustafa? Water them at once'. The servant came up to say dismally, 'They will not let me'. 'God's mercy!' shouted his master furiously, as he scrambled to his feet and hit the unfortunate Mustafa three or four sharp blows about the head and shoulders with his riding-stick. 'Go and ask them.' Mustafa looked hurt, astonished, and angry as though he would hit back, but thought better of it, and ran to the well.

The Harb, shocked, in pity made a place for him, and let his two camels drink from their water-trough. They whispered, 'Who is he?' and Mustapha said, 'Our Lord's cousin from Mecca'. At once they ran and untied a bundle from one of their saddles, and spread from it before the two riding camels fodder of the green leaves and buds of the thorn trees. They were used to gather this by striking the low bushes with a heavy staff, till the broken tips of the branches rained down on a cloth stretched over the ground beneath.

The young Sherif watched them contentedly. When his camel had fed, he climbed slowly and without apparent effort up its neck into the saddle, where he settled himself leisurely, and took an unctuous fare-well of us, asking God to requite the Arabs bountifully. They wished him a good journey; and he started southward, while Abdulla brought our camels, and we went off northward. Ten minutes later I heard a chuckle from old Tafas, and saw wrinkles of delight between his grizzled beard and moustache.

'What is upon you, Tafas?' said I.

'My Lord, you saw those two riders at the well?'

'The Sherif and his servant?'

'Yes; but they were Sherif Ali ibn el Hussein of Modhig, and his cousin, Sherif Mohsin, lords of the Harith, who are blood enemies of the Masruh. They feared they would be delayed or driven off the water if the Arabs knew them. So they pretended to be master and servant from Mecca. Did you see how Mohsin raged when Ali beat him? Ali is a devil. While only eleven years old he escaped from his father's house to his uncle, a robber of pilgrims by trade; and with him he lived by his hands for many months, till his father caught him. He was with our lord Feisal from the first day's battle in Medina, and led the Ateiba in the plains round Aar and Bir Derwish. It was all camel-fighting; and Ali would have no man with him who could not do as he did, run beside his camel, and leap with one hand into the saddle, carrying his rifle. The children of Harith are children of battle.' For the first time the old man's mouth was full of words.

CHAPTER XI

WHILE he spoke we scoured along the dazzling plain, now nearly bare of trees, and turning slowly softer under foot. At first it had been grey shingle, packed like gravel. Then the sand increased and the stones grew rarer, till we could distinguish the colours of the separate flakes, porphyry, green schist, basalt. At last it was nearly pure white sand, under which lay a harder stratum. Such going was like a pile-carpet for our camels' running. The particles of sand were clean and polished, and caught the blaze of sun like little diamonds in a reflection so fierce, that after a while I could not endure it. I frowned hard, and pulled the head-cloth forward in a peak over my eyes, and beneath them, too, like a beaver, trying to shut out the heat which rose in glassy waves off the ground, and beat up against my face. Eighty miles in front of us, the huge peak of Rudhwa behind Yenbo was looming and fading in the dazzle of vapour which hid its foot. Quite near in the plain rose the little shapeless hills of Hesna, which seemed to block the way. To our right was the steep ridge of Beni Ayub, toothed and narrow like a saw-blade, the first edge of the sheaf of mountains between the Tehama and the high scarp of the tableland about Medina. These Tareif Beni Ayub fell away on their north into a blue series of smaller hills, soft in character, behind which lofty range after range in a jagged stairway, red now the sun grew low, climbed up the towering central mass of Jebel Subh with its fantastic granite spires.

A little later we turned to the right, off the pilgrim road, and took a short cut across gradually rising ground of flat basalt ridges, buried in sand till only their topmost piles showed above the surface. It held moisture enough to be well grown over with hard wiry grass and shrubs up and down the slopes, on which a few sheep and goats were pasturing. There Tafas showed me a stone, which was the limit of the district of the Masruh, and told me with grim pleasure that he was now at home, in his tribal property, and might come off his guard.

Men have looked upon the desert as barren land, the free holding of whoever chose; but in fact each hill and valley in it had a man who was its acknowledged owner and would quickly assert the right of his family or clan to it, against aggression. Even the wells and trees had their masters, who allowed men to make firewood of the one and drink of the other freely, as much as was required for their need, but who would instantly check anyone trying to turn the property to account and to exploit it or its products among others for private benefit. The desert was held in a crazed communism by which Nature and the elements were for the free use of every known friendly person for his own purposes and no more. Logical outcomes were the reduction of this licence to privilege by the men of the desert, and their hardness to strangers unprovided with introduction or guarantee, since the common security lay in the common responsibility of kinsmen. Tafas, in his own country, could bear the burden of my safe-keeping lightly.

The valleys were becoming sharply marked, with clean beds of sand and shingle, and an occasional large boulder brought down by a flood. There were many broom bushes, restfully grey and green to the eye, and good for fuel, though useless as pasture. We ascended steadily till we rejoined the main track of the pilgrim road. Along this we held our way till sunset, when we came into sight of the hamlet of Bir el Sheikh. In the first dark as the supper fires were lighted we rode down its wide open street and halted. Tafas went into one of the twenty miserable huts, and in a few whispered words and long silences bought flour, of which with water he kneaded a dough cake two inches thick and eight inches across. This he buried in the ashes of a brushwood fire, provided for him by a Subh woman whom he seemed to know. When the cake was warmed he drew it out of the fire, and clapped it to shake off the dust; then we shared it together, while Abdulla went away to buy himself tobacco.

They told me the place had two stone-lined wells at the bottom of the southward slope, but I felt disinclined to go and look at them, for the long ride that day had tired my unaccustomed muscles, and the heat of the plain had been painful. My skin was blistered by it, and my eyes ached with the glare of light striking up at a sharp angle from the silver sand, and from the shining pebbles. The last two years I had spent in Cairo, at a desk all day or thinking hard in a little overcrowded office full of distracting noises, with a hundred rushing things to say, but no bodily need except to come and go each day between office and hotel. In consequence the novelty of this change was severe, since time had not been given me gradually to accustom myself to the pestilent beating of the Arabian sun, and the long monotony of camel pacing. There was to be another stage to-night, and a long day to-morrow before Feisal's camp would be reached.

So I was grateful for the cooking and the marketing, which spent one hour, and for the second hour of rest after it which we took by common consent; and sorry when it ended, and we re-mounted, and rode in pitch darkness up valleys and down valleys, passing in and out of bands of air, which were hot in the confined hollows, but fresh and stirring in the open places. The ground under foot must have been sandy, because the silence of our passage hurt my straining ears, and smooth, for I was always falling asleep in the saddle, to wake a few seconds later suddenly and sickeningly, as I clutched by instinct at the saddle post to recover my balance which had been thrown out by some irregular stride of the animal. It was too dark, and the forms of the country were too neutral, to hold my heavy-lashed, peering eyes. At length we stopped for good, long after midnight; and I was rolled up in my cloak and asleep in a most comfortable little sand-grave before Tafas had done knee-haltering my camel.

Three hours later we were on the move again, helped now by the last shining of the moon. We marched down Wadi Mared, the night of it dead, hot, silent, and on each side sharp-pointed hills standing up black and white in the exhausted air. There were many trees. Dawn finally came to us as we passed out of the narrows into a broad place, over whose flat floor an uneasy wind span circles, capriciously in the dust. The day strengthened always, and now showed Bir ibn Hassani just to our right. The trim settlement of absurd little houses, brown and white, holding together for security's sake, looked doll-like and more lonely than the desert, in the immense shadow of the dark precipice of Subh, behind. While we watched it, hoping to see life at its doors, the sun was rushing up, and the fretted cliffs, those thousands of feet above our heads, became outlined in hard refracted shafts of white light against a sky still sallow with the transient dawn.

We rode on across the great valley. A camel-rider, garrulous and old, came out from the houses and jogged over to join us. He named himself Khallaf, too friendly-like. His salutation came after a pause in a trite stream of chat; and when it was returned he tried to force us into conversation. However, Tafas grudged his company, and gave him short answers. Khallaf persisted, and finally, to improve his footing, bent down and burrowed in his saddle pouch till he found a small covered pot of enamelled iron, containing a liberal portion of the staple of travel in the Hejaz. This was the unleavened dough cake of yesterday, but crumbled between the fingers while still warm, and moistened with liquid butter till its particles would fall apart only reluctantly. It was then sweetened for eating with ground sugar, and scooped up like damp sawdust in pressed pellets with the fingers.

I ate a little, on this my first attempt, while Tafas and Abdulla played at it vigorously; so for his bounty Khallaf went half-hungry: deservedly for it was thought effeminate by the Arabs to carry a provision of food for a little journey of one hundred miles. We were now fellows, and the chat began again while Khallaf told us about the last fighting, and a reverse Feisal had had the day before. It seemed he had been beaten out of Kheif in the head of Wadi Safra, and was now at Hamra, only a little way in front of us; or at least Khallaf thought he was there: we might learn for sure in Wasta, the next village on our road. The fighting had not been severe; but the few casualties were all among the tribesmen of Tafas and Khallaf; and the names and hurts of each were told in order.

Meanwhile I looked about, interested to find myself in a new country. The sand and detritus of last night and of Bir el Sheikh had vanished. We were marching up a valley, from two hundred to five hundred yards in width, of shingle and light soil, quite firm, with occasional knolls of shattered green stone cropping out in its midst. There were many thorn trees, some of them woody acacias, thirty feet and more in height, beautifully green, with enough of tamarisk and soft scrub to give the whole a charming, well kept, park-like air now in the long soft shadows of the early morning. The swept ground was so flat and clean, the pebbles so variegated, their colours so joyously blended that they gave a sense of design to the landscape; and this feeling was strengthened by the straight lines and sharpness of the hills.

They rose on each hand regularly, precipices a thousand feet in height, of granite-brown and dark porphyry-coloured rock, with pink stains; and by a strange fortune these glowing hills rested on hundred-foot bases of the cross-grained stone, whose unusual colour suggested a thin growth of moss.

We rode along this beautiful place for about seven miles, to a low watershed, crossed by a wall of granite slivers, now little more than a shapeless heap, but once no doubt a barrier. It ran from cliff to cliff, and even far up the hill-sides, wherever the slopes were not too steep to climb. In the centre, where the road passed, had been two small enclosures like pounds. I asked Khallaf the purpose of the wall. He replied that he had been in Damascus and Constantinople and Cairo, and had many friends among the great men of Egypt. Did I know any of the English there? Khallaf seemed curious about my intentions and my history. He tried to trip me in Egyptian phrases. When I answered in the dialect of Aleppo he spoke of prominent Syrians of his acquaintance. I knew them, too; and he switched off into local politics, asking careful questions, delicately and indirectly, about the Sherif and his sons, and what I thought Feisal was going to do. I understood less of this than he, and parried inconsequentially. Tafas came to my rescue, and changed the subject. Afterwards we knew that Khallaf was in Turkish pay, and used to send frequent reports of what came past Bir ibn Hassani for the Arab forces.

Across the wall we were in an affluent of Wadi Safra, a more wasted and stony valley among less brilliant hills. It ran into another, far down which to the west lay a cluster of dark palm-trees, which the Arabs said was Jedida, one of the slave villages in Wadi Safra. We turned to the right, across another saddle, and then downhill for a few miles to a corner of tall cliffs. We rounded this and found ourselves suddenly in Wadi Safra, the valley of our seeking, and in the midst of Wasta, its largest village. Wasta seemed to be many nests of houses, clinging to the hill-sides each side the torrent-bed on banks of alluvial soil, or standing on detritus islands between the various deep-swept channels whose sum made up the parent valley.

Riding between two or three of these built-up islands, we made for the far bank of the valley. On our way was the main bed of the winter floods, a sweep of white shingle and boulders, quite flat. Down its middle, from palm-grove on the one side to palm-grove on the other, lay a reach of clear water, perhaps two hundred yards long and twelve feet wide, sand-bottomed, and bordered on each brink by a ten-foot lawn of thick grass and flowers. On it we halted a moment to let our camels put their heads down and drink their fill, and the relief of the grass to our eyes after the day-long hard glitter of the pebbles was so sudden that involuntarily I glanced up to see if a cloud had not covered the face of the sun.

We rode up the stream to the garden from which it ran sparkling in a stone-lined channel; and then we turned along the mud wall of the garden in the shadow of its palms, to another of the detached hamlets. Tafas led the way up its little street (the houses were so low that from our saddles we looked down upon their clay roofs), and near one of the larger houses stopped and beat upon the door of an uncovered court. A slave opened to us, and we dismounted in privacy. Tafas haltered the camels, loosed their girths, and strewed before them green fodder from a fragrant pile beside the gate. Then he led me into the guest-room of the house, a dark clean little mud-brick place, roofed with half palm-logs under hammered earth. We sat down on the palm-leaf mat which ran along the dais. The day in this stifling valley had grown very hot; and gradually we lay back side by side. Then the hum of the bees in the gardens without, and of the flies hovering over our veiled faces within, lulled us into sleep.

CHAPTER XII

BEFORE we awoke, a meal of bread and dates had been prepared for us by the people of the house. The dates were new, meltingly sweet and good, like none I had ever tasted. The owner of the property, a Harbi, was, with his neighbours, away serving Feisal; and his women and children were tenting in the hills with the camels. At the most, the tribal Arabs of Wadi Safra lived in their villages five months a year. For the other seasons the gardens were entrusted to slaves, negroes like the grown lads who brought in the tray to us, and whose thick limbs and plump shining bodies looked curiously out of place among the bird-like Arabs. Khallaf told me these blacks were originally from Africa, brought over as children by their nominal Takruri fathers, and sold during the pilgrimage, in Mecca. When grown strong they were worth from fifty to eighty pounds apiece, and were looked after carefully as befitted their price. Some became house or body servants with their masters; but the majority were sent out to the palm villages of these feverish valleys of running water, whose climate was too bad for Arab labour, but where they flourished and built themselves solid houses, and mated with women slaves, and did all the manual work of the holding.

They were very numerous — for instance, there were thirteen villages of them side by side in this Wadi Safra — so they formed a society of their own, and lived much at their pleasure. Their work was hard, but the supervision loose, and escape easy. Their legal status was bad, for they had no appeal to tribal justice, or even to the Sherif's courts; but public opinion and self-interest deprecated any cruelty towards them, and the tenet of the faith that to enlarge a slave is a good deed, meant in practice that nearly all gained freedom in the end. They made pocket-money during their service, if they were ingenious. Those I saw had property, and declared themselves contented. They grew melons, marrows, cucumber, grapes and tobacco for their own account, in addition to the dates, whose surplus was sent across to the Sudan by sailing dhow, and there exchanged for corn, clothing and the luxuries of Africa or Europe.

After the midday heat was passed we mounted again, and rode up the clear, slow rivulet till it was hidden within the palm-gardens, behind their low boundary walls of sun-dried clay. In and out between the tree roots were dug little canals a foot or two deep, so contrived that the stream might be let into them from the stone channel and each tree watered in its turn. The head of water was owned by the community, and shared out among the landowners for so many minutes or hours daily or weekly according to the traditional use. The water was a little brackish, as was needful for the best palms; but it was sweet enough in the wells of private water in the groves. These wells were very frequent, and found water three or four feet below the surface.

Our way took us through the central village and its market street. There was little in the shops; and all the place felt decayed. A genera- tion ago Wasta was populous (they said of a thousand houses); but one day there rolled a huge wall of water down Wadi Safra, the embank- ments of many palm-gardens were breached, and the palm trees swept away. Some of the islands on which houses had stood for centuries were submerged, and the mud houses melted back again into mud, killing or drowning the unfortunate slaves within. The men could have been replaced, and the trees, had the soil remained; but the gardens had been built up of earth carefully won from the normal freshets by years of labour, and this wave of water — eight feet deep, running in a race for three days — reduced the plots in its track to their primordial banks of stones.

A little above Wasta we came to Kharma, a tiny settlement with rich palm groves, where a tributary ran in from the north. Beyond Kharma the valley widened somewhat, to an average of perhaps four hundred yards, with a bed of fine shingle and sand, laid very smooth by the winter rains. The walls were of bare red and black rock, whose edges and ridges were sharp as knife blades, and reflected the sun like metal. They made the freshness of the trees and grass seem luxurious. We now saw parties of Feisal's soldiers, and grazing herds of their saddle camels. Before we reached Hamra every nook in the rocks or clump of trees was a bivouac. They cried cheery greetings to Tafas, who came to life again, waving back and calling to them, while he pressed on quickly to end his duty towards me.

Hamra opened on our left. It seemed a village of about one hundred houses, buried in gardens among mounds of earth some twenty feet in height. We forded a little stream, and went up a walled path between trees to the top of one of these mounds, where we made our camels kneel by the yard-gate of a long, low house. Tafas said something to a slave who stood there with silver-hilted sword in hand. He led me to an inner court, on whose further side, framed between the uprights of a black doorway, stood a white figure waiting tensely for me. I felt at first glance that this was the man I had come to Arabia to seek — the leader who would bring the Arab Revolt to full glory. Feisal looked very tall and pillar-like, very slender, in his long white silk robes and his brown head-cloth bound with a brilliant scarlet and gold cord. His eyelids were dropped; and his black beard and colourless face were like a mask against the strange, still watchfulness of his body. His hands were crossed in front of him on his dagger.

I greeted him. He made way for me into the room, and sat down on his carpet near the door. As my eyes grew accustomed to the shade, they saw that the little room held many silent figures, looking at me or at Feisal steadily. He remained staring down at his hands, which were twisting slowly about his dagger. At last he inquired softly how I had found the journey. I spoke of the heat and he asked how long from Rabegh, commenting that I had ridden fast for the season.

'And do you like our place here in Wadi Safra?'

'Well; but it is far from Damascus.'

The word had fallen like a sword in their midst. There was a quiver. Then everybody present stiffened where he sat, and held his breath for a silent minute. Some, perhaps, were dreaming of far off success: others may have thought it a reflection on their late defeat. Feisal at length lifted his eyes, smiling at me, and said, 'Praise be to God, there are Turks nearer us than that'. We all smiled with him; and I rose and excused myself for the moment.

[*facing:* FEYS]

CHAPTER XIII

UNDER tall arcades of palms with ribbed and groined branches, in a soft meadow, I found the trim camp of Egyptian Army soldiers with Nafi Bey, their Egyptian major, sent lately from the Sudan by Sir Reginald Wingate to help the Arab rebellion. They comprised a mountain battery and some machine-guns, and looked smarter than they felt. Nafi himself was an amiable fellow, kind and hospitable to me in spite of weak health and his resentment at having been sent so far away into the desert to serve in an unnecessary and toilsome war.

Egyptians, being home-loving persons and comfortable, found strangeness always a misery. In this bad instance they suffered hardship for a philanthropic end, which made it harder. They were fighting the Turks, for whom they had a sentimental regard, on behalf of the Arabs, an alien people speaking a language kindred to their own, but appearing therefore all the more unlike in character, and crude in life. The Arabs seemed hostile to the material blessings of civilization rather than appreciative of them. They met with a ribald hoot well-meaning attempts to furnish their bareness.

Englishmen being sure of their own absolute excellence would persist in help without grumbling overmuch; but the Egyptians lost faith. They had neither that collective sense of duty towards their State, nor that feeling of individual obligation to push struggling humanity up its road. The vicarious policemanship which was the strongest emotion of Englishmen towards another man's muddle, in their case was replaced by the instinct to pass by as discreetly far as possible on the other side. So, though all was well with these soldiers, and they had abundant rations and good health and no casualties, yet they found fault with the handling of the universe, and hoped this unexpected Englishman had come to set it right.

Feisal was announced with Maulud el Mukhlus, the Arab zealot or Tekrit, who, for rampant nationalism had been twice degraded in the Turkish Army, and had spent an exile of two years in Nejd as a secretary with Ibn Rashid. He had commanded the Turkish cavalry before

Shaiba, and had been taken by us there. As soon as he heard of the rebellion of the Sherif he had volunteered for him, and had been the first regular officer to join Feisal. He was now nominally his A.D.C.

Bitterly he complained that they were in every way ill-equipped. This was the main cause of their present plight. They got thirty thousand pounds a month from the Sherif, but little flour and rice, little barley, few rifles, insufficient ammunition, no machine-guns, no mountain guns, no technical help, no information.

I stopped Maulud there and said that my coming was expressly to learn what they lacked and to report it, but that I could work with them only if they would explain to me their general situation. Feisal agreed, and began to sketch to me the history of their revolt from its absolute beginning.

The first rush on Medina had been a desperate business. The Arabs were ill-armed and short of ammunition, the Turks in great force, since Fakhri's detachment had just arrived and the troops to escort von Stotzingen to Yemen were still in the town. At the height of the crisis the Beni Ali broke; and the Arabs were thrust out beyond the walls. The Turks then opened fire on them with their artillery; and the Arabs unused to this new arm, became terrified. The Ageyl and Ateiba got into safety and refused to move out again. Feisal and Ali ibn el Hussein vainly rode about in front of their men in the open, to show them that the bursting shells were not as fatal as they sounded. The demoralization deepened.

Sections of Beni Ali tribesmen approached the Turkish command with an offer to surrender, if their villages were spared. Fakhri played with them, and in the ensuing lull of hostilities surrounded the Awali suburb with his troops: then suddenly he ordered them to carry it by assault and to massacre every living thing within its walls. Hundreds of the inhabitants were raped and butchered, the houses fired, and living and dead alike thrown back into the flames. Fakhri and his men had served together and had learned the arts of both the slow and the fast kill upon the Armenians in the North.

This bitter taste of the Turkish mode of war sent a shock across Arabia; for the first rule of Arab war was that women were inviolable: the second that the lives and honour of children too young to fight with men were to be spared: the third, that property impossible to carry off should be left undamaged. The Arabs with Feisal perceived that they were opposed to new customs, and fell back out of touch to gain time to readjust themselves. There could no longer be any question of submission: the sack of Awali had opened blood feud upon blood feud, and put on them the duty of fighting to the end of their force: but it was plain now that it would be a long affair, and that with muzzle-loading guns for sole weapons, they could hardly expect to win.

So they fell back from the level plains about Medina into the hills across the Sultani-road, about Aar and Raha and Bir Abbas, where they rested a little, while Ali and Feisal sent messenger after messenger down to Rabegh, their sea-base, to learn when fresh stores and money and arms might be expected. The revolt had begun haphazard, on their father's explicit orders, and the old man, too independent to take his sons into his full confidence, had not worked out with them any arrangements for prolonging it. So the reply was only a little food. Later some Japanese rifles, most of them broken, were received. Such barrels as were still whole were so foul that the too-eager Arabs burst them on the first trial. No money was sent up at all: to take its place Feisal filled a decent chest with stones, had it locked and corded carefully, guarded on each daily march by his own slaves, and introduced meticulously into his tent each night. By such theatricals the brothers tried to hold a melting force.

At last Ali went down to Rabegh to inquire what was wrong with the organization. He found that Hussein Mabeirig, the local chief, had made up his mind that the Turks would be victorious (he had tried conclusions with them twice himself and had the worst of it), and accordingly decided theirs was the best cause to follow. As the stores for the Sherif were landed by the British he appropriated them and stored them away secretly in his own houses. Ali made a demonstration, and sent urgent messages for his half-brother Zeid to join him from Jidda with reinforcements. Hussein, in fear, slipped off to the hills, an outlaw. The two Sherifs took possession of his villages. In them they found great stores of arms, and food enough for their armies for a month. The temptation of a spell of leisured ease was too much for them: they settled down in Rabegh.

This left Feisal alone up country, and he soon found himself isolated, in a hollow situation, driven to depend upon his native resources. He bore it for a time, but in August took advantage of the visit of Colonel Wilson to the newly-conquered Yenbo, to come down and give a full explanation of his urgent needs. Wilson was impressed with him and his story, and at once promised him a battery of mountain guns and some maxims, to be handled by men and officers of the Egyptian Army garrison in the Sudan. This explained the presence of Nafi Bey and his units.

The Arabs rejoiced when they came, and believed they were now equals of the Turk; but the four guns were twenty-year-old Krupps, with a range of only three thousand yards; and their crews were not eager enough in brain and spirit for irregular fighting. However, they went forward with the mob and drove in the Turkish outposts, and then their supports, until Fakhri becoming seriously alarmed, came down himself, inspected the front, and at once reinforced the threatened detachment at Bir Abbas to some three thousand strong. The Turks had field guns and howitzers with them, and the added advantage of high ground for observation. They began to worry the Arabs by indirect fire, and nearly dropped a shell on Feisal's tent while all the head men were conferring within. The Egyptian gunners were asked to return the fire and smother the enemy guns. They had to plead that their weapons were useless, since they could not carry the nine thousand yards. They were derided; and the Arabs ran back again into the defiles.

Feisal was deeply discouraged. His men were tired. He had lost many of them. His only effective tactics against the enemy had been to chase in suddenly upon their rear by fast mounted charges, and many camels had been killed, or wounded or worn out in these expensive measures. He demurred to carrying the whole war upon his own neck while Abdulla delayed in Mecca, and Ali and Zeid at Rabegh. Finally he withdrew the bulk of his forces, leaving the Harb sub-tribes who lived by Bir Abbas to keep up pressure on the Turkish supply columns and communications by a repeated series of such raids as those which he himself found impossible to maintain.

Yet he had no fear that the Turks would again come forward against him suddenly. His failure to make any impression on them had not imbued him with the smallest respect for them. His late retirement to Hamra was not forced: it was a gesture of disgust because he was bored by his obvious impotence, and was determined for a little while to have the dignity of rest.

After all, the two sides were still untried. The armament of the Turks made them so superior at long range that the Arabs never got to grips. For this reason most of the hand-to-hand fighting had taken place at night, when the guns were blinded. To my ears they sounded oddly primitive battles, with torrents of words on both sides in a preliminary match of wits. After the foulest insults of the languages they knew would come the climax, when the Turks in frenzy called the Arabs 'English', and the Arabs screamed back 'German' at them. There were, of course, no Germans in the Hejaz, and I was the first English-man; but each party loved cursing, and any epithet would sting on the tongues of such artists.

I asked Feisal what his plans were now. He said that till Medina fell they were inevitably tied down there in Hejaz dancing to Fakhri's tune. In his opinion the Turks were aiming at the recapture of Mecca. The bulk of their strength was now in a mobile column, which they could move towards Rabegh by a choice of routes which kept the Arabs in constant alarm. A passive defence of the Subh hills had shown that the Arabs did not shine as passive resisters. When the enemy moved they must be countered by an offensive.

Feisal meant to retire further yet, to the Wadi Yenbo border of the great Juheina tribe. With fresh levies from them he would march eastwards towards the Hejaz Railway behind Medina, at the moment when Abdulla was advancing by the lava-desert to attack Medina from the East. He hoped that Ali would go up simultaneously from Rabegh, while Zeid moved into Wadi Safra to engage the big Turkish force at Bir Abbas, and keep it out of the main battle. By this plan Medina would be threatened or attacked on all sides at once. Whatever the success of the attack, the concentration from three sides would at least break up the prepared Turkish push-outwards on the fourth, and give Rabegh and the southern Hejaz a breathing space to equip themselves for effective defence, or counter-attack.

D

Maulud, who had sat fidgeting through our long, slow talk, could no longer restrain himself and cried out, 'Don't write a history of us. The needful thing is to fight and fight and kill them. Give me a battery of Schneider mountain guns and machine guns, and I will finish this off for you. We talk and talk and do nothing.' I replied as warmly; and Maulud, a magnificent fighter, who regarded a battle won as a battle wasted if he did not show some wound to prove his part in it, took me up. We wrangled while Feisal sat by and grinned delightedly at us.

This talk had been for him a holiday. He was encouraged even by the trifle of my coming; for he was a man of moods, flickering between glory and despair, and just now dead-tired. He looked years older than thirty-one; and his dark, appealing eyes, set a little sloping in his face, were bloodshot, and his hollow cheeks deeply lined and puckered with reflection. His nature grudged thinking, for it crippled his speed in action: the labour of it shrivelled his features into swift lines of pain. In appearance he was tall, graceful and vigorous, with the most beautiful gait, and a royal dignity of head and shoulders. Of course he knew it, and a great part of his public expression was by sigh and gesture.

His movements were impetuous. He showed himself hot-tempered and sensitive, even unreasonable, and he ran off soon on tangents. Appetite and physical weakness were mated in him, with the spur of courage. His personal charm, his imprudence, the pathetic hint of frailty as the sole reserve of this proud character made him the idol of his followers. One never asked if he were scrupulous; but later he showed that he could return trust for trust, suspicion for suspicion. He was fuller of wit than of humour.

His training in Abdul Hamid's entourage had made him past-master in diplomacy. His military service with the Turks had given him a working knowledge of tactics. His life in Constantinople and in the Turkish Parliament had made him familiar with European questions and manners. He was a careful judge of men. If he had the strength to realize his dreams he would go very far, for he was wrapped up in his work and lived for nothing else; but the fear was that he would wear himself out by trying to seem to aim always a little higher than the truth or that he would die of too much action. His men told me how, after a long spell of fighting, in which he had to guard himself, and lead the charges, and control and encourage them, he had collapsed physically and was carried away from his victory, unconscious, with the foam flecking his lips.

Meanwhile, here, as it seemed, was offered to our hand, which had only to be big enough to take it, a prophet who, if veiled, would give cogent form to the idea behind the activity of the Arab revolt. It was all and more than we had hoped for, much more than our halting course deserved. The aim of my trip was fulfilled.

My duty was now to take the shortest road to Egypt with the news and the knowledge gained that evening in the palm wood grew and blossomed in my mind into a thousand branches, laden with fruit and shady leaves, beneath which I sat and half-listened and saw visions, while the twilight deepened, and the night; until a line of slaves with lamps came down the winding paths between the palm trunks, and with Feisal and Maulud we walked back through the gardens to the little house, with its courts still full of waiting people, and to the hot inner room in which the familiars were assembled; and there we sat down together to the smoking bowl of rice and meat set upon the food-carpet for our supper by the slaves.

S O mixed was the company, Sherifs, Meccans, sheikhs of the Juheina and Ateiba, Mesopotamians, Ageyl, that I threw apples of discord, inflammatory subjects of talk amongst them, to sound their mettle and beliefs without delay. Feisal, smoking innumerable cigarettes, kept command of the conversation even at its hottest, and it was fine to watch him do it. He showed full mastery of tact, with a real power or disposing men's feelings to his wish. Storrs was as efficient; but Storrs paraded his strength, exhibiting all the cleverness and machinery, the movements of his hands which made the creatures dance. Feisal seemed to govern his men unconsciously: hardly to know how he stamped his mind on them, hardly to care whether they obeyed. It was as great art as Storrs'; and it concealed itself, for Feisal was born to it.

The Arabs loved him openly: indeed, these chance meetings made clear how to the tribes the Sherif and his sons were heroic. Sherif Hussein (Sayidna as they called him) was outwardly so clean and gentle-mannered as to seem weak; but this appearance hid a crafty policy, deep ambition, and an un-Arabian foresight, strength of character and obstinacy. His interest in natural history reinforced his sporting instincts, and made him (when he pleased) a fair copy of a Beduin prince, while his Circassian mother had endowed him with qualities foreign to both Turk and Arab, and he displayed considerable astuteness in turning now one, now another of his inherited assets to present advantage.

Yet the school of Turkish politics was so ignoble that not even the best could graduate from it unaffected. Hussein when young had been honest, outspoken ... and he learned not merely to suppress his speech, but to use speech to conceal his honest purpose. The art, over-indulged, became a vice from which he could not free himself. In old age ambiguity covered his every communication. Like a cloud it hid his decision of character, his worldly wisdom, his cheerful strength. Many denied him such qualities: but history gave proof.

One instance of his worldly wisdom was the upbringing of his sons. The Sultan had made them live in Constantinople to receive a Turkish education. Sherif Hussein saw to it that the education was general and good. When they came back to the Hejaz as young effendis in European clothes with Turkish manners, the father ordered them into Arab dress; and, to rub up their Arabic, gave them Meccan companions and sent them out into the wilds, with the Camel Corps, to patrol the pilgrim roads.

The young men thought it might be an amusing trip, but were dashed when their father forbade them special food, bedding, or soft-padded saddles. He would not let them back to Mecca, but kept them out for months in all seasons guarding the roads by day and by night, handling every variety of man, and learning fresh methods of riding and fighting. Soon they hardened, and became self-reliant, with that blend of native intelligence and vigour which so often comes in a crossed stock. Their formidable family group was admired and efficient, but curiously isolated in their world. They were natives of no country, lovers of no private plot of ground. They had no real confidants or ministers; and no one of them seemed open to another, or to the father, of whom they stood in awe.

The debate after supper was an animated one. In my character as a Syrian I made sympathetic reference to the Arab leaders who had been executed in Damascus by Jemal Pasha. They took me up sharply: the published papers had disclosed that these men were in touch with foreign Governments, and ready to accept French or British suzerainty as the price of help. This was a crime against Arab nationality, and Jemal had only executed the implied sentence. Feisal smiled, almost winked, at me. 'You see,' he explained, 'we are now of necessity tied to the British. We are delighted to be their friends, grateful for their help, expectant of our future profit. But we are not British subjects. We would be more at ease if they were not such disproportionate allies.'

I told a story of Abdulla el Raashid, on the way up to Hamra. He had groaned to me of the British sailors coming ashore each day at Rabegh. 'Soon they will stay nights, and then they will live here always, and take the country.' To cheer him I had spoken of millions of Englishmen now ashore in France, and of the French not afraid.

Whereat he had turned on me scornfully, asking if I meant to compare France with the land of Hejaz!

Feisal mused a little and said, 'I am not a Hejazi by upbringing; and yet, by God, I am jealous for it. And though I know the British do not want it, yet what can I say, when they took the Sudan, also not wanting it? They hunger for desolate lands, to build them up; and so, perhaps one day Arabia will seem to them precious. Your good and my good, perhaps they are different, and either forced good or forced evil will make a people cry with pain. Does the ore admire the flame which transforms it? There is no reason for offence, but a people too weak are clamant over their little own. Our race will have a cripple's temper till it has found its feet.'

The ragged, lousy tribesmen who had eaten with us astonished me by their familiar understanding of intense political nationality, an abstract idea they could hardly have caught from the educated classes of the Hejaz towns, from those Hindus, Javanese, Bokhariots, Sudanese, Turks, out of sympathy with Arab ideals, and indeed just then suffering a little from the force of local sentiment, springing too high after its sudden escape from Turkish control. Sherif Hussein had had the worldly wisdom to base his precepts on the instinctive belief of the Arabs that they were of the salt of the earth and self-sufficient. Then, enabled by his alliance with us to back his doctrine by arms and money, he was assured of success.

Of course, this success was not level throughout. The great body of Sherifs, eight hundred or nine hundred of them, understood his nationalistic doctrine and were his missionaries, successful missionaries thanks to the revered descent from the Prophet, which gave them the power to hold men's minds, and to direct their courses into the willing quietness of eventual obedience.

The tribes had followed the smoke of their racial fanaticism. The towns might sigh for the cloying inactivity of Ottoman rule: the tribes were convinced that they had made a free and Arab Government, and that each of them was It. They were independent and would enjoy themselves — a conviction and resolution which might have led to anarchy, if they had not made more stringent the family tie, and the bonds of kin-responsibility. But this entailed a negation of central power. The Sherif might have legal sovereignty abroad, if he liked the high-sounding toy; but home affairs were to be customary. The problem of the foreign theorists — 'Is Damascus to rule the Hejaz, or can Hejaz rule Damascus?' did not trouble them at all, for they would not have it set. The Semites' idea of nationality was the independence of clans and villages, and their ideal of national union was episodic combined resistance to an intruder. Constructive policies, an organized state, an extended empire, were not so much beyond their sight as hateful in it. They were fighting to get rid of Empire, not to win it.

The feeling of the Syrians and Mesopotamians in these Arab armies was indirect. They believed that by fighting in the local ranks, even here in Hejaz, they were vindicating the general rights of all Arabs to national existence; and without envisaging one State, or even a confederation of States, they were definitely looking northward, wishing to add an autonomous Damascus and Bagdad to the Arab family. They were weak in material resources, and even after success would be, since their world was agricultural and pastoral, without minerals, and could never be strong in modern armaments. Were it otherwise, we should have had to pause before evoking in the strategic centre of the Middle East new national movements of such abounding vigour.

Of religious fanaticism there was little trace. The Sherif refused in round terms to give a religious twist to his rebellion. His fighting creed was nationality. The tribes knew that the Turks were Moslems, and thought that the Germans were probably true friends of Islam. They knew that the British were Christians, and that the British were their allies. In the circumstances, their religion would not have been of much help to them, and they had put it aside. 'Christian fights Christian, so why should not Mohammedans do the same? What we want is a Government which speaks our own language of Arabic and will let us live in peace. Also we hate those Turks.'

CHAPTER XV

NEXT morning I was up early and out among Feisal's troops towards the side of Kheif, by myself, trying to feel the pulse of their opinions in a moment, by such tricks as those played upon their chiefs the night before. Time was of the essence of my effort, for it was necessary to gain in ten days the impressions which would ordinarily have been the fruit of weeks of observing in my crab-fashion that sideways-slipping affair of the senses. Normally I would go along all day, with the sounds immediate, but blind to every detail, only generally aware that there were things red, or things grey, or clear things about me. To-day my eyes had to be switched straight to my brain, that I might note a thing or two the more clearly by contrast with the former mistiness. Such things were nearly always shapes: rocks and trees, or men's bodies in repose or movement: not small things like flowers, nor qualities like colour.

Yet here was strong need of a lively reporter. In this drab war the least irregularity was a joy to all, and McMahon's strongest course was to exploit the latent imagination of the General Staff. I believed in the Arab movement, and was confident, before ever I came, that in it was the idea to tear Turkey into pieces; but others in Egypt lacked faith, and had been taught nothing intelligent of the Arabs in the field. By noting down something of the spirit of these romantics in the hills about the Holy Cities I might gain the sympathy of Cairo for the further measures necessary to help them.

The men received me cheerfully. Beneath every great rock or bush they sprawled like lazy scorpions, resting from the heat, and refreshing their brown limbs with the early coolness of the shaded stone. Because of my khaki they took me for a Turk-trained officer who had deserted to them, and were profuse in good-humoured but ghastly suggestions of how they should treat me. Most of them were young, though the term 'fighting man' in the Hejaz meant anyone between twelve and sixty sane enough to shoot. They were a tough-looking crowd, dark-coloured, some negroid. They were physically thin, but ex-

quisitely made, moving with an oiled activity altogether delightful to
watch. It did not seem possible that men could be hardier or harder.
They would ride immense distances day after day, run through sand
and over rocks bare-foot in the heat for hours without pain, and climb
their hills like goats. Their clothing was mainly a loose shirt, with
sometimes short cotton drawers, and a head-shawl usually of red cloth,
which acted towel or handkerchief or sack as required. They were
corrugated with bandoliers and fired joy-shots when they could.

They were in wild spirits, shouting that the war might last ten years.
It was the fattest time the hills had ever known. The Sherif was feeding
not only the fighting men, but their families, and paying two pounds a
month for a man, four for a camel. Nothing else would have performed
the miracle of keeping a tribal army in the field for five months on
end. It was our habit to sneer at Oriental soldiers' love of pay; but the
Hejaz campaign was a good example of the limitations of that argument.
The Turks were offering great bribes, and obtaining little service —
no active service. The Arabs took their money, and gave gratifying
assurances in exchange; yet these very tribes would be meanwhile in
touch with Feisal, who obtained service for his payment. The Turks
cut the throats of their prisoners with knives, as though they were
butchering sheep. Feisal offered a reward of a pound a head for
prisoners, and had many carried in to him unhurt. He also paid for
captured mules or rifles.

The actual contingents were continually shifting, in obedience to
the rule of flesh. A family would own a rifle, and the sons serve in turn
for a few days each. Married men alternated between camp and wife
and sometimes a whole clan would become bored and take a rest.
Consequently the paid men were more than those mobilized; and
policy often gave to great sheikhs, as wages, money that was a polite
bribe for friendly countenance. Feisal's eight thousand men were one
in ten camel-corps and the rest hill-men. They served only under their
tribal sheikhs, and near home, arranging their own food and transport.
Nominally each sheikh had a hundred followers. Sherifs acted as
group leaders, in virtue of their privileged position, which raised them
above the jealousies which shackled the tribesmen.

Blood feuds were nominally healed, and really suspended in the

Sherifian area: Billi and Juheina, Ateiba and Ageyl living and fighting side by side in Feisal's army. All the same, the members of one tribe were shy of those of another, and within the tribe no man would quite trust his neighbour. Each might be, usually was, whole-hearted against the Turk, but perhaps not quite to the point of failing to work off a family grudge upon a family enemy in the field. Consequently they could not attack. One company of Turks firmly entrenched in open country could have defied the entire army of them; and a pitched defeat, with its casualties, would have ended the war by sheer horror.

I concluded that the tribesmen were good for defence only. Their acquisitive recklessness made them keen on booty, and whetted them to tear up railways, plunder caravans, and steal camels; but they were too free-minded to endure command, or to fight in team. A man who could fight well by himself made generally a bad soldier, and these champions seemed to me no material for our drilling; but if we strengthened them by light automatic guns of the Lewis type, to be handled by themselves, they might be capable of holding their hills and serving as an efficient screen behind which we could build up, perhaps at Rabegh, an Arab regular mobile column, capable of meeting a Turkish force (distracted by guerilla warfare) on terms, and of defeating it piecemeal. For such a body of real soldiers no recruits would be forthcoming from Hejaz. It would have to be formed of the heavy unwarlike Syrian and Mesopotamian towns-folk already in our hands, and officered by Arabic-speaking officers trained in the Turkish army, men of the type and history of Aziz el Masri or Maulud. They would eventually finish the war by striking while the tribesmen skirmished about, and hindered and distracted the Turks by their pin-prick raids.

The Hejaz war, meanwhile, would be one of dervishes against regular troops. It was the fight of a rocky, mountainous, barren country (reinforced by a wild horde of mountaineers) against an enemy so enriched in equipment by the Germans as almost to have lost virtue for rough-and-tumble war. The hill-belt was a paradise for snipers; and Arabs were artists in sniping. Two or three hundred determined men knowing the ranges should hold any section of them; because the slopes were too steep for escalade. The valleys, which were the only practicable roads, for miles and miles were not so much valleys as chasms or gorges, sometimes two hundred yards across, but sometimes only twenty, full of twists and turns, one thousand or four thousand feet deep, barren of cover, and flanked each side by pitiless granite, basalt and porphyry, not in polished slopes, but serrated and split and piled up in thousands of jagged heaps of fragments as hard as metal and nearly as sharp.

It seemed to my unaccustomed eyes impossible that, without treachery on the part of the mountain tribes, the Turks could dare to break their way through. Even with treachery as an ally, to pass the hills would be dangerous. The enemy would never be sure that the fickle population might not turn again; and to have such a labyrinth of defiles in the rear, across the communications, would be worse than having it in front. Without the friendship of the tribes, the Turks would own only the ground on which their soldiers stood; and lines so long and complex would soak up thousands of men in a fortnight, and leave none in the battle-front.

The sole disquieting feature was the very real success of the Turks in frightening the Arabs by artillery. Aziz el Masri in the Turk-Italian war in Tripoli had found the same terror, but had found also that it wore off. We might hope that the same would happen here; but for the moment the sound of a fired cannon sent every man within earshot behind cover. They thought weapons destructive in proportion to their noise. They were not afraid of bullets, not indeed overmuch of dying: just the manner of death by shell-fire was unendurable. It seemed to me that their moral confidence was to be restored only by having guns, useful or useless, but noisy, on their side. From the magnificent Feisal down to the most naked stripling in the army the theme was artillery, artillery, artillery.

When I told them of the landing of the five-inch howitzers at Rabegh they rejoiced. Such news nearly balanced in their minds the check of their last retreat down Wadi Safra. The guns would be of no real use to them: indeed, it seemed to me that they would do the Arabs positive harm; for their virtues lay in mobility and intelligence, and by giving them guns we hampered their movements and efficiency. Only if we did not give them guns they would quit.

At these close quarters the bigness of the revolt impressed me. This well-peopled province, from Um Lejj to Kunfida, more than a fort-night's camel march, had suddenly changed its character from a rout of casual nomad pilferers to an eruption against Turkey, fighting her, not certainly in our manner, but fiercely enough, in spite of the religion which was to raise the East against us in a holy war. Beyond anything calculable in figures, we had let loose a passion of anti-Turkish feeling which embittered as it had been by generations of subjection, might die very hard. There was among the tribes in the fighting zone a nervous enthusiasm common, I suppose, to all national risings, but strangely disquieting to one from a land so long delivered that national freedom had become like the water in our mouths, tasteless.

Later I saw Feisal again, and promised to do my best for him. My chiefs would arrange a base at Yenbo, where the stores and supplies he needed would be put ashore for his exclusive use. We would try to get him officer-volunteers from among the prisoners of war captured in Mesopotamia or on the Canal. We would form gun crews and machine-gun crews from the rank and file in the internment camps, and provide them with such mountain guns and light machine-guns as were obtainable in Egypt. Lastly, I would advise that British Army officers, professionals, be sent down to act as advisers and liaison officers with him in the field.

This time our talk was of the pleasantest, and ended in warm thanks from him, and an invitation to return as soon as might be. I explained that my duties in Cairo excluded field work, but perhaps my chiefs would let me pay a second visit later on, when his present wants were filled and his movement was going forward prosperously. Meanwhile I would ask for facilities to go down to Yenbo, for Egypt, that I might get things on foot promptly. He at once appointed me an escort of fourteen Juheina Sherifs, all kinsmen of Mohammed Ali ibn Beidawi, the Emir of the Juheina. They were to deliver me intact in Yenbo to Sheikh Abd el Kadir el Abdo, its Governor.

CHAPTER XVI

LEAVING Hamra as dusk fell, we marched back down Wadi Safra until opposite Kharma, where we turned to the right up the side valley. It was closely grown with stiff brushwood through which we drove our camels strenuously, having tucked up the streamers of our saddle-bags to save them from being shredded by the thorns. Two miles later we began to climb the narrow pass of Dhifran, which gave evidence even by night of labour expended on the road. It had been artificially smoothed, and the stones piled at each side into a heavy wall of protection against the rush of water in the rains. Parts had been graded, and were at times carried on a causeway built seemingly six or eight feet high, of great blocks of uncut stone: but it had been breached at every turn by torrents, and was in terrible ruin.

The ascent lasted perhaps for a mile; and the steep descent on the other side was about the same. Then we got to the level and found ourselves in a much broken country of ridges, with an intricate net of wadies whose main flow was apparently towards the south-west. The going was good for our camels. We rode for about seven miles in the dark, and came to a well, Bir el Murra, in a valley bed under a very low bluff, on whose head the square courses of a small fort of ashlar stood out against the starry sky. Conceivably both fort and causeway had been built by an Egyptian Mameluke for the passage of his pilgrim-caravan from Yenbo.

We halted there for the night, sleeping for six hours, a long luxury upon the road, though this rest was broken twice by challenges from half-seen mounted parties who had found our bivouac. Afterwards we wandered among more small ridges until the dawn showed gentle valleys of sand with strange hills of lava hemming us about. The lava here was not the blue-black cinder-stone of the fields about Rabegh: it was rust-coloured, and piled in huge crags of flowing surface and bent and twisted texture, as though played with oddly while yet soft. The sand, at first a carpet about the foot of the dolerate, gradually gained on it. The hills got lower, with the sand banked up against them in greater drifts, till even the crests were sand-spattered, and at last drowned beyond sight. So, as the sun became high and painfully fierce, we led out upon a waste of dunes, rolling southward for miles down hill to the misty sea, where it lay grey-blue in the false distance of the heat.

The dunes were narrow. By half-past seven we were on a staring plain of glassy sand mixed with shingle, overspread by tall scrub and thorn bushes, with some good acacia trees. We rode very fast across this, myself in some discomfort; for I was not a skilled rider: the movement exhausted me, while sweat ran down my forehead and dripped smart-ingly into my gritty, sun-cracked eyelids. Sweat was actually welcome when a drop fell from the end of a tuft of hair, to strike on the cheek cold and sudden and unexpected like a splash; but these refreshments were too few to pay for the pain of heat. We pressed on, while the sand yielded to pure shingle, and that again hardened into the bed of a great valley, running down by a shallow, interwoven mouth towards the sea.

We crossed over a rise, and from the far side opened a wide view, which was the delta of Wadi Yenbo, the largest valley of Northern Hejas. It seemed a vivid copse of tamarisk and thorn. To the right, some miles up the valley, showed darkly the palm-groves of Nakhl Mubarak, a village and gardens of the Beni Ibrahim Juheina in the distance, ahead of us, lay the massive Jebel Rudhwa, brooding always so instantly over Yenbo, though more than twenty miles away. We had seen it from Masturah, for it was one of the great hills of Hejaz, the more wonderful because it lifted itself in one clear edge from flat Tehama to crest. My companions felt at home in its protection; so, as the plain was now dancing with unbearable heat, we took shade under the branches of a leafy acacia beside the path, and slumbered through the middle day.

In the afternoon we watered our camels at a brackish little water hole in the sand bed of a branch watercourse, before a trim hedge of the feathery tamarisk, and then pushed on for two more happy hours. At last we halted for the night in typical Tehama country of bare slowly-swelling sand and shingle ridges, with shallow valleys.

The Sherifs lit a fire of aromatic wood to bake bread and boil coffee;

and we slept sweetly with the salt sea air cool on our chafed faces. We rose at two in the morning, and raced our camels over a featureless plain of hard shingle and wet sand to Yenbo, which stood up with walls and towers on a reef of coral rag twenty feet above our level. They took me straight through the gates by crumbling, empty streets — Yenbo had been half a city of the dead since the Hejaz Railway opened — to the house of Abd el Kader, Feisal's agent, a well-informed, efficient, quiet and dignified person, with whom we had had correspondence when he was postmaster in Mecca, and the Survey in Egypt had been making stamps for the new State. He had just been transferred here.

With Abd el Kader, in his picturesque rambling house looking over the deserted square, whence so many Medina caravans had started, I stayed four days waiting for the ship, which seemed as if it might fail me at the rendezvous. However, at last the *Suva* appeared, with Captain Boyle, who took me back to Jidda. It was my first meeting with Boyle. He had done much in the beginning of the revolt, and was to do much more for the future: but I failed to make a good return impression. I was travel-stained and had no baggage with me. Worst of all I wore a native head-cloth, put on as a compliment to the Arabs. Boyle disapproved.

Our persistence in the hat (due to a misunderstanding of the ways of heat-stroke) had led the East to see significance in it, and after long thought their wisest brains concluded that Christians wore the hideous thing that its broad brim might interpose between their weak eyes and the uncongenial sight of God. So it reminded Islam continually that God was miscalled and misliked by Christians. The British thought this prejudice reprehensible (quite unlike our hatred of a head-cloth) one to be corrected at any price. If the people would not have us hatted, they should not have us any way. Now as it happened I had been educated in Syria before the war to wear the entire Arab outfit when necessary without strangeness, or sense of being socially compromised. The skirts were a nuisance in running up stairs, but the head-cloth was even convenient in such a climate. So I had accepted it when I rode inland, and must now cling to it under fire of naval disapproval, till some shop should sell me a cap.

In Jidda was the *Euryalus*, with Admiral Wemyss, bound for Port

Sudan that Sir Rosslyn might visit Sir Reginald Wingate at Khartoum. Sir Reginald, as Sirdar of the Egyptian Army, had been put in command of the British military side of the Arab adventure in place of Sir Henry McMahon, who continued to direct its politics; and it was necessary for me to see him, to impart my impressions to him. So I begged the Admiral for a passage over sea, and a place in his train to Khartum. This he readily granted, after cross-questioning me himself at length.

I found that his active and broad intelligence had engaged his interest in the Arab Revolt from the beginning. He had come down again and again in his flagship to lend a hand when things were critical, and had gone out of his way twenty times to help the shore, which properly was Army business. He had given the Arabs guns and machine-guns, landing parties and technical help, with unlimited transport and naval co-operation, always making a real pleasure of requests, and fulfilling them in overflowing measure.

Had it not been for Admiral Wemyss' good will, and prescience, and the admirable way in which Captain Boyle carried out his wishes, the jealousy of Sir Archibald Murray might have wrecked the Sherif's rebellion at its start. As it was, Sir Rosslyn Wemyss acted godfather till the Arabs were on their feet; when he went to London; and Allenby, coming out fresh to Egypt, found the Arabs a factor on his battle front, and put the energies and resources of the Army at their disposal. This was opportune, and a fortunate twist of the whirligig; for Admiral Wemyss' successor in the naval command in Egypt was not considered helpful by the other services, though apparently he treated them no worse than he treated his own subordinates. A hard task, of course, to succeed Wemyss.

In Port Sudan we saw two British officers of the Egyptian Army waiting to embark for Rabegh. They were to command the Egyptian troops in Hejaz, and to do their best to help Aziz el Masri organize the Arab Regular Force, which was going to end the war from Rabegh. This was my first meeting with Joyce and Davenport, the two Englishmen to whom the Arab cause owed the greater part of its foreign debt of gratitude. Joyce worked for long beside me. Of Davenport's successes in the south we heard by constant report.

Khartum felt cool after Arabia, and nerved me to show Sir Reginald Wingate my long reports written in those days of waiting at Yenbo. I urged that the situation seemed full of promise. The main need was skilled assistance; and the campaign should go prosperously if some Regular British officers, professionally competent and speaking Arabic, were attached to the Arab leaders as technical advisers, to keep us in proper touch.

Wingate was glad to hear a hopeful view. The Arab Revolt had been his dream for years. While I was at Khartum chance gave him the power to play the main part in it; for the workings against Sir Henry McMahon came to a head, were successful, and ended in his recall to England. Sir Reginald Wingate was ordered down to Egypt in his stead. So after two or three comfortable days in Khartum, resting and reading the *Morte d'Arthur* in the hospitable palace, I went down towards Cairo, feeling that the responsible person had all my news. The Nile trip became a holiday.

Egypt was, as usual, in the throes of a Rabegh question. Some aeroplanes were being sent there; and it was being argued whether to send a brigade of troops after them or not. The head of the French Military Mission at Jidda, Colonel Bremond (Wilson's counterpart, but with more authority; for he was a practising light in native warfare, a success in French Africa, and an ex-chief of staff of a Corps on the Somme) strongly urged the landing of Allied forces in Hejaz. To tempt us he had brought to Suez some artillery, some machine-guns, and some cavalry and infantry, all Algerian Moslem rank and file, with French officers. These added to the British troops would give the force an international flavour.

Bremond's specious appreciation of the danger of the state of affairs in Arabia gained upon Sir Reginald. Wingate was a British General, commander of a nominal expeditionary force, the Hejaz Force, which in reality comprised a few liaison officers and a handful of storemen and instructors. If Bremond got his way he would be G.O.C. of a genuine brigade of mixed British and French troops, with all its pleasant machinery of responsibility and despatches, and its prospect of increment and official recognition. Consequently he wrote a guarded despatch, half-tending towards direct interference.

As my experience of Arab feeling in the Harb country had given me strong opinions on the Rabegh question (indeed, most of my opinions were strong), I wrote for General Clayton, to whose Arab Bureau I was now formally transferred, a violent memorandum on the whole subject. Clayton was pleased with my view that the tribes might defend Rabegh for months if lent advice and guns, but that they would certainly scatter to their tents again as soon as they heard of the landing of foreigners in force. Further, that the intervention-plans were technically unsound, for a brigade would be quite insufficient to defend the position, to forbid the neighbouring water-supplies to the Turks, and to block their road towards Mecca. I accused Colonel Bremond of having motives of his own, not military, nor taking account of Arab interests and of the importance of the revolt to us; and quoted his words and acts in Hejaz as evidence against him. They gave just plausible colour to my charge.

Clayton took the memorandum to Sir Archibald Murray, who, liking its acidity and force, promptly wired it all home to London as proof that the Arab experts asking this sacrifice of valuable troops from him were divided about its wisdom and honesty, even in their own camp. London asked for explanations; and the atmosphere slowly cleared, though in a less acute form the Rabegh question lingered for two months more.

My popularity with the Staff in Egypt, due to the sudden help I had lent to Sir Archibald's prejudices, was novel and rather amusing. They began to be polite to me, and to say that I was observant, with a pungent style, and character. They pointed out how good of them it was to spare me to the Arab cause in its difficulties. I was sent for by the Commander-in-Chief, but on my way to him was intercepted by a waiting and agitated aide, and led first into the presence of the Chief of Staff, General Lynden Bell. To such an extent had he felt it his duty to support Sir Archibald in his whimsies that people generally confounded the two as one enemy. So I was astonished when, as I came in, he jumped to his feet, leaped forward, and gripped me by the shoulder, hissing, 'Now you're not to frighten him: don't you forget what I say!'

My face probably showed bewilderment, for his one eye turned bland and he made me sit down, and talked nicely about Oxford, and what fun undergrads had, and the interest of my report of life in Feisal's ranks, and his hope that I would go back there to carry on what I had so well begun, mixing these amiabilities with remarks of how nervous the Commander-in-Chief was, and how worried about everything, and the need there was for me to give him a reassuring picture of affairs, and yet not a rosy picture, since they could not afford excursions either way.

I was hugely amused, inwardly, and promised to be good, but pointed out that my object was to secure the extra stores and arms and officers the Arabs needed, and how for this end I must enlist the interest, and, if necessary (for I would stick at nothing in the way of duty), even the excitement of the Commander-in-Chief; whereupon General Lynden Bell took me up, saying that supplies were his part, and in them he did everything without reference, and he thought he might at once, here and now, admit his new determination to do all he could for us.

I think he kept his word and was fair to us thereafter. I was very soothing to his chief.

BOOK II

OPENING THE ARAB
OFFENSIVE

Chapters XVII to XXVII

My *chiefs were astonished at such favourable news, but promised help, and meanwhile sent me back, much against my will, into Arabia. I reached Feisal's camp on the day the Turks carried the defences of Jebel Subh. By their so doing the entire basis of my confidence in a tribal war was destroyed.*

We havered for a while by Yenbo, hoping to retrieve the position: but the tribesmen proved to be useless for assault, and we saw that if the Revolt was to endure we must invent a new plan of campaign at once.

This was hazardous, as the promised British military experts had not yet arrived. However, we decided that to regain the initiative we must ignore the main body of the enemy, and concentrate far off on his railway flank. The first step towards this was to move our base to Wejh: which we proceeded to do in the grand manner.

CHAPTER XVII

CLAYTON a few days later told me to return to Arabia and Feisal. This being much against my grain I urged my complete unfitness for the job: said I hated responsibility — obviously the position of a conscientious adviser would be responsible — and that in all my life objects had been gladder to me than persons, and ideas than objects. So the duty of succeeding with men, of disposing them to any purpose, would be doubly hard to me. They were not my medium: I was not practised in that technique. I was unlike a soldier: hated soldiering. Of course, I had read the usual books (too many books), Clausewitz and Jomini, Mahan and Foch, had played at Napoleon's campaigns, worked at Hannibal's tactics, and the wars of Belisarius, like any other man at Oxford; but I had never thought myself into the mind of a real commander compelled to fight a campaign of his own.

Last of all I reminded Clayton, relevantly, that the Sirdar had telegraphed to London for certain regular officers competent to direct the Arab war. The reply was that they might be months arriving, and meanwhile Feisal must be linked to us, and his needs promptly notified to Egypt. So I had to go; leaving to others the Arab Bulletin I had founded, the maps I wished to draw, and the file of the war-changes of the Turkish Army, all fascinating activities in which my training helped me; to take up a role for which I felt no inclination. As our revolt succeeded, onlookers have praised its leadership: but behind the scenes lay all the vices of amateur control, experimental councils, divisions, whimsicality.

My journey was to Yenbo, now the special base of Feisal's army, where Garland single-handed was teaching the Sherifians how to blow up railways with dynamite, and how to keep army stores in systematic order. The first activity was the better. Garland was an enquirer in physics, and had years of practical knowledge of explosives. He had his own devices for mining trains and felling telegraphs and cutting metals; and his knowledge of Arabic and freedom from the theories of the ordinary sapper-school enabled him to teach the art of demolition to unlettered Beduin in a quick and ready way. His pupils admired a man who was never at a loss.

Incidentally he taught me to be familiar with high explosive. Sappers handled it like a sacrament, but Garland would shovel a handful of detonators into his pocket, with a string of primers, fuse, and fusees, and jump gaily on his camel for a week's ride to the Hejaz Railway. His health was poor and the climate made him regularly ill. A weak heart troubled him after any strenuous effort or crisis; but he treated these troubles as freely as he did detonators, and persisted till he had derailed the first train and broken the first culvert in Arabia. Shortly afterwards he died.

Things in Hejaz had changed a good deal in the elapsed month. Pursuing his former plan, Feisal had moved to Wadi Yenbo, and was trying to make safe his rear before going up to attack the railway in the grand manner. To relieve him of the burdensome Harb tribes, his young half-brother Zeid was on the way up from Rabegh to Wadi Safra, as a nominal subordinate of Sherif Ali. The advanced Harb clans were efficiently harrying the Turkish communications between Medina and Bir Abbas. They sent in to Feisal nearly every day a little convoy of captured camels, or rifles picked up after an engagement, or prisoners, or deserters.

Rabegh, shaken by the first appearance of Turkish aeroplanes on November the seventh, had been reassured by the arrival of a flight of four British Aeroplanes, B.E. machines, under Major Ross, who spoke Arabic so adeptly and was so splendid a leader that there could be no two minds as to the wise direction of his help. More guns came in week by week, till there were twenty-three, mostly obsolete, and of fourteen patterns. Ali had about three thousand Arab infantry; of whom two thousand were regulars in khaki, under Aziz el Masri. With them were nine hundred camel corps, and three hundred Egyptian troops. French gunners were promised.

Sherif Abdulla had at last left Mecca, on November the twelfth. A fortnight later he was much where he had meant to be, south, east and north-east of Medina, able to cut off its supplies from Kasim and Kuweit. Abdulla had about four thousand men with him, but only three machine-guns, and ten inefficient mountain guns captured at Taif and Mecca. Consequently he was not strong enough to carry out his further plan of a concerted attack on Medina with Ali and Feisal. He could only blockade it, and for this purpose posted himself at Henakiyeh, a desert place, eighty miles north-east of Medina, where he was too far away to be very useful.

The matter of the stores in the Yenbo base was being well handled. Garland had left the checking and issuing of them to Abd el Kader, Feisal's governor, who was systematic and quick. His efficiency was a great comfort to us, since it enabled us to keep our attention on more active things. Feisal was organizing his peasants, his slaves, and his paupers into formal battalions, an irregular imitation of the new model army of Aziz at Rabegh. Garland held bombing classes, fired guns, repaired machine-guns, wheels, and harness, and was armourer for them all. The feeling was busy and confident.

Feisal, who had not yet acted on our reminders of the importance of Wejh, was imagining an expedition of the Juheina to take it. Meanwhile he was in touch with the Billi, the numerous tribe with head-quarters in Wejh, and he hoped for support from them. Their paramount Sheikh, Suleiman Rifada, was temporizing, being really hostile; for the Turks had made him Pasha and decorated him; but his cousin Hamid was in arms for the Sherif, and had just captured a gratifying little caravan of seventy camels on the way from El Ula, with stores for the Turkish garrison of Wejh. As I was starting for Kheif Hussein to press the Wejh plan again on Feisal, news came in of a Turkish repulse near Bir ibn Hassani. A reconnaissance of their cavalry and camel corps had been pushed too far into the hills, and the Arabs had caught it and scattered it. Better and better yet.

SO I made a happy start with my sponsor for the journey, Sherif Abd el Kerim el Beidawi, half-brother of Mohammed, Emir of the Juheina, but, to my astonishment, of pure Abyssinian type. They told me later that his mother had been a slave-girl married by the old Emir late in life. Abd el Kerim was a man of middle height, thin and coal black, but debonaire, twenty-six years old; though he looked less, and had only a tiny tuft of beard on his sharp chin. He was restless and active, endowed with an easy, salacious humour. He hated the Turks, who had despised him for his colour (Arabs had little colour-feeling against Africans: it was the Indian who evoked their race-dislike), and was very merry and intimate with me. With him were three or four of his men, all well mounted; and we had a rapid journey, for Abd el Kerim was a famous rider who took pride in covering his stages at three times the normal speed. It was not my camel, and the weather was cool and clouded, with a taste of rain. So I had no objection.

After starting, we cantered for three unbroken hours. That had shaken down our bellies far enough for us to hold more food, and we stopped and ate bread and drank coffee till sunset, while Abd el Kerim rolled about his carpet in a dog-fight with one of the men. When he was exhausted he sat up; and they told stories and japed, till they were breathed enough to get up and dance. Everything was very free, very good-tempered, and not at all dignified.

When we re-started, an hour's mad race in the dusk brought us to the end of the Tehama, and to the foot of a low range of rock and sand. A month ago, coming from Hamra, we had passed south of this: now we crossed it, going up Wadi Agida, a narrow, winding, sandy valley between the hills. Because it had run in flood a few days earlier, the going was firm for our panting camels; but the ascent was steep and we had to take it at walking pace. This pleased me, but so angered Abd el Kerim, that when, in a short hour, we reached the watershed he thrust his mount forward again and led us at break-neck speed down hill in the yielding night (a fair road, fortunately, with sand and pebbles underfoot) for half an hour, when the land flattened out, and we came to the outlying plantations of Nakhl Mubarak, chief date-gardens of the southern Juheina.

As we got near we saw through the palm-trees flame, and the flame-lit smoke of many fires, while the hollow ground re-echoed with the roaring of thousands of excited camels, and volleying of shots or shoutings in the darkness of lost men, who sought through the crowd to rejoin their friends. As we had heard in Yenbo that the Nekhl were deserted, this tumult meant something strange, perhaps hostile. We crept quietly past an end of the grove and along a narrow street between man-high mud walls, to a silent group of houses. Abd el Kerim forced the courtyard door of the first on our left, led the camels within, and hobbled them down by the walls that they might remain unseen. Then he slipped a cartridge into the breech of his rifle and stole off on tiptoe down the street towards the noise to find out what was happening. We waited for him, the sweat of the ride slowly drying in our clothes as we sat there in the chill night, watching.

He came back after half an hour to say that Feisal with his camel corps had just arrived, and we were to go down and join him. So we led the camels out and mounted; and rode in file down another lane on a bank between houses, with a sunk garden of palms on our right. Its end was filled with a solid crowd of Arabs and camels, mixed together in the wildest confusion, and all crying aloud. We pressed through them, and down a ramp suddenly into the bed of Wadi Yenbo, a broad, open space: how broad could only be guessed from the irregular lines of watch-fires glimmering over it to a great distance. Also it was very damp; with slime, the relic of a shallow flood two days before, yet covering its stones. Our camels found it slippery under foot and began to move timidly.

We had no opportunity to notice this, or indeed anything, just now, except the mass of Feisal's army, filling the valley from side to side. There were hundreds of fires of thorn-wood, and round them were Arabs making coffee or eating, or sleeping muffled like dead men in their cloaks, packed together closely in the confusion of camels. So many camels in company made a mess indescribable, couched as they were or tied down all over the camping ground, with more ever coming in, and the old ones leaping up on three legs to join them, roaring with hunger and agitation. Patrols were going out, caravans being unloaded, and dozens of Egyptian mules bucking angrily over the middle of the scene.

We ploughed our way through this din, and in an island of calm at the very centre of the valley bed found Sherif Feisal. We halted our camels by his side. On his carpet, spread barely over the stones, he was sitting between Sherif Sharraf, the Kaimmakam both of the Imaret and of Taif, his cousin, and Maulud, the rugged, slashing old Mesopotamian patriot, now acting as his A.D.C. In front of him knelt a secretary taking down an order, and beyond him another reading reports aloud by the light of a silvered lamp which a slave was holding. The night was windless, the air heavy, and the unshielded flame poised there stiff and straight.

Feisal, quiet as ever, welcomed me with a smile until he could finish his dictation. After it he apologized for my disorderly reception, and waved the slaves back to give us privacy. As they retired with the on-lookers, a wild camel leaped into the open space in front of us, plunging and trumpeting. Maulud dashed at its head to drag it away; but it dragged him instead; and, its load of grass ropes for camel fodder coming untied, there poured down over the taciturn Sharraf, the lamp, and myself, an avalanche of hay. 'God be praised,' said Feisal gravely, 'that it was neither butter nor bags of gold.' Then he explained to me what unexpected things had happened in the last twenty-four hours on the battle front.

The Turks had slipped round the head of the Arab barrier forces in Wadi Safra by a side road in the hills, and had cut their retreat. The Harb, in a panic, had melted into the ravines on each side, and escaped through them in parties of twos and threes, anxious for their threatened families. The Turkish mounted men poured down the empty valley and over the Dhifran Pass to Bir Said, where Ghalib Bey, their com-mander, nearly caught the unsuspecting Zeid asleep in his tent. How-ever, warning came just in time. With the help of Sherif Abdulla ibn Thawab, an old Harith campaigner, Emir Zeid held up the enemy attack for long enough to get some of his tents and baggage packed on camels and driven away. Then he escaped himself; but his force melted into a loose mob of fugitives riding wildly through the night towards Yenbo.

Thereby the road to Yenbo was laid open to the Turks, and Feisal had rushed down here only an hour before our arrival, with five thousand men, to protect his base until something properly defensive could be arranged. His spy system was breaking down: the Harb, having lost their wits in the darkness, were bringing in wild and contradictory reports from one side and another about the strength of the Turks and their movements and intention. He had no idea whether they would strike at Yenbo or be content with holding the passes from Wadi Yenbo into Wadi Safra while they threw the bulk of their forces down the coast towards Rabegh and Mecca. The situation would be serious either way: the best that could happen would be if Feisal's presence here attracted them, and caused them to lose more days trying to catch his field army while we strengthened Yenbo. Meanwhile, he was doing all he could, quite cheerfully; so I sat down and listened to the news; or to the petitions, complaints and difficulties being brought in and settled by him summarily.

Sharraf beside me worked a busy tooth-stick back and forward along his gleaming jaws, speaking only once or twice an hour, in reproof of too-urgent suitors. Maulud ever and again leaned over to me, round Feisal's neutral body, eagerly repeating for our joint benefit any word of a report which might be turned to favour the launching of an instant and formal counter-attack.

This lasted till half-past four in the morning. It grew very cold as the damp of the valley rose through the carpet and soaked our clothes. The camp gradually stilled as the tired men and animals went one by one to sleep; a white mist collected softly over them and in it the fires became slow pillars of smoke. Immediately behind us, rising out of the bed of mist, Jebel Rudhwa, more steep and rugged than ever, was brought so close by the hushed moonlight that it seemed hanging over our heads.

Feisal at last finished the urgent work. We ate half-a-dozen dates, a frigid comfort, and curled up on the wet carpet. As I lay there in a shiver, I saw the Biasha guards creep up and spread their cloaks gently over Feisal, when they were sure that he was sleeping.

An hour later we got up stiffly in the false dawn (too cold to go on pretending and lying down) and the slaves lit a fire of palm-ribs to warm us, while Sharraf and myself searched for food and fuel enough for the moment. Messengers were still coming in from all sides with evil rumours of an immediate attack; and the camp was not far off panic. So Feisal decided to move to another position, partly because we should be washed out of this one if it rained anywhere in the hills, and partly to occupy his men's minds and work off their restlessness.

When his drums began to beat, the camels were loaded hurriedly. After the second signal everyone leaped into the saddle and drew off to left or right, leaving a broad lane up which Feisal rode, on his mare, with Sharraf a pace behind him, and then Ali, the standard-bearer, a splendid wild man from Nejd, with his hawk's face framed in long plaits of jet-black hair falling downward from his temples. Ali was dressed garishly, and rode a tall camel. Behind him were all the mob of sherifs and sheikhs and slaves — and myself — pell-mell. There were eight hundred in the bodyguard that morning.

Feisal rode up and down looking for a place to camp, and at last stopped on the further side of a little open valley just north of Nakhl Mubarak village; though the houses were so buried in the trees that few of them could be seen from outside. On the south bank of this valley, beneath some rocky knolls, Feisal pitched his two plain tents. Sharraf had his personal tent also; and some of the other chiefs came and lived by us. The guard put up their booths and shelters; and the Egyptian gunners halted lower down on our side, and dressed their twenty tents beautifully in line, to look very military. So in a little while we were populous, if hardly imposing in detail.

CHAPTER XIX

WE stayed here two days, most of which I spent in Feisal's company, and so got a deeper experience of his method of command, at an interesting season when the morale of his men was suffering heavily from the scare reports brought in, and from the defection of the Northern Harb. Feisal, fighting to make up their lost spirits, did it most surely by lending of his own to everyone within reach. He was accessible to all who stood outside his tent and waited for notice; and he never cut short petitions, even when men came in chorus with their grief in a song of many verses, and sang them around us in the dark. He listened always, and if he did not settle the case himself called Sharraf or Faiz to arrange it for him. This extreme patience was a further lesson to me of what native headship in Arabia meant.

His self-control seemed equally great. When Mirzuk el Tikheimi, his guest-master, came in from Zeid to explain the shameful story of their rout, Feisal just laughed at him in public and sent him aside to wait while he saw the sheikhs of the Harb and the Ageyl whose carelessness had been mainly responsible for the disaster. These he rallied gently, chaffing them for having done this or that, for having inflicted such losses or lost so much. Then he called back Mirzuk and lowered the tent-flap: a sign that there was private business to be done. I thought of the meaning of Feisal's name (the sword flashing downward in the stroke) and feared a scene, but he made room for Mirzuk on his carpet, and said, 'Come! tell us more of your "nights" and marvels of the battle: amuse us'. Mirzuk, a good-looking, clever lad (a little too sharp-featured) falling into the spirit of the thing, began, in his broad, Ateibi twang, to draw for us word-pictures of young Zeid in flight; of the terror of Ibn Thawab, that famous brigand; and, ultimate disgrace, of how the venerable el Hussein, father of Sherif Ali, the Harithi, had lost his coffee-pots!

Feisal, in speaking, had a rich musical voice, and used it carefully upon his men. To them he talked in tribal dialect, but with a curious, hesitant manner, as though faltering painfully among phrases, looking inward for the just word. His thought, perhaps, moved only by a little in front of his speech, for the phrases at last chosen were usually the simplest, which gave an effect emotional and sincere. It seemed possible, so thin was the screen of words, to see the pure and the very brave spirit shining out.

At other times he was full of humour — that invariable magnet of Arab goodwill. He spoke one night to the Rifaa sheikhs when he sent them forward to occupy the plain this side of Bir el Fagir, a tangled country of acacia and tamarisk thickets on the imperceptible watershed of the long depression uniting Bruka and Bir Said. He told them gently that the Turks were coming on, and that it was their duty to hold them up and give God the credit of their victory; adding that this would become impossible if they went to sleep. The old men — and in Arabia elders mattered more than youths — broke out into delighted speech, and, after saying that God would give him a victory, or rather two victories, capped their wishes with a prayer that his life might be prolonged in the accumulation of an unprecedented number of victories. What was better, they kept effective watch all night, in the strength of his exhortation.

The routine of our life in camp was simple. Just before daybreak the army Imam used to climb to the head of the little hill above the sleeping army, and thence utter an astounding call to prayer. His voice was harsh and very powerful, and the hollow, like a sounding-board, threw echoes at the hills which returned them with indignant interest. We were effectually roused, whether we prayed or cursed. As soon as he ended, Feisal's Imam cried gently and musically from just outside the tent. In a minute, one of Feisal's five slaves (all freed men, but refusing discharge till it was their pleasure: since it was good and not unprofitable to be my lord's servant) came round to Sharraf and myself with sweetened coffee. Sugar for the first cup in the chill of dawn was considered fit.

An hour or so later, the flap of Feisal's sleeping tent would be thrown back: his invitation to callers from the household. There would be four or five present; and after the morning's news a tray of breakfast would be carried in. The staple of this was dates in Wadi Yenbo; sometimes Feisal's Circassian grandmother would send him a box of her famous spiced cakes from Mecca; and sometimes Hejris, the body slave, would give us odd biscuits and cereals of his own trying. After breakfast we would play with bitter coffee and sweet tea in alternation, while Feisal's correspondence was dealt with by dictation to his secretaries. One of these was Faiz el Ghusein the adventurous; another was the Imam, a sad-faced person made conspicuous in the army by the baggy umbrella hanging from his saddle-bow. Occasionally a man was given private audience at this hour, but seldom; as the sleeping tent was strictly for the Sherif's own use. It was an ordinary bell tent, furnished with cigarettes, a camp-bed, a fairly good Kurd rug, a poor Shirazi, and the delightful old Baluch prayer-carpet on which he prayed.

At about eight o'clock in the morning, Feisal would buckle on his ceremonial dagger and walk across to the reception tent, which was floored with two horrible kilims. Feisal would sit down at the end of the tent facing the open side, and we with our backs against the wall, in a semicircle out from him. The slaves brought up the rear, and clustered round the open wall of the tent to control the besetting suppliants who lay on the sand in the tent-mouth, or beyond, waiting their turn. If possible, business was got through by noon, when the Emir liked to rise.

We of the household, and any guests, then reassembled in the living tent; and Hejris and Salem carried in the luncheon tray, on which were as many dishes as circumstances permitted. Feisal was an inordinate smoker, but a very light eater, and he used to make-believe with his fingers or a spoon among the beans, lentils, spinach, rice, and sweet cakes till he judged that we had had enough, when at a wave of his hand the tray would disappear, as other slaves walked forward to pour water for our fingers at the tent door. Fat men, like Mohammed Ibn Shefia, made a comic grievance of the Emir's quick and delicate meals, and would have food of their own prepared for them when they came away. After lunch we would talk a little, while sucking up two cups of coffee, and savouring two glasses full of syrup-like green tea. Then till two in the afternoon the curtain of the living tent was down, signifying that Feisal was sleeping, or reading, or doing private business. Afterwards he would sit again in the reception tent till he had finished with all who wanted him. I never saw an Arab leave him dissatisfied or hurt

— a tribute to his tact and to his memory; for he seemed never to halt for loss of a fact, nor to stumble over a relationship.

If there were time after second audience, he would walk with his friends, talking of horses or plants, looking at camels, or asking someone the names of the visible land features. The sunset prayer was at times public, though Feisal was not outwardly very pious. After it he saw people individually in the living tent, planning the night's reconnaissances and patrols — for most of the field-work was done after dark. Between six and seven there was brought in the evening meal, to which all present in headquarters were called by the slaves. It resembled the lunch, except that cubes of boiled mutton were sorted through the great tray of rice, *Medfa el Suhur*, the mainstay of appetite. We observed silence till all had eaten.

This meal ended our day, save for the stealthy offering by a bare-footed slave of a tray of tea-glasses at protracted intervals. Feisal did not sleep till very late, and never betrayed a wish to hasten our going. In the evening he relaxed as far as possible and avoided avoidable work. He would send out for some local sheikh to tell stories of the district, and histories of the tribe and its genealogy; or the tribal poets would sing us their war narratives: long traditional forms with stock epithets, stock sentiments, stock incidents grafted afresh on the efforts of each generation. Feisal was passionately fond of Arabic poetry, and would often provoke recitations, judging and rewarding the best verses of the night. Very rarely he would play chess, with the unthinking directness of a fencer, and brilliantly. Sometimes, perhaps for my benefit, he told stories of what he had seen in Syria, and scraps of Turkish secret history, or family affairs. I learned much of the men and parties in the Hejaz from his lips.

CHAPTER XX

S UDDENLY Feisal asked me if I would wear Arab clothes like his own while in the camp. I should find it better for my own part, since it was a comfortable dress in which to live Arab-fashion as we must do. Besides, the tribesmen would then understand how to take me. The only wearers of khaki in their experience had been Turkish officers, before whom they took up an instinctive defence. If I wore Meccan clothes, they would behave to me as though I were really one of the leaders; and I might slip in and out of Feisal's tent without making a sensation which he had to explain away each time to strangers.

I agreed at once, very gladly; for army uniform was abominable when camel-riding or when sitting about on the ground; and the Arab things, which I had learned to manage before the war, were cleaner and more decent in the desert. Hejris was pleased, too, and exercised his fancy in fitting me out in splendid white silk and gold-embroidered wedding garments which had been sent to Feisal lately (was it a hint?) by his great-aunt in Mecca. I took a stroll in the new looseness of them round the palm-gardens of Mubarak and Bruka, to accustom myself to their feel.

These villages were pleasant little places, built of mud brick on the high earth mounds encircling the palm-gardens. Nakhl Mubarak lay to the north, and Bruka just south of it across a thorny valley. The houses were small, mud-washed inside, cool, and very clean, furnished with a mat or two, a coffee mortar, and food pots and trays. The narrow streets were shaded by an occasional well-grown tree. The earth embankments round the cultivated areas were sometimes fifty feet in height, and had been for the most part artificially formed from the surplus earth dug out between the trees, from household rubbish and from stones gathered out of the Wadi.

The banks were to defend the crops from flood. Wadi Yenbo otherwise would soon have filled the gardens, since these, to be irrigable, must be below the valley floor. The narrow plots were divided by fences of palm-ribs or by mud walls, with narrow streams of sweet water in raised channels round them. Each garden gate was over water, with a bridge of three or four parallel palm-logs built up to it for the passage of donkeys or camels. Each plot had a mud sluice, scooped away when its turn for watering came. The palms, regularly planted in ordered lines and well cared for, were the main crop; but between them were grown barley, radishes, marrows, cucumbers, tobacco and henna. Villages higher up Wadi Yenbo were cool enough to grow grapes.

Feisal's stand in Nakhl Mubarak could in the nature of things only be a pause, and I felt that I had better get back to Yenbo, to think seriously about our amphibious defence of this port. The Navy having promised its every help. We settled that I should consult Zeid, and act with him as seemed best. Feisal gave me a magnificent bay camel for the trip back. We marched through the Agida hills by a new road, Wadi Messarih, because of a scare of Turkish patrols on the more direct line. Bedr ibn Shefia was with me; and we did the distance gently in a single stage of six hours, getting to Yenbo before dawn. Being tired after three strenuous days of little sleep among constant alarms and excitements I went straight to Garland's empty house (he was living on board ship in the harbour) and fell asleep on a bench; but afterwards I was called out again by the news that Sherif Zeid was coming, and went down to the walls to see the beaten force ride in.

There were about eight hundred of them, quiet, but in no other way mortified by their shame. Zeid himself seemed finely indifferent. As he entered the town he turned and cried to Abd el Kadir, the Governor, riding behind him, 'Why, your town is ruinous! I must telegraph to my father for forty masons to repair the public buildings.' And this actually he did. I had telegraphed to Captain Boyle that Yenbo was gravely threatened, and Boyle at once replied that his fleet would be there in time, if not sooner. This readiness was an opportune consolation: worse news came along next day. The Turks, by throwing a strong force forward from Bir Said against Nakhl Mubarak, had closed with Feisal's levies while they were yet unsteady. After a short fight, Feisal had broken off, yielded his ground, and was retreating here. Our war seemed entering its last act. I took my camera, and from the parapet of the Medina gate got a fine photograph of the brothers coming in. Feisal had nearly two thousand men with him, but none of the Juheina tribesmen. It looked like treachery and a real defection of the tribes, things which both of us had ruled out of court as impossible.

I called at once at his house and he told me the history. The Turks had come on with three battalions and a number of mule-mounted infantry and camelry. Their command was in the hands of Ghalib Bey, who handled his troops with great keenness, acting as he did under the eye of the Corps Commander. Fakhru Pasha privately accompanied the expedition, whose guide and go-between with the Arabs was Dakhil-Allah el Kadhi, the hereditary law-giver of the Juheina, a rival of Sherif Mohammed Ali el Beidawi, and after him the second man in the tribe.

They got across Wadi Yenbo to the groves of Bruka in their first onset, and thus threatened the Arab communications with Yenbo. They were also able to shell Nakhl Mubarak freely with their seven guns. Feisal was not a whit dismayed, but threw out the Juheina on his left to work down the great valley. His centre and right he kept in Nakhl Mubarak, and he sent the Egyptian artillery to take post in Jebel Agida, to deny that to the Turks. Then he opened fire on Bruka with his own two fifteen-pounders.

Rasim, a Syrian officer, formerly a battery commander in the Turkish Army, was fighting these two guns; and he made a great demonstration with them. They had been sent down as a gift from Egypt, anyhow, old rubbish thought serviceable for the wild Arabs, just as the sixty thousand rifles supplied the Sherif were condemned weapons, relics of the Gallipoli campaign. So Rasim had no sights, nor range-finder, no range tables, no high explosive.

His distance might have been six thousand yards; but the fuses of his shrapnel were Boer War antiquities, full of green mould, and, if they burst, it was sometimes short in the air, and sometimes grazing. However, he had no means of getting his ammunition away if things went wrong, so he blazed off at speed, shouting with laughter at this fashion of making war; and the tribesmen seeing the commandant so merry took heart of grace themselves. 'By God,' said one, 'those are the real guns: the Importance of their noise!' Rasim swore that the Turks were dying in heaps; and the Arabs charged forward warmly at his word.

Things were going well; and Feisal had the hope of a decisive success when suddenly his left wing in the valley wavered, halted; finally it turned its back on the enemy and retired tumultuously to the camping ground. Feisal, in the centre, galloped to Rasim and cried that the Juheina had broken and he was to save the guns. Rasim yoked up the teams and trotted away to Wadi Agida, wherein the Egyptians were taking counsel pavidly with one another. After him streamed the Ageyl and the Atban, the men of Ibn Shefia, the Harb and Biasha. Feisal and his household composed the rear, and in deliberate procession they moved down towards Yenbo, leaving the Juheina with the Turks on the battlefield.

As I was still hearing of this sad end and cursing with him the traitor Beidawi brothers, there was a stir about the door, and Abd el Kerim broke through the slaves, swung up to the dais, kissed Feisal's head-rope in salutation, and sat down beside us. Feisal with a gasping stare at him, said, 'How?' and Abd el Kerim explained their dismay at the sudden flight of Feisal, and how he with his brother and their gallant men had fought the Turks for the whole night, alone, without artillery, till the palm-groves became untenable and they too had been driven through Wadi Agida. His brother, with half the manhood of the tribe, was just entering the gate. The others had fallen back up Wadi Yenbo for water.

'And why did you retire to the camp-ground behind us during the battle?' asked Feisal. 'Only to make ourselves a cup of coffee,' said Abd el Kerim. 'We had fought from sunrise and it was dusk: we were very tired and thirsty.' Feisal and I lay back and laughed: then we went to see what could be done to save the town.

The first step was simple. We sent all the Juheina back to Wadi Yenbo with orders to mass at Kheif, and keep up a steady pressure on the Turkish line of communications. They were also to push sniping parties down the Agida hills. This diversion would hold up so many of the Turks that they would be unable to bring against Yenbo a force superior in number to the defenders, who in addition had the advantage of a good position. The town on the top of its flat reef of coral rose perhaps twenty feet above the sea, and was compassed by water on two sides. The other two sides looked over flat stretches of sand, soft in places, destitute of cover for miles, and with no fresh water upon them anywhere. In daylight, if defended by artillery and machine-gun fire, they should be impregnable.

The artillery was arriving every minute; for Boyle, as usual far better than his word, had concentrated five ships on us in less than twenty-four hours. He put the monitor *M.*31, whose shallow draught fitted her for the job, in the end of the south-eastern creek of the harbour, whence she could rake the probable direction of a Turkish advance with her six-inch guns. Crocker, her captain, was very anxious to let off those itching guns. The larger ships were moored to fire over the town at longer range, or to rake the other flank from the northern harbour. The searchlights of *Dufferin* and *M.* 31 crossed on the plain beyond the town.

The Arabs, delighted to count up the quantity of vessels in the harbour, were prepared to contribute their part to the night's entertainment. They gave us good hope there would be no further panic: but to reassure them fully they needed some sort of rampart to defend, mediæval fashion: it was no good digging trenches, partly because the ground was coral rock, and, besides, they had no experience of trenches and might not have manned them confidently. So we took the crumbling, salt-riddled wall of the place, doubled it with a second, packed earth between the two, and raised them till our sixteenth-century bastions were rifle-proof at least, and probably proof against the Turkish mountain guns. Outside the bastions we put barbed wire, festooned between cisterns on the rain catchments beyond the walls. We dug in machine-gun nests in the best angles, and manned them with Feisal's regular gunners. The Egyptians, like everyone else given a place in the scheme, were gratifyingly happy. Garland was engineer-in-chief and chief adviser.

After sun-down the town quivered with suppressed excitement. So long as the day lasted there had been shouts and joy-shots and wild bursts of frenzy among the workmen; but when dark came, they went back to feed and a hush fell. Nearly everyone sat up that night. There was one alarm about eleven o'clock. Our outposts had met the enemy only three miles outside the town. Garland, with a crier, went through the few streets, and called the garrison. They tumbled straight out and went to their places in dead silence without a shot or a loose shout. The seamen on the minaret sent warning to the ships, whose combined searchlights began slowly to traverse the plain in complex intersections, drawing pencils of wheeling light across the flats which the attacking force must cross. However, no sign was made and no cause given us to open fire.

Afterwards, old Dakhil Allah told me he had guided the Turks down to rush Yenbo in the dark that they might stamp out Feisal's army once for all; but their hearts had failed them at the silence and the blaze of lighted ships from end to end of the harbour, with the eerie beams of the searchlights revealing the bleakness of the glacis they would have to cross. So they turned back: and that night, I believe, the Turks lost their war. Personally, I was on the *Suva*, to be undisturbed, and sleeping splendidly at last; so I was grateful to Dakhil Allah for the prudence which he preached the Turks, as though we might perhaps have won a a glorious victory, I was ready to give much more for just that eight hours' unbroken rest.

CHAPTER XXI

NEXT day the crisis had passed: the Turks had clearly failed. The Juheina were active in their flank position from Wadi Yenbo. Garland's architectural efforts about the town became impressive. Sir Archibald Murray, to whom Feisal had appealed for a demonstration in Sinai to prevent further withdrawals of Turks for service at Medina, sent back an encouraging reply, and everybody was breathing easily. A few days later Boyle dispersed the ships, promising another lightning concentration upon another warning; and I took the opportunity to go down to Rabegh, where I met Colonel Bremond, the great bearded chief of the French Military Mission, and the only real soldier in Hejaz. He was still using his French detachment in Suez as a lever to move a British Brigade into Rabegh; and, since he suspected I was not wholly of his party, he made an effort to convert me.

In the course of the argument which followed, I said something about the need of soon attacking Medina; for, with the rest of the British, I believed that the fall of Medina was a necessary preliminary to any further progress of the Arab Revolt. He took me up sharply, saying that it was in no wise proper for the Arabs to take Medina. In his view, the Arab Movement had attained its maximum utility by the mere rebellion in Mecca; and military operations against Turkey were better in the unaided hands of Great Britain and France. He wished to land Allied troops at Rabegh, because it would quench the ardour of the tribes by making the Sherif suspect in their eyes. The foreign troops would then be his main defence, and his preservation be our work and option, until the end of the war, when Turkey was defeated, the victorious Powers could extract Medina by treaty from the Sultan, and confer it upon Hussein, with the legal sovereignty of Hejaz, as his rewards for faithful service.

I had not his light confidence in our being strong enough to dispense with small allies; so I said shortly that my opinions were opposed to his. I laid the greatest weight on the immediate conquest of Medina, and was advising Feisal to seize Wejh, in order to prolong his threat against the railway. In sum, to my mind, the Arab Movement would not justify its creation if the enthusiasm of it did not carry the Arabs into Damascus.

This was unwelcome to him; for the Sykes-Picot Treaty of 1916 between France and England had been drawn by Sykes for this very eventuality; and, to reward it, stipulated the establishment of independent Arab states in Damascus, Aleppo and Mosul, districts which would otherwise fall to the unrestricted control of France. Neither Sykes nor Picot had believed the thing really possible; but I knew that it was, and believed that after it the vigour of the Arab Movement would prevent the creation — by us or others — in Western Asia of unduly 'colonial' schemes of exploitation.

Bremond took refuge in his technical sphere, and assured me, on his honour as a staff-officer, that for Feisal to leave Yenbo and go to Wejh was military suicide; but I saw no force in the arguments which he threw at me volubly; and told him so. It was a curious interview, that, between an old soldier and a young man in fancy dress; and it left a bad taste in my mouth. The Colonel, like his countrymen, was a realist in love, and war. Even in situations of poetry the French remained incorrigible prose-writers, seeing by the directly-thrown light of reason and understanding, not through the half-closed eye, mistily, by things' essential radiance, in the manner of the imaginative British: so the two races worked ill together on a great undertaking. However, I controlled myself enough not to tell any Arab of the conversation, but sent a full account of it to Colonel Wilson, who was shortly coming up to see Feisal for a discussion of the Wejh prospect in all its bearings.

Before Wilson arrived the centre of Turkish gravity changed abruptly. Fakhri Pasha had seen the hopelessness of attacking Yenbo, or of driving after the intangible Juheina in Kheif Hussein. Also he was being violently bombed in Nakhl Mubarak itself by a pair of British seaplanes which did hardy flights over the desert and got well into the enemy on two occasions, despite their shrapnel.

Consequently he decided to fall back in a hurry on Bir Said, leaving a small force there to check the Juheina, and to move down the Sultani road towards Rabegh with the bulk of his men. These changes were no doubt partly impelled by the unusual vigour of Ali at Rabegh. As soon as Ali had heard of Zeid's defeat he had sent him reinforcements and guns; and when Feisal himself collapsed he decided to move north with all his army, to attack the Turks in Wadi Safra and draw them off Yenbo. Ali had nearly seven thousand men; and Feisal felt that if the move was synchronized with one on his part, Fakhri's force might be crushed between them in the hills. He telegraphed, suggesting this, asking for a delay of a few days till his shaken men were ready.

Ali was strung up and would not wait. Feisal therefore rushed Zeid out to Masahali in Wadi Yenbo to make preparations. When these were complete he sent Zeid on to occupy Bir Said, which was done successfully. He then ordered the Juheina forward in support. They demurred; for ibn Beidawi was jealous of Feisal's growing power among his tribes, and wanted to keep himself indispensable. Feisal rode unattended to Nakhl Mubarak, and in one night convinced the Juheina that he was their leader. Next morning they were all moving, while he went on to collect the northern Harb on the Tasha Pass to interrupt the Turkish retreat in Wadi Safra. He had nearly six thousand men; and if Ali took the southern bank of the valley the weak Turks would be between two fires.

Unfortunately it did not happen. When actually on the move he heard from Ali that, after a peaceful recovery of Bir ibn Hassani, his men had been shaken by false reports of disloyalty among the Subh, and had fallen back in rapid disorder to Rabegh.

In this ominous pause Colonel Wilson came up to Yenbo to persuade us of the necessity of an immediate operation against Wejh. An amended plan had been drawn up whereby Feisal would take the whole force of the Juheina, and his permanent battalions, against Wejh with the maximum of naval help. This strength would make success reasonably sure, but it left Yenbo empty and defenceless. For the moment Feisal dreaded incurring such a risk. He pointed out, not unreasonably, that the Turks in his neighbourhood were still mobile; that Ali's force had proved hollow, unlikely to defend even Rabegh against serious attack; and that, as Rabegh was the bulwark of Mecca, sooner than see it lost he must throw away Yenbo and ferry himself and men thither to die fighting on its beach.

To reassure him, Wilson painted the Rabegh force in warm colours.

E*

Feisal checked his sincerity by asking for his personal word that the Rabegh garrison, with British naval help, would resist enemy attack till Wejh fell. Wilson looked for support round the silent deck of the *Dufferin* (on which we were conferring), and nobly gave the required assurance: a wise gamble, since without it Feisal would not move; and this diversion against Wejh, the only offensive in the Arabs' power, was their last chance not so much of securing a convincing siege of Medina, as of preventing the Turkish capture of Mecca. A few days later he strengthened himself by sending Feisal direct orders from his father, the Sherif, to proceed to Wejh at once, with all his available troops.

Meanwhile the Rabegh situation grew worse. The enemy in Wadi Safra and the Sultani road were estimated at nearly five thousand men. The Harb of the north were suppliant to them for preservation of their palm-groves. The Harb of the south, those of Hussein Mabeirig, notoriously waited their advance to attack the Sherifians in the rear. At a conference of Wilson, Bremond, Joyce, Ross and others, held in Rabegh on Christmas Eve, it was decided to lay out on the beach by the aerodrome a small position, capable of being held under the ship's guns by the Egyptians, the Flying Corps and a seamen's landing party from the *Minerva*, for the few hours needed to embark or destroy the stores. The Turks were advancing step by step; and the place was not in condition to resist one well-handled battalion supported by field artillery.

However, Fakhri was too slow. He did not pass Bir el Sheikh in any force till near the end of the first week in January, and seven days later was still not ready to attack Khoreiba, where Ali had an outpost of a few hundred men. The patrols were in touch; and an assault was daily expected, but as regularly delayed.

In truth the Turks were meeting with unguessed difficulties. Their headquarters were faced by a heavy sick rate among the men, and a growing weakness of the animals: both symptoms of overwork and lack of decent food. Always the activity of the tribesmen behind their back hampered them. Clans might sometimes fall away from the Arab cause, but did not therefore become trustworthy adherents of the Turks, who soon found themselves in ubiquitously hostile country. The tribal raids in the first fortnight of January caused them average daily losses of forty camels and some twenty men killed and wounded, with corresponding expense in stores.

These raids might occur at any point from ten miles seaward of Medina itself for the next seventy miles through the hills. They illustrated the obstacles in the way of the new Turkish Army with its half-Germanized complexity of equipment, when, from a distant rail-head with no made roads, it tried to advance through extremely rugged and hostile country. The administrative developments of scientific war had clogged its mobility and destroyed its dash; and troubles grew in geometrical rather than arithmetical progression for each new mile its commanding officers put between themselves and Medina, their ill-found, insecure and inconvenient base.

The situation was so unpromising for the Turks that Fakhri was probably half glad when the forthcoming sudden moves of Abdulla and Feisal in the last days of 1916 altered the strategic conception of the Hejaz war, and hurried the Mecca expedition (after January the eighteenth 1917) back from the Sultani and the Fara and the Gaha roads, back from Wadi Safra, to hold a passive defence of trenches within sight of the walls of Medina; a static position which endured till the Armistice ended the war and involved Turkey in the dismal surrender of the Holy City and its helpless garrison.

FEISAL was a fine, hot workman, whole-heartedly doing a thing when he had agreed to it. He had pledged his word that he would go at once to Wejh; so he and I sat down together on new-year's day for consideration of what this move meant to us and to the Turks. Around us, stretching up and down the Wadi Yenbo for miles, in little groups round palm-gardens, under the thicker trees, and in all the side tributaries, wherever there was shelter from the sun and rain, or good grazing for the camels, were the soldiers of our army. The mountaineers, half-naked footmen, had grown few. Most of the six thousand present were mounted men of substance. Their coffee hearths were outlined from afar by the camel saddles, pitched in circles round the fire as elbow-rests for men reclining between meals. The Arabs' physical perfection let them lie relaxed to the stony ground like lizards, moulding themselves to its roughness in corpse-like abandon.

They were quiet but confident. Some, who had been serving Feisal for six months or more, had lost that pristine heat of eagerness which had so thrilled me in Hamra; but they had gained experience in compensation; and staying-power in the ideal was fatter and more important for us than an early fierceness. Their patriotism was now conscious; and their attendance grew more regular as the distance from their homes increased. Tribal independence of orders was still maintained; but they had achieved a mild routine in camp life and on the march. When the Sherif came near they fell into a ragged line, and together made the bow and sweep of the arm to the lips, which was the official salute. They did not oil their guns: they said lest the sand clog them; also they had no oil, and it was better rubbed in to soften wind-chaps on their skin; but the guns were decently kept, and some of the owners could shoot at long range.

In mass they were not formidable, since they had no corporate spirit, nor discipline nor mutual confidence. The smaller the unit the better its performance. A thousand were a mob, ineffective against a company of trained Turks: but three or four Arabs in their hills would stop a dozen Turks. Napoleon remarked this of the Mamelukes. We were yet too breathless to turn our hasty practice into principle: our tactics were empirical snatchings of the first means to escape difficulty. But we were learning like our men.

From the battle of Nakhl Mubarak we abandoned the brigading of Egyptian troops with irregulars. We embarked the Egyptian officers and men, after turning over their complete equipment to Rasim, Feisal's gunner, and Abdulla el Deleimi, his machine-gun officer. They built up Arab companies out of local material, with a stiffening of Turk-trained Syrian and Mesopotamian deserters. Maulud, the fire-eating A.D.C., begged fifty mules off me, put across them fifty of his trained infantrymen, and told them they were cavalry. He was a martinet, and a born mounted officer, and by his spartan exercises the much-beaten mule-riders grew painfully into excellent soldiers, instantly obedient and capable of formal attack! They were prodigies in the Arab ranks. We telegraphed for another fifty mules, to double the dose of mounted infantry, since the value of so tough a unit for reconnaissance was obvious.

Feisal suggested taking nearly all the Juheina to Wejh with him and adding to them enough of the Harb and Billi, Ateiba and Ageyl to give the mass a many-tribed character. We wanted this march, which would be in its way a closing act of the war in Northern Hejaz, to send a rumour through the length and breadth of Western Arabia. It was to be the biggest operation of the Arabs in their memory; dismissing those who saw it to their homes, with a sense that their world had changed indeed; so that there would be no more silly defections and jealousies of clans behind us in future, to cripple us with family politics in the middle of our fighting.

Not that we expected immediate opposition. We bothered to take this unwieldy mob with us to Wejh, in the teeth of efficiency and experience, just because there was no fighting in the bill. We had intangible assets on our side. In the first place, the Turks had now engaged their surplus strength in attacking Rabegh, or rather in prolonging their occupied area so as to attack Rabegh. It would take them days to transfer back north. Then the Turks were stupid, and we reckoned on their not hearing all at once of our move, and on their not believing its first tale, and not seeing till later what chances it had given them. If we did our march in three weeks we should probably take Wejh by surprise. Lastly, we might develop the sporadic raiding activity of the Harb into conscious operations, to take booty, if possible, in order to be self-supporting; but primarily to lock up large numbers of Turks in defence positions. Zeid agreed to go down to Rabegh to organize similar pin-pricks in the Turks' rear. I gave him letters to the captain of the *Dufferin*, the Yenbo guardship, which would ensure him a quick passage down: for all who knew of the Wejh scheme were agog to help it.

To exercise my own hand in the raiding genre I took a test party of thirty-five Mahamid with me from Nakhl Mubarak, on the second day of 1917, to the old blockhouse-well of my first journey from Rabegh to Yenbo. When dark came we dismounted, and left our camels with ten men to guard them against possible Turkish patrols. The rest of us climbed up Dhifran: a painful climb, for the hills were of knife-sharp strata turned on edge and running in oblique lines from crest to foot. They gave abundance of broken surface, but no sure grip, for the stone was so minutely cracked that any segment would come away from its matrix, in the hand.

The head of Dhifran was cold and misty, and time dragged till dawn. We disposed ourselves in crevices of the rock, and at last saw the tips of bell-tents three hundred yards away beneath us to the right, behind a spur. We could not get a full view, so contented ourselves with putting bullets through their tops. A crowd of Turks turned out and leaped like stags into their trenches. They were very fast targets, and probably suffered little. In return they opened rapid fire in every direction, and made a terrific row; as if signalling the Hamra force to turn out in their help. As the enemy were already more than ten to one, the reinforcements might have prevented our retreat: so we crawled gently back till we could rush down into the first valley, where we fell over two scared Turks, unbuttoned, at their morning exercise. They were ragged, but something to show, and we dragged them homeward, where their news proved useful.

Feisal was still nervous over abandoning Yenbo, hitherto his indispensable base, and the second sea-port of Hejaz: and when casting

about for further expedients to distract the Turks from its occupation
we suddenly remembered Sidi Abdulla in Henakiyeh. He had some
five thousand irregulars, and a few guns and machine-guns, and the
reputation of his successful (if too slow) siege of Taif. It seemed a
shame to leave him wasting in the middle of the wilderness. A first
idea was that he might come to Kheibar, to threaten the railway north
of Medina: but Feisal improved my plan vastly, by remembering
Wadi Ais, the historic valley of springs and palm-villages flowing
through the impregnable Juheina hills from behind Rudhwa eastward
to the Hamdh valley near Hedia. It lay just one hundred kilometres
north of Medina, a direct threat on Fakhri's railway communications
with Damascus. From it Abdulla could keep up his arranged blockade
of Medina from the east, against caravans from the Persian Gulf. Also
it was near Yenbo, which could easily feed him there with munitions
and supplies.

The proposal was obviously an inspiration and we sent off Raja el
Khuluwi at once to put it to Abdulla. So sure were we of his adopting
it that we urged Feisal to move away from Wadi Yenbo northward on
the first stage to Wejh, without waiting a reply.

CHAPTER XXIII

HE agreed, and we took the wide upper road through Wadi Messarih, for Owais, a group of wells about fifteen miles to the north of Yenbo. The hills were beautiful to-day. The rains of December had been abundant, and the warm sun after them had deceived the earth into believing it was spring. So a thin grass had come up in all the hollows and flat places. The blades (single, straight and very slender) shot up between the stones. If a man bent over from his saddle and looked downward he would see no new colour in the ground; but, by looking foward, and getting a distant slope at a flat angle with his eye, he could feel a lively mist of pale green here and there over the surface of slate-blue and brown-red rock. In places the growth was strong, and our painstaking camels had become prosperous, grazing on it.

The starting signal went, but only for us and the Ageyl. The other units of the army, standing each man by his couched camel, lined up beside our road, and, as Feisal came near, saluted him in silence. He called back cheerfully, 'Peace upon you', and each head sheikh returned the phrase. When we had passed they mounted, taking the time from their chiefs, and so the forces behind us swelled till there was a line of men and camels winding along the narrow pass towards the watershed for as far back as the eye reached.

Feisal's greetings had been the only sounds before we reached the crest of the rise where the valley opened out and became a gentle forward slope of soft shingle and flint bedded in sand: but there ibn Dakhil, the keen sheikh of Russ, who had raised this contingent of Ageyl two years before to aid Turkey, and had brought it over with him intact to the Sherif when the revolt came, dropped back a pace or two, marshalled our following into a broad column of ordered ranks, and made the drums strike up. Everyone burst out singing a full-throated song in honour of Emir Feisal and his family.

The march became rather splendid and barbaric. First rode Feisal in white, then Sharraf at his right in red head-cloth and henna-dyed tunic and cloak, myself on his left in white and scarlet, behind us three banners of faded crimson silk with gilt spikes, behind them the drummers playing a march, and behind them again the wild mass of twelve hundred bouncing camels of the bodyguard, packed as closely as they could move, the men in every variety of coloured clothes and the camels nearly as brilliant in their trappings. We filled the valley to its banks with our flashing stream.

At the mouth of Messarih, a messenger rode up with letters to Feisal from Abd el Kader, in Yenbo. Among them was one three days' old for me from the *Dufferin* to say that she would not embark Zeid till she had seen me and heard details of the local situation. She was in the Sherm, a lonely creek eight miles up the coast from the port, where the officers could play cricket on the beach without the plague of flies pervading Yenbo. Of course, they cut themselves off from news by staying so far away: it was a point of old friction between us. Her well-meaning commander had not the breadth of Boyle, the fiery politician and revolutionary constitutionalist, nor the brain of Linberry, of the *Hardinge*, who filled himself with the shore gossip of every port he touched, and who took pains to understand the nature of all classes on his beat.

Apparently I had better race off to *Dufferin* and regulate affairs. Zeid was a nice fellow, but would assuredly do something quaint in his enforced holiday; and we needed peace just then. Feisal sent some Ageyl with me and we made speed for Yenbo: indeed, I got there in three hours, leaving my disgusted escort (who said they would wear out neither camels nor bottoms for my impatience) half way back on the road across the plain so wearily well known to me. The sun, which had been delightful overhead in the hills, now, in the evening, shone straight into our faces with a white fury, before which I had to press my hand as shield over my eyes. Feisal had given me a racing camel (a present from the Emir of Nejd to his father), the finest and roughest animal I had ridden. Later she died of overwork, mange, and necessary neglect on the road to Akaba.

On arrival in Yenbo things were not as expected. Zeid had been embarked, and the *Dufferin* had started that morning for Rabegh. So I sat down to count what we needed of naval help on the way to Wejh, and to scheme out means of transport. Feisal had promised to wait at Owais till he got my report that everything was ready.

The first check was a conflict between the civil and military powers. Abd el Kader, the energetic but temperamental governor, had been cluttered up with duties as our base grew in size, till Feisal added to him a military commandant, Tewfik Bey, a Syrian from Homs, to care for ordnance stores. Unfortunately, there was no arbiter to define ordnance stores. That morning they fell out over empty arms-chests. Abd el Kadir locked the store and went to lunch. Tewfik came down to the quay with four men, a machine-gun and a sledge hammer, and opened the door. Abd el Kader got into a boat, and rowed out to the British guardship — the tiny *Espiègle* — and told her embarrassed but hospitable captain that he had come to stay. His servant brought him food from the shore and he slept the night in a camp-bed on the quarter-deck.

I wanted to hurry, so began to solve the deadlock by making Abd el Kadir write to Feisal for his decision and by making Tewfik hand over the store to me. We brought the trawler *Arethusa* near the sloop, that Abd el Kader might direct the loading of the disputed chests from his ship, and lastly brought Tewfik off to the *Espiègle* for a temporary reconciliation. It was made easy by an accident, for, as Tewfik saluted his guard of honour at the gangway (not strictly regular, this guard, but politic), his face beamed and he said: 'This ship captured me at Kurna', pointing to the trophy of the nameplate of the Turkish gunboat *Marmaris*, which the *Espiègle* had sunk in action on the Tigris. Abd el Kadir was as interested in the tale as Tewfik, and the trouble ceased.

Sharraf came into Yenbo next day as Emir, in Feisal's place. He was a powerful man, perhaps the most capable of all the Sherifs in the army, but devoid of ambition: acting out of duty, not from impulse. He was rich, and had been for years chief justice of the Sherif's court. He knew and handled tribesmen better than any man, and they feared him, for he was severe and impartial, and his face was sinister, with a left eyebrow which drooped (the effect of an old blow) and gave him an air of forbidding hardness. The surgeon of the *Suva* operated on the eye and repaired much of the damage, but the face remained one to rebuke liberties or weakness. I found him good to work with, very clearheaded, wise and kind, with a pleasant smile — his mouth became soft then, while his eyes remained terrible — and a determination to do fittingly, always.

We agreed that the risk of the fall of Yenbo while we hunted ₁Wejh was great, and that it would be wise to empty it of stores. Boyle gave me an opportunity by signalling that either *Dufferin* or *Hardinge* would be made available for transport. I replied that as difficulties would be severe I preferred *Hardinge*! Captain Warren, whose ship intercepted the message, felt it superfluous, but it brought along *Hardinge* in the best temper two days later. She was an Indian troop-ship, and her lowest troop-deck had great square ports along the water level. Linberry opened these for us, and we stuffed straight in eight thousand rifles, three million rounds of ammunition, thousands of shells, quantities of rice and flour, a shed-full of uniforms, two tons of high explosive, and all our petrol, pell-mell. It was like posting letters in a box. In no time she had taken a thousand tons of stuff.

Boyle came in eager for news. He promised the *Hardinge* as depot ship throughout, to land food and water whenever needed, and this solved the main difficulty. The Navy were already collecting. Half the Red Sea Fleet would be present. The admiral was expected and landing parties were being drilled on every ship. Everyone was dyeing white duck khaki-coloured, or sharpening bayonets, or practising with rifles.

I hoped silently, in their despite, that there would be no fighting. Feisal had nearly ten thousand men, enough to fill the whole Billi country with armed parties and carry off everything not to heavy or too hot. The Billi knew it, and were now profuse in their loyalties to the Sherif, completely converted to Arab nationality.

It was sure that we would take Wejh: the fear was lest numbers of Feisal's host die of hunger or thirst on the way. Supply was my business and rather a responsibility. However, the country to Um Lejj, half way, was friendly: nothing tragic could happen so far as that: therefore, we sent word to Feisal that all was ready, and he left Owais on the very day that Abdulla replied welcoming the Ais plan and promising an immediate start thither. The same day came news of my relief. New-combe, the regular colonel being sent to Hejaz as chief of our military mission had arrived in Egypt and his two staff officers, Cox and Vickery, were actually on their way down the Red Sea, to join this expedition.

Boyle took me to Um Lejj in the *Suva*, and we went ashore to get the news. The sheikh told us that Feisal would arrive to-day, at Bir el Waheidi, the water supply, four miles inland. We sent up a message for him and then walked over to the fort which Boyle had shelled some months before from the *Fox*. It was just a rubble barrack, and Boyle looked at the ruins and said: 'I'm rather ashamed of myself for smashing such a potty place.' He was a very professional officer, alert, business-like and official; sometimes a little intolerant of easy-going things and people. Red-haired men are seldom patient. 'Ginger Boyle', as they called him, was warm.

While we were looking over the ruins four grey ragged elders of the village came up and asked leave to speak. They said that some months before a sudden two-funnelled ship had come up and destroyed their fort. They were now required to re-build it for the police of the Arab Government. Might they ask the generous captain of this peace-able one-funnelled ship for a little timber, or for other material help towards the restoration? Boyle was restless at their long speech, and snapped at me, 'What is it? What do they want?' I said, 'Nothing; they were describing the terrible effect of the *Fox's* bombardment.' Boyle looked round him for a moment and smiled grimly, 'It's a fair mess'.

Next day Vickery arrived. He was a gunner, and in his ten years' service in the Sudan had learned Arabic, both literary and colloquial, so well that he would quit us of all need of an interpreter. We arranged to go up with Boyle to Feisal's camp to make the time-table for the attack, and after lunch Englishmen and Arabs got to work and dis-cussed the remaining march to Wejh.

We decided to break the army into sections: and that these should proceed independently to our concentration place of Abu Zereibat in Hamdh, after which there was no water before Wejh; but Boyle agreed that the *Hardinge* should take station for a single night in Sherm Habban — supposed to be a possible harbour — and land twenty tons of water for us on the beach. So that was settled.

For the attack on Wejh we offered Boyle an Arab landing party of several hundred Harb and Juheina peasantry and freed men, under Saleh ibn Shefia, a negroid boy of good courage (with the faculty of friendliness) who kept his men in reasonable order by conjurations and appeals, and never minded how much his own dignity was outraged by them or by us. Boyle accepted them and decided to put them on another deck of the many-stomached *Hardinge*. They, with the naval party, would land north of the town, where the Turks had no post to block a landing, and whence Wejh and its harbour were best turned.

Boyle would have at least six ships, with fifty guns to occupy the Turks' minds, and a seaplane ship to direct the guns. We would be at Abu Zereibat on the twentieth of the month: at Habban for the *Hardinge's* water on the twenty-second: and the landing party should go ashore at dawn on the twenty-third, by which time our mounted men would have closed all roads of escape from the town.

The news from Rabegh was good; and the Turks had made no attempt to profit by the nakedness of Yenbo. These were our hazards, and when Boyle's wireless set them at rest we were mightily encouraged. Abdulla was almost in Ais: we were half-way to Wejh: the initiative had passed to the Arabs. I was so joyous that for a moment I forgot my self-control, and said exultingly that in a year we would be tapping on the gates of Damascus. A chill came over the feeling in the tent and my hopefulness died. Later, I heard that Vickery had gone to Boyle and vehemently condemned me as a braggart and visionary; but, though the outburst was foolish, it was not an impossible dream, for five months later I was in Damascus, and a year after that I was its *de facto* Governor.

Vickery had disappointed me, and I had angered him. He knew I was militarily incompetent and thought me politically absurd. I knew he was the trained soldier our cause needed, and yet he seemed blind to its power. The Arabs nearly made shipwreck through this blindness of European advisers, who would not see that rebellion was not war: indeed, was more of the nature of peace — a national strike perhaps. The conjunction of Semites, an idea, and an armed prophet held illimitable possibilities; in skilled hands it would have been, not Damascus, but Constantinople which was reached in 1918.

CHAPTER XXIV

EARLY next morning, having seen that the *Hardinge* was unloading without friction, I went ashore to Sheikh Yusuf, and found him helping his Bisha police, the frightened villagers and a squad of old Maulud's men to throw a quick barricade across the end of the main street. He told me that fifty wild mules, without halter or bridle or saddle, had been loosed on shore that morning from a ship. By luck rather than skill they had been stampeded into the market-place: the exits were now safely barred, and there they must remain, ramping about the stalls, till Maulud, to whom they were addressed, invented saddlery in the wilderness. This was the second batch of fifty mules for the mounted unit, and by the chance of our fear at Yenbo we, fortunately, had spare ropes and bits enough for them on board the *Hardinge*. So by noon the shops were again open, and the damage paid for.

I went up to Feisal's camp, which was busy. Some of the tribes were drawing a month's wages; all were getting eight days' food; tents and heavy baggage were being stored; and the last arrangement for the march being made. I sat and listened to the chatter of the staff: Faiz el Ghusein, Beduin sheikh, Turkish official, chronicler of the Armenian massacres, now secretary; Nesib el Bekri, Damascene land-owner, and Feisal's host in Syria, now exiled from his country with a death-sentence over him; Sami, Nesib's brother, graduate of the Law School, and now assistant paymaster; Shefik el Eyr, ex-journalist, now assistant secretary, a little white-faced man, and furtive, with a whispering manner, honest in his patriotism, but in life perverse, and so a nasty colleague.

Hassan Sharaf, the headquarters' doctor, a noble man who had put not merely his life, but his purse to service in the Arab cause, was plaintive with excess of disgust at finding his phials smashed and their drugs confounded in the bottom of his chest. Shefik rallying him, said, 'Do you expect a rebellion to be comfortable?' and the contrast with the pale misery of their manner delighted us. In hardships the humour of triteness outweighed a whole world of wit.

With Feisal in the evening we talked of the coming marches. The first stage was short: to Semna, where were palm-groves and wells of abundant water. After that there was choice of ways, to be determined only when our scouts returned with reports as to ponded rain-water. By the coast, the straight road, it was sixty dry miles to the next well, and our multitude of footmen would find that long.

The army at Bir el Waheida amounted to five thousand one hundred camel-riders, and five thousand three hundred men on foot, with four Krupp mountain guns, and ten machine-guns: and for transport we had three hundred and eighty baggage camels. Everything was cut to the lowest, far below the standard of the Turks. Our start was set for January the eighteenth just after noon, and punctually by lunch-time Feisal's work was finished. We were a merry party: Feisal himself, relaxed after responsibility, Abd el Kerim, never very serious, Sherif Jabar, Nasib and Sami, Shefik, Hassan Sharaf and myself. After lunch the tent was struck. We went to our camels, where they were couched in a circle, saddled and loaded, each held short by the slave standing on its doubled fore-leg. The kettle drummer, waiting beside ibn Dakhil, who commanded the bodyguard, rolled his drum seven or eight times, and everything became still. We watched Feisal. He got up from his rug, on which he had been saying a last word to Abd el Kerim, caught the saddle-pommels in his hands, put his knee on the side and said aloud, 'Make God your agent'. The slave released the camel, which sprang up. When it was on its feet Feisal passed his other leg across its back, swept his skirts and his cloak under him by a wave of the arm, and settled himself in the saddle.

As his camel moved we had jumped for ours, and the whole mob rose together, some of the beasts roaring, but the most quiet, as trained she-camels should be. Only a young animal, a male or ill-bred, would grumble on the road, and self-respecting Beduins did not ride such, since the noise might give them away by night or in surprise attacks. The camels took their first abrupt steps, and we riders had quickly to hook our legs round the front cantles, and pick up the head-stalls to check the pace. We then looked where Feisal was, and tapped our mounts' heads gently round, and pressed them on the shoulders with our bare feet till they were in line beside him. Ibn Dakhil came up, and after a glance at the country and the direction of march passed a short order for the Ageyl to arrange themselves in wings, out to right and left of us for two or three hundred yards, camel marching by camel in line as near as the accidents underfoot permitted. The manœuvre was neatly done.

These Ageyl were Nejd townsmen, the youth of Aneyza, Boreida or Russ, who had contracted for service as regular camel corps for a term of years. They were young, from sixteen to twenty-five, and nice fellows, large-eyed, cheery, a bit educated, catholic, intelligent, good companions on the road. There was seldom a heavy one. Even in repose (when most Eastern faces emptied themselves of life) these lads remained keen-looking and handsome. They talked a delicate and elastic Arabic, and were mannered, often foppish, in habit. The docility and reasonableness of their town-bred minds made them look after themselves and their masters without reiterated instructions. Their fathers dealt in camels, and they had followed the trade from infancy; consequently they wandered instinctively, like Beduin; while the decadent softness in their nature made them biddable, tolerant of the harshness and physical punishment which in the East were the outward proofs of discipline. They were essentially submissive; yet had the nature of soldiers, and fought with brains and courage when familiarly led.

Not being a tribe they had no blood enemies, but passed freely in the desert: the carrying trade and chaffer of the interior lay in their hands. The gains of the desert were poor, but enough to tempt them abroad, since the conditions of their home-life were uncomfortable. The Wahabis, followers of a fanatical Moslem heresy, had imposed their strict rules on easy and civilized Kasim. In Kasim there was but little coffee-hospitality, much prayer and fasting, no tobacco, no artistic dalliance with women, no silk clothes, no gold and silver head-ropes or ornaments. Everything was forcibly pious or forcibly puritanical.

It was a natural phenomenon, this periodic rise at intervals of little more than a century, of ascetic creeds in Central Arabia. Always the votaries found their neighbours' beliefs cluttered with inessential things, which became impious in the hot imagination of their preachers. Again and again they had arisen, had taken possession, soul and body, of the tribes, and had dashed themselves to pieces on the urban Semites, merchants and concupiscent men of the world. About their comfortable possessions the new creeds ebbed and flowed like the tides or the changing seasons, each movement with the seeds of early death in its excess of rightness. Doubtless they must recur so long as the causes — sun, moon, wind, acting in the emptiness of open spaces, weigh without check on the unhurried and uncumbered minds of the desert-dwellers.

However, this afternoon the Ageyl were not thinking of God, but of us, and as ibn Dakhil ranged them to the right and left they fell eagerly into rank. There came a warning patter from the drums and the poet of the right wing burst into strident song, a single invented couplet, of Feisal and the pleasure he would afford us at Wejh. The right wing listened to the verse intently, took it up and sang it together once, twice and three times, with pride and self-satisfaction and derision. However, before they could brandish it a fourth time the poet of the left wing broke out in extempore reply, in the same metre, in answering rhyme, and capping the sentiment. The left wing cheered it in a roar of triumph, the drums tapped again, the standard-bearers threw out their great crimson banners, and the whole guard, right, left and centre, broke together into the rousing regimental chorus,

> 'I've lost Britain, and I've lost Gaul,
> I've lost Rome, and, worst of all,
> I've lost Lalage — '

only it was Nejd they had lost, and the women of the Maabda, and their future lay from Jidda towards Suez. Yet it was a good song, with a rhythmical beat which the camels loved, so that they put down their heads, stretched their necks out far and with lengthened pace shuffled forward musingly while it lasted.

Our road to-day was easy for them, since it was over firm sand slopes, long, slowly-rising waves of dunes, bare-backed, but for scrub in the folds, or barren palm-trees solitary in the moist depressions. Afterwards in a broad flat, two horsemen came cantering across from the left to greet Feisal. I knew the first one, dirty old blear-eyed Mohammed Ali el Beidawi, Emir of the Juheina: but the second looked strange. When he came nearer I saw he was in khaki uniform, with a cloak to cover it and a silk head-cloth and head-rope, much awry. He looked up, and there was Newcombe's red and peeling face, with straining eyes and vehement mouth, a strong, humorous grin between the jaws. He had arrived at Um Lejj this morning, and hearing we were only just off, had seized Sheikh Yusuf's fastest horse and galloped after us.

I offered him my spare camel and an introduction to Feisal, whom he greeted like an old school-friend; and at once they plunged into the midst of things, suggesting, debating, planning at lightning speed. Newcombe's initial velocity was enormous, and the freshness of the day and the life and happiness of the Army gave inspiration to the march and brought the future bubbling out of us without pain.

We passed Ghowashia, a ragged grove of palms, and marched over a lava-field easily, its roughnesses being drowned in sand just deep enough to smooth them, but not deep enough to be too soft. The tops of the highest lava-piles showed through. An hour later we came suddenly to a crest which dropped as a sand slope, abrupt and swept and straight enough to be called a sand-cliff, into a broad splendid valley of rounded pebbles. This was Semna, and our road went down the steep, through terraces of palms.

The wind had been following our march, and so it was very still and warm at bottom of the valley in lee of the great bank of sand. Here was our water, and here we would halt till the scouts returned from seeking rain-pools in front of us; for so Abd el Kerim, our chief guide, had advised. We rode the four hundred yards across the valley and up the further slopes till we were safe from floods, and there Feisal tapped his camel lightly on the neck till she sank to her knees with a scrape of shingle pushed aside, and settled herself. Hejris spread the carpet for us, and with the other Sherifs we sat and jested while the coffee was made hot.

I maintained against Feisal the greatness of Ibrahim Pasha, leader of Milli-Kurds, in North Mesopotamia. When he was to march, his women rose before dawn, and footing noiselessly overhead on the taut tentcloth, unskewered the strips of it, while others beneath held and removed the poles till all was struck and divided into camel-loads, and loaded. Then they drove off, so that the Pasha awoke alone on his pallet in the open air where at night he had lain down in the rich inner compartment of his palace-tent.

He would get up at leisure and drink coffee on his carpet: and after-wards the horses would be brought, and they would ride towards the new camping ground. But if on his way he thirsted he would crisp his fingers to the servants, and the coffee man would ride up beside him with his pots ready and his brazier burning on a copper bracket of the saddle, to serve the cup on the march without breaking stride; and at sunset they would find the women waiting in the erected tent, as it had been on the evening before.

To-day had a grey weather, so strange after the many thronging suns, that Newcombe and I walked stooping to look where our shadows had gone, as we talked of what I hoped, and of what he wanted. They were the same thing, so we had brain-leisure to note Semna and its fine groves of cared-for palms between little hedges of dead thorn; with here and there huts of reed and palm-rib, to shelter the owners and their families at times of fertilization and harvest. In the lowest gardens and in the valley bed were the shallow wood-lined wells, whose water was, they said, fairly sweet and never-failing: but so little fluent that to water our host of camels took the night.

Feisal wrote letters from Semna to twenty-five leaders of the Billi and Howeitat and Beni Atiyeh, saying that he with his army would be instantly in Wejh and they must see to it. Mohammed Ali bestirred himself, and since almost all our men were of his tribe, was useful in arranging the detachments and detailing them their routes for the morrow. Our water-scouts had come in, to report shallow pools at two points well-spaced on the coast road. After cross-questioning them we decided to send four sections that way, and the other five by the hills: in such a fashion we thought we should arrive soonest and safest at Abu Zereibat.

The route was not easy to decide with the poor help of the Musa Juheina, our informants. They seemed to have no unit of time smaller than the half-day, or of distance between the span and the stage; and a stage might be from six to sixteen hours according to the man's will and camel. Intercommunication between our units was hindered because often there was no one who could read or write, in either. Delay, confusion, hunger and thirst marred this expedition. These might have been avoided had time let us examine the route beforehand. The animals were without food for nearly three days, and the men marched the last fifty miles on half a gallon of water, with nothing to eat. It did not in any way dim their spirit, and they trotted into Wejh gaily enough, hoarsely singing, and executing mock charges: but Feisal said that another hot and barren midday would have broken both their speed and their energy.

When business ended, Newcombe and I went off to sleep in the tent Feisal had lent us as a special luxury. Baggage conditions were so hard and important for us that we rich took pride in faring like the men, who could not transport unnecessary things: and never before had I had a tent of my own. We pitched it at the very edge of a bluff of the foot-hills; a bluff no wider than the tent and rounded, so that the slope went straight down from the pegs of the door-flap. There we found sitting and waiting for us Abd el Kerim, the young Beidawi Sherif, wrapped up to the eyes in his head-cloth and cloak, since the evening was chill and threatened rain. He had come to ask me for a mule, with saddle and bridle. The smart appearance of Maulud's little company in breeches and puttees, and their fine new animals in the market at Um Lejj, had roused his desire.

I played with his eagerness, and put him off, advancing a condition that he should ask me after our successful arrival at Wejh; and with this he was content. We hungered for sleep, and at last he rose to go, but, chancing to look across the valley, saw the hollows beneath and about us winking with the faint camp-fires of the scattered contingents. He called me out to look, and swept his arm round, saying half-sadly, 'We are no longer Arabs but a People'.

He was half-proud too, for the advance on Wejh was their biggest effort; the first time in memory that the manhood of a tribe, with trans-port, arms, and food for two hundred miles, had left its district and marched into another's territory without the hope of plunder or the stimulus of blood feud. Abd el Kerim was glad that his tribe had shown this new spirit of service, but also sorry; for to him the joys of life were a fast camel, the best weapons, and a short sharp raid against his neigh-bour's herd: and the gradual achievement of Feisal's ambition was making such joys less and less easy for the responsible.

CHAPTER XXV

DURING the morning it rained persistently; and we were glad to see more water coming to us, and so comfortable in the tents at Semna that we delayed our start till the sun shone again in the early afternoon. Then we rode westward down the valley in the fresh light. First behind us came the Ageyl. After them Abd el Kerim led his Gufa men, about seven hundred of them mounted, with more than that number following afoot. They were dressed in white, with large headshawls of red and black striped cotton, and they waved green palm-branches instead of banners.

Next to them rode Sherif Mohammed Ali abu Sharrain, an old patriarch with a long curling grey beard and an upright carriage of himself. His three hundred riders were Ashraf, of the Aiaishi (Juheina) stock, known Sherifs, but only acknowledged in the mass, since they had not inscribed pedigrees. They wore rusty-red tunics henna-dyed, under black cloaks, and carried swords. Each had a slave crouched behind him on the crupper to help him with rifle and dagger in the fight, and to watch his camel and cook for him on the road. The slaves, as befitted slaves of poor masters, were very little dressed. Their strong, black legs gripped the camels' woolly sides as in a vice, to lessen the shocks inevitable on their bony perches, while they had knotted up their rags of shirts into the plaited thong about their loins to save them from the fouling of the camels and their staling on the march. Semna water was medicinal, and our animals' dung flowed like green soup down their hocks that day.

Behind the Ashraf came the crimson banner of our last tribal detachment, the Rifaa, under Owdi ibn Zuweid, the old wheedling sea-pirate who had robbed the Stotzingen Mission and thrown their wireless and their Indian servants into the sea at Yenbo. The sharks presumably refused the wireless, but we had spent fruitless hours dragging for it in the harbour. Owdi still wore a long, rich, fur-lined German officer's greatcoat, a garment little suited to the climate but, as he insisted, magnificent booty. He had about a thousand men, three-quarters of them on foot, and next him marched Rasim, the gunner commandant, with his four old Krupp guns on the pack-mules, just as we had lifted them from the Egyptian Army.

Rasim was a sardonic Damascene, who rose laughing to every crisis and slunk about sore-headed with grievances when things went well. On this day there were dreadful murmurings, for alongside him rode Abdulla el Deleimi, in charge of machine-guns, a quick, clever, super-ficial but attractive officer, much of the professional type, whose great joy was to develop some rankling sorrow in Rasim till it discharged full blast on Feisal or myself. To-day I helped him by smiling to Rasim that we were moving at intervals of a quarter-day in echelon of sub-tribes. Rasim looked over the new-washed underwood, where raindrops glistened in the light of the sun setting redly across the waves below a ceiling of clouds, and looked too at the wild mob of Beduins racing here and there on foot after birds and rabbits and giant lizards and jerboas and one another; and assented sourly, saying that he too would shortly become a sub-tribe, and echelon himself half a day to one side or other, and be quit of flies.

At first starting a man in the crowd had shot a hare from the saddle, but because of the risk of wild shooting Feisal had then forbidden it, and those later put up by our camels' feet were chased with sticks. We laughed at the sudden commotion in the marching companies: cries, and camels swerving violently, their riders leaping off and laying out wildly with their canes to kill or to be pickers-up of a kill. Feisal was happy to see the army win so much meat, but disgusted at the shameless Juheina appetite for lizards and jerboas.

We rode over the flat sand, among the thorn trees, which here were plentiful and large, till we came out on the sea-beach and turned north-ward along a broad, well-beaten track, the Egyptian pilgrim road. It ran within fifty yards of the sea, and we could go up it thirty or forty singing files abreast. An old lava-bed half buried in sand jutted out from the hills four or five miles inland, and made a promontory. The road cut across this, but at the near side were some mud flats, on which shallow reaches of water burned in the last light of the west. This was our expected stage, and Feisal signalled the halt. We got off our camels and stretched ourselves, sat down or walked before supper to the sea and bathed by hundreds, a splashing, screaming, mob of fish-like naked men of all earth's colours.

Supper was to look forward to, as a Juheina that afternoon had shot a gazelle for Feisal. Gazelle meat we found better than any other in the desert, because this beast, however barren the land and dry the water-holes, seemed to own always a fat juicy body.

The meal was the expected success. We retired early, feeling too full: but soon after Newcombe and myself had stretched out in our tent we were quickened by a wave of excitement travelling up the lines; running camels, shots, and shouts. A breathless slave thrust his head under the flap crying, 'News! news! Sherif Bey is taken'. I jumped up and ran through the gathering crowd to Feisal's tent, which was already beset by friends and servants. With Feisal sat, portentously and un-naturally collected in the din, Raja, the tribesman who had taken to Abdulla word to move into Wadi Ais. Feisal was radiant, his eyes swollen with joy, as he jumped up and shouted to me through the voices, 'Abdulla has captured Eshref Bey'. Then I knew how big and good the event was.

Eshref was a notorious adventurer in the lower levels of Turkish politics. In his boyhood, near his Smyrna home, he had been just a brigand, but with years he became a revolutionary, and when he was finally captured Abd el Hamid exiled him to Medina for five coloured years. At first he was closely confined there, but one day he broke the privy window and escaped to Shehad, the bibulous Emir, in his suburb of Awali. Shahad was, as usual, at war with the Turks and gave him sanctuary; but Eshref, finding life dull, at last borrowed a fine mare and rode to the Turkish barracks. On its square was the officer-son of his enemy the Governor drilling a company of gendarmes. He galloped him down, slung him across his saddle, and made away before the astonished police could protest.

He took to Jebel Ohod, an uninhabited place, driving his prisoner before him, calling him his ass, and lading upon him thirty loaves and the skins of water necessary for their nourishment. To recover his son, the Pasha gave Eshref liberty on parole and five hundred pounds. He bought camels, a tent, and a wife, and wandered among the tribes till the Young Turk revolution. Then he reappeared in Constantinople and became a bravo, doing Enver's murders. His services earned the appointment of inspector of refugee-relief in Macedonia, and he retired a year later with an assured income from landed estate.

When war broke out he went down to Medina with funds, and letters from the Sultan to Arabian neutrals; his mission being to open communications with the isolated Turkish garrison in Yemen. His track on the first stage of the journey had happened to cross Abdulla's, on his way to Wadi Ais, near Kheibar, and some of the Arabs, watching their camels during a midday halt, had been stopped by Eshref's men and questioned. They said they were Heteym, and Abdulla's army a supply caravan going to Medina. Eshref released one with orders to bring the rest for examination, and this man told Abdulla of soldiers camped up on the hill.

Abdulla was puzzled and sent horsemen to investigate. A minute later he was startled by the sudden chatter of a machine-gun. He leaped to the conclusion that the Turks had sent out a flying column to cut him off, and ordered his mounted men to charge them desperately. They galloped over the machine-gun, with few casualties, and scattered the Turks. Eshref fled on foot to the hill-top. Abdulla offered a reward of a thousand pounds for him; and near dusk he was found, wounded, and captured by Sherif Fauzan el Harith, in a stiff fight.

In the baggage were twenty thousand pounds in coin, robes of honour, costly presents, some interesting papers, and camel loads of rifles and pistols. Abdulla wrote an exultant letter to Fakhri Pasha, (telling him of the capture), and nailed it to an uprooted telegraph pole between the metals, when he crossed the railway next night on his unimpeded way to Wadi Ais. Raja had left him there, camped in quiet and in ease. The news was a double fortune for us.

Between the joyful men slipped the sad figure of the Imam, who raised his hand. Silence fell for an instant. 'Hear me', he said, and intoned an ode in praise of the event, to the effect that Abdulla was especially favoured, and had attained quickly to the glory which Feisal was winning slowly but surely by hard work. The poem was creditable as the issue of only sixteen minutes, and the poet was rewarded in gold.

Then Feisal saw a gaudy jewelled dagger at Raja's belt. Raja stammered it was Eshref's. Feisal threw him his own and pulled the other off, to give it in the end to Colonel Wilson. 'What did my brother say to Eshref?' 'Is this your return for our hospitality?' While Eshref had replied like Suckling, 'I can fight, Whether I am i' the wrong or right, Devoutly!'

'How many millions did the Arabs get?' gasped greedy old Mohammed Ali, when he heard of Abdulla to the elbows in the captured chest, flinging gold by handfuls to the tribes. Raja was everywhere in hot demand, and he slept a richer man that night, deservedly, for Abdulla's march to Ais made the Medina situation sure. With Murray pressing in Sinai, Feisal nearing Wejh, and Abdulla between Wejh and Medina, the position of the Turks in Arabia became defensive only. The tide of our ill-fortune had turned; and the camp, seeing our glad faces was noisy until dawn.

Next day we rode easily. A breakfast suggested itself, upon our finding some more little water-pools, in a bare valley flowing down from El Sukhur, a group of three extraordinary hills like granite bubbles blown through the earth. The journey was pleasant, for it was cool; there were a lot of us; and we two Englishmen had a tent in which we could shut ourselves up and be alone. A weariness of the desert was the living always in company, each of the party hearing all that was said and seeing all that was done by the others day and night. Yet the craving for solitude seemed part of the delusion of self-sufficiency, a factitious making-rare of the person to enhance its strangeness in its own estimation. To have privacy, as Newcombe and I had, was ten thousand times more restful than the open life, but the work suffered by the creation of such a bar between the leaders and men. Among the Arabs there were no distinctions, traditional or natural, except the unconscious power given a famous sheikh by virtue of his accomplishment; and they taught me that no man could be their leader except he ate the ranks' food, wore their clothes, lived level with them, and yet appeared better in himself.

In the morning we pressed towards Abu Zereibat with the early sun incandescent in a cloudless sky, and the usual eye-racking dazzle and dance of sunbeams on polished sand or polished flint. Our path rose slightly at a sharp limestone ridge with eroded flanks, and we looked over a sweeping fall of bare, black gravel between us and the sea, which now lay about eight miles to the westward: but invisible.

Once we halted and began to feel that a great depression lay in front of us; but not till two in the afternoon after we had crossed a basalt outcrop did we look out over a trough fifteen miles across, which was Wadi Hamdh, escaped from the hills. On the north-west spread the great delta through which Hamdh spilled itself by twenty mouths; and we saw the dark lines, which were thickets of scrub in the flood channels of the dried beds, twisting in and out across the flat from the hill-edge beneath us, till they were lost in the sun-haze twenty miles away beyond us to our left, near the invisible sea. Behind Hamdh rose sheer from the plain a double hill, Jebel Raal: hog-backed but for a gash which split it in the middle. To our eyes, sated with small things, it was a fair sight, this end of a dry river longer than the Tigris; the greatest valley in Arabia, first understood by Doughty, and as yet unexplored; while Raal was a fine hill, sharp and distinctive, which did honour to the Hamdh.

Full of expectation we rode down the gravel slopes, on which tufts of grass became more frequent, till at three o'clock we entered the Wadi itself. It proved a bed about a mile wide, filled with clumps of *asla* bushes, round which clung sandy hillocks each a few feet high. Their sand was not pure, but seamed with lines of dry and brittle clay, last indications of old flood levels. These divided them sharply into layers, rotten with salty mud and flaking away, so that our camels sank in, fetlock-deep, with a crunching noise like breaking pastry. The dust rose up in thick clouds, thickened yet more by the sunlight held in them; for the dead air of the hollow was a-dazzle.

The ranks behind could not see where they were going, which was difficult for them, as the hillocks came closer together, and the river-bed slit into a maze of shallow channels, the work of partial floods year after year. Before we gained the middle of the valley everything was overgrown by brushwood, which sprouted sideways from the mounds and laced one to another with tangled twigs as dry, dusty and brittle as old bone. We tucked in the streamers of our gaudy saddle-bags, to prevent their being jerked off by the bushes, drew cloaks tight over our clothes, bent our heads down to guard our eyes and crashed through like a storm amongst reeds. The dust was blinding and choking, and the snapping of the branches, grumbles of the camels, shouts and laughter of the men, made a rare adventure.

CHAPTER XXVI

BEFORE we quite reached the far bank the ground suddenly cleared at a clay bottom, in which stood a deep brown water-pool, eighty yards long and about fifteen yards wide. This was the flood-water of the Abu Zereibat, our goal. We went a few yards further, through the last scrub, and reached the open north bank where Feisal had appointed the camp. It was a huge plain of sand and flints, running to the very feet of Raal, with room on it for all the armies of Arabia. So we stopped our camels, and the slaves unloaded them and set up the tents; while we walked back to see the mules, thirsty after their long day's march, rush with the foot-soldiers into the pond, kicking and splashing with pleasure in the sweet water. The abundance of fuel was an added happiness, and in whatever place they chose to camp each group of friends had a roaring fire — very welcome, as a wet evening mist rose eight feet out of the ground and our woollen cloaks stiffened and grew cold with its silver beads in their coarse woof.

It was a black night, moonless, but above the fog very brilliant with stars. On a little mound near our tents we collected and looked over the rolling white seas of fog. Out of it arose tent-peaks, and tall spires of melting smoke, which became luminous underneath when the flames licked higher into the clean air, as if driven by the noises of the unseen army. Old Auda ibn Zuweid corrected me gravely when I said this to him, telling me, 'It is not an army, it is a world which is moving on Wejh'. I rejoiced at his insistence, for it had been to create this very feeling that we had hampered ourselves with an unwieldy crowd of men on so difficult a march.

That evening the Billi began to come in to us shyly, and swear fealty, for the Hamdh Valley was their boundary. Amongst them Hamid el Rifada rode up with a numerous company to pay his respects to Feisal. He told us that his cousin, Suleiman Pasha, the paramount of the tribe, was at Abu Ajaj, fifteen miles north of us, trying desperately for once to make up the mind which had chopped and balanced profitably throughout a long life. Then, without warning or parade, Sherif Nasir of Medina came in. Feisal leaped up and embraced him, and led him over to us.

Nasir made a splendid impression, much as we had heard, and much as we were expecting of him. He was the opener of roads, the fore-runner of Feisal's movement, the man who had fired his first shot in Medina, and who was to fire our last shot at Muslimieh beyond Aleppo on the day that Turkey asked for an armistice, and from beginning to end all that could be told of him was good.

He was a brother of Shehad, the Emir of Medina. Their family was descended from Hussein, the younger of Ali's children, and they were the only descendants of Hussein considered Ashraf, not Saada. They were Shias, and had been since the days of Kerbela, and in Hejaz were respected only second to the Emirs of Mecca. Nasir himself was a man of gardens, whose lot had been unwilling war since boyhood. He was now about twenty-seven. His low, broad forehead matched his sensitive eyes, while his weak pleasant mouth and small chin were clearly seen through a clipped black beard.

He had been up here for two months, containing Wejh, and his last news was that the outpost of Turkish camel corps upon our road had withdrawn that morning towards the main defensive position.

We slept late the following day, to brace ourselves for the necessary hours of talk. Feisal carried most of this upon his own shoulders. Nasir supported him as second in command, and the Beidawi brothers sat by to help. The day was bright and warm, threatening to be hot later, and Newcombe and I wandered about looking at the watering, the men, and the constant affluence of newcomers. When the sun was high a great cloud of dust from the east heralded a larger party and we walked back to the tents to see Mirzuk el Tikheimi, Feisal's sharp, mouse-featured guest-master, ride in. He led his clansmen of the Juheina past the Emir at a canter, to make a show. They stifled us with their dust, for his van of a dozen sheikhs carrying a large red flag and a large white flag drew their swords and charged round and round our tents. We admired neither their riding nor their mares: perhaps because they were a nuisance to us.

About noon the Wuld Mohammed Harb, and the mounted men of the ibn Shefia battalion came in: three hundred men, under Sheikh

Salih and Mohammed ibn Shefia. Mohammed was a tubby, vulgar little man of fifty-five, common-sensible and energetic. He was rapidly making a name for himself in the Arab army, for he would get done any manual work. His men were the sweepings of Wadi Yenbo, landless and without family, or labouring Yenbo townsmen, hampered by no inherited dignity. They were more docile than any other of our troops except the white-handed Ageyl who were too beautiful to be made into labourers.

We were already two days behind our promise to the Navy, and Newcombe decided to ride ahead this night to Habban. There he would meet Boyle and explain that we must fail the *Hardinge* at the rendezvous, but would be glad if she could return there on the evening of the twenty-fourth, when we should arrive much in need of water. He would also see if the naval attack could not be delayed till the twenty-fifth to preserve the joint scheme.

After dark there came a message from Suleiman Rifada, with a gift-camel for Feisal to keep if he were friendly, and to send back if hostile. Feisal was vexed, and protested his inability to understand so feeble a man. Nasir asserted, 'Oh, it's because he eats fish. Fish swells the head, and such behaviour follows'. The Syrians and Mesopotamians, and men of Jidda and Yenbo laughed loudly, to shew that they did not share this belief of the upland Arab, that a man of his hands was disgraced by tasting the three mean foods – chickens, eggs and fish. Feisal said, with mock gravity, 'You insult the company, we like fish'. Others protested, 'We abandon it, and take refuge in God', and Mirzuk to change the current said, 'Suleiman is an unnatural birth, neither raw nor ripe'.

In the morning, early, we marched in a straggle for three hours down Wadi Hamdh. Then the valley went to the left, and we struck out across a hollow, desolate, featureless region. To-day was cold: a hard north wind drove into our faces down the grey coast. As we marched we heard intermittent heavy firing from the direction of Wejh, and feared that the Navy had lost patience and were acting without us. However, we could not make up the days we had wasted, so we pushed on for the whole dull stage, crossing affluent after affluent of Hamdh. The plain was striped with these wadies, all shallow and

straight and bare, as many and as intricate as the veins in a leaf. At last
we re-entered Hamdh, at Kurna, and though its clay bottoms held only
mud, decided to camp.

While we were settling in there was a sudden rush. Camels had been
seen pasturing away to the east, and the energetic of the Juheina
streamed out, captured them, and drove them in. Feisal was furious,
and shouted to them to stop, but they were too excited to hear him. He
snatched his rifle, and shot at the nearest man; who, in fear, tumbled out
of his saddle, so that the others checked their course. Feisal had them
up before him, laid about the principals with his camel-stick, and
impounded the stolen camels and those of the thieves till the whole
tally was complete. Then he handed the beasts back to their Billi
owners. Had he not done so it would have involved the Juheina in a
private war with the Billi, our hoped-for allies of the morrow, and
might have checked extension beyond Wejh. Our success lay in bond
to such trifles.

Next morning we made for the beach, and up it to Habban at four
o'clock. The *Hardinge* was duly there, to our relief, and landing water:
although the shallow bay gave little shelter, and the rough sea rolling
in made boat-work hazardous. We reserved first call for the mules, and
gave what water was left to the more thirsty of the footmen; but it was
a difficult night, and crowds of suffering men lingered jostling about
the tanks in the rays of the searchlight, hoping for another drink, if the
sailors should venture in again.

I went on board, and heard that the naval attack had been carried
out as though the land army were present, since Boyle feared the Turks
would run away if he waited. As a matter of fact, the day we reached
Abu Zereibat, Ahmed Tewfik Bey, Turkish Governor, had addressed
the garrison, saying that Wejh must be held to the last drop of blood.
Then at dusk he had got on to his camel and ridden off to the railway
with the few mounted men fit for flight. The two hundred infantry
determined to do his abandoned duty against the landing party; but
they were out-numbered three to one, and the naval gun-fire was too
heavy to let them make proper use of their positions. So far as the
Hardinge knew, the fighting was not ended, but Wejh town had been
occupied by seamen and Saleh's Arabs.

CHAPTER XXVII

PROFITABLE rumours excited the army, which began to trickle off northward soon after midnight. At dawn we rallied the various contingents on Wadi Miya, twelve miles south of the town, and advanced on it in order, meeting a few scattered Turks, of whom one party put up a short resistance. The Ageyl dismounted, to strip off their cloaks, head-cloths and shirts; and went on in brown half-nakedness, which they said would ensure clean wounds if they were hit: also their precious clothes would not be damaged. Ibn Dakhil in command obtained a quiet regularity of obedience. They advanced by alternate companies, in open order, at intervals of four or five yards, with even-numbered companies in support, making good use of the poor cover which existed.

It was pretty to look at the neat, brown men in the sunlit sandy valley, with the turquoise pool of salt water in the midst to set off the crimson banners which two standard bearers carried in the van. They went along in a steady lope, covering the ground at nearly six miles an hour, dead silent, and reached and climbed the ridge without a shot fired. So we knew the work had been finished for us and trotted forward to find the boy Saleh, son of ibn Shefia, in possession of the town. He told us that his casualties had been nearly twenty killed; and later we heard that a British lieutenant of the Air Service had been mortally wounded in a seaplane reconnaissance, and one British seaman hurt in the foot.

Vickery, who had directed the battle, was satisfied, but I could not share his satisfaction. To me an unnecessary action, or shot, or casualty, was not only waste but sin. I was unable to take the professional view that all successful actions were gains. Our rebels were not materials, like soldiers, but friends of ours, trusting our leadership. We were not in command nationally, but by invitation; and our men were volunteers, individuals, local men, relatives, so that a death was a personal sorrow to many in the army. Even from the purely military point of view the assault seemed to me a blunder.

The two hundred Turks in Wejh had no transport and no food, and if left alone a few days must have surrendered. Had they escaped, it would not have mattered the value of an Arab life. We wanted Wejh as a base against the railway and to extend our front; the smashing and killing in it had been wanton.

The place was inconveniently smashed. Its townspeople had been warned by Feisal of the coming attack, and advised either to forestall it by revolt or to clear out; but they were mostly Egyptians from Kosseir, who preferred the Turks to us, and decided to wait the issue; so the Shefa men and the Biasha found the houses packed with fair booty and made a sweep of it. They robbed the shops, broke open doors, searched every room, smashed chests and cupboards, tore down all fixed fittings, and slit each mattress and pillow for hidden treasure; while the fire of the fleet punched large holes in every prominent wall or building.

Our main difficulty was the landing of stores. The *Fox* had sunk the local lighters and rowing boats and there was no sort of quay; but the resourceful *Hardinge* thrust herself into the harbour (which was wide enough but much too short) and landed our stuff in her own cutters. We raised a tired working party of ibn Shefa followers, and with their clumsy or languid help got enough food into the place for the moment's needs. The townspeople had returned hungry, and furious, at the state of what had been their property; and began their revenge by stealing everything unguarded, even slitting open the rice-bags on the beach and carrying away quantities in their held-up skirts. Feisal corrected this by making the pitiless Maulud Town-governor. He brought in his rough-riders and in one day of wholesale arrest and summary punishment persuaded everyone to leave things alone. After that Wejh had the silence of fear.

Even in the few days which elapsed before I left for Cairo the profits of our spectacular march began to come in. The Arab movement had now no opponent in Western Arabia, and had passed beyond danger of collapse. The vexed Rabegh question died: and we had learnt the first rules of Beduin warfare. When regarded backward from our benefits of new knowledge the deaths of those regretted twenty men in the Wejh streets seemed not so terrible. Vickery's impatience was justified, perhaps, in cold blood.

BOOK III

A RAILWAY DIVERSION

Chapters XXVIII to XXXVIII

OUR *taking Wejh had the wished effect upon the Turks, who abandoned their advance towards Mecca for a passive defence of Medina and its Railway. Our experts made plans for attacking them.*

The Germans saw the danger of envelopment, and persuaded Enver to order the instant evacuation of Medina. Sir Archibald Murray begged us to put in a sustained attack to destroy the retreating enemy.

Feisal was soon ready in his part: and I went off to Abdulla to get his co-operation. On the way I fell sick and while lying alone with empty hands was driven to think about the campaign. Thinking convinced me that our recent practice had been better than our theory.

So on recovery I did little to the Railway, but went back to Wejh with novel ideas. I tried to make the others admit them, and adopt deployment as our ruling principle; and to put preaching even before fighting. They preferred the limited and direct objective of Medina. So I decided to slip off to Akaba by myself on test of my own theory.

CHAPTER XXVIII

IN Cairo the yet-hot authorities promised gold, rifles, mules, more machine-guns, and mountain guns; but these last, of course, we never got. The gun question was an eternal torment. Because of the hilly, trackless country, field guns were no use to us; and the British Army had no mountain guns except the Indian ten-pounder, which was serviceable only against bows and arrows. Bremond had some excellent Schneider sixty-fives at Suez, with Algerian gunners, but he regarded them principally as his lever to move allied troops into Arabia. When we asked him to send them down to us with or without men, he would reply, first that the Arabs would not treat the crews properly, and then that they would not treat the guns properly. His price was a British brigade for Rabegh; and we would not pay it.

He feared to make the Arab Army formidable — an argument one could understand — but the case of the British Government was incomprehensible. It was not ill-will, for they gave us all else we wanted; nor was it niggardliness, for their total help to the Arabs, in materials and money, exceeded ten millions. I believe it was sheer stupidity. But it was maddening to be unequal to many enterprises and to fail in others, for the technical reason that we could not keep down the Turkish artillery because its guns outranged ours by three or four thousand yards. In the end, happily, Bremond over-reached himself, after keeping his batteries idle for a year at Suez. Major Cousse, his successor, ordered them down to us, and by their help we entered Damascus. During that idle year they had been to each Arab officer who entered Suez, a silent incontrovertible proof of French malice towards the Arab movement.

We received a great reinforcement to our cause in Jaafar Pasha, a Bagdadi officer from the Turkish Army. After distinguished service in the German and Turkish armies, he had been chosen by Enver to organize the levies of the Sheikh el Senussi. He went there by submarine, made a decent force of the wild men, and showed tactical ability against the British in two battles. Then he was captured and lodged in the citadel at Cairo with the other officer prisoners of war. He escaped one night, slipping down a blanket-rope towards the moat; but the blankets failed under the strain, and in the fall he hurt his ankle, and was re-taken helpless. In hospital he gave his parole, and was enlarged after paying for the torn blanket. But one day he read in an Arabic newspaper of the Sherif's revolt, and of the execution by the Turks of prominent Arab Nationalists — his friends — and realized that he had been on the wrong side.

Feisal had heard of him, of course, and wanted him as commander-in-chief of his regular troops, whose improvement was now our main effort. We knew that Jaafar was one of the few men with enough of reputation and personality to weld their difficult and reciprocally disagreeable elements into an army. King Hussein, however, would not have it. He was old and narrow, and disliked Mesopotamians and Syrians: Mecca must deliver Damascus. He refused the services of Jaafar. Feisal had to accept him on his own responsibility.

In Cairo were Hogarth and George Lloyd, and Storrs and Deedes, and many old friends. Beyond them the circle of Arabian well-wishers was now strangely increased. In the army our shares rose as we showed profits. Lynden Bell stood firmly our friend and swore that method was coming out of the Arab madness. Sir Archibald Murray realized with a sudden shock that more Turkish troops were fighting the Arabs than were fighting him, and began to remember how he had always favoured the Arab revolt. Admiral Wemyss was as ready to help now as he had been in our hard days round Rabegh. Sir Reginald Wingate, High Commissioner in Egypt, was happy in the success of the work he had advocated for years. I grudged him this happiness; for McMahon, who took the actual risk of starting it, had been broken just before prosperity began. However, that was hardly Wingate's fault.

In the midst of my touching the slender stops of all these quills there came a rude surprise. Colonel Bremond called to felicitate me on the capture of Wejh, saying that it confirmed his belief in my military talent, and encouraged him to expect my help in an extension of our success. He wanted to occupy Akaba with an Anglo-French force and naval help. He pointed out the importance of Akaba, the only Turkish port left in the Red Sea, the nearest to the Suez Canal, the nearest to the

Hejaz Railway, on the left flank of the Beersheba army; suggesting its occupation by a composite brigade, which should advance up Wadi Itm for a crushing blow at Maan. He began to enlarge on the nature of the ground.

I told him that I knew Akaba from before the war, and felt that his scheme was technically impossible. We could take the beach of the gulf; but our forces there, as unfavourably placed as on a Gallipoli beach, would be under observation and gun-fire from the coastal hills: and these granite hills, thousands of feet high, were impracticable for heavy troops: the passes through them being formidable defiles, very costly to assault or to cover. In my opinion, Akaba, whose importance was all and more than he said, would be best taken by Arab irregulars descending from the interior without naval help.

Bremond did not tell me (but I knew) that he wanted the landing at Akaba to head off the Arab movement, by getting a mixed force in front of them (as at Rabegh), so that they might be confined to Arabia, and compelled to waste their efforts against Medina. The Arabs still feared that the Sherif's alliance with us was based on a secret agreement to sell them at the end, and such a Christian invasion would have confirmed these fears and destroyed their co-operation. For my part, I did not tell Bremond (but he knew) that I meant to defeat his efforts and to take the Arabs soon into Damascus. It amused me, this childishly-conceived rivalry of vital aims, but he ended his talk ominously by saying that, anyhow, he was going down to put the scheme to Feisal in Wejh.

Now, I had not warned Feisal that Bremond was a politician. Newcombe was in Wejh, with his friendly desire to get moves on. We had not talked over the problem of Akaba. Feisal knew neither its terrain nor its tribes. Keenness and ignorance would lend an ear favourable to the proposal. It seemed best for me to hurry down there and put my side on its guard, so I left the same afternoon for Suez and sailed that night. Two days later, in Wejh, I explained myself; so that when Bremond came after ten days and opened his heart, or part of it, to Feisal, his tactics were returned to him with improvements.

The Frenchman began by presenting six Hotchkiss automatics complete with instructors. This was a noble gift; but Feisal took the opportunity to ask him to increase his bounty by a battery of the quick-firing mountain guns at Suez, explaining that he had been sorry to leave the Yenbo area for Wejh, since Wejh was so much further from his objective — Medina — but it was really impossible for him to assault the Turks (who had French artillery) with rifles or with the old guns supplied him by the British Army. His men had not the technical excellence to make a bad tool prevail over a good one. He had to exploit his only advantages — numbers and mobility — and, unless his equipment could be improved, there was no saying where this protraction of his front might end!

Bremond tried to turn it off by belittling guns as useless for Hejaz warfare (quite right, this, practically). But it would end the war at once if Feisal made his men climb about the country like goats and tear up the railway. Feisal, angry at the metaphor (impolite in Arabic), looked at Bremond's six feet of comfortable body, and asked if he had ever tried to 'goat' himself. Bremond referred gallantly to the question of Akaba, and the real danger to the Arabs in the Turks remaining there: insisting that the British, who had the means for an expedition thither, should be pressed to undertake it. Feisal, in reply, gave him a geographical sketch of the land behind Akaba (I recognized the less dashing part of it myself) and explained the tribal difficulties and the food problem — all the points which made it a serious obstacle. He ended by saying that, after the cloud of orders, counter-orders and confusion over the allied troops for Rabegh, he really had not the face to approach Sir Archibald Murray so soon with another request for an excursion.

Bremond had to retire from the battle in good order, getting in a Parthian shot at me, where I sat spitefully smiling, by begging Feisal to insist that the British armoured cars in Suez be sent down to Wejh. But even this was a boomerang, since they had started! After he had gone, I returned to Cairo for a cheerful week, in which I gave my betters much good advice. Murray, who had growlingly earmarked Tullibardine's brigade for Akaba, approved me still further when I declared against that side-show too. Then to Wejh.

CHAPTER XXIX

LIFE in Wejh was interesting. We had now set our camp in order. Feisal pitched his tents (here an opulent group: living tents, reception tents, staff tents, guest tents, servants') about a mile from the sea, on the edge of the coral shelf which ran up gently from the beach till it ended in a steep drop facing east and south over broad valleys radiating star-like from the land-locked harbour. The tents of soldiers and tribesmen were grouped in these sandy valleys, leaving the chill height for ourselves; and very delightful in the evening we northerners found it when the breeze from the sea carried us a murmur of the waves, faint and far off, like the echo of traffic up a by-street in London.

Immediately beneath us were the Ageyl, an irregular close group of tents. South of these were Rasim's artillery; and by him for company, Abdulla's machine-gunners, in regular lines, with their animals picketed out in those formal rows which were incense to the professional officer and convenient if space were precious. Further out the market was set plainly on the ground, a boiling swell of men always about the goods. The scattered tents and shelters of the tribesmen filled each gully or windless place. Beyond the last of them lay open country, with camel-parties coming in and out by the straggling palms of the nearest, too-brackish well. As background were the foothills, reefs and clusters like ruined castles, thrown up craggily to the horizon of the coastal range.

As it was the custom in Wejh to camp wide apart, very wide apart, my life was spent in moving back and forth, to Feisal's tents, to the English tents, to the Egyptian Army tents, to the town, the port, the wireless station, tramping all day restlessly up and down these coral paths in sandals or barefoot, hardening my feet, getting by slow degrees the power to walk with little pain over sharp and burning ground, tempering my already trained body for greater endeavour.

Poor Arabs wondered why I had no mare; and I forbore to puzzle them by incomprehensible talk of hardening myself, or confess I would rather walk than ride for sparing of animals: yet the first was true and the second true. Something hurtful to my pride, disagreeable, rose at the sight of these lower forms of life. Their existence struck a servile reflection upon our human kind: the style in which a God would look on us; and to make use of them, to lie under an avoidable obligation to them, seemed to me shameful. It was as with the negroes, tom-tom playing themselves to red madness each night under the ridge. Their faces, being clearly different from our own, were tolerable; but it hurt that they should possess exact counterparts of all our bodies.

Feisal, within, laboured day and night at his politics, in which so few of us could help. Outside, the crowd employed and diverted us with parades, joy-shooting, and marches of victory. Also there were accidents. Once a group, playing behind our tents, set off a seaplane bomb, dud relic of Boyle's capture of the town. In the explosion their limbs were scattered about the camp, marking the canvas with red splashes which soon turned a dull brown and then faded pale. Feisal had the tents changed and ordered the bloody ones to be destroyed: the frugal slaves washed them. Another day a tent took fire, and part-roasted three of our guests. The camp crowded round and roared with laughter till the fire died down, and then, rather shamefacedly, we cared for their hurts. The third day, a mare was wounded by a falling joy-bullet, and many tents were pierced.

One night the Ageyl mutinied against their commandant, ibn Dakhil, for fining them too generally and flogging them too severely. They rushed his tent, howling and shooting, threw his things about and beat his servants. That not being enough to blunt their fury, they began to remember Yenbo, and went off to kill the Ateiba. Feisal from our bluff saw their torches and ran barefoot amongst them, laying on with the flat of his sword like four men. His fury delayed them while the slaves and horsemen, calling for help, dashed downhill with rushes and shouts and blows of sheathed swords. One gave him a horse on which he charged down the ringleaders, while we dispersed groups by firing Very lights into their clothing. Only two were killed and thirty wounded. Ibn Dakhil resigned next day.

Murray had given us two armoured-cars, Rolls-Royces, released from the campaign in East Africa. Gilman and Wade commanded, and their crews were British, men from the A.S.C. to drive and from the Machine Gun Corps to shoot. Having them in Wejh made things more difficult for us, because the food we had been eating and the water we had been drinking were at once medically condemned; but English company was a balancing pleasure, and the occupation of pushing cars and motor-bicycles through the desperate sand about Wejh was great. The fierce difficulty of driving across country gave the men arms like boxers, so that they swung their shoulders professionally as they walked. With time they became skilled, developing a style and art of sand-driving, which got them carefully over the better ground and rushed them at speed over soft places. One of these soft places was the last twenty miles of plain in front of Jebel Raal. The cars used to cross it in little more than half an hour, leaping from ridge to ridge of the dunes and swaying dangerously around their curves. The Arabs loved the new toys. Bicycles they called devil-horses, the children of cars, which themselves were sons and daughters of trains. It gave us three generations of mechanical transport.

The Navy added greatly to our interests in Wejh. The *Espiègle* was sent by Boyle as station ship, with the delightful orders to 'do everything in her power to co-operate in the many plans which would be suggested to her by Colonel Newcombe, while letting it be clearly seen that she was conferring a favour'. Her commander Fitzmaurice (a good name in Turkey), was the soul of hospitality and found quiet amusement in our work on shore. He helped us in a thousand ways; above all in signalling; for he was a wireless expert, and one day at noon the *Northbrook* came in and landed an army wireless set, on a light lorry, for us. As there was no one to explain it, we were at a loss; but Fitzmaurice raced ashore with half his crew, ran the car to a fitting site, rigged the masts professionally, started the engine, and connected up to such effect that before sunset he had called the astonished *Northbrook* and held a long conversation with her operator. The station increased the efficiency of the base at Wejh and was busy day and night, filling the Red Sea with messages in three tongues, and twenty different sorts of army cypher-codes.

CHAPTER XXX

FAKHRI Pasha was still playing our game. He held an entrenched line around Medina, just far enough out to make it impossible for the Arabs to shell the city. (Such an attempt was never made or imagined.) The other troops were being distributed along the railway, in strong garrisons at all water stations between Medina and Tebuk, and in smaller posts between these garrisons, so that daily patrols might guarantee the track. In short, he had fallen back on as stupid a defensive as could be conceived. Garland had gone south-east from Wejh, and Newcombe north-east, to pick holes in it with high explosives. They would cut rails and bridges, and place automatic mines for running trains.

The Arabs had passed from doubt to violent optimism, and were promising exemplary service. Feisal enrolled most of the Billi, and the Moahib, which made him master of Arabia between the railway and the sea. He then sent the Juheina to Abdulla in Wadi Ais.

He could now prepare to deal solemnly with the Hejaz Railway; but with a practice better than my principles, I begged him first to delay in Wejh and set marching an intense movement among the tribes beyond us, that in the future our revolt might be extended, and the railway threatened from Tebuk (our present limit of influence) northward as far as Maan. My vision of the course of the Arab war was still purblind. I had not seen that the preaching was victory and the fighting a delusion. For the moment, I roped them together, and, as Feisal fortunately liked changing men's minds rather than breaking railways, the preaching went the better.

With his northern neighbours, the coastal Howeitat, he had already made a beginning: but we now sent to the Beni Atiyeh, a stronger people to the north-east; and gained a great step when the chief, Asi ibn Atiyeh, came in and swore allegiance. His main motive was jealousy of his brothers, so that we did not expect from him active help; but the bread and salt with him gave us freedom of movement across his tribe's territory. Beyond lay various tribes owning obedience to

Nuri Shaalan, the great Emir of the Ruwalla, who, after the Sherif and ibn Saud and ibn Rashid, was the fourth figure among the precarious princes of the desert.

Nuri was an old man, who had ruled his Anazeh tribesmen for thirty years. His was the chief family of the Rualla, but Nuri had no precedence among them at birth, nor was he loved, nor a great man of battle. His leadership had been acquired by sheer force of character. To gain it he had killed two of his brothers. Later he had added Sherarat and others to the number of his followers, and in all their desert his word was absolute law. He had none of the wheedling diplomacy of the ordinary sheikh; a word, and there was an end of opposition, or of his opponent. All feared and obeyed him; to use his roads we must have his countenance.

Fortunately, this was easy. Feisal had secured it years ago, and had retained it by interchange of gifts from Medina and Yenbo. Now, from Wejh, Fais el Ghusein went up to him and on the way crossed ibn Dughmi, one of the chief men of the Ruwalla, coming down to us with the desirable gift of some hundreds of good baggage camels. Nuri, of course, still kept friendly with the Turks. Damascus and Bagdad were his markets, and they could have half-starved his tribe in three months, had they suspected him; but we knew that when the moment came we should have his armed help, and till then anything short of a breach with Turkey.

His favour would open to us the Sirhan, a famous roadway, camping ground, and chain of water-holes, which in a series of linked depressions extended from Jauf, Nuri's capital, in the south-east, northwards to Azrak, near Jebel Druse, in Syria. It was the freedom of the Sirhan we needed to reach the tents of the Eastern Howeitat, those famous abu Tayi, of whom Auda, the greatest fighting man in northern Arabia, was chief. Only by means of Auda abu Tayi could we swing the tribes from Maan to Akaba so violently in our favour that they would help us take Akaba and its hills from their Turkish garrisons: only with his active support could we venture to thrust out from Wejh on the long trek to Maan. Since our Yenbo days we had been longing for him and trying to win him to our cause.

We made a great step forward at Wejh; ibn Zaal, his cousin and a war-leader of the abu Tayi, arrived on the seventeenth of February, which was in all respects a fortunate day. At dawn there came in five chief men of the Sherarat from the desert east of Tebuk, bringing a present of eggs of the Arabian ostrich, plentiful in their little frequented desert. After them, the slaves showed in Dhaif-Allah, abu Tiyur, a cousin of Hamd ibn Jazi, paramount of the central Howeitat of the Maan plateau. These were numerous and powerful; splendid fighters; but blood enemies of their cousins, the nomad abu Tayi, because of an old-grounded quarrel between Auda and Hamd. We were proud to see them coming thus far to greet us, yet not content, for they were less fit than the abu Tayi for our purposed attack against Akaba.

On their heels came a cousin of Nawwaf, Nuri Shaalan's eldest son, with a mare sent by Nawwaf to Feisal. The Shaalan and the Jazi, being hostile, hardened eyes at one another; so we divided the parties and improvised a new guest-camp. After the Rualla, was announced the abu Tageiga chief of the sedentary Howeitat of the coast. He brought his tribe's respectful homage and the spoils of Dhaba and Moweilleh, the two last Turkish outlets on the Red Sea. Room was made for him on Feisal's carpet, and the warmest thanks rendered him for his tribe's activity; which carried us to the borders of Akaba, by tracks too rough for operations of force, but convenient for preaching and still more so for getting news.

In the afternoon, ibn Zaal arrived, with ten other of Auda's chief followers. He kissed Feisal's hand once for Auda and then once for himself, and, sitting back, declared that he came from Auda to present his salutations and to ask for orders. Feisal, with policy, controlled his outward joy, and introduced him gravely to his blood enemies, the Jazi Howeitat. Ibn Zaal acknowledged them distantly. Later, we held great private conversations with him and dismissed him with rich gifts, richer promises, and Feisal's own message to Auda that his mind would not be smooth till he had seen him face to face in Wejh. Auda was an immense chivalrous name, but an unknown quantity to us, and in so vital a matter as Akaba we could not afford a mistake. He must come down that we might weigh him, and frame our future plans actually in his presence, and with his help.

Except that all its events were happy, this day was not essentially unlike Feisal's every day. The rush of news made my diary fat. The roads to Wejh swarmed with envoys and volunteers and great sheikhs riding in to swear allegiance. The contagion of their constant passage made the lukewarm Billi ever more profitable to us. Feisal swore new adherents solemnly on the Koran between his hands, 'to wait while he waited, march when he marched, to yield obedience to no Turk, to deal kindly with all who spoke Arabic (whether Bagdadi, Aleppine, Syrian, or pure-blooded) and to put independence above life, family, and goods'.

He also began to confront them at once, in his presence, with their tribal enemies, and to compose their feuds. An account of profit and loss would be struck between the parties, with Feisal modulating and interceding between them, and often paying the balance, or contributing towards it from his own funds, to hurry on the pact. During two years Feisal so laboured daily, putting together and arranging in their natural order the innumerable tiny pieces which made up Arabian society, and combining them into his one design of war against the Turks. There was no blood feud left active in any of the districts through which he had passed, and he was Court of Appeal, ultimate and unchallenged, for western Arabia.

He showed himself worthy of this achievement. He never gave a partial decision, nor a decision so impracticably just that it must lead to disorder. No Arab ever impugned his judgements, or questioned his wisdom and competence in tribal business. By patiently sifting out right and wrong, by his tact, his wonderful memory, he gained authority over the nomads from Medina to Damascus and beyond. He was recognized as a force transcending tribe, superseding blood chiefs, greater than jealousies. The Arab movement became in the best sense national, since within it all Arabs were at one, and for it private interests must be set aside; and in this movement chief place, by right of application and by right of ability, had been properly earned by the man who filled it for those few weeks of triumph and longer months of disillusion after Damascus had been set free.

CHAPTER XXXI

URGENT messages from Clayton broke across this cheerful work with orders to wait in Wejh for two days and meet the *Nur el Bahr*, an Egyptian patrol ship, coming down with news. I was not well and waited with more excellent grace. She arrived on the proper day, and disembarked MacRury, who gave me a copy of long telegraphic instructions from Jemal Pasha to Fakhri in Medina. These, emanating from Enver and the German staff in Constantinople, ordered the instant abandonment of Medina, and evacuation of the troops by route march in mass, first to Hedia, thence to El Ula, thence to Tebuk, and finally to Maan, where a fresh rail-head and entrenched position would be constituted.

This move would have suited the Arabs excellently; but our army of Egypt was perturbed at the prospect of twenty-five thousand Anatolian troops, with far more than the usual artillery of a corps, descending suddenly on the Beersheba front. Clayton, in his letter, told me the development was to be treated with the utmost concern, and every effort made to capture Medina, or to destroy the garrison when they came out. Newcombe was on the line, doing a vigorous demolition-series, so that the moment's responsibility fell on me. I feared that little could be done in time, for the message was days old, and the evacuation timed to begin at once.

We told Feisal the frank position, and that Allied interests in this case demanded the sacrifice, or at least the postponement of immediate advantage to the Arabs. He rose, as ever, to a proposition of honour, and agreed instantly to do his best. We worked out our possible resources and arranged to move them into contact with the railway. Sherif Mastur, an honest, quiet old man, and Rasim, with tribesmen, mule-mounted infantry, and a gun, were to proceed directly to Fagair, the first good water-base north of Wadi Ais, to hold up our first section of railway, from Abdulla's area northward.

Ali ibn el Hussein, from Jeida, would attack the next section of line northward from Mastur. We told ibn Mahanna to get close to El Ula, and watch it. We ordered Sherif Nasir to stay near Kalaat et Muadhdham, and keep his men in hand for an effort. I wrote asking Newcombe to come in for news. Old Mohammed Ali was to move from Dhaba to an oasis near Tebuk, so that if the evacuation got so far we should be ready. All our hundred and fifty miles of line would thus be beset, while Feisal himself, at Wejh, stood ready to bring help to whatever sector most needed him.

My part was to go off to Abdulla in Wadi Ais, to find out why he had done nothing for two months, and to persuade him, if the Turks came out, to go straight at them. I hoped we might deter them from moving by making so many small raids on this lengthy line that traffic would be seriously disorganized, and the collection of the necessary food-dumps for the army at each main stage be impracticable. The Medina force, being short of animal transport, could carry little with them. Enver had instructed them to put guns and stores on trains; and to enclose these trains in their columns and march together up the railway. It was an unprecedented manœuvre, and if we gained ten days to get in place, and they then attempted anything so silly, we should have a chance of destroying them all.

Next day I left Wejh, ill and unfit for a long march, while Feisal in his haste and many preoccupations had chosen me a travelling party of queer fellows. There were four Rifaa and one Merawi Juheina as guides, and Arslan, a Syrian soldier-servant, who prepared bread and rice for me and acted besides as butt to the Arabs; four Ageyl, a Moor, and an Ateibi, Suleiman. The camels, thin with the bad grazing of this dry Billi territory, would have to go slowly.

Delay after delay took place in our starting, until nine at night, and then we moved unwillingly: but I was determined to get clear of Wejh somehow before morning. So we went four hours and slept. Next day we did two stages of five hours each, and camped at Abu Zereibat, in our old ground of the winter. The great pool had shrunk little in the two months, but was noticeably more salt. A few weeks later it was unfit to drink. A shallow well near by was said to afford tolerable water. I did not look for it, since boils on my back and heavy fever made painful the jolting of the camel, and I was tired.

Long before dawn we rode away, and having crossed Hamdh got

confused in the broken surfaces of Agunna, an area of low hills. When day broke we recovered direction and went over a watershed steeply down into El Khubt, a hill-locked plain extending to the Sukhur, the granite bubbles of hills which had been prominent on our road up from Um Lejj. The ground was luxuriant with colocynth, whose runners and fruits looked festive in the early light. The Juheina said both leaves and stalks were excellent food for such horses as would eat them, and defended from thirst for many hours. The Ageyl said that the best aperient was to drink camel-milk from cups of the scooped-out rind. The Ateibi said that he was sufficiently moved if he just rubbed the juice of the fruit on the soles of his feet. The Moor Hamed said that the dried pith made good tinder. On one point however they were all agreed, that the whole plant was useless or poisonous as fodder for camels.

This talk carried us across the Khubt, a pleasant three miles, and through a low ridge into a second smaller section. We now saw that, of the Sukhur, two stood together to the north-east, great grey striated piles of volcanic rock, reddish coloured where protected from the burning of the sun and the bruising of sandy winds. The third Sakhara, which stood a little apart, was the bubble rock which had roused my curiosity. Seen from near by, it more resembled a huge football half-buried in the ground. It, too, was brown in colour. The south and east faces were quite smooth and unbroken, and its regular, domed head was polished and shining and had fine cracks running up and over it like stitched seams: altogether one of the strangest hills in Hejaz, a country of strange hills. We rode gently towards it, through a thin shower of rain which came slanting strangely and beautifully across the sunlight. Our path took up between the Sakhara and the Sukhur by a narrow gorge with sandy floor and steep bare walls. Its head was rough. We had to scramble up shelves of coarse-faced stone, and along a great fault in the hill-side between two tilted red reefs of hard rock. The summit of the pass was a knife-edge, and from it we went down an encumbered gap, half-blocked by one fallen boulder which had been hammered over with the tribal marks of all the generations of men who had used this road. Afterwards there opened tree-grown spaces, collecting grounds in winter for the sheets of rain which poured off the glazed sides of the Sukhur. There were granite outcrops here and there, and a fine silver sand underfoot in the still damp water-channels. The drainage was towards Heiran.

We then entered a wild confusion of granite shards, piled up hap-hazard into low mounds, in and out of which we wandered any way we could find practicable going for our hesitating camels. Soon after noon this gave place to a broad wooded valley, up which we rode for an hour, till our troubles began again; for we had to dismount and lead our animals up a narrow hill-path with broken steps of rock so polished by long years of passing feet that they were dangerous in wet weather. They took us over a great shoulder of the hills and down among more small mounds and valleys, and afterwards by another rocky zigzag descent into a torrent-bed. This soon became too confined to admit the passage of laden camels, and the path left it to cling pre-cariously to the hill-side with a cliff above and cliff below. After fifteen minutes of this we were glad to reach a high saddle on which former travellers had piled little cairns of commemoration and thank-fulness. Of such a nature had been the road-side cairns of Masturah, on my first Arabian journey, from Rabegh to Feisal.

We stopped to add one to the number, and then rode down a sandy valley into Wadi Hanbag, a large, well-wooded tributary of Hamdh. After the broken country in which we had been prisoned for hours, the openness of Hanbag was refreshing. Its clean white bed swept on northward through the trees in a fine curve under precipitous hills of red and brown, with views for a mile or two up and down its course. There were green weeds and grass growing on the lower sand-slopes of the tributary, and we stopped there for half an hour to let our starved camels eat the juicy, healthy stuff.

They had not so enjoyed themselves since Bir el Waheidi, and tore at it ravenously, stowing it away unchewed inside them, pending a fit time for leisurely digestion. We then crossed the valley to a great branch opposite our entry. This Wadi Kitan was also beautiful. Its shingle face without loose rocks, was plentifully grown over with trees. On the right were low hills, on the left great heights called the Jidhwa, in parallel ridges of steep broken granite, very red now that the sun was setting amid massed cloud-banks of boding rain.

At last we camped, and when the camels were unloaded and driven out to pasture, I lay down under the rocks and rested. My body was very sore with headache and high fever, the accompaniments of a sharp attack of dysentery which had troubled me along the march and had laid me out twice that day in short fainting fits, when the more difficult parts of the climb had asked too much of my strength. Dysentery of this Arabian coast sort used to fall like a hammer blow, and crush its victims for a few hours, after which the extreme effects passed off; but it left men curiously tired, and subject for some weeks to sudden breaks of nerve.

My followers had been quarrelling all day; and while I was lying near the rocks a shot was fired. I paid no attention; for there were hares and birds in the valley; but a little later Suleiman roused me and made me follow him across the valley to an oppposite bay in the rocks, where one of the Ageyl, a Boreida man, was lying stone dead with a bullet through his temples. The shot must have been fired from close by; because the skin was burnt about one wound. The remaining Ageyl were running frantically about; and when I asked what it was Ali, their head man, said that Hamed the Moor had done the murder. I suspected Suleiman, because of the feud between the Atban and Ageyl which had burned up in Yenbo and Wejh; but Ali assured me that Suleiman had been with him three hundred yards further up the valley gathering sticks when the shot was fired. I sent all out to search for Hamed, and crawled back to the baggage, feeling that it need not have happened this day of all days when I was in pain.

As I lay there I heard a rustle, and opened my eyes slowly upon Hamed's back as he stooped over his saddle-bags, which lay just beyond my rock. I covered him with a pistol and then spoke. He had put down his rifle to lift the gear; and was at my mercy till the others came. We held a court at once; and after a while Hamed confessed that, he and Salem having had words, he had seen red and shot him suddenly. Our inquiry ended. The Ageyl, as relatives of the dead man, demanded blood for blood. The others supported them; and I tried vainly to talk the gentle Ali round. My head was aching with fever and I could not think; but hardly even in health, with all eloquence, could I have begged Hamed off; for Salem had been a friendly fellow and his sudden murder a wanton crime.

Then rose up the horror which would make civilized man shun justice like a plague if he had not the needy to serve him as hangmen for wages. There were other Moroccans in our army; and to let the Ageyl kill one in feud meant reprisals by which our unity would have been endangered. It must be a formal execution, and at last, desperately, I told Hamed that he must die for punishment, and laid the burden of his killing on myself. Perhaps they would count me not qualified for feud. At least no revenge could lie against my followers; for I was a stranger and kinless.

I made him enter a narrow gully of the spur, a dank twilight place overgrown with weeds. Its sandy bed had been pitted by trickles of water down the cliffs in the late rain. At the end it shrank to a crack a few inches wide. The walls were vertical. I stood in the entrance and gave him a few moments' delay which he spent crying on the ground. Then I made him rise and shot him through the chest. He fell down on the weeds shrieking, with the blood coming out in spurts over his clothes, and jerked about till he rolled nearly to where I was. I fired again, but was shaking so that I only broke his wrist. He went on calling out, less loudly, now lying on his back with his feet towards me, and I leant forward and shot him for the last time in the thick of his neck under the jaw. His body shivered a little, and I called the Ageyl; who buried him in the gully where he was. Afterwards the wakeful night dragged over me, till, hours before dawn, I had the men up and made them load, in my longing to be set free of Wadi Kitan. They had to lift me into the saddle.

CHAPTER XXXII

DAWN found us crossing a steep short pass out of Wadi Kitan into the main drainage valley of these succeeding hills. We turned aside into Wadi Reimi, a tributary, to get water. There was no proper well, only a seepage hole in the stony bed of the valley; and we found it partly by our noses: though the taste, while as foul, was curiously unlike the smell. We refilled our water-skins. Arslan baked bread, and we rested for two hours. Then we went on through Wadi Amk, an easy green valley which made comfortable marching for the camels.

When the Amk turned westward we crossed it, going up between piles of the warped grey granite (like cold toffee) which was common up-country in the Hejaz. The defile culminated at the foot of a natural ramp and staircase: badly broken, twisting, and difficult for camels, but short. Afterwards we were in an open valley for an hour, with low hills to the right and mountains to the left. There were water pools in the crags, and Merawin tents under the fine trees which studded the flat. The fertility of the slopes was great: on them grazed flocks of sheep and goats. We got milk from the Arabs: the first milk my Ageyl had been given in the two years of drought.

The track out of the valley when we reached its head was execrable, and the descent beyond into Wadi Marrakh almost dangerous; but the view from the crest compensated us. Wadi Marrakh, a broad, peaceful avenue, ran between two regular straight walls of hills to a circus four miles off where valleys from left, right and front seemed to meet. Artificial heaps of uncut stone were piled about the approach. As we entered it, we saw that the grey hill-walls swept back on each side in a half-circle. Before us, to the south, the curve was barred across by a straight wall or step of blue-black lava, standing over a little grove of thorn trees. We made for these and lay down in their thin shade, grateful in such sultry air for any pretence of coolness.

The day, now at its zenith, was very hot; and my weakness had so increased that my head hardly held up against it. The puffs of feverish wind pressed like scorching hands against our faces, burning our eyes. My pain made me breathe in gasps through the mouth; the wind cracked my lips and seared my throat till I was too dry to talk, and drinking became sore; yet I always needed to drink, as my thirst would not let me lie still and get the peace I longed for. The flies were a plague.

The bed of the valley was of fine quartz gravel and white sand. Its glitter thrust itself between our eyelids; and the level of the ground seemed to dance as the wind moved the white tips of stubble grass to and fro. The camels loved this grass, which grew in tufts, about sixteen inches high, on slate-green stalks. They gulped down great quantities of it until the men drove them in and couched them by me. At the moment I hated the beasts, for too much food made their breath stink; and they rumblingly belched up a new mouthful from their stomachs each time they had chewed and swallowed the last, till a green slaver flooded out between their loose lips over the side teeth, and dripped down their sagging chins.

Lying angrily there, I threw a stone at the nearest, which got up and wavered about behind my head: finally it straddled its back legs and staled in wide, bitter jets; and I was so far gone with the heat and weakness and pain that I just lay there and cried about it unhelping. The men had gone to make a fire and cook a gazelle one of them had fortunately shot; and I realized that on another day this halt would have been pleasant to me; for the hills were very strange and their colours vivid. The base had the warm grey of old stored sunlight; while about their crests ran narrow veins of granite-coloured stone, generally in pairs, following the contour of the skyline like the rusted metals of an abandoned scenic railway. Arslan said the hills were combed like cocks, a sharper observation.

After the men had fed we re-mounted, and easily climbed the first wave of the lava flood. It was short, as was the second, on the top of which lay a broad terrace with an alluvial plot of sand and gravel in its midst. The lava was a nearly clean floor of iron-red rock-cinders, over which were scattered fields of loose stone. The third and other steps ascended to the south of us: but we turned east, up Wadi Gara.

Gara had, perhaps, been a granite valley down whose middle the lava had flowed, slowly filling it, and arching itself up in a central heap. On each side were deep troughs, between the lava and the hill-side. Rain water flooded these as often as storms burst in the hills. The lava flow, as it coagulated, had been twisted like a rope, cracked, and bent back irregularly upon itself. The surface was loose with fragments through which many generations of camel parties had worn an inadequate and painful track.

We struggled along for hours, going slowly, our camels wincing at every stride as the sharp edges slipped beneath their tender feet. The paths were only to be seen by the droppings along them, and by the slightly bluer surfaces of the rubbed stones. The Arabs declared them impassable after dark, which was to be believed, for we risked laming our beasts each time our impatience made us urge them on. Just before five in the afternoon, however, the way got easier. We seemed to be near the head of the valley, which grew narrow. Before us on the right, an exact cone-crater, with tidy furrows scoring it from lip to foot, promised good going; for it was made of black ash, clean as though sifted, with here and there a bank of harder soil, and cinders. Beyond it was another lava-field, older perhaps than the valleys, for its stones were smoothed, and between them were straths of flat earth, rank with weeds. In among these open spaces were Beduin tents, whose owners ran to us when they saw us coming; and, taking our head-stalls with hospitable force, led us in.

They proved to be Sheikh Fahad el Hansha and his men: old and garrulous warriors who had marched with us to Wejh, and had been with Garland on that great occasion when his first automatic mine had succeeded under a troop train near Toweira station. Fahad would not hear of my resting quietly outside his tent, but with the reckless equality of the desert men urged me into an unfortunate place inside among his own vermin. There he plied me with bowl after bowl of diuretic camel-milk between questions about Europe, my home tribe, the English camel-pasturages, the war in the Hejaz and the wars elsewhere, Egypt and Damascus, how Feisal was, why did we seek Abdulla, and by what perversity did I remain Christian, when their hearts and hands waited to welcome me to the Faith?

So passed long hours till ten at night, when the guest-sheep was carried in, dismembered royally over a huge pile of buttered rice. I ate as manners demanded, twisted myself up in my cloak, and slept; my bodily exhaustion, after those hours of the worst imaginable marching, proofing me against the onslaught of lice and fleas. The illness, however, had stimulated my ordinarily sluggish fancy, which ran riot this night in dreams of wandering naked for a dark eternity over interminable lava (like scrambled egg gone iron-blue, and very wrong), sharp as insect-bites underfoot; and with some horror, perhaps a dead Moor, always climbing after us.

In the morning we woke early and refreshed, with our clothes stinging-full of fiery points feeding on us. After one more bowl of milk proffered us by the eager Fahad, I was able to walk unaided to my camel and mount her actively. We rode up the last piece of Wadi Gara to the crest, among cones of black cinders from a crater to the south. Thence we turned to a branch valley, ending in a steep and rocky chimney, up which we pulled our camels.

Beyond we had an easy descent into Wadi Murrmiya, whose middle bristled with lava like galvanized iron, on each side of which there were smooth sandy beds, good going. After a while we came to a fault in the flow, which served as a track to the other side. By it we crossed over, finding the lava pocketed with soils apparently of extreme richness, for in them were leafy trees and lawns of real grass, starred with flowers, the best grazing of all our ride, looking the more wonderfully green because of the blue-black twisted crusts of rock about. The lava had changed its character. Here were no piles of loose stones, as big as a skull or a man's hand, rubbed and rounded together; but bunched and crystallized fronds of metallic rock, altogether impassable for bare feet.

Another watershed conducted us to an open place where the Jeheina had ploughed some eight acres of the thin soil below a thicket of scrub. They said there were like it in the neighbourhood other fields, silent witnesses to the courage and persistence of the Arabs. It was called Wadi Chetf, and after it was another broken river of lava, the worst yet encountered. A shadowy path zigzagged across it. We lost one camel with a broken fore-leg, the result of a stumble in a pot-hole; and the many bones which lay about showed that we were not the only party to suffer misfortune in the passage. However, this ended our lava, according to the guides, and we went thence forward along easy valleys with finally a long run up a gentle slope till dusk. The going was so good and the cool of the day so freshened me that we did not halt at nightfall, after our habit, but pushed on for an hour across the basin of Murrmiya into the basin of Wadi Ais, and there, by Tleih, we stopped for our last camp in the open.

I rejoiced that we were so nearly in, for fever was heavy on me. I was afraid that perhaps I was going to be really ill, and the prospect of falling into the well-meaning hands of tribesmen in such a state was not pleasant. Their treatment of every sickness was to burn holes in the patient's body at some spot believed to be the complement of the part affected. It was a cure tolerable to such as had faith in it, but torture to the unbelieving: to incur it unwillingly would be silly, and yet certain; for the Arabs' good intentions, selfish as their good digestions, would never heed a sick man's protesting.

The morning was easy, over open valleys and gentle rides into Wadi Ais. We arrived at Abu Markha, its nearest watering-place, just a few minutes after Sherif Abdulla had dismounted there, and while he was ordering his tents to be pitched in an acacia glade beyond the well. He was leaving his old camp at Bir el Amri, lower down the valley, as he had left Murabba, his camp before, because the ground had been fouled by the careless multitude of his men and animals. I gave him the documents from Feisal, explaining the situation in Medina, and the need we had of haste to block the railway. I thought he took it coolly; but, without argument, went on to say that I was a little tired after my journey, and with his permission would lie down and sleep a while. He pitched me a tent next his great marquee, and I went into it and rested myself at last. It had been a struggle against faintness day-long in the saddle to get here at all: and now the strain was ended with the delivery of my message, I felt that another hour would have brought the breaking point.

CHAPTER XXXIII

ABOUT ten days I lay in that tent, suffering a bodily weakness which made my animal self crawl away and hide till the shame was passed. As usual in such circumstances my mind cleared, my senses became more acute, and I began at last to think consecutively of the Arab Revolt, as an accustomed duty to rest upon against the pain. It should have been thought out long before, but at my first landing in Hejaz there had been a crying need for action, and we had done what seemed to instinct best, not probing into the why, nor formulating what we really wanted at the end of all. Instinct thus abused without a basis of past knowledge and reflection had grown intuitive, feminine, and was now bleaching my confidence; so in this forced inaction I looked for the equation between my book-reading and my movements, and spent the intervals of uneasy sleeps and dreams in plucking at the tangle of our present.

As I have shown, I was unfortunately as much in command of the campaign as I pleased, and was untrained. In military theory I was tolerably read, my Oxford curiosity having taken me past Napoleon to Clausewitz and his school, to Caemmerer and Moltke, and the recent Frenchmen. They had all seemed to be one-sided; and after looking at Jomini and Willisen, I had found broader principles in Saxe and Guibert and the eighteenth century. However, Clausewitz was intellectually so much the master of them, and his book so logical and fascinating, that unconsciously I accepted his finality, until a comparison of Kuhne and Foch disgusted me with soldiers, wearied me of their officious glory, making me critical of all their light. In any case, my interest had been abstract, concerned with the theory and philosophy of warfare especially from the metaphysical side.

Now, in the field everything had been concrete, particularly the tiresome problem of Medina; and to distract myself from that I began to recall suitable maxims on the conduct of modern, scientific war. But they would not fit, and it worried me. Hitherto, Medina had been an obsession for us all; but now that I was ill, its image was not clear, whether it was that we were near to it (one seldom liked the attainable), or whether it was that my eyes were misty with too constant staring at the butt. One afternoon I woke from a hot sleep, running with sweat and pricking with flies, and wondered what on earth was the good of Medina to us? Its harmfulness had been patent when we were at Yenbo and the Turks in it were going to Mecca: but we had changed all that by our march to Wejh. To-day we were blockading the railway, and they only defending it. The garrison of Medina, reduced to an inoffensive size, were sitting in trenches destroying their own power of movement by eating the transport they could no longer feed. We had taken away their power to harm us, and yet wanted to take away their town. It was not a base for us like Wejh, nor a threat like Wadi Ais. What on earth did we want it for?

The camp was bestirring itself after the torpor of the midday hours; and noises from the world outside began to filter in to me past the yellow lining of the tent-canvas, whose every hole and tear was stabbed through by a long dagger of sunlight. I heard the stamping and snorting of the horses plagued with flies where they stood in the shadow of the trees, the complaint of camels, the ringing of coffee mortars, distant shots. To their burden I began to drum out the aim in war. The books gave it pat — the destruction of the armed forces of the enemy by the one process — battle. Victory could be purchased only by blood. This was a hard saying for us. As the Arabs had no organized forces, a Turkish Foch would have no aim? The Arabs would not endure casualties. How would our Clausewitz buy his victory. Von der Goltz had seemed to go deeper, saying it was necessary not to annihilate the enemy, but to break his courage. Only we showed no prospect of ever breaking anybody's courage.

However, Goltz was a humbug, and these wise men must be talking metaphors; for we were indubitably winning our war; and as I pondered slowly, it dawned on me that we had won the Hejaz war. Out of every thousand square miles of Hejaz nine hundred and ninety-nine were now free. Did my provoked jape at Vickery, that rebellion was more like peace than like war, hold as much truth as haste? Perhaps in war the absolute did rule, but for peace a majority was good enough. If we held the rest, the Turks were welcome to the tiny fraction on which they stood, till peace or Doomsday showed them the futility of clinging to our window-pane.

I brushed off the same flies once more from my face patiently, content to know that the Hejaz War was won and finished with: won from the day we took Wejh, if we had had wit to see it. Then I broke the thread of my argument again to listen. The distant shots had grown and tied themselves into long, ragged volleys. They ceased. I strained my ears for the other sounds which I knew would follow. Sure enough across the silence came a rustle like the dragging of a skirt over the flints, around the thin walls of my tent. A pause, while the camel-riders drew up: and then the soggy tapping of canes on the thick of the beasts' necks to make them kneel.

They knelt without noise: and I timed it in my memory: first the hesitation, as the camels, looking down, felt the soil with one foot for a soft place; then the muffled thud and the sudden loosening of breath as they dropped on their fore-legs, since this party had come far and were tired; then the shuffle as the hind legs were folded in, and the rocking as they tossed from side to side thrusting outward with their knees to bury them in the cooler subsoil below the burning flints, while the riders, with a quick soft patter of bare feet, like birds over the ground, were led off tacitly either to the coffee hearth or to Abdulla's tent, according to their business. The camels would rest there, uneasily switching their tails across the shingle till their masters were free and looked to their stabling.

I had made a comfortable beginning of doctrine, but was left still to find an alternative end and means of war. Ours seemed unlike the ritual of which Foch was priest; and I recalled him, to see a difference in kind between him and us. In his modern war — absolute war he called it — two nations professing incompatible philosophies put them to the test of force. Philosophically, it was idiotic, for while opinions were arguable, convictions needed shooting to be cured; and the struggle could end only when the supporters of the one immaterial principle had no more means of resistance against the supporters of the other. It sounded like a twentieth-century restatement of the wars of religion, whose logical end was utter destruction of one creed, and whose protagonists believed that God's judgement would prevail. This might do for France and Germany, but would not represent the British attitude. Our Army was not intelligently maintaining a philosophic conception in Flanders or on the Canal. Efforts to make our men hate the enemy usually made them hate the fighting. Indeed Foch had knocked out his own argument by saying that such war depended on levy in mass, and was impossible with professional armies; while the old army was still the British ideal, and its manner the ambition of our ranks and our files. To me the Foch war seemed only an exterminative variety, no more absolute than another. One could as explicably call it 'murder war'. Clausewitz enumerated all sorts of war ... personal wars, joint-proxy duels, for dynastic reasons ... expulsive wars, in party politics ... commercial wars, for trade objects ... two wars seemed seldom alike. Often the parties did not know their aim, and blundered till the march of events took control. Victory in general habit leaned to the clear-sighted, though fortune and superior intelligence could make a sad muddle of nature's 'inexorable' law.

I wondered why Feisal wanted to fight the Turks, and why the Arabs helped him, and saw that their aim was geographical, to extrude the Turk from all Arabic-speaking lands in Asia. Their peace ideal of liberty could exercise itself only so. In pursuit of the ideal conditions we might kill Turks, because we disliked them very much; but the killing was a pure luxury. If they would go quietly the war would end. If not, we would urge them, or try to drive them out. In the last resort, we should be compelled to the desperate course of blood and the maxims of 'murder war', but as cheaply as could be for ourselves, since the Arabs fought for freedom, and that was a pleasure to be tasted only by a man alive. Posterity was a chilly thing to work for, no matter how much a man happened to love his own, or other people's already-produced children.

At this point a slave slapped my tent-door, and asked if the Emir might call. So I struggled into more clothes, and crawled over to his great tent to sound the depth of motive in him. It was a comfortable place, luxuriously shaded and carpeted deep in strident rugs, the aniline-dyed spoils of Hussein Mabeirig's house in Rabegh. Abdulla passed most of his day in it, laughing with his friends, and playing games with Mohammed Hassan, the court jester. I set the ball of conversation rolling between him and Shakir and the chance sheikhs among whom was the fire-hearted Ferhan el Aida, the son of Doughty's Motlog; and I was rewarded, for Abdulla's words were definite. He contrasted his hearers' present independence with their past servitude to Turkey, and roundly said that talk of Turkish heresy, or the immoral doctrine of *Yeni-Turan*, or the illegitimate Caliphate was beside the point. It was Arab country, and the Turks were in it: that was the one issue. My argument preened itself.

The next day a great complication of boils developed out, to conceal my lessened fever, and to chain me down yet longer in impotence upon my face in this stinking tent. When it grew too hot for dreamless dozing, I picked up my tangle again, and went on ravelling it out, considering now the whole house of war in its structural aspect, which was strategy, in its arrangements, which were tactics, and in the sentiment of its inhabitants, which was psychology; for my personal duty was command, and the commander, like the master architect, was responsible for all.

The first confusion was the false antithesis between strategy, the aim in war, the synoptic regard seeing each part relative to the whole, and tactics, the means towards a strategic end, the particular steps of its staircase. They seemed only points of view from which to ponder the elements of war, the Algebraical element of things, a Biological element of lives, and the Psychological element of ideas.

The Algebraical element looked to me a pure science, subject to mathematical law, inhuman. It dealt with known variables, fixed conditions, space and time, inorganic things like hills and climates and railways, with mankind in type-masses too great for individual variety, with all artificial aids and the extensions given our faculties by mechanical invention. It was essentially formulable.

Here was a pompous, professorial beginning. My wits, hostile to the abstract, took refuge in Arabia again. Translated into Arabic, the algebraic factor would first take practical account of the area we wished to deliver, and I began idly to calculate how many square miles: sixty: eighty: one hundred: perhaps one hundred and forty thousand square miles. And how would the Turks defend all that? No doubt by a trench line across the bottom, if we came like an army with banners;

but suppose we were (as we might be) an influence, an idea, a thing intangible, invulnerable, without front or back, drifting about like a gas? Armies were like plants, immobile, firm-rooted, nourished through long stems to the head. We might be a vapour, blowing where we listed. Our kingdoms lay in each man's mind; and as we wanted nothing material to live on, so we might offer nothing material to the killing. It seemed a regular soldier might be helpless without a target, owning only what he sat on, and subjugating only what, by order, he could poke his rifle at.

Then I figured out how many men they would need to sit on all this ground, to save it from our attack-in-depth, sedition putting up her head in every unoccupied one of those hundred thousand square miles. I knew the Turkish Army exactly, and even allowing for their recent extension of faculty by aeroplanes and guns and armoured trains (which made the earth a smaller battlefield) still it seemed they would have need of a fortified post every four square miles, and a post could not be less than twenty men. If so, they would need six hundred thousand men to meet the illwills of all the Arab peoples, combined with the active hostility of a few zealots.

How many zealots could we have? At present we had nearly fifty thousand: sufficient for the day. It seemed the assets in this element of war were ours. If we realized our raw materials and were apt with them, then climate, railway, desert, and technical weapons could also be attached to our interests. The Turks were stupid; the Germans behind them dogmatical. They would believe that rebellion was absolute like war, and deal with it on the analogy of war. Analogy in human things was fudge, anyhow; and war upon rebellion was messy and slow, like eating soup with a knife.

This was enough of the concrete; so I sheered off ἐπιστήμη, the mathematical element, and plunged into the nature of the biological factor in command. Its crisis seemed to be the breaking point, life and death, or less finally, wear and tear. The war-philosophers had properly made an art of it, and had elevated one item, 'effusion of blood', to the height of an essential, which became humanity in battle, an act touching every side of our corporal being, and very warm. A line of variability. Man, persisted like leaven through its estimates, making them irregular,

The components were sensitive and illogical, and generals guarded themselves by the device of a reserve, the significant medium of their art. Goltz had said that if you knew the enemy's strength, and he was fully deployed, then you could dispense with a reserve: but this was never. The possibility of accident, of some flaw in materials was always in the general's mind, and the reserve unconsciously held to meet it.

The 'felt' element in troops, not expressible in figures, had to be guessed at by the equivalent of Plato's δόξα, and the greatest commander of men was he whose intuitions most nearly happened. Nine-tenths of tactics were certain enough to be teachable in schools; but the irrational tenth was like the kingfisher flashing across the pool, and in it lay the test of generals. It could be ensued only by instinct (sharpened by thought practising the stroke) until at the crisis it came naturally, a reflex. There had been men whose δόξα so nearly approached perfection that by its road they reached the certainty of ἐπιστήμη. The Greeks might have called such genius for command νόησις had they bothered to rationalize revolt.

My mind see-sawed back to apply this to ourselves, and at once knew that it was not bounded by mankind, that it applied also to materials. In Turkey things were scarce and precious, men less esteemed than equipment. Our cue was to destroy, not the Turk's army, but his minerals. The death of a Turkish bridge or rail, machine or gun or charge of high explosive, was more profitable to us than the death of a Turk. In the Arab Army at the moment we were chary both of materials and of men. Governments saw men only in mass; but our men, being irregulars, were not formations, but individuals. An individual death, like a pebble dropped in water, might make but a brief hole; yet rings of sorrow widened out therefrom. We could not afford casualties.

Materials were easier to replace. It was our obvious policy to be superior in some one tangible branch; gun-cotton or machine-guns or whatever could be made decisive. Orthodoxy had laid down the maxim, applied to men, of being superior at the critical point and moment of attack. We might be superior in equipment in one dominant moment or respect; and for both things and men we might give the doctrine a twisted negative side, for cheapness' sake, and be weaker than the enemy everywhere except in that one point or matter. The decision of what was critical would always be ours. Most wars were wars of contact, both forces striving into touch to avoid tactical surprise. Ours should be a war of detachment. We were to contain the enemy by the silent threat of a vast unknown desert, not disclosing ourselves till we attacked. The attack might be nominal, directed not against him, but against his stuff; so it would not seek either his strength or his weakness, but his most accessible material. In railway-cutting it would be usually an empty stretch of rail; and the more empty, the greater the tactical success. We might turn our average into a rule (not a law, since war was antinomian) and develop a habit of never engaging the enemy. This would chime with the numerical plea for never affording a target. Many Turks on our front had no chance all the war to fire on us, and we were never on the defensive except by accident and in error.

The corollary of such a rule was perfect 'intelligence', so that we could plan in certainty. The chief agent must be the general's head; and his understanding must be faultless, leaving no room for chance. Morale, if built on knowledge, was broken by ignorance. When we knew all about the enemy we should be comfortable. We must take more pains in the service of news than any regular staff.

I was getting through my subject. The algebraical factor had been translated into terms of Arabia, and fitted like a glove. It promised victory. The biological factor had dictated to us a development of the tactical line most in accord with the genius of our tribesmen. There remained the psychological element to build up into an apt shape. I went to Xenophon and stole, to name it, his word *diathetics*, which had been the art of Cyrus before he struck.

Of this our 'propaganda' was the stained and ignoble offspring. It was the pathic, almost the ethical, in war. Some of it concerned the crowd, an adjustment of its spirit to the point where it became useful to exploit in action, and the pre-direction of this changing spirit to a certain end. Some of it concerned the individual, and then it became a rare art of human kindness, transcending, by purposed emotion, the gradual logical sequence of the mind. It was more subtle than tactics, and better worth doing, because it dealt with uncontrollables, with subjects incapable of direct command. It considered the capacity for mood of our men, their complexities and mutability, and the cultivation of whatever in them promised to profit our intention. We had to arrange their minds in order of battle just as carefully and as formally as other officers would arrange their bodies. And not only our own men's minds, though naturally they came first. We must also arrange the minds of the enemy, so far as we could reach them; then those other minds of the nation supporting us behind the firing line, since more than half the battle passed there in the back; then the minds of the enemy nation waiting the verdict; and of the neutrals looking on; circle beyond circle.

There were many humiliating material limits, but no moral impossibilities; so that the scope of our diathetical activities was unbounded. On it we should mainly depend for the means of victory on the Arab front: and the novelty of it was our advantage. The printing press, and each newly-discovered method of communication favoured the intellectual above the physical, civilization paying the mind always from the body's funds. We kindergarten soldiers were beginning our art of war in the atmosphere of the twentieth century, receiving our weapons without prejudice. To the regular officer, with the tradition of forty generations of service behind him, the antique arms were the most honoured. As we had seldom to concern ourselves with what our men did, but always with what they thought, the diathetic for us would be more than half the command. In Europe it was set a little aside, and entrusted to men outside the General Staff. In Asia the regular elements were so weak that irregulars could not let the metaphysical weapon rust unused.

Battles in Arabia were a mistake, since we profited in them only by the ammunition the enemy fired off. Napoleon had said it was rare to find generals willing to fight battles; but the curse of this war was that so few would do anything else. Saxe had told us that irrational battles were the refuges of fools: rather they seemed to me impositions on the side which believed itself weaker, hazards made unavoidable either by lack of land room or by the need to defend a material property dearer than the lives of soldiers. We had nothing material to lose, so our best line was to defend nothing and to shoot nothing. Our cards were

G*

speed and time, not hitting power. The invention of bully beef had profited us more than the invention of gunpowder, but gave us strategical, rather than tactical strength, since in Arabia range was more than force, space greater than the power of armies.

I had now been eight days lying in this remote tent, keeping my ideas general,* till my brain, sick of unsupported thinking, had to be dragged to its work by an effort of will, and went off into a doze whenever that effort was relaxed. The fever passed: my dysentery ceased; and with restored strength the present again became actual to me. Facts concrete and pertinent thrust themselves into my reveries; and my inconstant wit bore aside towards all these roads of escape. So I hurried into line my shadowy principles, to have them once precise before my power to evoke them faded.

It seemed to me proven that our rebellion had an unassailable base, guarded not only from attack, but from the fear of attack. It had a sophisticated alien enemy, disposed as an army of occupation in an area greater than could be dominated effectively from fortified posts. It had a friendly population, of which some two in the hundred were active, and the rest quietly sympathetic to the point of not betraying the movements of the minority. The active rebels had the virtues of secrecy and self-control, and the qualities of speed, endurance and independence of arteries of supply. They had technical equipment enough to paralyse the enemy's communications. A province would be won when we had taught the civilians in it to die for our ideal of freedom. The presence of the enemy was secondary. Final victory seemed certain, if the war lasted long enough for us to work it out.

---

* Not perhaps as successfully as here. I thought out my problems mainly in terms of Hejaz, illustrated by what I knew of its men and its geography. These would have been too long if written down; and the argument has been compressed into an abstract form in which it smells more of the lamp than of the field. All military writing does, worse luck.

CHAPTER XXXIV

OBVIOUSLY I was well again, and I remembered the reason of my journey to Wadi Ais. The Turks meant to march out of Medina, and Sir Archibald Murray wanted us to attack them in professional form. It was irksome that he should come butting into our show from Egypt, asking from us alien activities. Yet the British were the bigger; and the Arabs lived only by grace of their shadow. We were yoked to Sir Archibald Murray, and must work with him, to the point of sacrificing our non-essential interests for his, if they would not be reconciled. At the same time we could not possibly act alike. Feisal might be a free gas: Sir Archibald's army, probably the most cumbrous in the world, had to be laboriously pushed forward on its belly. It was ridiculous to suppose it could keep pace with ethical conceptions as nimble as the Arab Movement: doubtful even if it would understand them. However, perhaps by hindering the railway we could frighten the Turks off their plan to evacuate Medina, and give them reason to remain in the town on the defensive: a conclusion highly serviceable to both Arabs and English, though possibly neither would see it, yet.

Accordingly, I wandered into Abdulla's tent, announcing my complete recovery and an ambition to do something to the Hejaz railway. Here were men, guns, machine-guns, explosives and automatic mines: enough for a main effort. But Abdulla was apathetic. He wanted to talk about the Royal families of Europe, or the Battle of the Somme: the slow march of his own war bored him. However, Sherif Shakir, his cousin and second in command, was fired to enthusiasm, and secured us licence to do our worst. Shakir loved the Ateiba, and swore they were the best tribe on earth; so we settled to take mostly Ateiba with us. Then we thought we might have a mountain gun, one of the Egyptian Army Krupp veterans, which had been sent by Feisal to Abdulla from Wejh as a present.

Shakir promised to collect the force, and we agreed that I should go in front (gently, as befitted my weakness) and search for a target. The nearest and biggest was Aba el Naam Station. With me went Raho, Algerian officer in the French Army, and member of Bremond's mission, a very hard-working and honest fellow. Our guide was Mohammed el Kadhi, whose old father, Dakhil-Allah, hereditary lawman of the Juheina, had guided the Turks down to Yenbo last December. Mohammed was eighteen, solid and silent natured. Sherif Fauzan el Harith, the famous warrior who had captured Eshref at Janbila, escorted us, with about twenty Ateiba and five or six Juheina adventurers.

We left on March the twenty-sixth, while Sir Archibald Murray was attacking Gaza; and rode down Wadi Ais; but after three hours the heat proved too much for me, and we stopped by a great sidr tree (lote or ju-jube, but the fruit was scarce) and rested under it the midday hours. Sidr trees cast heavy shade: there was a cool east wind, and few flies. Wadi Ais was luxuriant with thorn trees and grass, and its air full of white butterflies and scents of wild flowers; so that we did not remount till late in the afternoon, and then did only a short march, leaving Wadi Ais by the right, after passing in an angle of the valley a ruined terrace and cistern. Once there had been villages in this part, with the underground waters carefully employed in their frequent gardens; but now it was waste.

The following morning we had two hours' rough riding around the spurs of Jebel Serd into Wadi Turaa, a historic valley, linked by an easy pass to Wadi Yenbo. We spent this midday also under a tree, near some Juheina tents, where Mohammed guested while we slept. Then we rode on rather crookedly for two more hours, and camped after dark. By ill luck an early spring scorpion stung me severely on the left hand while I lay down to sleep. The place swelled up; and my arm became stiff and sore.

At five next morning, after a long night, we restarted, and passed through the last hills, out into the Jurf, an undulating open space which ran up southward to Jebel Antar, a crater with a split and castellated top, making it a landmark. We turned half-right in the plain, to get under cover of the low hills which screened it from Wadi Hamdh, in whose bed the railway lay. Behind these hills we rode southward till opposite Aba el Naam. There we halted to camp, close to the enemy but quite in safety. The hill-top commanded them; and we climbed it before sunset for a first view of the station.

The hill was, perhaps, six hundred feet high and steep, and I made many stages of it, resting on my way up: but the sight from the top was good. The railway was some three miles off. The station had a pair of large, two-storied houses of basalt, a circular water-tower, and other buildings. There were bell-tents, huts and trenches, but no sign of guns. We could see about three hundred men in all.

We heard that the Turks patrolled their neighbourhood actively at night. A bad habit this: so we sent off two men to lie by each block-house, and fire a few shots after dark. The enemy, thinking it a prelude to attack, stood-to in their trenches all night, while we were comfortably sleeping; but the cold woke us early with a restless dawn wind blowing across the Jurf, and singing in the great trees round our camp. As we climbed to our observation point the sun conquered the clouds and an hour later it grew very hot.

We lay like lizards in the long grass round the stones of the foremost cairn upon the hill-top and saw the garrison parade. Three hundred and ninety-nine infantry, little toy men, ran about when the bugle sounded, and formed up in stiff lines below the black building till there was more bugling: then they scattered, and after a few minutes the smoke of cooking fires went up. A herd of sheep and goats in charge of a little ragged boy issued out towards us. Before he reached the foot of the hills there came a loud whistling down the valley from the north, and a tiny, picture-book train rolled slowly into view across the hollow sounding bridge and halted just outside the station, panting out white puffs of steam.

The shepherd lad held on steadily, driving his goats with shrill cries up our hill for the better pasture on the western side. We sent two Juheina down behind a ridge beyond sight of the enemy, and they ran from each side and caught him. The lad was of the outcast Heteym, pariahs of the desert, whose poor children were commonly sent on hire as shepherds to the tribes about them. This one cried continually, and made efforts to escape as often as he saw his goats straying uncared-for about the hill. In the end the men lost patience and tied him up roughly, when he screamed for terror that they would kill him.

Fauzan had great ado to make him quiet, and then questioned him about his Turkish masters. But all his thoughts were for the flock: his eyes followed them miserably while the tears made edged and crooked tracks down his dirty face.

Shepherds were a class apart. For the ordinary Arab the hearth was a university, about which their world passed and where they heard the best talk, the news of their tribe, its poems, histories, love tales, lawsuits and bargainings. By such constant sharing in the hearth councils they grew up masters of expression, dialecticians, orators, able to sit with dignity in any gathering and never at a loss for moving words. The shepherds missed the whole of this. From infancy they followed their calling, which took them in all seasons and weathers, day and night, into the hills and condemned them to loneliness and brute company. In the wilderness, among the dry bones of nature, they grew up natural, knowing nothing of man and his affairs; hardly sane in ordinary talk; but very wise in plants, wild animals and the habits of their own goats and sheep, whose milk was their chief sustenance. With manhood they became sullen, while a few turned dangerously savage, more animal than man, haunting the flocks, and finding the satisfaction of their adult appetites in them, to the exclusion of more licit affections.

For hours after the shepherd had been suppressed only the sun moved in our view. As it climbed we shifted our cloaks to filter its harshness, and basked in luxurious warmth. The restful hill-top gave me back something of the sense-interests which I had lost since I had been ill. I was able to note once more the typical hill scenery, with its hard stone crests, its sides of bare rock, and lower slopes of loose sliding screes, packed, as the base was approached, solidly with a thin dry soil. The stone itself was glistening, yellow, sunburned stuff; metallic in ring, and brittle; splitting red or green or brown as the case might be. From every soft place sprouted thorn-bushes; and there was frequent grass, usually growing from one root in a dozen stout blades, knee-high and straw-coloured: the heads were empty ears between many-feathered arrows of silvery down. With these, and with a shorter grass, whose bottle-brush heads of pearly grey reached only to the ankle, the hill-sides were furred white and bowed themselves lowly towards us with each puff of the casual wind.

Verdure it was not, but excellent pasturage; and in the valleys were bigger tufts of grass, coarse, waist-high and bright green when fresh though they soon faded to the burned yellow of ordinary life. They grew thickly in all the beds of water-ribbed sand and shingle, between the occasional thorn trees, some of which stood forty feet in height. The sidr trees, with their dry, sugary fruit, were rare. But bushes of browned tamarisk, tall broom, other varieties of coarse grass, some flowers, and everything which had thorns, flourished about our camp, and made it a rich sample of the vegetation of the Hejaz highlands. Only one of the plants profited ourselves, and that was the hemeid: a sorrel with fleshy heart-shaped leaves, whose pleasant acidity stayed our thirst.

At dusk we climbed down again with the goat-herd prisoner, and what we could gather of his flock. Our main body would come this night, so that Fauzan and I wandered out across the darkling plain till we found a pleasant gun-position in some low ridges not two thousand yards from the station. On our return, very tired, fires were burning among the trees. Shakir had just arrived, and his men and ours were roasting goat-flesh contentedly. The shepherd was tied up behind my sleeping place, because he had gone frantic when his charges were unlawfully slaughtered. He refused to taste the supper; and we only forced bread and rice into him by the threat of dire punishment if he insulted our hospitality. They tried to convince him that we should take the station next day and kill his masters; but he would not be comforted, and afterwards, for fear lest he escape, had to be lashed to his tree again.

After supper Shakir told me that he had brought only three hundred men instead of the agreed eight or nine hundred. However, it was his war, and therefore his tune, so we hastily modified the plans. We would not take the station; we would frighten it by a frontal artillery attack, while we mined the railway to the north and south, in the hope of trapping that halted train. Accordingly we chose a party of Garland-trained dynamiters who should blow up something north of the bridge at dawn, to seal that direction; while I went off with high explosive and a machine-gun with its crew to lay a mine to the south of the station, the probable direction from which the Turks would seek or send help, in their emergency.

Mohammed el Khadi guided us to a deserted bit of line just before midnight. I dismounted and fingered its thrilling rails for the first time during the war. Then, in an hour's busy work, we laid the mine, which was a trigger action to fire into twenty pounds of blasting gelatine when the weight of the locomotive overhead deflected the metals. Afterwards we posted the machine-gunners in a little bush-screened watercourse, four hundred yards from and fully commanding the spot where we hoped the train would be derailed. They were to hide there; while we went on to cut the telegraph, that isolation might persuade Aba el Naam to send their train for reinforcements, as our main attack developed.

So we rode another half-hour, and then turned in to the line, and again were fortunate to strike an unoccupied place. Unhappily the four remaining Juheina proved unable to climb a telegraph pole, and I had to struggle up it myself. It was all I could do, after my illness; and when the third wire was cut the flimsy pole shook so that I lost grip, and came slipping down the sixteen feet upon the stout shoulders of Mohammed, who ran in to break my fall, and nearly got broken himself. We took a few minutes to breathe, but afterwards were able to regain our camels. Eventually we arrived in camp just as the others had saddled up to go forward.

Our mine-laying had taken four hours longer than we had planned and the delay put us in the dilemma either of getting no rest, or of letting the main body march without us. Finally by Shakir's will we let them go, and fell down under our trees for an hour's sleep, without which I felt I should collapse utterly. The time was just before day-break, an hour when the uneasiness of the air affected trees and animals, and made even men-sleepers turn over sighingly. Mohammed, who wanted to see the fight, awoke. To get me up he came over and cried the morning prayer-call in my ear, the raucous voice sounding battle, murder, and sudden death across my dreams. I sat up and rubbed the sand out of red-rimmed aching eyes, as we disputed vehemently of prayer and sleep. He pleaded that there was not a battle every day, and showed the cuts and bruises sustained during the night in helping me. By my blackness and blueness I could feel for him, and we rode off to catch the army, after loosing the still unhappy shepherd boy, with advice to wait for our return.

A band of trodden untidiness in a sweep of gleaming water-rounded sand showed us the way, and we arrived just as the guns opened fire. They did excellently, and crashed in all the top of one building, damaged the second, hit the pump-room, and holed the water-tank. One lucky shell caught the front waggon of the train in the siding, and it took fire furiously. This alarmed the locomotive, which uncoupled and went off southward. We watched her hungrily as she approached our mine, and when she was on it there came a soft cloud of dust and a report and she stood still. The damage was to the front part, as she was reversed and the charge had exploded late; but, while the drivers got out, and jacked up the front wheels and tinkered at them, we waited and waited in vain for the machine-gun to open fire. Later we learned that the gunners, afraid of their loneliness, had packed up and marched to join us when we began shooting. Half an hour after, the repaired engine went away towards Jebel Antar, going at a foot pace and clanking loudly; but going none the less.

Our Arabs worked in towards the station, under cover of the bombardment, while we gnashed our teeth at the machine-gunners. Smoke clouds from the fired trucks screened the Arab advance which wiped out one enemy outpost, and captured another. The Turks withdrew their surviving detachments to the main position, and waited rigorously in their trenches for the assault, which they were in no better spirit to repel than we were to deliver. With our advantages in ground the place would have been a gift to us, if only we had had some of Feisal's men to charge home.

Meanwhile the wood, tents and trucks in the station were burning, and the smoke was too thick for us to shoot, so we broke off the action. We had taken thirty prisoners, a mare, two camels and some more sheep; and had killed and wounded seventy of the garrison, at a cost to ourselves of one man slightly hurt. Traffic was held up for three days of repair and investigation. So we did not wholly fail.

CHAPTER XXXV

WE left two parties in the neighbourhood to damage the line on the next day and the next, while we rode to Abdullah's camp on April the first. Shakir, splendid in habit, held a grand parade on entry, and had thousands of joy-shots fired in honour of his partial victory. The easy-going camp made carnival.

In the evening I went wandering in the thorn-grove behind the tents, till I began to see through the thick branches a wild light, from bursts of raw flame; and across the flame and smoke came the rhythm of drums, in tune with hand-clapping, and the deep roar of a tribal chorus. I crept up quietly, and saw an immense fire, ringed by hundreds of Ataiba sitting on the ground one by the other, gazing intently on Shakir, who, upright and alone in their midst, performed the dance of their song. He had put off his cloak, and wore only his white head-veil and white robes: the powerful firelight was reflected by these and by his pale, ravaged face. As he sang he threw back his head, and at the close of each phrase raised his hands, to let the full sleeves run back upon his shoulders, while he waved his bare arms weirdly. The tribe around him beat time with their hands, or bayed out the refrains at his nod. The grove of trees where I stood outside the circle of light was thronged with Arabs of stranger tribes, whispering, and watching the Atban.

In the morning we determined on another visit to the line, for fuller trial of the automatic mine-action which had half-failed at Aba el Naam. Old Dakhil-Allah said that he would come with me himself on this trip, the project of looting a train had tempted him. With us went some forty of the Juheina, who seemed to me stouter men than the high-bred Ateiba. However, one of the chiefs of the Ataiba, Sultan el Abbud, a boon friend of Abdulla and Shakir, refused to be left behind. This good-tempered but hare-brained fellow, sheikh of a poor section of the tribe, had had more horses killed under him in battle than any other Ateibi warrior. He was about twenty-six and a great rider; full of quips and fond of practical jokes, very noisy: tall and strong, with a big, square head, wrinkled forehead, and deep-set bright eyes. A young moustache and beard hid his ruthless jaw and the wide, straight mouth, with white teeth gleaming and locked like a wolf's.

We took a machine-gun and its soldier crew of thirteen with us, to settle our train when caught. Shakir, with his grave courtesy to the Emir's guest, set us on our road for the first half-hour. This time we kept to the Wadi Ais almost to its junction with Hamdh, finding it very green and full of grazing, since it had flooded twice already in this winter. At last we bore off to the right over a ditch on to a flat, and there slept in the sand, rather distressed by a shower of rain which sent little rills over the ground about midnight: but the next morning was bright and hot, and we rode into the huge plain where the three great valleys, Tubja, Ais and Jizil, flowed into and became one with Hamdh. The course of the main stream was overgrown by asla wood, just as at Abu Zereibat, with the same leprous bed of hummocky sand-blisters: but the thicket was only two hundred yards broad, and beyond it the plain with its grained intricacy of shallow torrent-beds stretched for yet further miles. At noon we halted by a place like a wilderness garden, waist deep in juicy grass and flowers, upon which our happy camels gorged themselves for an hour and then sat down, full and astonished.

The day seemed to be hotter and hotter: the sun drew close, and scorched us without intervening air. The clean, sandy soil was so baked that my bare feet could not endure it, and I had to walk in sandals, to the amusement of the Juheina, whose thick soles were proof even against slow fire. As the afternoon passed on the light became dim, but the heat steadily increased with an oppression and sultriness which took me by surprise. I kept turning my head to see if some mass was not just behind me, shutting off the air.

There had been long rolls of thunder all morning in the hills, and the two peaks, Serd and Jasim, were wrapped in folds of dark blue and yellow vapour, which looked motionless and substantial. At last I saw that part of the yellow cloud off Serd was coming slowly against the wind in our direction raising scores of dust devils before its feet.

The cloud was nearly as high as the hill. While it approached, two dust-spouts, tight and symmetrical chimneys, advanced, one on the right and one on the left of its front. Dakhil-Allah responsibly looked ahead and to each side for shelter, but saw none. He warned me that the storm would be heavy.

When it got near, the wind, which had been scorching our faces with its hot breathlessness, changed suddenly; and, after waiting a moment, blew bitter cold and damp upon our backs. It also increased greatly in violence, and at the same time the sun disappeared, blotted out by thick rags of yellow air over our heads. We stood in a horrible light, ochreous and fitful. The brown wall of cloud from the hills was now very near, rushing changelessly upon us with a loud grinding sound. Three minutes later it struck, wrapping about us a blanket of dust and stinging grains of sand, twisting and turning in violent eddies, and yet advancing eastward at the speed of a strong gale.

We had put our camels' backs to the storm, to march before it: but these internal whirling winds tore our tightly-held cloaks from our hands, filled our eyes, and robbed us of all sense of direction by turning our camels right or left from their course. Sometimes they were blown completely round: once we clashed helplessly together in a vortex, while large bushes, tufts of grass, and even a small tree were torn up by the roots in dense waves of soil about them, and driven against us, or blown over our heads with dangerous force. We never were blinded — it was always possible to see for seven or eight feet to each side — but it was risky to look out, as, in addition to the certain sand-blast, we never knew if we should not meet a flying tree, a rush of pebbles, or a spout of grass-laden dust.

This storm lasted for eighteen minutes, and then leaped forward from us as suddenly as it had come. Our party was scattered over a square mile or more, and before we could rally, while we, our clothes and our camels were yet smothered in dust, yellow and heavy with it from head to foot, down burst torrents of thick rain and muddied us to the skin. The valley began to run in plashes of water, and Dakhil-Allah urged us across it quickly. The wind chopped once more, this time to the north, and the rain came driving before it in harsh sheets of spray. It beat through our woollen cloaks in a moment, and moulded them and our shirts to our bodies, and chilled us to the bone.

We reached the hill-barrier in mid-afternoon, but found the valley bare and shelterless, colder than ever. After riding up it for three or four miles we halted, and climbed a great crag to see the railway which, they said, lay just beyond. On the height the wind was so terrible that we could not cling to the wet slippery rocks against the slapping and bellying of our cloaks and skirts. I took mine off, and climbed the rest of the way half-naked, more easily, and hardly colder than before. But the effort proved useless, the air being too thick for observation. So I worked down, cut and bruised, to the others; and dressed numbly. On our way back we suffered the only casualty of this trip. Sultan had insisted on coming with us, and his Ateibi servant, who must follow him though he had no head for heights, slipped in one bad place with a fall of forty feet to the stones, and plunged down headlong.

When we got back my hands and feet were too broken to serve me longer, and I lay down and shivered for an hour or so while the others buried the dead man in a side valley. On their return they met suddenly an unknown rider on a camel, crossing their track. He fired at them. They fired back, snap-shooting through the rain, and the evening swallowed him. This was disquieting, for surprise was our main ally, and we could only hope that he would not return to warn the Turks that there were raiders in the neighbourhood.

After the heavy camels with the explosives caught us, we mounted again to get closer to the line; but we had no more than started when brazenly down the visible wind in the misted valley came the food-call of Turkish bugles. Dakhil-Allah thrust his ear forward in the direction of the sound, and understood that over there lay Madahrij, the small station below which we meant to operate. So we steered on the hateful noise, hateful because it spoke of supper and of tents, whereas we were shelterless, and on such a night could not hope to make ourselves a fire and bake bread from the flour and water in our saddle-bags, and consequently must go hungry.

We did not reach the railway till after ten o'clock at night, in conditions of invisibility which made it futile to choose a machine-gun position. At random I pitched upon kilometre 1,121 from Damascus for the mine. It was a complicated mine, with a central trigger to fire simultaneous charges thirty yards apart: and we hoped in this way to get the locomotive whether it was going north or south. Burying the mine took four hours, for the rain had caked the surface and rotted it. Our feet made huge tracks on the flat and on the bank, as though a school of elephants had been dancing there. To hide these marks was out of the question, so we did the other thing, trampling about for hundreds of yards, even bringing up our camels to help, until it looked as though half an army had crossed the valley, and the mine-place was no better and no worse than the rest. Then we went back a safe distance behind some miserable mounds, and cowered down in the open, waiting for day. The cold was intense. Our teeth chattered, and we trembled and hissed involuntarily, while our hands drew in like claws.

At dawn the clouds had disappeared, and a red sun promised, over the very fine broken hills beyond the railway. Old Dakhil-Allah, our active guide and leader in the night, now took general charge, and sent us out singly and in pairs to all the approaches of our hiding-place. He himself crawled up the ridge before us to watch events upon the railway through his glasses. I was praying that there might be no events till the sun had gained power and warmed me, for the shivering fit still jerked me about. However, soon the sun was up and unveiled, and things improved. My clothes were drying. By noon it was nearly as hot as the day before, and we were gasping for shade, and thicker clothes, against the sun.

First of all, though, at six in the morning, Dakhil-Allah reported a trolley, which came from the south, and passed over the mine harmlessly — to our satisfaction, for we had not laid a beautiful compound charge for just four men and a sergeant. Then sixty men sallied out from Madahrij. This disturbed us till we saw that they were to replace five telegraph poles blown down by the storm of the afternoon before. Then at seven-thirty a patrol of eleven men went down the line: two inspecting each rail minutely, three marching each side of the bank looking for cross-tracks, and one, presumably the N.C.O., walking grandly along the metals with nothing to do.

However, to-day they did find something, when they crossed our footprints about kilometre 1,121. They concentrated there upon the permanent way, stared at it, stamped, wandered up and down, scratched the ballast; and thought exhaustively. The time of their search passed slowly for us: but the mine was well hidden, so that eventually they wandered on contentedly towards the south, where they met the Hedia patrol, and both parties sat together in the cool shade of a bridge-arch, and rested after their labours. Meanwhile the train, a heavy train, came along from the south. Nine of its laden trucks held women and children from Medina, civil refugees being deported to Syria, with their household stuff. It ran over the charges without explosion. As artist I was furious; as commander deeply relieved: women and children were not proper spoil.

The Juheina raced to the crest where Dakhil-Allah and myself lay hidden, when they heard the train coming, to see it blown in pieces. Our stone headwork had been built for two, so that the hill-top, a bald cone conspicuously opposite the working party, became suddenly and visibly populous. This was too much for the nerves of the Turks, who fled back into Madahrij, and thence, at about five thousand yards, opened a brisk rifle fire. They must also have telephoned to Hedia, which soon came to life: but since the nearest outpost on that side was about six miles off, its garrisons held their fire, and contented themselves with selections on the bugle, played all day. The distance made it grave and beautiful.

Even the rifle shooting did us no harm; but the disclosure of ourselves was unfortunate. At Madahrij were two hundred men and at Hedia eleven hundred, and our retreat was by the plain of Hamdh on which Hedia stood. Their mounted troops might sally out and cut our rear. The Juheina had good camels, and so were safe; but the machine-gun was a captured German sledge-Maxim: a heavy load for its tiny mule. The servers were on foot, or on other mules: their top speed would be only six miles an hour, and their fighting value, with a single gun, not high. So after a council of war we rode back with them half-way through the hills, and there dismissed them, with fifteen Juheina, towards Wadi Ais.

This made us mobile, and Dakhil-Allah, Sultan, Mohammed and I rode back with the rest of our party for another look at the line. The sunlight was now terrific, with faint gusts of scorching heat blowing up at us out of the south. We took refuge about ten o'clock under some spacious trees, where we baked bread and lunched, in nice view of the line, and shaded from the worst of the sun. About us, over the gravel, circles of pale shadow from the crisping leaves ran to and fro, like grey, indeterminate bugs, as the slender branches dipped reluctantly in the wind. Our picnic annoyed the Turks, who shot or trumpeted at us incessantly through the middle day and till evening, while we slept in turn.

About five they grew quiet, and we mounted and rode slowly across the open valley towards the railway. Madahrij revived in a paroxysm of fire, and all the trumpets of Hedia blared again. The monkey-pleasure of pulling large and impressive legs was upon us. So when we reached the line we made our camels kneel down beside it, and, led by Dakhil-Allah as Imam, performed a sunset prayer quietly between the rails. It was probably the first prayer of the Juheina for a year or so, and I was a novice, but from a distance we passed muster, and the Turks stopped shooting in bewilderment. This was the first and last time I ever prayed in Arabia as a Moslem.

After the prayer it was still much too light to hide our actions: so we sat round on the embankment smoking, till dusk, when I tried to go off by myself and dig up the mine, to learn, for service on the next occasion, why it had failed. However, the Juheina were as interested in that as I. Along they came in a swarm and clustered over the metals during the search. They brought my heart into my throat, for it took me an hour to find just where the mine was hidden. Laying a Garland mine was shaky work, but scrabbling in pitch darkness up and down a hundred yards of railway, feeling for a hair-trigger buried in the ballast, seemed, at the time, an almost uninsurable occupation. The two charges connected with it were so powerful that they would have rooted out seventy yards of track; and I saw visions of suddenly blowing up, not only myself, but my whole force, every moment. To be sure, such a feat would have properly completed the bewilderment of the Turks!

At last I found it, and ascertained by touch that the lock had sunk one sixteenth of an inch, due to bad setting by myself or because the ground had subsided after the rain. I firmed it into its place. Then, to explain ourselves plausibly to the enemy, we began blowing up things to the north of the mine. We found a little four-arch bridge and put it into the air. Afterwards we turned to rails and cut about two hundred: and while the men were laying and lighting charges I taught Mohammed to climb a splintery pole; together we cut the wires, and with their purchase dragged down other poles. All was done at speed, for we feared lest Turks come after us: and when our explosive work was finished we ran back like hares to our camels, mounted them, and trotted without interruption down the windy valley once more to the plain of Hamdh.

There we were in safety, but old Dakhil-Allah was too pleased with the mess we had made of the line to go soberly. When we were on the sandy flat he beat up his camel into a canter, and we pounded madly after him through the colourless moonlight. The going was perfect, and we never drew rein for three hours, till we over-rode our machine-gun and its escort camping on the road home. The soldiers heard our rout yelling through the night, thought us enemies of sorts, and let fly at us with their Maxim: but it jammed after half a belt, and they, being tailors from Mecca, were unhandy with it. So no one was hurt, and we captured them mirthfully.

In the morning we slept lazily long, and breakfasted at Rubiaan, the first well in Wadi Ais. Afterwards we were smoking and talking, about to bring in the camels, when suddenly we felt the distant shock of a great explosion behind us on the railway. We wondered if the mine had been discovered or had done its duty. Two scouts had been left to report, and we rode slowly; for them, and because the rain two days ago had brought down Wadi Ais once more in flood, and its bed was all flecked over with shallow pools of soft, grey water, between banks of silvery mud, which the current had rippled into fish-scales. The warmth of the sun made the surface like fine glue, on which our helpless camels sprawled comically, or went down with a force and complete-ness surprising in such dignified beasts. Their tempers were roughened each time by our fit of mirth.

The sunlight, the easy march and the expectation of the scouts' news made everything gay, and we developed social virtues: but our limbs, stiff from the exertions of yesterday, and our abundant food, deter-mined us to fall short of Abu Markha for the night. So, near sunset, we chose a dry terrace in the valley to sleep upon. I rode up it first and turned and looked at the men reined in below me in a group, upon their bay camels like copper statues in the fierce light of the setting sun; they seemed to be burning with an inward flame.

Before bread was baked the scouts arrived, to tell us that at dawn the Turks had been busy round our damages; and a little later a locomotive with tracks of rails, and a crowded labour gang on top, had come up from Hedia, and had exploded the mine fore and aft of its wheels. This was everything we had hoped, and we rode back to Abdulla's camp on a morning of perfect springtime, in a singing company. We had proved that a well-laid mine would fire; and that a well-laid mine was difficult even for its maker to discover. These points were of importance; for Newcombe, Garland and Hornby were now out upon the railway, harrying it: and mines were the best weapon yet discovered to make the regular working of their trains costly and uncertain for our Turkish enemy.

CHAPTER XXXVI

DESPITE his kindness and charm, I could not like Abdullah or his camp: perhaps because I was not sociable, and these people had no personal solitude: perhaps because their good humour showed me the futility of my more than Palomides' pains, not merely to seem better than myself, but to make others better. Whereas nothing was futile in the atmosphere of higher thinking and responsibility which ruled at Feisal's. Abdulla passed his merry day in the big cool tent accessible only to friends, limiting suppliants or new adherents or the hearing of disputes to one public session in the afternoon. For the rest he read the papers, ate carefully, slept. Especially he played games, either chess with his staff or practical jokes with Mohammed Hassan. Mohammed, nominally Muedhdhin, was really court fool. A tiresome old fool I found him, as my illness left me less even than usual in jesting mood.

Abdulla and his friends, Shakir, Fauzan, and the two sons of Hamza among the Sherifs, with Sultan el Abbud and Hoshan, from the Ateiba, and ibn Mesfer, the guest-master, would spend much of the day and all the evening hours tormenting Mohammed Hassan. They stabbed him with thorns, stoned him, dropped sun-heated pebbles down his back, set him on fire. Sometimes the jest would be elaborate, as when they laid a powder trail under the rugs, and lured Mohammed Hassan to sit on its end. Once Abdulla shot a coffee-pot off his head thrice from twenty yards, and then rewarded his long-suffering servility with three months' pay.

Abdulla would sometimes ride a little, or shoot a little, and return exhausted to his tent for massage; and afterwards reciters would be introduced to soothe his aching head. He was fond of Arabic verses and exceptionally well read. The local poets found him a profitable audience. He was also interested in history and letters, and would have grammatical disputations in his tent and adjudge money prizes.

He affected to have no care for the Hejaz situation, regarding the autonomy of the Arabs as assured by the promises of Great Britain to his father, and leaning at ease against this prop. I longed to tell him that the half-witted old man had obtained from us no concrete or unqualified undertaking of any sort, and that their ship might founder on the bar of his political stupidity; but that would have been to give away my English masters, and the mental tug of war between honesty and loyalty, after swaying a while, settled again expediently into deadlock.

Abdulla professed great interest in the war in Europe, and studied it closely in the Press. He was also acquainted with Western politics, and had learned by rote the courts and ministries of Europe, even to the name of the Swiss President. I remarked again how much the comfortable circumstance that we still had a King made for the reputation of England in this world of Asia. Ancient and artificial societies like this of the Sherifs and feudal chieftains of Arabia found a sense of honourable security when dealing with us in such proof that the highest place in our state was not a prize for merit or ambition.

Time slowly depressed my first, favourable, opinion of Abdulla's character. His constant ailments, which once aroused compassion, became fitter for contempt when their causes were apparent in laziness and self-indulgence, and when he was seen to cherish them as occupations of his too-great leisure. His casual attractive fits of arbitrariness now seemed feeble tyranny disguised as whims; his friendliness became caprice; his good humour love of pleasure. The leaven of insincerity worked through all the fibres of his being. Even his simplicity appeared false upon experience; and inherited religious prejudice was allowed rule over the keenness of his mind because it was less trouble to him than uncharted thought. His brain often betrayed its intricate pattern, disclosing idea twisted tightly over idea into a strong cord of design; and thus his indolence marred his scheming, too. The webs were constantly unravelling through his carelessness in leaving them unfinished. Yet they never separated into straight desires, or grew into effective desires. Always he watched out of the corner of his bland and open eye our returns to his innocent-sounding questions, reading an insect-subtlety of significant meaning into every hesitation or uncertainty or honest mistake.

One day I entered to find him sitting upright and wide-eyed with a spot of red in either cheek. Sergeant Prost, his old tutor, had just come from Colonel Bremond, innocent bearer of a letter which pointed out how the British were wrapping up the Arabs on all sides — at Aden, at Gaza, at Bagdad — and hoped that Abdulla realized his situation. He asked hotly what I thought of it. In answer I fell back on artifice, and replied in a pretty phrase that I hoped he would suspect our honesty when he found us backbiting our allies in private letters. The delicately poisoned Arabic pleased him, and he paid us the edged compliment of saying that he knew we were sincere, since otherwise we would not be represented at Jeddah by Colonel Wilson. There, characteristically, his subtlety hanged itself, not perceiving the double subtlety which negatived him. He did not understand that honesty might be the best-paying cat's paw of rogues, and Wilson, too, downright readily or quickly to suspect evil in the dignitaries above him.

Wilson never told even a half-truth. If instructed to inform the King diplomatically that the subsidy of the month could not at present be increased, he would ring up Mecca and say 'Lord, Lord, there is no more money'. As for lying, he was not merely incapable of it, but also shrewd enough to know that it was the worst gambit against players whose whole life had passed in a mist of deceits, and whose perceptions were of the finest. The Arab leaders showed a completeness of instinct, a reliance upon intuition, the unperceived foreknown, which left our centrifugal minds gasping. Like women, they understood and judged quickly, effortlessly, unreasonably. It almost seemed as though the Oriental exclusion of woman from politics had conferred her particular gifts upon the men. Some of the speed and secrecy of our victory, and its regularity, might perhaps be ascribed to this double endowment's offsetting and emphasizing the rare feature that from end to end of it there was nothing female in the Arab movement, but the camels.

The outstanding figure of Abdulla's entourage was Sherif Shakir, a man of twenty-nine, and companion since boyhood of the four Emirs. His mother was Circassian, as had been his grandmother. From them he obtained his fair complexion; but the flesh of his face was torn away by smallpox. From its white ruin two restless eyes looked out, very bright and big; for the faintness of his eyelashes and eyebrows made his stare directly disconcerting. His figure was tall, slim, almost boyish from the continual athletic activity of the man. His sharp, decided, but pleasant voice frayed out if he shouted. His manner while delightfully frank, was abrupt, indeed imperious; with a humour as cracked as his cackling laugh.

This bursting freedom of speech seemed to respect nothing on earth except King Hussein: towards himself he exacted deference, more so than did Abdulla, who was always playing tricks with his companions, the bevy of silk-clad fellows who came about him when he would be easy. Shakir joined wildly in the sport, but would smartingly punish a liberty. He dressed simply, but very cleanly, and, like Abdulla, spent public hours with toothpick and toothstick. He took no interest in books and never wearied his head with meditation, but was intelligent and interesting in talk. He was devout, but hated Mecca, and played backgammon while Abdulla read the Koran. Yet by fits he would pray interminably.

In war he was the man at arms. His feats made him the darling of the tribes. He, in turn, described himself as a Bedawi, and an Ateibi and imitated them. He wore his black hair in plaits down each side of his face, and kept it glossy with butter, and strong by frequent washings in camel urine. He encouraged nits, in deference to the Beduin proverb that a deserted head showed an ungenerous mind: and wore the *brîm*, a plaited girdle of thin leathern thongs wrapped three or four times round the loins to confine and support the belly. He owned splendid horses and camels: was considered the finest rider in Arabia: ready for a match with anyone.

Shakir gave me the sense that he preferred a fit of energy to sustained effort: but there was balance and shrewdness behind his mad manner. Sherif Hussein had used him on embassies to Cairo before the war, to arrange private business with the Khedive of Egypt. The Beduin figure must have looked strange in the stucco splendour of the Abdin. Abdulla had unlimited admiration for Shakir and tried to see the world with his eyes of gay carelessness. Between them they seriously complicated my mission to Wadi Ais.

CHAPTER XXXVII

OF the tactical situation, Abdulla made very little, pretending pettishly that it was Feisal's business. He had come to Wadi Ais to please his younger brother, and there he would stay. He would not go on raids himself, and hardly encouraged those who did. I detected jealousy of Feisal in this, as if he wished ostentatiously to neglect military operations to prevent unbecoming comparison with his brother's performance. Had Shakir not helped me in the first instance, I might have had delay and difficulty in getting started, though Abdulla would have ceded in time and graciously permitted anything not calling directly upon his own energies. However, there were now two parties on the railway, with reliefs enough to do a demolition of some sort every day or so. Much less interference than this would suffice to wreck the working of trains, and by making the maintenance of the Turkish garrison at Medina just a shade less difficult than its evacuation would serve the interests of British and Arab alike. So I judged my work in Wadi Ais sufficiently done, and well done.

I longed to get north again quit of this relaxing camp. Abdulla might let me do all I wanted, but would do nothing of his own: whereas for me the best value of the revolt lay in the things which the Arabs attempted without our aid. Feisal was the working enthusiast with the one idea of making his ancient race justify its renown by winning freedom with its own hands. His lieutenants Nasir or Sharraf or Ali ibn el Hussein seconded his plans with head and heart, so that my part became only synthetic. I combined their loose showers of sparks into a firm flame: transformed their series of unrelated incidents into a conscious operation.

We left on the morning of April the tenth, after pleasant farewells from Abdulla. My three Ageyl were again with me; and Arslan, the little Syrian Punch-figure, very conscious of Arab dress, and of the droll outlook and manners of all Bedouins. He rode disgracefully and endured sorrow the whole way at the uneasy steps of his camels: but he salved his self-respect by pointing out that in Damascus no decent man would ride a camel, and his humour by showing that in Arabia no one but a Damascene would ride so bad a camel as his. Mohammed el Kadhi was our guide, with six Juheina.

We marched up Wadi Tleih as we had come, but branched off to the right, avoiding the lava. We had brought no food, so stopped at some tents for hospitality of their rice and milk. This spring-time in the hills was the time of plenty for the Arabs, whose tents were full of sheep-milk and goat-milk and camel-milk, with everyone well fed and well looking. Afterwards we rode, in weather like a summer's day in England, for five hours down a narrow, flood-swept valley, Wadi Osman, which turned and twisted in the hills but gave an easy road. The last part of the march was after dark, and when we stopped, Arslan was missing. We fired volleys and lit fires hoping he would come upon us; but till dawn there was no sign, and the Juheina ran back and forward in doubting search. However, he was only a mile behind, fast asleep under a tree.

A short hour later we stopped at the tents of a wife of Dakhil-Allah, for a meal, Mohammed allowed himself a bath, a fresh braiding of his luxuriant hair, and clean clothes. They took very long about the food, and it was not till near noon that at last it came: a great bowl of saffron-rice, with a broken lamb littered over it. Mohammed, who felt it his duty in my honour to be dainty in service, arrested the main dish, and took from it the fill of a small copper basin for him and me. Then he waved the rest of the camp on to the large supply. Mohammed's mother knew herself old enough to be curious about me. She questioned me about the women of the tribe of Christians and their way of life, marvelling at my white skin, and the horrible blue eyes which looked, she said, like the sky shining through the eye-sockets of an empty skull.

Wadi Osman to-day was less irregular in course, and broadened slowly. After two hours and a half it twisted suddenly to the right through a gap, and we found ourselves in Hamdh, in a narrow, cliff-walled gorge. As usual the edges of the bed of hard sand were bare; and the middle bristled with hamdh-asla trees, in grey, salty, bulging scabs. Before us were flood-pools of sweet water, the largest of them nearly three hundred feet long, and sharply deep. Its narrow bed was cut into the

light impervious clay. Mohammed said its water would remain till the year's end, but would soon turn salt and useless.

After drinks we bathed in it, and found it full of little silver fish like sardines: all ravenous. We loitered after bathing, prolonging our bodily pleasure; and remounting in the dark, rode for six miles, till sleepy. Then we turned away to higher ground for the night's camp. Wadi Hamdh differed from the other wild valleys of Hejaz, in its chill air. This was, of course, most obvious at night, when a white mist, glazing the valley with a salt sweat, lifted itself some feet up and stood over it motionless. But even by day, and in sunshine the Hamdh felt damp and raw and unnatural.

Next morning we started early and passed large pools in the valley; but only a few were fit to drink: the rest had gone green and brackish with the little white fish floating, dead and pickled, in them. Afterwards we crossed the bed, and struck northward over the plain of Ugila, where Ross, our flight commander from Wejh, had lately made an aerodrome. Arab guards were sitting by his petrol, and we breakfasted from them, and afterwards went along Wadi Methar to a shady tree, where we slept four hours.

In the afternoon everyone was fresh, and the Juheina began to match their camels against one another. At first it was two and two, but the others joined, till they were six abreast. The road was bad, and finally, one lad cantered his animal into a heap of stones. She slipped, so that he crashed off and broke an arm. It was a misfortune: but Mohammed coolly tied him up with rags and camel-girths, and left him at ease under a tree to rest a little before riding back to Ugila for the night. The Arabs were casual about broken bones. In a tent at Wadi Ais I had seen a youth whose forearm had set crookedly; realizing this, he had dug into himself with a dagger till he had bared the bone, re-broken it, and set it straight; and there he lay, philosophically enduring the flies, with his left forearm huge under healing mosses and clay, waiting for it to be well.

In the morning we pushed on to Khauthila, a well, where we watered the camels. The water was impure and purged them. We rode again in the evening for another eight miles, intending to race straight through to Wejh in a long last day. So we got up soon after midnight,

H

and before daylight were coming down the long slope from Raal into the plain, which extended across the mouths of Hamdh into the sea. The ground was scarred with motor tracks, exciting a lively ambition in the Juheina to hurry on and see the new wonders of Feisal's army. Fired by this, we did a straight march of eight hours, unusually long for these Hejaz Bedouin.

We were then reasonably tired, both men and camels, since we had had no food after breakfast the day before. Therefore it seemed fit to the boy Mohammed to run races. He jumped from his camel, took off his clothes, and challenged us to race to the clump of thorns up the slope in front, for a pound English. Everybody took the offer, and the camels set off in a mob. The distance, about three-quarters of a mile, uphill, over heavy sand, proved probably more than Mohammed had bargained for. However, he showed surprising strength and won, though by inches: then he promptly collapsed, bleeding from mouth and nose. Some of our camels were good, and they went their fastest when pitted against one another.

The air here was very hot and heavy for natives of the hills, and I feared there might be consequences of Mohammed's exhaustion: but after we had rested an hour and made him a cup of coffee he got going again and did the six remaining hours into Wejh as cheerfully as ever; continuing to play the little pranks which had brightened our long march from Abu Markha. If one man rode quietly behind another's camel, poked his stick suddenly up its rump, and screeched, it mistook him for an excited male, and plunged off at a mad gallop, very disconcerting to the rider. A second good game was to cannon one galloping camel with another, and crash it into a near tree. Either the tree went down (valley trees in the light Hejaz soil were notably unstable things) or the rider was scratched and torn; or, best of all, he was swept quite out of his saddle, and left impaled on a thorny branch, if not dropped violently to the ground. This counted as a bull, and was very popular with everyone but him.

The Bedu were odd people. For an Englishman, sojourning with them was unsatisfactory unless he had patience wide and deep as the sea. They were absolute slaves of their appetite, with no stamina of mind, drunkards for coffee, milk or water, gluttons for stewed meat, shameless beggars of tobacco. They dreamed for weeks before and after their rare sexual exercises, and spent the intervening days titillating themselves and their hearers with bawdy tales. Had the circumstances of their lives given them opportunity they would have been sheer sensualists. Their strength was the strength of men geographically beyond temptation: the poverty of Arabia made them simple, continent, enduring. If forced into civilized life they would have succumbed like any savage race to its diseases, meanness, luxury, cruelty, crooked dealing, artifice; and, like savages, they would have suffered them exaggeratedly for lack of inoculation.

If they suspected that we wanted to drive them either they were mulish or they went away. If we comprehended them, and gave time and trouble to make things tempting to them, then they would go to great pains for our pleasure. Whether the results achieved were worth the effort, no man could tell. Englishmen, accustomed to greater returns, would not, and, indeed, could not, have spent the time, thought and tact lavished every day by sheikhs and emirs for such meagre ends. Arab processes were clear, Arab minds moved logically as our own, with nothing radically incomprehensible or different, except the premiss: there was no excuse or reason, except our laziness and ignorance, whereby we could call them inscrutable or Oriental, or leave them misunderstood.

They would follow us, if we endured with them, and played the game according to their rules. The pity was, that we often began to do so, and broke down with exasperation and threw them over, blaming them for what was a fault in our own selves. Such strictures like a general's complaint of bad troops, were in reality a confession of our faulty foresight, often made falsely out of mock modesty to show that, though mistaken, we had at least the wit to know our fault.

CHAPTER XXXVIII

CLEANLINESS made me stop outside Wejh and change my filthy clothes. Feisal, when I reported, led me into the inner tent to talk. It seemed that everything was well. More cars had arrived from Egypt: Yenbo was emptied of its last soldiers and stores: and Sharraf himself had come up, with an unexpected unit, a new machine-gun company of amusing origin. We had left thirty sick and wounded men in Yenbo when we marched away; also heaps of broken weapons, with two British armourer-sergeants repairing them. The sergeants, who found time hang heavily, had taken mended maxims and patients and combined them into a machine-gun company so thoroughly trained by dumb show that they were as good as the best we had.

Rabegh also was being abandoned. The aeroplanes from it had flown up here and were established. Their Egyptian troops had been shipped after them, with Joyce and Goslett and the Rabegh staff, who were now in charge of things at Wejh. Newcombe and Hornby were up country tearing at the railway day and night, almost with their own hands for lack of helpers. The tribal propaganda was marching forward: all was for the best, and I was about to take my leave when Suleiman, the guest-master, hurried in and whispered to Feisal, who turned to me with shining eyes, trying to be calm, and said, 'Auda is here'. I shouted, 'Auda abu Tayi', and at that moment the tent-flap was drawn back, before a deep voice which boomed salutations to Our Lord, the Commander of the Faithful. There entered a tall, strong figure, with a haggard face, passionate and tragic. This was Auda, and after him followed Mohammed, his son, a child in looks, and only eleven years old in truth.

Feisal had sprung to his feet. Auda caught his hand and kissed it, and they drew aside a pace or two and looked at each other—a splendidly unlike pair, typical of much that was best in Arabia, Feisal the prophet, and Auda the warrior, each filling his part to perfection, and immediately understanding and liking the other. They sat down. Feisal introduced

us one by one, and Auda with a measured word seemed to register
each person.

We had heard much of Auda, and were banking to open Akaba with
his help; and after a moment I knew, from the force and directness of
the man, that we would attain our end. He had come down to us like
a knight-errant, chafing at our delay in Wejh, anxious only to be
acquiring merit for Arab freedom in his own lands. If his performance
was one-half his desire, we should be prosperous and fortunate. The
weight was off all minds before we went to supper.

We were a cheerful party; Nasib, Faiz, Mohammed el Dheilan
Auda's politic cousin, Zaal his nephew, and Sherif Nasir, resting in
Wejh for a few days between expeditions. I told Feisal odd stories of
Abdulla's camp, and the joy of breaking railways. Suddenly Auda
scrambled to his feet with a loud 'God forbid', and flung from the tent.
We stared at one another, and there came a noise of hammering
outside. I went after to learn what it meant, and there was Auda bent
over a rock pounding his false teeth to fragments with a stone. 'I had
forgotten,' he explained, 'Jemal Pasha gave me these. I was eating my
Lord's bread with Turkish teeth!' Unfortunately he had few teeth of
his own, so that henceforward eating the meat he loved was difficulty
and after-pain, and he went about half-nourished till we had taken
Akaba, and Sir Reginald Wingate sent him a dentist from Egypt to
make an Allied set.

Auda was very simply dressed, northern fashion, in white cotton
with a red Mosul head-cloth. He might be over fifty, and his black hair
was streaked with white; but he was still strong and straight, loosely
built, spare, and as active as a much younger man. His face was
magnificent in its lines and hollows. On it was written how truly the
death in battle of Annad, his favourite son, cast sorrow over all his life
when it ended his dream of handing on to future generations the greatness of the name of Abu Tayi. He had large eloquent eyes, like black
velvet in richness. His forehead was low and broad, his nose very high
and sharp, powerfully hooked: his mouth rather large and mobile: his
beard and moustaches had been trimmed to a point in Howeitat style,
with the lower jaw shaven underneath.

Centuries ago the Howeitat came from Hejaz, and their nomad clans prided themselves on being true Bedu. Auda was their master type. His hospitality was sweeping; except to very hungry souls, inconvenient. His generosity kept him always poor, despite the profits of a hundred raids. He had married twenty-eight times, had been wounded thirteen times; whilst the battles he provoked had seen all his tribesmen hurt and most of his relations killed. He himself had slain seventy-five men, Arabs, with his own hand in battle: and never a man except in battle. Of the number of dead Turks he could give no account: they did not enter the register. His Toweiha under him had become the first fighters of the desert, with a tradition of desperate courage, a sense of superiority which never left them while there was life and work to do: but which had reduced them from twelve hundred men to less than five hundred, in thirty years as the standard of nomadic fighting rose.

Auda raided as often as he had opportunity, and as widely as he could. He had seen Aleppo, Basra, Wejh, and Wadi Dawasir on his expeditions: and was careful to be at enmity with nearly all tribes in the desert, that he might have proper scope for raids. After his robber-fashion, he was as hard-headed as he was hot-headed, and in his maddest exploits there would be a cold factor of possibility to lead him through. His patience in action was extreme: and he received and ignored advice, criticism, or abuse, with a smile as constant as it was very charming. If he got angry his face worked uncontrollably, and he burst into a fit of shaking passion, only to be assuaged after he had killed: at such times he was a wild beast, and men escaped his presence. Nothing on earth would make him change his mind or obey an order to do the least thing he disapproved; and he took no heed of men's feelings when his face was set.

He saw life as a saga. All the events in it were significant: all personages in contact with him heroic. His mind was stored with poems of old raids and epic tales of fights, and he overflowed with them on the nearest listener. If he lacked listeners, he would very likely sing them to himself in his tremendous voice, deep and resonant and loud. He had no control over his lips, and was therefore terrible to his own interests and hurt his friends continually. He spoke of himself in the third person, and was so sure of his fame that he loved to shout out stories against himself. At times he seemed taken by a demon of mischief, and in public assembly would invent and utter on oath appalling tales of the private life of his hosts or guests: and yet with all this he was modest, as simple as a child, direct, honest, kind-hearted, and warmly loved even by those to whom he was most embarrassing — his friends.

Joyce lived near the beach, beside the spread lines of the Egyptian troops in an imposing array of large tents and small tents, and we talked over things done or to do. Every effort was still directed against the railway. Newcombe and Garland were near Muadhdham with Sherif Sharraf and Maulud. They had many Billi, the mule-mounted infantry, and guns and machine-guns, and hoped to take the fort and railway station there. Newcombe meant then to move all Feisal's men forward very close to Medain Salih, and, by taking and holding a part of the line, to cut off Medina and compel its early surrender. Wilson was coming up to help in this operation, and Davenport would take as many of the Egyptian army as he could transport, to reinforce the Arab attack.

All this programme was what I had believed necessary for the further progress of the Arab Revolt when we took Wejh. I had planned and arranged some of it myself. But now, since that happy fever and dysentery in Abdulla's camp had given me leisure to meditate upon the strategy and tactics of irregular war, it seemed that not merely the details but the essence of this plan were wrong. It therefore became my business to explain my changed ideas, and if possible to persuade my chiefs to follow me into the new theory.

So I began with three propositions. Firstly, that irregulars would not attack places, and so remained incapable of forcing a decision. Secondly, that they were as unable to defend a line or point as they were to attack it. Thirdly, that their virtue lay in depth, not in face.

The Arab war was geographical, and the Turkish Army an accident. Our aim was to seek the enemy's weakest material link and bear only on that till time made their whole length fail. Our largest resources, the Beduin on whom our war must be built, were unused to formal operations, but had assets of mobility, toughness, self-assurance, knowledge of the country, intelligent courage. With them dispersal was strength. Consequently we must extend our front to its maximum, to impose on the Turks the longest possible passive defence, since that was, materially, their most costly form of war.

Our duty was to attain our end with the greatest economy of life, since life was more precious to us than money or time. If we were patient and superhuman-skilled, we could follow the direction of Saxe and reach victory without battle, by pressing our advantages mathematical and psychological. Fortunately our physical weakness was not such as to demand this. We were richer than the Turks in transport, machine-guns, cars, high explosive. We could develop a highly mobile, highly equipped striking force of the smallest size, and use it successively at distributed points of the Turkish line, to make them strengthen their posts beyond the defensive minimum of twenty men. This would be a short cut to success.

We must not take Medina. The Turk was harmless there. In prison in Egypt he would cost us food and guards. We wanted him to stay at Medina, and every other distant place, in the largest numbers. Our ideal was to keep his railway just working, but only just, with the maximum of loss and discomfort. The factor of food would confine him to the railways, but he was welcome to the Hejaz Railway, and the Trans-Jordan railway, and the Palestine and Syrian railways for the duration of the war, so long as he gave us the other nine hundred and ninety-nine thousandths of the Arab world. If he tended to evacuate too soon, as a step to concentrating in the small area which his numbers could dominate effectually, then we should have to restore his confidence by reducing our enterprises against him. His stupidity would be our ally, for he would like to hold, or to think he held, as much of his old provinces as possible. This pride in his imperial heritage would keep him in his present absurd position — all flanks and no front.

In detail I criticized the ruling scheme. To hold a middle point of the railway would be expensive, for the holding force might be threatened from each side. The mixture of Egyptian troops with tribesmen was a moral weakness. If there were professional soldiers present, the Beduin would stand aside and watch them work, glad to be excused the leading part. Jealousy, superadded to inefficiency, would be the outcome. Further, the Billi country was very dry, and the maintenance of a large force up by the line technically difficult.

Neither my general reasoning, however, nor my particular objections had much weight. The plans were made, and the preparations advanced. Everyone was too busy with his own work to give me specific authority to launch out on mine. All I gained was a hearing, and a qualified admission that my counter-offensive might be a useful diversion. I was working out with Auda abu Tayi a march to the Howeitat in their spring pastures of the Syrian desert. From them we might raise a mobile camel force, and rush Akaba from the eastward without guns or machine-guns.

The eastern was the unguarded side, the line of least resistance, the easiest for us. Our march would be an extreme example of a turning movement, since it involved a desert journey of six hundred miles to capture a trench within gunfire of our ships: but there was no practicable alternative, and it was so entirely in the spirit of my sick-bed ruminations that its issue might well be fortunate, and would surely be instructive. Auda thought all things possible with dynamite and money, and that the smaller clans about Akaba would join us. Feisal, who was already in touch with them, also believed that they would help if we won a preliminary success up by Maan and then moved in force against the port. The Navy raided it while we were thinking, and their captured Turks gave us such useful information that I became eager to go off at once.

The desert route to Akaba was so long and so difficult that we could take neither guns nor machine-guns, nor stores nor regular soldiers. Accordingly the element I would withdraw from the railway scheme was only my single self; and, in the circumstances, this amount was negligible, since I felt so strongly against it that my help there would have been half-hearted. So I decided to go my own way, with or without orders. I wrote a letter full of apologies to Clayton, telling him that my intentions were of the best: and went.

BOOK IV

EXTENDING TO AKABA

Chapters XXXIX to LIV

THE *port of Akaba was naturally so strong that it could be taken only by surprise from inland: but the opportune adherence to Feisal of Auda abu Tayi made us hope to enrol enough tribesmen in the eastern desert for such a descent upon the coast.*

Nasir, Auda, and I set off together on the long ride. Hitherto Feisal had been the public leader: but his remaining in Wejh threw the ungrateful load of this northern expedition upon myself. I accepted it and its dishonest implication as our only means of victory. We tricked the Turks and entered Akaba with good fortune.

CHAPTER XXXIX

BY May the ninth all things were ready, and in the glare of mid-afternoon we left Feisal's tent, his good wishes sounding after us from the hill-top as we marched away. Sherif Nasir led us: his lucent goodness, which provoked answering devotion even from the depraved, made him the only leader (and a benediction) for forlorn hopes. When we broke our wishes to him he had sighed a little, for he was body-weary after months of vanguard-service, and mind-weary too, with the passing of youth's careless years. He feared his maturity as it grew upon him, with its ripe thought, its skill, its finished art; yet which lacked the poetry of boyhood to make living a full end of life. Physically, he was young yet; but his changeful and mortal soul was ageing quicker than his body — going to die before it, like most of ours.

Our short stage was to the fort of Sebeil, inland Wejh, where the Egyptian pilgrims used to water. We camped by their great brick tank, in shade of the fort's curtain wall, or of the palms, and put to rights the deficiencies which this first march had shown. Auda and his kinsmen were with us; also Nesib el Bekri, the politic Damascene, to represent Feisal to the villagers of Syria. Nesib had brains and position, and the character of a previous successful, desert-journey: his cheerful endurance of adventure, rare among Syrians, marked him out as our fellow, as much as his political mind, his ability, his persuasive good-humoured eloquence, and the patriotism which often overcame his native passion for the indirect. Nesib chose Zeki, a Syrian officer, as his companion. For escort we had thirty-five Ageyl under ibn Dgheithir, a man walled into his own temperament: remote, abstracted, self-sufficient. Feisal made up a purse of twenty-thousand pounds in gold — all he could afford and more than we asked for — to pay the wages of the new men we hoped to enrol, and to make such advances as should stimulate the Howeitat to swiftness.

This inconvenient load of four hundred weight of gold we shared out between us, against the chance of accident upon the road. Sheikh Yusuf, now back in charge of supply, gave us each a half-bag of flour, whose forty-five pounds were reckoned a man's pinched ration for six weeks. This went slung on the riding-saddle, and Nasir took enough on baggage camels to distribute a further fourteen pounds per man when we had marched the first fortnight, and had eaten room for it in our bags.

We had a little spare ammunition and some spare rifles as presents; and loaded six camels with light packs of blasting gelatine for rails or trains or bridges in the north. Nasir, a great Emir in his own place, also carried a good tent in which to receive visitors, and a camel load of rice for their entertainment: but the last we ate between us with huge comfort, as the unrelieved dietary of water-bread and water, week after week, grew uninspiring. Being beginners in this style of travelling, we did not know that dry flour, the lightest food, was therefore the best for a long journey. Six months later neither Nasir nor myself wasted transport and trouble on the rice-luxury.

My Ageyl — Mukheymer, Merjan, Ali — had been supplemented by Mohammed, a blowsy obedient peasant boy from some village in Hauran, and by Gasim, of Maan, a fanged and yellow-faced outlaw, who fled into the desert to the Howeitat, after killing a Turkish official in a dispute over cattle tax. Crimes against tax-gatherers had a sympathetic aspect for all of us, and this gave Gasim a specious rumour of geniality, which actually was far from truth.

We seemed a small party to win a new province, and so apparently others thought; for presently Lamotte, Bremond's representative with Feisal, rode up to take a farewell photograph of us. A little later Yusuf arrived, with the good doctor, and Shefik, and Nesib's brothers, to wish us success on our march. We joined in a spacious evening meal, whose materials the prudent Yusuf had brought with him. His not-slender heart perhaps misgave him at the notion of a bread supper: or was it the beautiful desire to give us a last feast before we were lost in the wilderness of pain and evil refreshment?

After they had gone we loaded up, and started before midnight on another stage of our journey to the oasis of Kurr. Nasir, our guide, had grown to know this country nearly as well as he did his own.

While we rode through the moonlit and starry night, his memory was dwelling very intimately about his home. He told me of their stone-paved house whose sunk halls had vaulted roofs against the summer heat, and of the gardens planted with every kind of fruit tree in shady paths about which they could walk at ease, mindless of the sun. He told me of the wheel over the well, with its machinery of leathern trip-buckets, raised by oxen upon an inclined path of hard-trodden earth; and of how the water from its reservoir slid in concrete channels by the borders of the paths; or worked fountains in the court beside the great vine-trellised swimming tank, lined with shining cement, within whose green depth he and his brother's household used to plunge at midday.

Nasir, though usually merry, had a quick vein of suffering in him, and to-night he was wondering why he, an Emir of Medina, rich and powerful and at rest in that garden-palace, had thrown up all to become the weak leader of desperate adventures in the desert. For two years he had been outcast, always fighting beyond the front line of Feisal's armies, chosen for every particular hazard, the pioneer in each advance; and, meanwhile, the Turks were in his house, wasting his fruit trees and chopping down his palms. Even, he said, the great well, which had sounded with the creak of the bullock wheels for six hundred years, had fallen silent; the garden, cracked with heat, was becoming waste as the blind hills over which we rode.

After four hours' march we slept for two, and rose with the sun. The baggage camels, weak with the cursed mange of Wejh, moved slowly, grazing all day as they went. We riders, light-mounted, might have passed them easily; but Auda, who was regulating our marches, forbade, because of the difficulties in front, for which our animals would need all the fitness we could conserve in them. So we plodded soberly on for six hours in great heat. The summer sun in this country of white sand behind Wejh, could dazzle the eyes cruelly, and the bare rocks each side our path threw off waves of heat which made our heads ache and swim. Consequently, by eleven of the forenoon we were mutinous against Auda's wish still to hold on. So we halted and lay under trees till half-past two, each of us trying to make a solid, though shifting shadow for himself by means of a doubled blanket caught across the thorns of overhanging boughs.

We rode again, after this break, for three gentle hours over level bottoms, approaching the walls of a great valley; and found the green garden of El Kurr lying just in front of us. White tents peeped from among the palms. While we dismounted, Rasim and Abdulla, Mahmud, the doctor, and even old Maulud, the cavalryman, came out to welcome us. They told us that Sherif Sharraf, whom we wished to meet at Abu Raga, our next stopping place, was away raiding for a few days. This meant that there was no hurry, so we made holiday at El Kurr for two nights.

It contented me: for the trouble of boils and fever which had shackled me in Wadi Ais had come afresh, more strongly, making each journey a pain, and each rest a blessed relaxation of my will strung to go on — a chance to add patience to a scant reserve. So I lay still, and received into my mind the sense of peace, the greenness and the presence of water which made this garden in the desert beautiful and haunting, as though pre-visited. Or was it merely that long ago we had seen fresh grass growing in the spring?

The inhabitant of Kurr, the only sedentary Belluwi, hoary Dhaif-Allah, laboured day and night with his daughters in the little terraced plot which he had received from his ancestors. It was built out of the south edge of the valley in a bay defended against flood by a massive wall of unhewn stone. In its midst opened the well of clear cold water, above which stood a balance-cantilever of mud and rude poles. By this Dhaif-Allah, morning and evening when the sun was low, drew up great bowls of water and spilled them into clay runnels contrived through his garden among the tree roots. He grew low palms, for their spreading leaves shaded his plants from the sun which otherwise might in that stark valley wither them, and raised young tobacco (his most profitable crop); with smaller plots of beans and melons, cucumbers and egg-plants, in due season.

The old man lived with his women in a brushwood hut beside the well, and was scornful of our politics, demanding what more to eat or drink these sore efforts and bloody sacrifices would bring. We gently teased him with notions of liberty; with freedom of the Arab countries for the Arabs. 'This Garden, Dhaif-Allah, should it not be your very own?' However, he would not understand, but stood up to strike himself proudly on the chest, crying, 'I — I am Kurr'.

He was free and wanted nothing for others; and only his garden for himself. Nor did he see why others should not become rich in a like frugality. His felt skull-cap, greased with sweat to the colour and consistence of lead, he boasted had been his grandfather's, bought when Ibrahim Pasha was in Wejh a century before: his other necessary garment was a shirt, and annually, with his tobacco, he would buy the shirt of the new year for himself; one for each of his daughters, and one for the old woman — his wife.

Still we were grateful to him, for, besides that he showed an example of contentment to us slaves of unnecessary appetite, he sold vegetables; and on them, and on the tinned bounty of Rasim and Abdulla and Mahmud, we lived richly. Each evening round the fires they had music, not the monotonous open-throated roaring of the tribes, nor the exciting harmony of the Ageyl, but the falsetto quarter tones and trills of urban Syria. Maulud had musicians in his unit; and bashful soldiers were brought up each evening to play guitars and sing café songs of Damascus or the love verses of their villages. In Abdulla's tent, where I was lodged, distance, the ripple of the fragrant out-pouring water, and the tree-leaves softened the music, so that it became dully pleasant to the ear.

Often, too, Nesib el Bekri would take out his manuscript of the songs of Selim el Jezairi, that fierce unscrupulous revolutionary who, in his leisure moments between campaigns, the Staff College, and the bloody missions he fulfilled for the Young Turks, his masters, had made up verses in the common speech of the people about the freedom which was coming to his race. Nesib and his friends had a swaying rhythm in which they would chant these songs, putting all hope and passion into the words, their pale Damascus faces moon-large in the firelight, sweating. The soldier camp would grow dead silent till the stanza ended, and then from every man would come a sighing, longing echo of the last note. Only old Dhaif-Allah went on splashing out his water, sure that after we had finished with our silliness someone would yet need and buy his greenstuff.

CHAPTER XL

TO townsmen this garden was a memory of the world before we went mad with war and drove ourselves into the desert: to Auda there was an indecency of exhibition in the plant-richness, and he longed for an empty view. So we cut short our second night in paradise and at two in the morning went on up the valley. It was pitch dark, the very stars in the sky being unable to cast light into the depths where we were wandering. To-night Auda was guide, and to make us sure of him he lifted up his voice in an interminable 'ho, ho, ho' song of the Howeitat; an epic chanted on three bass notes, up and down, back and forward, in so round a voice that the words were indistinguishable. After a little we thanked him for the singing, since the path went away to the left, and our long line followed his turn by the echoes of his voice rolling about the torn black clouds in the moonlight.

On this long journey Sherif Nasir and Auda's sour-smiling cousin, Mohammed el Dheilan, took pains with my Arabic, giving me by turn lessons in the classical Medina tongue, and in the vivid desert language. At the beginning my Arabic had been a halting command of the tribal dialects of the Middle Euphrates (a not impure form), but now it became a fluent mingling of Hejaz slang and north-tribal poetry with household words and phrases from the limpid Nejdi, and book forms from Syria. The fluency had a lack of grammar, which made my talk a perpetual adventure for my hearers. Newcomers imagined I must be the native of some unknown illiterate district; a shot-rubbish ground of disjected Arabic parts of speech.

However, as yet I understood not three words of Auda's, and after half an hour his chant tired me, while the old moon climbed slowly up the sky, sailed over the topmost hills and threw a deceitful light, less sure than darkness into our valley. We marched until the early sun, very trying to those who had ridden all night, opposed us.

Breakfast was off our own flour, thus lightening at last, after days of hospitality, our poor camels' food-load. Sharraf being not yet in Abu Raga, we made no more of haste than water-difficulties compelled;

and, after food, again put up our blanket roofs and lay till afternoon, fretfully dodging after their unstable shadow, getting moist with heat and the constant pricking of flies.

At last Nasir gave the marching signal, and we went on up the defile, with slightly pompous hills each side, for four hours; when we agreed to camp again in the valley bed. There was abundant brushwood for fuel; and up the cliff on our right were rock-pools of fresh water, which gave us a delicious drink. Nasir was wrought up; he commanded rice for supper, and the friends to feed with us.

Our rule of march was odd and elaborate. Nasir, Auda, and Nesib were so many separate, punctilious houses, admitting the supremacy of Nasir only because I lived with him as a guest and furnished them with the example of respect. Each required to be consulted on the details of our going, and where and when we should halt. This was inevitable with Auda, a child of battle who had never known a master, since, as a tiny boy, he had first ridden his own camel. It was advisable with Nesib, a Syrian of the queasy Syrian race; jealous; hostile to merit, or to its acknowledgement.

Such people demanded a war-cry and banner from outside to combine them, and a stranger to lead them, one whose supremacy should be based on an idea: illogical, undeniable, discriminant: which instinct might accept and reason find no rational basis to reject or approve. For this army of Feisal's the conceit was that an Emir of Mecca, a descendant of the prophet, a Sherif, was an other-worldly dignitary whom sons of Adam might reverence without shame. This was the binding assumption of the Arab movement; it was this which gave it an effective, if imbecile unanimity.

In the morning we rode at five. Our valley pinched together, and we went round a sharp spur, ascending steeply. The track became a bad goat-path, zigzagging up a hill-side too precipitous to climb except on all fours. We dropped off our camels and led them by the head-stalls. Soon we had to help each other, a man urging the camels from behind, another pulling them from the front, encouraging them over the worst places, adjusting their loads to ease them.

Parts of the track were dangerous, where rocks bulged out and narrowed it, so that the near half of the load grazed and forced the animal to the cliff-edge. We had to re-pack the food and explosives; and, in spite of all our care, lost two of our feeble camels in the pass. The Howeitat killed them where they lay broken, stabbing a keen dagger into the throat-artery near the chest, while the neck was strained tight by pulling the head round to the saddle. They were at once cut up and shared out as meat.

The head of the pass we were glad to find not a range but a spacious plateau which sloped slowly before us to the east. The first yards were rough and rocky, overgrown with low mats of thorns like ling; but afterwards we came to a valley of white shingle, in whose bed a Beduin woman was filling her water-skin with a copper cup, ladling milky water, quite pure and sweet, from a little hole a foot wide, scraped elbow deep in the pebbles. This was Abu Saad, and for its name's sake and for its water, and the joints of red meat bumping on our saddles, we settled we would stay here one night, filling up yet more of the time which must be filled before Sharraf came back from his expedition against the railway.

So we rode on four more miles, to camp under spreading trees, in close-grown thickets of thorn-scrub, hollow underneath like booths. By day these made tent-ribs for our blankets stretched against the masterful sun. At night they were bowers for our sleeping-places. We had learned to sleep with nothing overhead but moon and stars, and nothing either side to keep distant the winds and noises of the night; and by contrast it was strange, but quieting, to rest within walls, with a roof above; even though walls and roof were only interlacing twigs making a darker mesh against the star-scattered sky.

For myself, I was ill again; a fever increasing upon me, and my body very sore with boils and the rubbing of my sweaty saddle. When Nasir, without my prompting, had halted at the half-stage, I turned and thanked him warmly, to his astonishment. We were now on the limestone of the Shefa crest. Before us lay a great dark lava-field, and short of it a range of red and black banded sandstone cliffs with conical tops. The air on the high tableland was not so warm; and morning and evening there blew across us a free current which was refreshing after the suspended stillness of the valleys.

We breakfasted on our camel meat, and started more gaily the next morning down a gently-falling plateau of red sandstone. Then we came to the first break of surface, a sharp passage to the bottom of a shrub-grown, sandy valley, on each side of which sandstone precipices and pinnacles, gradually growing in height as we went down, detached themselves sharply against the morning sky. It was shadowed in the bottom, and the air tasted wet and decayed, as though sap was drying out into it. The edges of the cliffs about us were clipped strangely, like fantastic parapets. We wound on, ever deeper into the earth until, half an hour later, by a sharp corner we entered Wadi Jizil, the main gutter of these sandstone regions, whose end we had seen near Hedia.

Jizil was a deep gorge some two hundred yards in width, full of tamarisk sprouting from the bed of drifted sand, as well as from the soft twenty-foot banks, heaped up wherever an eddy in flood or wind had laid the heavier dust under the returns of cliffs. The walls each side were of regular bands of sandstone, streaked red in many shades. The union of dark cliffs, pink floors, and pale green shrubbery was beautiful to eyes sated with months of sunlight and sooty shadow. When evening came, the declining sun crimsoned one side of the valley with its glow, leaving the other in purple gloom.

Our camp was on some swelling dunes of weedy sand in an elbow of the valley, where a narrow cleft had set up a back-wash and scooped out a basin in which a brackish remnant of last winter's flood was caught. We sent a man for news up the valley to an oleander thicket where we saw the white peaks of Sharraf's tents. They expected him next day; so we passed two nights in this strange-coloured, echoing place. The brackish pool was fit for our camels, and in it we bathed at noon. Then we ate and slept generously, and wandered in the nearer valleys to see the horizontal stripes of pink and brown and cream and red which made up the general redness of the cliffs, delighting in the varied patterns of thin pencillings of lighter or darker tint which were drawn over the plain body of rock. One afternoon I spent behind some shepherd's fold of sandstone blocks in warm soft air and sunlight, with a low burden of the wind plucking at the rough wall-top above my head. The valley was instinct with peace, and the wind's continuing noise made even it seem patient.

My eyes were shut and I was dreaming, when a youthful voice made me see an anxious Ageyli, a stranger, Daud, squatting by me. He appealed for my compassion. His friend Farraj had burned their tent in a frolic, and Saad, captain of Sharraf's Ageyl was going to beat him in punishment. At my intercession he would be released. Saad happened, just then, to visit me, and I put it to him, while Daud sat watching us, his mouth slightly, eagerly, open; his eyelids narrowed over large, dark eyes, and his straight brows furrowed with anxiety. Daud's pupils, set a little in from the centre of the eyeball, gave him an air of acute readiness.

Saad's reply was not comforting. The pair were always in trouble, and of late so outrageous in their tricks that Sharraf, the severe, had ordered an example to be made of them. All he could do for my sake was to let Daud share the ordained sentence. Daud leaped at the chance, kissed my hand and Saad's, and ran off up the valley; while Saad, laughing, told me stories of the famous pair. They were an instance of the eastern boy and boy affection which the segregation of women made inevitable. Such friendships often led to manly loves of a depth and force beyond our flesh-steeped conceit. When innocent they were hot and unashamed. If sexuality entered, they passed into a give and take, unspiritual relation, like marriage.

Next day Sharraf did not come. Our morning passed with Auda talking of the march in front, while Nasir with forefinger and thumb flicked sputtering matches from the box across his tent at us. In the midst of our merriment two bent figures, with pain in their eyes, but crooked smiles upon their lips, hobbled up and saluted. These were Daud the hasty and his love-fellow, Farraj; a beautiful, soft-framed, girlish creature, with innocent, smooth face and swimming eyes. They said they were for my service. I had no need of them; and objected that after their beating they could not ride. They replied they had now come bare-backed. I said I was a simple man who disliked servants about him. Daud turned away, defeated and angry; but Farraj pleaded that we must have men, and they would follow me for company and out of gratitude. While the harder Daud revolted, he went over to Nasir and knelt in appeal, all the woman of him evident in his longing. At the end, on Nasir's advice, I took them both, mainly because they looked so young and clean.

CHAPTER XLI

SHARRAF delayed to come until the third morning, but then we heard him loudly, for the Arabs of his raiding force fired slow volleys of shots into the air, and the echoes were thrown about the windings of the valley till even the barren hills seemed to join in the salute. We dressed in our cleanest to go and call on him. Auda wore the splendours he had bought at Wejh: a mouse-coloured greatcoat of broadcloth with velvet collar, and yellow elastic-sided boots: these below his streaming hair and ruined face of a tired tragedian! Sharraf was kind to us, for he had captured prisoners on the line and blown up rails and a culvert. One piece of his news was that in Wadi Diraa, on our road, were pools of rain-water, new fallen and sweet. This would shorten our waterless march to Fejr by fifty miles, and remove its danger of thirst; a great benefit, for our total water carriage came to about twenty gallons, for fifty men; too slender a margin of safety.

Next day we left Abu Raga near mid-afternoon, not sorry, for this beautiful place had been unhealthy for us and fever had bothered us during our three days in its confined bed. Auda led us up a tributary valley which soon widened into the plain of the Shegg — a sand flat. About it, in scattered confusion, sat small islands and pinnacles of red sandstone, grouped like seracs, wind-eroded at the bases till they looked very fit to fall and block the road; which wound in and out between them, through narrows seeming to give no passage, but always opening into another bay of blind alleys. Through this maze Auda led un-hesitatingly; digging along on his camel, elbows out, hands poised swaying in the air by his shoulders.

There were no footmarks on the ground, for each wind swept like a great brush over the sand surface, stippling the traces of the last travellers till the surface was again a pattern of innumerable tiny virgin waves. Only the dried camel droppings, which were lighter than the sand and rounded like walnuts, escaped over its ripples.

They rolled about, to be heaped in corners by the skirling winds. It was perhaps by them, as much as by his unrivalled road-sense, that

Auda knew the way. For us, the rock shapes were constant speculation and astonishment; their granular surfaces and red colour and the curved chiselling of the sand-blast upon them softened the sunlight, to give our streaming eyes relief.

In the mid-march we perceived five or six riders coming from the railway. I was in front with Auda, and we had that delicious thrill 'Friend or enemy?' of meeting strangers in the desert, whilst we circumspectly drew across to the vantage side which kept the rifle-arm free for a snap shot; but when they came nearer we saw they were of the Arab forces. The first, riding loosely on a hulking camel, with the unwieldy Manchester-made timber saddle of the British Camel Corps, was a fair-haired, shaggy-bearded Englishman in tattered uniform. This we guessed must be Hornby, Newcombe's pupil, the wild engineer who vied with him in smashing the railway. After we had exchanged greetings, on this our first meeting, he told me that Newcombe had lately gone to Wejh to talk over his difficulties with Feisal and make fresh plans to meet them.

Newcombe had constant difficulties owing to excess of zeal, and his habit of doing four times more than any other Englishman would do: ten times what the Arabs thought needful or wise. Hornby spoke little Arabic; and Newcombe not enough to persuade, though enough to give orders; but orders were not in place inland. The persistent pair would cling for weeks to the railway edge, almost without helpers, often without food, till they had exhausted either explosives or camels and had to return for more. The barrenness of the hills made their trips hungry for camels, and they wore out Feisal's best animals in turn. In this Newcombe was chief sinner, for his journeys were done at the trot; also, as a surveyor, he could not resist a look from each high hill over the country he crossed, to the exasperation of his escort who must either leave him to his own courses (a lasting disgrace to abandon a companion of the road) or founder their own precious and irreplaceable camels in keeping pace with him. 'Newcombe is like fire', they used to complain; 'he burns friend and enemy'; and they admired his amazing energy with nervous shrinking lest they should be his next friendly victims.

Arabs told me Newcombe would not sleep except head on rails, and that Hornby would worry the metals with his teeth when gun-cotton failed. These were legends, but behind them lay a sense of their joint insatiate savagery in destroying till there was no more to destroy. Four Turkish labour battalions they kept busy, patching culverts, relaying sleepers, jointing new rails; and gun-cotton had to come in increasing tons to Wejh to meet their appetites. They were wonderful, but their too-great excellence discouraged our feeble teams, making them ashamed to exhibit their inferior talent: so Newcombe and Hornby remained as individualists, barren of the seven-fold fruits of imitation.

At sunset we reached the northern limit of the ruined sandstone land, and rode up a new level, sixty feet higher than the old, blue-black and volcanic, with a scattered covering of worn basalt-blocks, small as a man's hand, neatly bedded like cobble paving over a floor of fine, hard black cinder-debris of themselves. The rain in its long pelting seemed to have been the agent of these stony surfaces by washing away the lighter dust from above and between, till the stones, set closely side by side and as level as a carpet, covered all the face of the plain and shielded from direct contact with weather the salty mud which filled the interstices of the lava flow beneath. It grew easier going, and Auda ventured to carry on after the light had failed, marching upon the Polar Star.

It was very dark; a pure night enough, but the black stone underfoot swallowed the light of the stars, and at seven o'clock, when at last we halted, only four of our party were with us. We had reached a gentle valley, with a yet damp, soft, sandy bed, full of thorny brush-wood, unhappily useless as camel food. We ran about tearing up these bitter bushes by the roots and heaping them in a great pyre, which Auda lit. When the fire grew hot a long black snake wormed slowly out into our group; we must have gathered it, torpid, with the twigs. The flames went shining across the dark flat, a beacon to the heavy camels which had lagged so much to-day that it was two hours before the last group arrived, the men singing their loudest, partly to encourage themselves and their hungry animals over the ghostly plain, partly so that we might know them friends. We wished their slowness slower, because of our warm fire.

In the night some of our camels strayed and our people had to go looking for them so long, that it was nearly eight o'clock, and we had baked bread and eaten, before again we started. Our track lay across more lava-field, but to our morning strength the stones seemed rarer, and waves or hard surfaces of laid sand often drowned them smoothly with a covering as good to march on as a tennis court. We rode fast over this for six or seven miles, and then turned west of a low cinder-crater across the flat, dark, stony watershed which divided Jizil from the basin in which the railway ran. These great water systems up here at their springing were shallow sandy beds, scoring involved yellow lines across the blue-black plain. From our height the lie of the land was patent for miles, with the main features coloured in layers, like a map.

We marched steadily till noon, and then sat out on the bare ground till three; an uneasy halt made necessary by our fear that the dejected camels, so long accustomed only to the sandy tracks of the coastal plain, might have their soft feet scorched by the sun-baked stones, and go lame with us on the road. After we mounted, the going became worse and we had continually to avoid large fields of piled basalt, or deep yellow watercourses which cut through the crust into the soft stone beneath. After a while red sandstone again cropped out in crazy chimneys, from which the harder layers projected knife-sharp in level shelves beyond the soft crumbling rock. At last these sandstone ruins became plentiful, in the manner of yesterday, and stood grouped about our road in similar chequered yards of light and shade. Again we marvelled at the sureness with which Auda guided our little party through the mazy rocks.

They passed, and we re-entered volcanic ground. Little pimply craters stood about, often two or three together, and from them spines of high, broken basalt led down like disordered causeways across the barren ridges; but these craters looked old, not sharp and well-kept like those of Ras Gara, near Wadi Ais, but worn and degraded, some-times nearly to surface level by a great bay broken into their central hollow. The basalt which ran out from them was a coarse bubbled rock like Syrian dolerite. The sand-laden winds had ground its exposed surfaces to a pitted smoothness like orange-rind, and the sunlight had faded out its blue to a hopeless grey.

Between craters the basalt was strewn in small tetrahedra, with angles rubbed and rounded, stone tight to stone like tesseræ upon a bed of pink-yellow mud. The ways worn across such flats by the constant passage of camels were very evident, since the slouching tread had pushed the blocks to each side of the path, and the thin mud of wet weather had run into these hollows and now inlaid them palely against the blue. Less-used roads for hundreds of yards were like narrow ladders across the stone-fields, for the tread of each foot was filled in with clean yellow mud, and ridges or bars of the blue-grey stone remained between each stepping place. After a stretch of such stone-laying would be a field of jet-black basalt cinders, firm as concrete in the sun-baked mud, and afterwards a valley of soft, black sand, with more crags of weathered sandstone rising from the blackness, or from waves of the wind-blown red and yellow grains of their own decay.

Nothing in the march was normal or reassuring. We felt we were in an ominous land, incapable of life, hostile even to the passing of life, except painfully along such sparse roads as time had laid across its face. We were forced into a single file of weary camels, picking a hesitant way step by step through the boulders for hour after hour. At last Auda pointed ahead to a fifty-root ridge of large twisted blocks, lying coursed one upon the other as they had writhed and shrunk in their cooling. There was the limit of lava; and he and I rode on together and saw in front of us an open rolling plain (Wadi Aish) of fine scrub and golden sand, with green bushes scattered here and there. It held a very little water in holes which someone had scooped after the rainstorm of three weeks ago. We camped by them and drove our unladen camels out till sunset, to graze for the first adequate time since Abu Raga.

While they were scattered over the land, mounted men appeared on the horizon to the east, making towards the water. They came on too quickly to be honest, and fired at our herdsmen; but the rest of us ran at once upon the scattered reefs and knolls, shooting or shouting. Hearing us so many they drew off as fast as their camels would go; and from the ridge in the dusk we saw them a bare dozen in all, scampering away towards the line. We were glad to see them avoid us so thoroughly. Auda thought they were a Shammar patrol.

At dawn we saddled up for the short stage to Diraa, the water pools of which Sharraf had told us. The first miles were through the grateful sand and scrub of Wadi Aish, and afterwards we crossed a simple lava flat. Then came a shallow valley, more full of sandstone pillars and mushrooms and pinnacles than anywhere yesterday. It was a mad country, of nine-pins from ten to sixty feet in height. The sand-paths between them were wide enough for one only, and our long column wound blindly through, seldom a dozen of us having common sight at once. This ragged thicket of stone was perhaps a third of a mile in width, and stretched like a red copse to right and left across our path.

Beyond it a graded path over black ledges of rotten stone led us to a plateau strewn with small, loose, blue-black basalt shards. After a while we entered Wadi Diraa, and marched down its bed for an hour or more, sometimes over loose grey stone, sometimes along a sandy bottom between low lips of rock. A deserted camp with empty sardine tins gave proof of Newcombe and Hornby. Behind were the limpid pools, and we halted there till afternoon; for we were now quite near the railway, and had to drink our stomachs full and fill our few water-skins, ready for the long dash to Fejr.

In the halt Auda came down to see Farraj and Daud dress my camel with butter for relief against the intolerable itch of mange which had broken out recently on its face. The dry pasturage of the Billi country and the infected ground of Wejh had played havoc with our beasts. In all Feisal's stud of riding-camels there was not one healthy; in our little expedition every camel was weakening daily. Nasir was full of anxiety lest many break down in the forced march before us and leave their riders stranded in the desert.

We had no medicines for mange and could do little for it in spite of our need. However, the rubbing and anointing did make my animal more comfortable, and we repeated it as often as Farraj or Daud could find butter in our party. These two boys were giving me great satis-faction. They were brave and cheerful beyond the average of Arab servant-kind. As their aches and pains wore off they showed them-selves active, good riders, and willing workmen. I liked their freedom towards myself and admired their instinctive understanding with one another against the demands of the world.

CHAPTER XLII

BY a quarter to four we were in the saddle, going down Wadi Diraa, into steep and high ridges of shifting sand, sometimes with a cap of harsh red rock jutting from them. After a while, three or four of us, in advance of the main body, climbed a sand-peak on hands and knees to spy out the railway. There was no air, and the exercise was more than we required; but our reward was immediate, for the line showed itself quiet and deserted-looking, on a green flat at the mouth of the deep valley down which the rest of the company was marching circumspectly with ready weapons.

We checked the men at the bottom of their narrow sand-fold, whilst we studied the railway. Everything was indeed peaceful and empty, even to the abandoned blockhouse in a rich patch of rank grass and weeds between us and the line. We ran to the edge of the rock-shelf, leaped out from it into the fine dry sand, and rolled down in a magnificent slide till we came to an abrupt and rather bruising halt in the level ground beside the column. We mounted, to hurry our camels out to the grazing, and leaving them there ran over to the railway and shouted the others on.

This unmolested crossing was blessed, for Sharraf had warned us seriously against the enemy patrols of mule-riding infantry and camel corps, reinforced from the entrenched posts by infantry on trolleys mounting machine-guns. Our riding beasts we chased into the grass to feed for a few minutes, while the heavy camels marched over the valley, the line, and the farther flat, till sheltered in the sand and rock mouths of the country beyond the railway. Meanwhile the Ageyl amused us by fixing gun-cotton or gelatine charges about our crossing-place to as many of the rails as we had time to reach, and when our munching camels had been dragged away into safety on the far side of the line, we began in proper order to light the fuses, filling the hollow valley with the echoes of repeated bursts.

Auda had not before known dynamite, and with a child's first pleasure was moved to a rush of hasty poetry on its powerful glory.

We cut three telegraph wires, and fastened the free ends to the saddles of six riding-camels of the Howeitat. The astonished team struggled far into the eastern valleys with the growing weight of twanging, tangling wire and the bursting poles dragging after them. At last they could no longer move. So we cut them loose and rode laughing after the caravan.

For five miles we proceeded in the growing dusk, between ridges which seemed to run down like fingers from some knuckle in front of us. At last their rise and fall became too sharp to be crossed with safety by our weak animals in the dark, and we halted. The baggage and the bulk of our riders were still ahead of us, keeping the advantage they had gained while we played with the railway. In the night we could not find them, for the Turks were shouting hard and shooting at shadows from their stations on the line behind us; and we judged it prudent to keep quiet ourselves, not lighting fires nor sending up signals to attract attention.

However, ibn Dgheithir, in charge of the main body, had left a connecting file behind, and so before we had fallen asleep, two men came in to us, and reported that the rest were securely camped in the hidden fold of a steep sand-bank a little further on. We threw our saddle-bags again across our camels, and plodded after our guides in the murky dark (to-night was almost the last night of the moon) till we reached their hushed picket on the ridge, and bedded ourselves down beside them without words.

In the morning Auda had us afoot before four, going uphill, till at last we climbed a ridge, and plunged over, down a sand slope. Into it our camels sank knee-deep, held upright despite themselves by its clinging. They were able to make forward only by casting themselves on and down its loose face, breaking their legs out of it by their bodies' weight. At the bottom we found ourselves in the head-courses of a valley, which trended towards the railway. Another half-hour took us to the springing of this, and we breasted the low edge of the plateau which was the watershed between Hejaz and Sirhan. Ten yards more, and we were beyond the Red Sea slope of Arabia, fairly embarked upon the mystery of its central drainage.

Seemingly it was a plain, with an illimitable view downhill to the east, where one gentle level after another slowly modulated into a distance only to be called distance because it was a softer blue, and more hazy. The rising run flooded this falling plain with a perfect level of light, throwing up long shadows of almost imperceptible ridges, and the whole life and play of a complicated ground-system — but a transient one; for, as we looked at it, the shadows drew in towards the dawn, quivered a last moment behind their mother-banks, and went out as though at a common signal. Full morning had begun: the river of sunlight, sickeningly in the full-face of us moving creatures, poured impartially on every stone of the desert over which we had to go.

Auda struck out north-eastward, aiming for a little saddle which joined the low ridge of Ugula to a lofty hill on the divide, to our left or north about three miles away. We crossed the saddle after four miles, and found beneath our feet little shallow runnels of watercourses in the ground. Auda pointed to them, saying that they ran to Nebk in Sirhan, and that we would follow their swelling bed northward and eastward to the Howeitat in their summer camp.

A little later we were marching over a low ridge of slivers of sandstone with the nature of slate, sometimes quite small, but other times great slabs ten feet each way and, perhaps, four inches thick. Auda ranged up beside my camel, and pointing with his riding-stick told me to write down on my map the names and nature of the land. The valleys on our left were the Seyal Abu Arad, rising in Selhub, and fed by many successors from the great divide, as it prolonged itself northward to Jebel Rufeiya by Tebuk. The valleys on our right were the Siyul el Kelb, from Ugula Agidat el Jemelein, Lebda and the other ridges which bent round us in a strung bow eastward and north-eastward carrying the great divide as it were in a foray out across the plain. These two water systems united fifty miles before us in Fejr, which was a tribe, its well, and the valley of its well. I cried Auda mercy of his names, swearing I was no writer-down of unspoiled countries, or pandar to geographical curiosity; and the old man, much pleased, began to tell me personal notes and news of the chiefs with us, and in front upon our line of march. His prudent talk whiled away the slow passage of abominable desolation.

The Fejr Bedouin, whose property it was, called our plain El Houl because it was desolate; and to-day we rode in it without seeing signs of life, no tracks of gazelle, no lizards, no burrowing of rats, not even any birds. We, ourselves, felt tiny in it, and our urgent progress across its immensity was a stillness or immobility of futile effort. The only sounds were the hollow echoes, like the shutting down of pavements over vaulted places, of rotten stone slab on stone slab when they tilted under our camels' feet, and the low but piercing rustle of the sand, as it crept slowly westward before the hot wind along the worn sandstone, under the harder overhanging caps which gave each reef its eroded, rind-like shape.

It was a breathless wind, with the furnace taste sometimes known in Egypt when a khamsin came; and, as the day went on and the sun rose in the sky it grew stronger, more filled with the dust of the Nefudh, the great sand desert of Northern Arabia, close by us over there, but invisible through the haze. By noon it blew a half-gale, so dry that our shrivelled lips cracked open, and the skin of our faces chapped; while our eyelids, gone granular, seemed to creep back and bare our shrinking eyes. The Arabs drew their head-clothes tightly across their noses, and pulled the brow-folds forward like vizors with only a narrow, loose-flapping slit of vision.

At this stifling price they kept their flesh unbroken, for they feared the sand particles which would wear open the chaps into a painful wound: but, for my own part, I always rather liked a khamsin, since its torment seemed to fight against mankind with ordered conscious malevolence, and it was pleasant to outface it so directly, challenging its strength, and conquering its extremity. There was pleasure also in the salt sweat-drops which ran singly down the long hair over my fore-head, and dripped like ice-water on my cheek. At first, I played at catching them in my mouth; but, as we rode further into the desert and the hours passed, the wind became stronger, thicker in dust, more terrible in heat. All semblance of friendly contest passed. My camel's pace became sufficient increase to the irritation of the choking waves, whose dryness broke my skin and made my throat so painful that for three days afterwards I could eat little of our stodgy bread. When evening at last came to us I was content that my burned face still felt the other and milder air of darkness.

We plodded on all the day (even without the wind forbidding us there could have been no more luxury halts under the shadow of blankets if we would arrive unbroken men with strong camels at el Fejr), and nothing made us widen an eye or think a thought till after three in the afternoon. Then, above two natural tumuli, we came to a cross-ridge swelling at last into a hill. Auda huskily spat extra names at me.

Beyond it a long slope, slow degrees of a washed gravel surface with stripings of an occasional torrent-bed, went down westward. Auda and I trotted ahead together for relief against the intolerable slowness of the caravan. This side the sunset glow a modest wall of hills barred our way to the north. Shortly afterwards the Seil abu Arad, turning east, swept along our front in a bed a fair mile wide; it was inches deep with scrub as dry as dead wood, which crackled and split with little spurts of dust when we began to gather it for a fire to show the others where we had made the halt. We gathered and gathered vigorously, till we had a great cock ready for lighting. Then we found that neither of us had a match.

The mass did not arrive for an hour or more, when the wind had altogether died away, and the evening, calm and black and full of stars, had come down on us. Auda set a watch through the night, for this district was in the line of raiding parties, and in the hours of darkness there were no friends in Arabia. We had covered about fifty miles this day; all we could at a stretch, and enough according to our programme. So we halted the night hours; partly because our camels were weak and ill, and grazing meant much to them, and partly because the Howeitat were not intimate with this country, and feared to lose their way if they should ride too boldly without seeing.

CHAPTER XLIII

BEFORE dawn the following day we started down the bed of Seil Abu Arad till the white sun came up over the Zibliyat hills ahead of us. We turned more north to cut off an angle of the valley, and halted for half an hour till we saw the main body coming. Then Auda, Nasir and myself, unable longer to endure passively the hammer strokes of the sun upon our bowed heads, pushed forward at a jerky trot. Almost at once we lost sight of the others in the lymph-like heat-vapour throbbing across the flat: but the road was evident, down the scrubby bed of Wadi Fejr.

At the height of noon we reached the well of our desire. It was about thirty feet deep, stone-steyned, seemingly ancient. The water was abundant, slightly brackish, but not ill-tasting when drunk fresh: though it soon grew foul in a skin. The valley had flooded in some burst of rain the year before, and therefore contained much dry and thirsty pasturage: to this we loosed our camels. The rest came up, and drew water and baked bread. We let the camels crop industriously till nightfall, then watered them again, and pounded them under the bank a half mile from the water, for the night: thus leaving the well un-molested in case raiders should need it in the dark hours. Yet our sentries heard no one.

As usual we were off before dawn, though we had an easy march before us; but the heated glare of the desert became so painful that we designed to pass the midday in some shelter. After two miles the valley spread out, and later we came to a low, broken cliff on the east bank opposite the mouth of Seil Raugha. Here the country looked more green, and we asked Auda to fetch us game. He sent Zaal one way and rode westward himself across the open plain which stretched beyond view, while we turned in to the cliffs and found beneath their fallen crags and undercut ledges abundant shady nooks, cool against the sun and restful for our unaccustomed eyes.

The hunters returned before noon, each with a good gazelle. We had filled our water-skins at Fejr, and could use them up, for the water

[*facing:* AUDA ABU]

of Abu Ajaj was near: so there was feasting on bread and meat in our stone dens. These indulgences, amid the slow fatigue of long unbroken marches, were grateful to the delicate townsfolk among us: to myself, and to Zeki and Nesib's Syrian servants, and in a lesser degree to Nesib himself. Nasir's courtesy as host, and his fount of native kindliness, made him exquisite in attention to us whenever the road allowed. To his patient teaching I owed most of my later competence to accompany tribal Arabs on the march without ruining their range and speed.

We rested till two in the afternoon, and reached our stage, Khabr Ajaj, just before sunset, after a dull ride over a duller plain which pro-longed Wadi Fejr to the eastward for many miles. The pool was of this year's rain, already turned thick; and brackish; but good for camels and just possible for men to drink. It lay in a shallow double depression by Wadi Fejr, whose flood had filled it two feet deep over an area two hundred yards across. At its north end was a low sandstone tump. We had thought to find Howeitat here; but the ground was grazed bare and the water fouled by their animals, while they themselves were gone. Auda searched for their tracks, but could find none: the wind-storms had swept the sand-face into clean new ripples. However, since they had come down here from Tubaik, they must have gone on and out into Sirhan: so, if we went away northward, we should find them.

The following day, despite the interminable lapse of time, was only our fourteenth from Wejh; and its sun rose upon us again marching. In the afternoon we at last left Wadi Fejr to steer for Arfaja in Sirhan, a point rather east of north. Accordingly, we inclined right, over flats of limestone and sand, and saw a distant corner of the Great Nefudh, the famous belts of sand-dune which cut off Jebel Shammar from the Syrian Desert. Palgrave, the Blunts, and Gertrude Bell amongst the storied travellers had crossed it, and I begged Auda to bear off a little and let us enter it, and their company: but he growled that men went to the Nefudh only of necessity, when raiding, and that the son of his father did not raid on a tottering, mangy camel. Our business was to reach Arfaja alive.

So we wisely marched on, over monotonous, glittering sand; and over those worse stretches, 'Giaan', of polished mud, nearly as white and smooth as laid paper, and often whole miles square. They blazed

I

back the sun into our faces with glassy vigour, so we rode with its light raining direct arrows upon our heads, and its reflection glancing up from the ground through our inadequate eyelids. It was not a steady pressure, but a pain ebbing and flowing; at one time piling itself up and up till we nearly swooned; and then falling away coolly, in a moment of false shadow like a black web crossing the retina: these gave us a moment's breathing space to store new capacity for suffering, like the struggles to the surface of a drowning man.

We grew short-answered to one another; but relief came toward six o'clock, when we halted for supper, and baked ourselves fresh bread. I gave my camel what was left of my share, for the poor animal went tired and hungry in these bad marches. She was the pedigree camel given by Ibn Saud of Nejd to King Hussein and by him to Feisal; a splendid beast; rough, but sure-footed on hills, and great-hearted. Arabs of means rode none but she-camels, since they went smoother under the saddle than males, and were better tempered and less noisy: also, they were patient and would endure to march long after they were worn out, indeed until they tottered with exhaustion and fell in their tracks and died: whereas the coarser males grew angry, flung themselves down when tired, and from sheer rage would die there unnecessarily.

After dark we crawled for three hours, reaching the top of a sand-ridge. There we slept thankfully, after a bad day of burning wind, dust blizzards, and drifting sand which stung our inflamed faces, and at times in the greater gusts, wrapped the sight of our road from us and drove our complaining camels up and down. But Auda was anxious about the morrow, for another hot head-wind would delay us a third day in the desert, and we had no water left: so he called us early in the night, and we marched down into the plain of the Bisaita (so called in derision, for its huge size and flatness), before day broke. Its fine surface-litter of sun-browned flints was restfully dark after sunrise for our streaming eyes, but hot and hard going for our camels, some of which were already limping with sore feet.

Camels brought up on the sandy plains of the Arabian coast had delicate pads to their feet; and if such animals were taken suddenly inland for long marches over flints or other heat-retaining ground, their soles would burn, and at last crack in a blister; leaving quick flesh, two inches or more across, in the centre of the pad. In this state they could march as ever over sand; but if, by chance, the foot came down on a pebble, they would stumble, or flinch as though they had stepped on fire, and in a long march might break down altogether unless they were very brave. So we rode carefully, picking the softest way, Auda and myself in front.

As we went, some little puffs of dust scurried into the eye of the wind. Auda said they were ostriches. A man ran up to us with two great ivory eggs. We settled to breakfast on this bounty of the Biseita, and looked for fuel; but in twenty minutes found only a wisp of grass. The barren desert was defeating us. The baggage train passed, and my eye fell on the loads of blasting gelatine. We broached a packet, shredding it carefully into a fire beneath the egg propped on stones, till the cookery was pronounced complete. Nasir and Nesib, really interested, dismounted to scoff at us. Auda drew his silver-hilted dagger and chipped the top of the first egg. A stink like a pestilence went across our party. We fled to a clean spot, rolling the second egg hot before us with gentle kicks. It was fresh enough, and hard as a stone. We dug out its contents with the dagger on to the flint flakes which were our platters, and ate it piecemeal; persuading even Nasir, who in his life before had never fallen so low as egg-meat, to take his share. The general verdict was: tough and strong, but good in the Biseita.

Zaal saw an oryx; stalked it on foot, and killed it. The better joints were tied upon the baggage camels for the next halt, and our march continued. Afterwards the greedy Howeitat saw more oryx in the distance and went after the beasts, who foolishly ran a little; then stood still and stared till the men were near, and, too late, ran away again. Their white shining bellies betrayed them; for, by the magnification of the mirage, they winked each move to us from afar.

CHAPTER XLIV

I WAS too weary, and too little sporting, to go out of the straight way for all the rare beasts in the world; so I rode after the caravan, which my camel overhauled quickly with her longer stride. At the tail of it were my men, walking. They feared that some of their animals would be dead before evening, if the wind blew stronger, but were leading them by hand in hope of getting them in. I admired the contrast between Mohammed the lusty, heavy-footed peasant, and the lithe Ageyl, with Farraj and Daud dancing along, barefooted, delicate as thoroughbreds. Only Gasim was not there: they thought him among the Howeitat, for his surliness offended the laughing soldiery and kept him commonly with the Beduin, who were more of his kidney.

There was no one behind, so I rode forward wishing to see how his camel was: and at last found it, riderless, being led by one of the Howeitat. His saddle-bags were on it, and his rifle and his food, but he himself nowhere; gradually it dawned on us that the miserable man was lost. This was a dreadful business, for in the haze and mirage the caravan could not be seen two miles, and on the iron ground it made no tracks: afoot he would never overtake us.

Everyone had marched on, thinking him elsewhere in our loose line; but much time had passed and it was nearly midday, so he must be miles back. His loaded camel was proof that he had not been forgotten asleep at our night halt. The Ageyl ventured that perhaps he had dozed in the saddle and fallen, stunning or killing himself: or perhaps someone of the party had borne him a grudge. Anyway they did not know. He was an ill-natured stranger, no charge on any of them, and they did not greatly care.

True: but it was true also that Mohammed, his countryman and fellow, who was technically his road-companion, knew nothing of the desert, had a foundered camel, and could not turn back for him.

If I sent him, it would be murder. That shifted the difficulty to my shoulders. The Howeitat, who would have helped, were away in the mirage out of sight, hunting or scouting. Ibn Dgheithir's Ageyl were so clannish that they would not put themselves about except for one another. Besides Gasim was my man: and upon me lay the responsibility of him.

I looked weakly at my trudging men, and wondered for a moment if I could change with one, sending him back on my camel to the rescue. My shirking the duty would be understood, because I was a foreigner: but that was precisely the plea I did not dare set up, while I yet presumed to help these Arabs in their own revolt. It was hard, anyway, for a stranger to influence another people's national movement, and doubly hard for a Christian and a sedentary person to sway Moslem nomads. I should make it impossible for myself if I claimed, simultaneously, the privileges of both societies.

So, without saying anything, I turned my unwilling camel round, and forced her, grunting and moaning for her camel friends, back past the long line of men, and past the baggage into the emptiness behind. My temper was very unheroic, for I was furious with my other servants, with my own play-acting as a Beduin, and most of all with Gasim, a gap-toothed, grumbling fellow, skrimshank in all our marches, bad-tempered, suspicious, brutal, a man whose engagement I regretted, and of whom I had promised to rid myself as soon as we reached a discharging-place. It seemed absurd that I should peril my weight in the Arab adventure for a single worthless man.

My camel seemed to feel it also, by her deep grumbling; but that was a constant recourse of ill-treated camels. From calfhood they were accustomed to live in droves, and some grew too conventional to march alone: while none would leave their habitual party without loud grief and unwillingness, such as mine was showing. She turned her head back on her long neck, lowing to the rest, and walked very slowly, and bouncingly. It needed careful guidance to hold her on the road, and a tap from my stick at every pace to keep her moving. However, after a mile or two, she felt better, and began to go forward less constrainedly, but still slowly. I had been noting our direction all these days with my oil compass, and hoped, by its aid, to return nearly to our starting place, seventeen miles away.

Before twenty minutes, the caravan was out of sight, and it was borne in on me how really barren the Bisaita was. Its only marks were the old sanded samh pits, across all possible of which I rode, because my camel tracks would show in them, and be so many blazes of the way back. This samh was the wild flour of the Sherarat; who, poor in all but camel-stocks, made it a boast to find the desert sufficient for their every need. When mixed with dates and loosened with butter, it was good food.

The pits, little threshing floors, were made by pushing aside the flints over a circle of ten feet across. The flints, heaped up round the rim of the pit, made it inches deep, and in this hollow place the women collected and beat out the small red seed. The constant winds, sweeping since over them, could not indeed put back the flint surface (that would perhaps be done by the rain in thousands of winters), but had levelled them up with pale blown sand, so that the pits were grey eyes in the black stony surface.

I had ridden about an hour and a half, easily, for the following breeze had let me wipe the crust from my red eyes and look forward almost without pain: when I saw a figure, or large bush, or at least something black ahead of me. The shifting mirage disguised height or distance; but this thing seemed moving, a little east of our course. On chance I turned my camel's head that way, and in a few minutes saw that it was Gasim. When I called he stood confusedly; I rode up and saw that he was nearly blinded and silly, standing there with his arms held out to me, and his black mouth gaping open. The Ageyl had put our last water in my skin, and this he spilled madly over his face and breast, in haste to drink. He stopped babbling, and began to wail out his sorrows. I sat him, pillion, on the camel's rump; then stirred her up and mounted.

At our turn the beast seemed relieved, and moved forward freely. I set an exact compass course, so exact that often I found our old tracks, as little spurts of paler sand scattered over the brown-black flint. In spite of our double weight the camel began to stride out, and at times she even put her head down and for a few paces developed that fast and most comfortable shuffle to which the best animals, while young, were broken by skilled riders. This proof of reserve spirit in her rejoiced me, as did the little time lost in search.

Gasim was moaning impressively about the pain and terror of his thirst: I told him to stop; but he went on, and began to sit loosely; until at each step of the camel he bumped down on her hinder quarters with a crash, which, like his crying, spurred her to greater pace. There was danger in this, for we might easily founder her so. Again I told him to stop, and when he only screamed louder, hit him and swore that for another sound I would throw him off. The threat, to which my general rage gave colour, worked. After it he clung on grimly without sound.

Not four miles had passed when again I saw a black bubble, lunging and swaying in the mirage ahead. It split into three, and swelled. I wondered if they were enemy. A minute later the haze unrolled with the disconcerting suddenness of illusion; and it was Auda with two of Nasir's men come back to look for me. I yelled jests and scoffs at them for abandoning a friend in the desert. Auda pulled his beard and grumbled that had he been present I would never have gone back. Gasim was transferred with insults to a better rider's saddle-pad, and we ambled forward together.

Auda pointed to the wretched hunched-up figure and denounced me, 'For that thing, not worth a camel's price . . .' I interrupted him with 'Not worth a half-crown, Auda', and he, delighted in his simple mind, rode near Gasim, and struck him sharply, trying to make him repeat, like a parrot, his price. Gasim bared his broken teeth in a grin of rage and afterwards sulked on. In another hour we were on the heels of the baggage camels, and as we passed up the inquisitive line of our caravan, Auda repeated my joke to each pair, perhaps forty times in all, till I had seen to the full its feebleness.

Gasim explained that he had dismounted to ease nature, and had missed the party afterwards in the dark: but, obviously, he had gone to sleep, where he dismounted, with the fatigue of our slow, hot journeying. We rejoined Nasir and Nesib in the van. Nesib was vexed with me, for perilling the lives of Auda and myself on a whim. It was clear to him that I reckoned they would come back for me. Nasir was shocked at his ungenerous outlook, and Auda was glad to rub into a townsman the paradox of tribe and city; the collective responsibility and group-brotherhood of the desert, contrasted with the isolation and competitive living of the crowded districts.

Over this little affair hours had passed, and the rest of the day seemed not so long; though the heat became worse, and the sand-blast stiffened in our faces till the air could be seen and heard, whistling past our camels like smoke. The ground was flat and featureless till five o'clock, when we saw low mounds ahead, and a little later found ourselves in comparative peace, amid sand-hills coated slenderly with tamarisk. These were the Kaseim of Sirhan. The bushes and the dunes broke the wind, it was sunset, and the evening mellowed and reddened on us from the west. So I wrote in my diary that Sirhan was beautiful.

Palestine became a land of milk and honey to those who had spent forty years in Sinai: Damascus had the name of an earthly paradise to the tribes which could enter it only after weeks and weeks of painful marching across the flint-stones of this northern desert: and likewise the Kaseim of Arfaja in which we spent that night, after five days across the blazing Houl in the teeth of a sand-storm, looked fresh and countryfied. They were raised only a few feet above the Biseita, and from them valleys seemed to run down towards the east into a huge depression where lay the well we wanted: but now that we had crossed the desert and reached the Sirhan safely, the terror of thirst had passed and we knew fatigue to be our chief ill. So we agreed to camp for the night where we were, and to make beacon fires for the slave of Nuri Shaalan, who, like Gasim, had disappeared from our caravan to-day.

We were not greatly perturbed about him. He knew the country and his camel was under him. It might be that he had intentionally taken the direct way to Jauf, Nuri's capital, to earn the reward of first news that we came with gifts. However it was, he did not come that night, nor next day; and when, months after, I asked Nuri of him, he replied that his dried body had lately been found, lying beside his un-plundered camel far out in the wilderness. He must have lost himself in the sand-haze and wandered till his camel broke down; and there died of thirst and heat. Not a long death — even for the very strongest a second day in summer was all — but very painful; for thirst was an active malady; a fear and panic which tore at the brain and reduced the bravest man to a stumbling babbling maniac in an hour or two: and then the sun killed him.

CHAPTER XLV

HAVING not a mouthful of water we of course ate nothing: which made it a continent night. Yet the certainty of drink on the morrow let us sleep easily, lying on our bellies to prevent the inflation of foodlessness. Arab habit was to fill themselves to vomiting point at each well, and either to go dry to the next; or, if they carried water, to use it lavishly at the first halt, drinking and bread-making. As my ambition was to avoid comment upon my difference, I copied them, trusting with reason that their physical superiority was not great enough to trap me into serious harm. Actually I only once went ill with thirst.

Next morning we rode down slopes, over a first ridge, and a second, and a third; each three miles from the other; till at eight o'clock we dismounted by the wells of Arfaja, the sweet-smelling bush so called being fragrant all about us. We found the Sirhan not a valley, but a long fault draining the country on each side of it and collecting the waters into the successive depressions of its bed. The ground surface was of flinty gravel, alternating with soft sand; and the aimless valleys seemed hardly able to trace their slow and involved levels between the loose sand-dunes, over which blew the feathery tamarisk; its whipcord roots binding the slopes together.

The unlined wells were dug about eighteen feet, to water creamy to the touch with a powerful smell and brackish taste. We found it delicious, and since there was greenstuff about, good for camel food, decided to stay here the day while we searched for the Howeitat by sending to Maigua, the southernmost well of the Sirhan. So we should establish whether they were behind us; and if they were not, could march towards the north with confidence that we were on their track.

Hardly, however, had our messenger ridden off when one of the Howeitat saw riders hiding in the scrub to the northward of us.

Instantly they called to arms. Mohammed el Dheilan, first into the saddle, with other Toweiha galloped out against the supposed enemy;

Nasir and I mustered the Ageyl (whose virtue lay not in fighting Beduin-fashion with Beduins) and placed them in sets about the dune so as reasonably to defend the baggage. However, the enemy got off. Mohammed returned after half an hour to say that he had not made relentless pursuit for pity of the condition of his camel. He had seen only three tracks and supposed that the men had been scouts of a Shammar raiding party in the neighbourhood, Arfaja being commonly infested by them.

Auda called up Zaal, his nephew, the keenest eye of all the Howeitat, and told him to go out and discover the enemy's number and intention. Zaal was a lithe metallic man, with a bold appraising look, cruel lips, and a thin laugh, full of the brutality which these nomad Howeitat had caught from the peasantry. He went off and searched; but found the thicket of brushwood about us full of tracks; while the tamarisk kept the wind off the sandy floor, and made it impossible to distinguish particularly the footprints of to-day.

The afternoon passed peacefully, and we lulled ourselves, though we kept a sentry on the head of the great dune behind the water-holes. At sunset I went down and washed myself in the smarting brine; and on my way back halted at the Ageyl fire to take coffee with them, while listening to their Nejdi Arabic. They began to tell me long stories of Captain Shakespear, who had been received by ibn Saud in Riyadh as a personal friend, and had crossed Arabia from the Persian Gulf to Egypt; and been at last killed in battle by the Shammar in a set-back which the champions of Nejd had suffered during one of their periodic wars.

Many of the Ageyl of ibn Dgheithir had travelled with him, as escort or followers, and had tales of his magnificence and of the strange seclusion in which he kept himself day and night. The Arabs, who usually lived in heaps, suspected some ulterior reason for any too careful privacy. To remember this, and to foreswear all selfish peace and quiet while wandering with them, was one of the least pleasant lessons of the desert war: and humiliating, too, for it was a part of pride with Englishmen to hug solitude; ourselves finding ourselves to be remarkable, when there was no competition present.

While we talked the roasted coffee was dropped with three grains of cardamom into the mortar. Abdulla brayed it; with the dring-drang, dring-drang pestle strokes of village Nejd, two equal pairs of *legato* beats. Mohammed el Dheilan heard, came silently across the sand and sank down, slowly, groaningly, camel-like, on the ground by me. Mohammed was a companionable fellow; a powerful, thinking man with much wry humour, and an affection of sour craft, sometimes justified by his acts, but generally disclosing a friendly cynical nature. In build he was unusually strong and well-grown, not much under six feet in height; a man of perhaps thirty-eight, determined and active, with a high-coloured face ruggedly lined, and very baffling eyes.

He was second man of the Abu Tayi; richer and having more followers than Auda, and with more taste for the luscious. He had a little house in Maan, landed property (and it was whispered, 'cattle') near Tafileh. Under his influence the war parties of the Abu Tayi rode out delicately, with sunshades to defend them from the fierce rays of the sun and with bottles of mineral water in their saddle-bags, as refreshment upon the journey. He was the brain of the tribal councils and directed their politics. His sore-headed critical spirit pleased me; and often I used his intelligence and greed to convert him to my party before broaching a new idea.

The long ride in company had made companions of our minds and bodies. The hazardous goal was in our thoughts, day and night; consciously and unconsciously we were training ourselves; reducing our wills to the single purpose which oftenest engrossed these odd moments of talk about an evening fire. And we were so musing while the coffee-maker boiled up his coffee, tapped it down again, made a palm-fibre mat to strain it before he poured (grounds in the cup were evil manners), when there came a volley from the shadowy dunes east of us and one of the Ageyl toppled forward into the centre of the firelit circle with a screech.

Mohammed with his massive foot thrust a wave of sand over the fire and in the quick blinding darkness we rolled behind banks of tamarisk and scattered to get rifles, while our outlying pickets began to return the fire, aiming hurriedly towards the flashes. We had unlimited ammunition in our hand, and did not stint to show it.

Gradually the enemy slackened, astonished perhaps at our preparedness. Finally his fire stopped, and we held our own, listening for a rush or for attack from a new quarter. For half an hour we lay still; and silent, but for the groans, and at last the death struggle of the man hit with the first volley. Then we were impatient of waiting longer. Zaal went out to report what was happening to the enemy. After another half-hour he called to us that no one was left within reach. They had ridden away: about twenty of them, in his trained opinion.

Despite Zaal's assurances, we passed a restless night, and in the morning before dawn we buried Assaf, our first casualty, and moved off northward, keeping the bottom of the hollow, with the sand-hills mostly on our left. We rode for five hours and then halted for breakfast on the south bank of a great spill of torrent-beds running down into the Sirhan from the south-west. Auda told me these were the mouths of Seil Fejr, the valley whose head we had seen at Selhub and whose bed we had followed right across the Houl.

The grazing was better than at Arfaja, and we allowed our camels the four hours of noon to fill themselves — a poor proceeding, for the midday grazing was not profitable to them, though we enjoyed ourselves in the shadow of our blankets, sleeping out the sleep we had missed the night before. Here in the open, away from all possibility of hidden approach, was no fear of disturbance, and our displayed strength and confidence might dissuade the invisible enemy. Our desire was to fight Turks, and this inter-Arab business was sheer waste. In the afternoon we rode on twelve miles to a sharp group of firm sand-hills, enclosing an open space big enough for us, and commanding the country round about. We halted there, in anticipation of another night attack.

Next morning we did a fast march of five hours (our camels being full of life after their ease of yesterday) to an oasis-hollow of stunted palm-trees, with tamarisk clumps here and there, and plentiful water, about seven feet underground, tasting sweeter than the water of Arfaja. Yet this also upon experience proved 'Sirhan water', the first drink of which was tolerable, but which refused a lather to soap, and developed (after two days in closed vessels) a foul smell and a taste destructive to the intended flavour of coffee, tea, or bread.

Verily we were tiring of Wadi Sirhan, though Nesib and Zeki still designed works of plantation and reclamation here for the Arab Government when by them established. Such vaulting imagination was typical of Syrians, who easily persuaded themselves of possibilities, and as quickly reached forward to lay their present responsibilities on others. 'Zeki,' said I one day, 'your camel is full of mange.' 'Alas, and alack,' agreed he mournfully, 'in the evening, very quickly, when the sun is low, we shall dress her skin with ointment.'

During our next ride I mentioned mange once again. 'Aha,' said Zeki, 'it has given me a full idea. Conceive the establishment of a Veterinary Department of State, for Syria, when Damascus is ours. We shall have a staff of skilled surgeons, with a school of probationers and students, in a central hospital, or rather central hospitals, for camels and for horses, and for donkeys and cattle, even (why not?) for sheep and goats. There must be scientific and bacteriological branches to make researches into universal cures for animal disease. And what about a library of foreign books? ... and district hospitals to feed the central, and travelling inspectors ...' With Nesib's eager collaboration he carved Syria into four inspectorates general, and many sub-inspectorates.

Again on the morrow there was mention of mange. They had slept on their labour, and the scheme was rounding out. 'Yet, my dear, it is imperfect; and our nature stops not short of perfection. We grieve to see you thus satisfied to snatch the merely opportune. It is an English fault.' I dropped into their vein. 'O Nesib,' said I, 'and O Zeki, will not perfection, even in the least of things, entail the ending of this world? Are we ripe for that? When I am angry I pray God to swing our globe into the fiery sun, and prevent the sorrows of the not-yet-born: but when I am content, I want to lie for ever in the shade, till I become a shade myself.' Uneasily they shifted the talk to stud farms, and on the sixth day the poor camel died. Very truly, 'Because', as Zeki pointed out, 'you did not dress her'. Auda, Nasir, and the rest of us kept our beasts going by constant care. We could, perhaps, just stave the mange off till we should reach the camp of some well-provided tribe, and be able to procure medicines, with which to combat the disease whole-heartedly.

A mounted man came bearing down upon us. Tension there was, for a moment; but then the Howeitat hailed him. He was one of their herdsmen, and greetings were exchanged in an unhurried voice, as was proper in the desert, where noise was a low-bred business at the best, and urban at its worst.

He told us the Howeitat were camped in front, from Isawiya to Nebk, anxiously waiting our news. All was well with their tents. Auda's anxiety passed and his eagerness kindled. We rode fast for an hour to Isawiya and the tents of Ali abu Fitna, chief of one of Auda's clans. Old Ali, rheumy-eyed, red and unkempt, into whose jutting beard a long nose perpetually dripped, greeted us warmly and urged us to the hospitality of his tent. We excused ourselves as too many, and camped near by under some thorns, while he and the other tent-holders made estimate of our numbers, and prepared feasts for us in the evening, to each group of tents its little batch of visitors. The meal took hours to produce, and it was long after dark when they called us to it. I woke and stumbled across, ate, made my way back to our couched camels and slept again.

Our march was prosperously over. We had found the Howeitat: our men were in excellent fettle: we had our gold and our explosives still intact. So we drew happily together in the morning to a solemn council on action. There was agreement that first we should present six thousand pounds to Nuri Shaalan, by whose sufferance we were in Sirhan. We wanted from him liberty to stay while enrolling and preparing our fighting men; and when we moved off we wanted him to look after their families and tents and herds.

These were great matters. It was determined that Auda himself should ride to Nuri on embassy, because they were friends. Nuri's was too near and too big a tribe for Auda to fight, however lordly his delight in war. Self-interest, accordingly, had prompted the two great men to an alliance: and acquaintance had bred a whimsical regard, by virtue of which each suffered the other's oddities with patience. Auda would explain to Nuri what we hoped to do, and Feisal's desire that he make a public demonstration of adherence to Turkey. Only so could he cover us, while still pleasing the Turks.

CHAPTER XLVI

MEANWHILE we would stay with Ali abu Fitna, moving
gently northward with him towards Nebk, where Auda
would tell all the Abu Tayi to collect. He would be back
from Nuri before they were united. This was the business, and we
laded six bags of gold into Auda's saddle-bags, and off he went.
Afterwards the chiefs of the Fitenna waited on us, and said they were
honoured to feast us twice a day, forenoon and sunset, so long as we
remained with them; and they meant what they said. Howeitat
hospitality was unlimited — no three-day niggardliness for them of the
nominal desert law — and importunate, and left us no honourable
escape from the entirety of the nomad's dream of well-being.

Each morning, between eight and ten, a little group of blood mares
under an assortment of imperfect saddlery would come to our camping
place, and on them Nasir, Nesib, Zeki and I would mount, and with
perhaps a dozen of our men on foot would move solemnly across the
valley by the sandy paths between the bushes. Our horses were led by
our servants, since it would be immodest to ride free or fast. So
eventually we would reach the tent which was to be our feast-hall for
that time; each family claiming us in turn, and bitterly offended if
Zaal, the adjudicator, preferred one out of just order.

As we arrived, the dogs would rush out at us, and be driven off by
onlookers — always a crowd had collected round the chosen tent — and
we stepped in under the ropes to its guest half, made very large for the
occasion and carefully dressed with its wall-curtain on the sunny side
to give us the shade. The bashful host would murmur and vanish
again out of sight. The tribal rugs, lurid red things from Beyrout, were
ready for us, arranged down the partition curtain, along the back wall
and across the dropped end, so that we sat down on three sides of an
open dusty space. We might be fifty men in all.

The host would reappear, standing by the pole; our local fellow-
guests, el Dheilan, Zaal and other sheikhs, reluctantly let themselves be
placed on the rugs between us, sharing our elbow-room on the pack-

271

saddles, padded with folded felt rugs, over which we leaned. The front of the tent was cleared, and the dogs were frequently chased away by excited children, who ran across the empty space pulling yet smaller children after them. Their clothes were less as their years were less, and their pot-bodies rounder. The smallest infants of all, out of their fly-black eyes, would stare at the company, gravely balanced on spread legs, stark-naked, sucking their thumbs and pushing out expectant bellies towards us.

Then would follow an awkward pause, which our friends would try to cover, by showing us on its perch the household hawk (when possible a sea-bird taken young on the Red Sea coast) or their watch-cockerel, or their greyhound. Once a tame ibex was dragged in for our admiration: another time an oryx. When these interests were exhausted they would try and find a small talk to distract us from the household noises, and from noticing the urgent whispered cookery-directions wafted through the dividing curtain with a powerful smell of boiled fat and drifts of tasty meat-smoke.

After a silence the host or a deputy would come forward and whisper 'Black or white?' an invitation for us to choose coffee or tea. Nasir would always answer 'Black', and the slave would be beckoned forward with the beaked coffee-pot in one hand, and three or four clinking cups of white ware in the other. He would dash a few drops of coffee into the uppermost cup, and proffer it to Nasir; then pour the second for me, and the third for Nesib; and pause while we turned the cups about in our hands, and sucked them carefully, to get appreciatively from them the last richest drop.

As soon as they were empty his hand was stretched to clap them noisily one above the other, and toss them out with a lesser flourish for the next guest in order, and so on round the assembly till all had drunk. Then back to Nasir again. This second cup would be tastier than the first, partly because the pot was yielding deeper from the brew, partly because of the heel-taps of so many previous drinkers present in the cups; whilst the third and fourth rounds, if the serving of the meat delayed so long, would be of surprising flavour.

However, at last, two men came staggering through the thrilled crowd, carrying the rice and meat on a tinned copper tray or shallow bath, five feet across, set like a great brazier on a foot. In the tribe there was only this one food-bowl of the size, and an incised inscription ran round it in florid Arabic characters: 'To the glory of God, and in trust of mercy at the last, the property of His poor suppliant, Auda abu Tayi'. It was borrowed by the host who was to entertain us for the time; and, since my urgent brain and body made me wakeful, from my blankets in the first light I would see the dish going across country, and by marking down its goal would know where we were to feed that day.

The bowl was now brim-full, ringed round its edge by white rice in an embankment a foot wide and six inches deep, filled with legs and ribs of mutton till they toppled over. It needed two or three victims to make in the centre a dressed pyramid of meat such as honour pre- scribed. The centre-pieces were the boiled, upturned heads, propped on their severed stumps of necks, so that the ears, brown like old leaves, flapped out on the rice surface. The jaws gaped emptily upward, pulled open to show the hollow throat with the tongue, still pink, clinging to the lower teeth; and the long incisors whitely crowned the pile, very prominent above the nostrils' pricking hair and the lips which sneered away blackly from them.

This load was set down on the soil of the cleared space between us, where it steamed hotly, while a procession of minor helpers bore small cauldrons and copper vats in which the cooking had been done. From them, with much-bruised bowls of enamelled iron, they ladled out over the main dish all the inside and outside of the sheep; little bits of yellow intestine, the white tail-cushion of fat, brown muscles and meat and bristly skin, all swimming in the liquid butter and grease of the seething. The bystanders watched anxiously, muttering satisfactions when a very juicy scrap plopped out.

The fat was scalding. Every now and then a man would drop his baler with an exclamation, and plunge his burnt fingers, not re- luctantly, in his mouth to cool them: but they persevered till at last their scooping rang loudly on the bottoms of the pots; and, with a gesture of triumph, they fished out the intact livers from their hiding place in the gravy and topped the yawning jaws with them.

Two raised each smaller cauldron and tilted it, letting the liquid splash down upon the meat till the rice-crater was full, and the loose grains at the edge swam in the abundance: and yet they poured, till, amid cries of astonishment from us, it was running over, and a little pool congealing in the dust. That was the final touch of splendour, and the host called us to come and eat.

We feigned a deafness, as manners demanded: at last we heard him, and looked surprised at one another, each urging his fellow to move first; till Nasir rose coyly, and after him we all came forward to sink on one knee round the tray, wedging in and cuddling up till the twenty-two for whom there was barely space were grouped around the food. We turned back our right sleeves to the elbow, and, taking lead from Nasir with a low 'In the name of God the merciful, the loving-kind', we dipped together.

The first dip, for me, at least, was always cautious, since the liquid fat was so hot that my unaccustomed fingers could seldom bear it: and so I would toy with an exposed and cooling lump of meat till others' excavations had drained my rice-segment. We would knead between the fingers (not soiling the palm), neat balls of rice and fat and liver and meat cemented by gentle pressure, and project them by leverage of the thumb from the crooked fore-finger into the mouth. With the right trick and the right construction the little lump held together and came clean off the hand; but when surplus butter and odd fragments clung, cooling, to the fingers, they had to be licked carefully to make the next effort slip easier away.

As the meat pile wore down (nobody really cared about rice: flesh was the luxury) one of the chief Howeitat eating with us would draw his dagger, silver hilted, set with turquoise, a signed masterpiece of Mohammed ibn Zari, of Jauf,* and would cut criss-cross from the larger bones long diamonds of meat easily torn up between the fingers; for it was necessarily boiled very tender, since all had to be disposed of with the right hand which alone was honourable.

Our host stood by the circle, encouraging the appetite with pious

---

* The most famous sword-smith of my time was ibn Bani, a craftsman of the Ibn Rashid dynasty of Hail. He rode once on foray with the Shammar against the Rualla, and was captured. When Nuri recognized him, he shut up with him in prison ibn Zari, his own sword-smith, swearing they should not come out till their work was indistinguishable. So ibn Zari improved greatly in the skill of his craft, while remaining in design the better artist.

ejaculations. At top speed we twisted, tore, cut and stuffed: never speaking, since conversation would insult a meal's quality, though it was proper to smile thanks when an intimate guest passed a select fragment, or when Mohammed el Dheilan gravely handed over a huge barren bone with a blessing. On such occasions I would return the compliment with some hideous impossible lump of guts, a flippancy which rejoiced the Howeitat, but which the gracious, aristocratic Nasir saw with disapproval.

At length some of us were nearly filled, and began to play and pick; glancing sideways at the rest till they too grew slow, and at last ceased eating, elbow on knee, the hand hanging down from the wrist over the tray edge to drip, while the fat, butter and scattered grains of rice cooled into a stiff white grease which gummed the fingers together. When all had stopped, Nasir meaningly cleared his throat, and we rose up together in haste with an explosive 'God requite it you, O host', to group ourselves outside among the tent-ropes while the next twenty guests inherited our leaving.

Those of us who were nice would go to the end of the tent where the flap of the roof-cloth, beyond the last poles, drooped down as an end curtain; and on this clan handkerchief (whose coarse goat-hair mesh was pliant and glossy with much use) would scrape the thickest of the fat from the hands. Then we would make back to our seats, and re-take them sighingly; while the slaves, leaving aside their portion, the skulls of the sheep, would come round our rank with a wooden bowl of water, and a coffee-cup as dipper, to splash over our fingers, while we rubbed them with the tribal soap-cake.

Meantime the second and third sittings by the dish were having their turn, and then there would be one more cup of coffee, or a glass of syrup-like tea; and at last the horses would be brought and we would slip out to them, and mount, with a quiet blessing to the hosts as we passed by. When our backs were turned the children would run in disorder upon the ravaged dish, tear our gnawed bones from one another, and escape into the open with valuable fragments to be devoured in security behind some distant bush: while the watchdogs of all the camp prowled round snapping, and the master of the tent fed the choicest offal to his greyhound.

CHAPTER XLVII

WE feasted on the first day once, on the second twice, on the third twice; at Isawiya: and then, on May the thirtieth, we saddled and rode easily for three hours, past an old sanded lava-field to a valley in which seven-foot wells of the usual brackish water lay all about us. The Abu Tayi struck camp when we struck, and journeyed at our side, and camped around us: so to-day for the first time I was spectator from the midst of an Arab tribe, and actor in the routine of its march.

It was strangely unlike the usual desert-constancy. All day the grey-green expanse of stones and bushes quivered like a mirage with the movement of men on foot; and horsemen; men on camels; camels bearing the hunched black loads which were the goat-hair tent-cloths; camels swaying curiously, like butterflies, under the winged and fringed howdahs of the women; camels tusked like mammoths or tailed like birds with the cocked or dragging tent-poles of silvery poplar. There was no order nor control nor routine of march, other than the wide front, the self-contained parties, the simultaneous start, which the insecurity of countless generations had made instinctive. The difference was that the desert, whose daily sparseness gave value to every man, to-day seemed with their numbers suddenly to come alive.

The pace was easy; and we, who had been guarding our own lives for weeks, found it a relaxation beyond feeling to know ourselves so escorted as to share the light liability of danger with a host. Even our most solemn riders let themselves go a little, and the wilder ones became licentious. First amongst these, of course, were Farraj and Daud, my two imps, whose spirits not all the privations of our road had quelled for a moment. About their riding places in our line of march centred two constant swirls of activity or of accident, according as their quenchless mischief found a further expression.

On my dry patience they grated a little, because the plague of snakes which had been with us since our first entry into Sirhan to-day rose to memorable height, and became a terror. In ordinary times, so the Arabs said, snakes were little worse here than elsewhere by water in the desert: but this year the valley seemed creeping with horned vipers and puff-adders, cobras and black snakes. By night movement was dangerous: and at last we found it necessary to walk with sticks, beating the bushes each side while we stepped warily through on bare feet.

We could not lightly draw water after dark, for there were snakes swimming in the pools or clustering in knots around their brinks. Twice puff-adders came twisting into the alert ring of our debating coffee-circle. Three of our men died of bites; four recovered after great fear and pain, and a swelling of the poisoned limb. Howeitat treatment was to bind up the part with snake-skin plaster, and read chapters of the Koran to the sufferer until he died. They also pulled thick Damascene ankle-boots, red, with blue tassels and horse-shoe heels, over their horny feet when they went late abroad.

A strange thing was the snakes' habit, at night, of lying beside us, probably for warmth, under or on the blanket. When we learned this our rising was with infinite care, and the first up would search round his fellows with a stick till he could pronounce them unencumbered. Our party of fifty men killed perhaps twenty snakes daily; at last they got so on our nerves that the boldest of us feared to touch ground; while those who, like myself, had a shuddering horror of all reptiles longed that our stay in Sirhan might end.

Not so Farraj and Daud. To them, this was a new and splendid game. They troubled us continually with alarms, and furious beatings upon the head of every harmless twig or root which caught their fancy. At last, in our noon-halt, I charged them strictly not to let the cry of snake again pass their lips aloud; and then, sitting by our traps upon the sand, we had peace. To live on the floor, whence it was so far to arise and walk, disposed to inaction, and there was much to think about so that it may have been an hour afterwards before I noticed the offending pair smiling and nudging one another. My eyes idly followed their eyes to the neighbouring bush under which a brown snake lay coiled, glittering at me.

Quickly I moved myself, and cried to Ali, who jumped in with his riding-cane and settled it. I told him to give the two boys a swinging half-dozen each, to teach them not again to be literal at my expense. Nasir, slumbering behind me, heard and with joy shouted to add six from himself. Nesib copied him, and then Zeki, and then ibn Dgheithir, till half the men were clamouring for revenge. The culprits were abashed when they saw that all the hides and all the sticks in the party would hardly expiate their account: however, I saved them the weight of it, and instead we proclaimed them moral bankrupts, and set them under the women to gather wood and draw water for the tents.

So they laboured shamefully for the two days we spent at Abu Tarfeiyat; where on the first day we feasted twice and on the second day twice. Then Nesib broke down, and on plea of illness took refuge inside Nasir's tent, and ate dry bread thankfully. Zeki had been ailing on the road, and his first effort at the Howeitat sodden meat and greasy rice had prostrated him. He also lay within the tent, breathing disgust and dysentery against us. Nasir's stomach had had long experience of tribal ways and stood the test grandly. It was incumbent on him, for the honour of our guesting, to answer every call; and for greater honour, he constrained me always to go with him. So we two leaders represented the camp each day, with a decent proportion of the hungering Ageyl.

Of course it was monotonous; but the crystal happiness in our hosts was a return satisfaction for our eyes, and to have shattered it a crime. Oxford or Medina had tried to cure Nasir and me of superstitious prejudice; and had complicated us to the point of regaining simplicity. These people were achieving in our cause the height of nomadic ambition, a continued orgy of seethed mutton. My heaven might have been a lonely, soft arm-chair, a book-rest, and the complete poets, set in Caslon, printed on tough paper: but I had been for twenty-eight years well-fed, and if Arab imagination ran on food-bowls, so much the more attainable their joy. They had been provident expressly on our account. A few days before we came, a drover had guested with them; and, by Auda's order, they had bought his fifty sheep to entertain us worthily. In fifteen meals (a week) we had consumed them all, and the hospitality guttered out.

Digestion returned, and with it our power of movement. We were very weary of Sirhan. The landscape was of a hopelessness and sadness deeper than all the open deserts we had crossed. Sand, or flint, or a desert of bare rocks was exciting sometimes, and in certain lights had the monstrous beauty of sterile desolation: but there was something sinister, something actively evil in this snake-devoted Sirhan, proliferant of salt water, barren palms, and bushes which served neither for grazing nor for firewood.

Accordingly we marched one day, and another, beyond Ghutti, whose weak well was nearly sweet. When we got near Ageila, we saw that it was held by many tents, and presently a troop came out to meet us. They were Auda abu Tayi, safely back from Nuri Shaalan, with the one-eyed Durzi ibn Dughmi, our old guest at Wejh. His presence proved Nuri's favour, as did their strong escort of Rualla horse; who, bareheaded and yelling, welcomed us to Nuri's empty house with a great show of spears and wild firing of rifles and revolvers at full gallop through the dust.

This modest manor had some fruitful palms, enclosed, and they had pitched beside the garden a Mesopotamian tent of white canvas. Here, also, stood Auda's tent, a huge hall seven poles long and three wide; and Zaal's tent was near it, and many others; and through the afternoon we received fusillades of honour, deputations, and gifts of ostrich eggs, or Damascus dainties, or camels, or scraggy horses, while the air was loud about us with the cries of Auda's volunteers demanding service, immediate service, against the Turks.

Affairs looked well, and we set three men to make coffee for the visitors, who came in to Nasir one by one or group by group, swearing allegiance to Feisal and to the Arab Movement, in the Wejh formula; and promising to obey Nasir, and to follow after him with their contingents. Besides their formal presents, each new party deposited on our carpet their privy, accidental gift of lice; and long before sunset Nasir and I were in a fever, with relay after relay of irritation. Auda had a stiff arm, the effect of an old wound in the elbow joint, and so could not scratch all of himself; but experience had taught him a way of thrusting a cross-headed camel-stick up his left sleeve and turning it round and round inside against his ribs, which method seemed to relieve his itch more than our claws did ours.

CHAPTER XLVIII

NEBK, to be our next halt, had plentiful water, with some grazing. Auda had appointed it our rallying place, because of the convenient nearness of the Blaidat, or 'salt hamlets'. In it he and Sherif Nasir sat down for days, to consider enrolling the men, and to prepare the road along which we would march, by approaching the tribes and the sheikhs who lived near. Leisure remained for Nesib, Zeki and myself. As usual, the unstable Syrian judgement, not able to consist in the narrow point of virtue, staggered to the circumference. In the heady atmosphere of first enthusiasm they ignored Akaba and, despised the plain purpose which had led us here. Nesib knew the Shaalans and the Druses. His mind enrolled them, not the Howeitat; struck at Deraa, not Maan: occupied Damascus, not Akaba. He pointed out that the Turks were all unready: that we were sure to gain our first objective, by sheer surprise: that therefore our objective should be the highest. Damascus was indicated by the finger of inevitable fate.

I pointed him in vain to Feisal yet in Wejh: to the British yet the wrong side of Gaza: to the new Turkish army massing in Aleppo to recover Mesopotamia. I showed how we in Damascus would be unsupported: without resources or organizations: without a base: without even a line of communication with our friends. But Nesib was towering above geography, and beyond tactics, and only sordid means would bring him down. So I went to Auda, and said that with the new objective cash and credit would go to Nuri Shaalan, and not to him: I went to Nasir, and used influence and our liking for one another to keep him on my plan; fanning high the too easily-lit jealousy between a Sherif and a Damascene; between an authentic Shia descendant of Ali and the martyred Hussein, and a very doubtfully reputed descendant of the 'successor' Abu Bekr.

For our movement, the point was life and death. I was sure that if we took Damascus we should not hold it six weeks, for Murray could not instantly attack the Turks, nor would sea-transport be available at the moment's notice to land a British army at Beyrout: and in losing

Damascus we should lose our supporters (only their first flush was profitable: a rebellion which stood still or went back was lost) without having gained Akaba, which was the last base in safe water; and in my judgement the only door, except the Middle Euphrates, which we could unlock for an assuredly successful entry into Syria.

Akaba's special value to the Turks was that, when they pleased, it might be constituted a threat to the right flank of the British Army. At the end of 1914 their higher command had thought to make it their main route to the Canal: but they found the food and water difficulties great, and adopted the Beersheba route. Now, however, the British had left the Canal positions and had thrust forward to Gaza and Beersheba. This made the feeding of the Turkish army easier by shortening its line. Consequently, the Turks had surplus transport. Akaba was also of greater geographical value than of old, since it now lay behind the British right, and a small force operating from it would threaten either El Arish or Suez effectively.

The Arabs needed Akaba: firstly, to extend their front, which was their tactical principle; and, secondly, to link up with the British. If they took it the act gave them Sinai, and made positive junction between them and Sir Archibald Murray. Thus having become really useful, they would obtain material help. The human frailty of Murray's Staff was such that nothing but physical contact with our success could persuade them of our importance. Murray was friendly: but if we became his right wing he would equip us properly, almost without the asking. Accordingly, for the Arabs, Akaba spelt plenty in food, money, guns, advisers. I wanted contact with the British; to act as the right wing of the Allies in the conquest of Palestine and Syria; and to assert the Arabic-speaking peoples' desire or desert of freedom and self-government. In my view, if the revolt did not reach the main battle-field against Turkey it would have to confess failure, and remain a side-show of a side-show. I had preached to Feisal, from our first meeting, that freedom was taken, not given.

Both Nasir and Auda fortunately answered to my whispers; and, after recriminations, Nesib left us, and rode with Zeki to the Druse Mountain, there to do the preliminary work necessary to the launching of his great Damascus scheme. I knew his incapacity to create; but it was not in my mind to permit even a half-baked rising there, to spoil our future material. So I was careful to draw his teeth before he started, by taking from him most of the money Feisal had shared out to him. The fool made this easy for me, as he knew he had not enough for all he wanted; and, measuring the morality of England by his own pettiness, came to me for the promise of more if he raised a Syrian movement independent of Feisal, under his own leadership. I had no fear of so untoward a miracle; and, instead of calling him rat, gave my ready promise for future help, if he would for the present give me his balance, to get us to Akaba, where I would make funds available for the general need. He yielded to my condition with a bad grace: and Nasir was delighted to get two bags of money unexpectedly.

Yet the optimism of Nesib had its effect upon me; while I still saw the liberation of Syria happening in steps, of which Akaba was the indispensable first. I now saw these steps coming close together; and as soon as Nesib was out of the way planned to go off myself, rather in his fashion, on a long tour of the north country. I felt that one more sight of Syria would put straight the strategic ideas given me by the Crusaders and the first Arab conquest, and adjust them to the two new factors — the railways, and Murray in Sinai.

Also a rash adventure suited my abandoned mood. It should have been happiness, this lying out free as air, with the visible life striving its utmost along my own path; but the knowledge of the axe I was secretly grinding destroyed all my assurance.

The Arab Revolt had begun on false pretences. To gain the Sherif's help our Cabinet had offered, through Sir Henry McMahon, to support the establishment of native governments in parts of Syria and Mesopotamia, 'saving the interests of our ally, France'. The last modest clause concealed a treaty (kept secret, till too late, from McMahon, and therefore from the Sherif) by which France, England and Russia agreed to annex some of these promised areas, and to establish their respective spheres of influence over all the rest.

Rumours of the fraud reached Arab ears, from Turkey. In the East persons were more trusted than institutions. So the Arabs, having tested my friendliness and sincerity under fire, asked me, as a free agent, to endorse the promises of the British Government. I had had no previous or inner knowledge of the McMahon pledges and the Sykes-Picot treaty, which were both framed by war-time branches of the Foreign Office. But, not being a perfect fool, I could see that if we won the war the promises to the Arabs were dead paper. Had I been an honourable adviser I would have sent my men home, and not let them risk their lives for such stuff. Yet the Arab inspiration was our main tool in winning the Eastern war. So I assured them that England kept her word in letter and spirit. In this comfort they performed their fine things: but, of course, instead of being proud of what we did together, I was continually and bitterly ashamed.

Clear sight of my position came to me one night, when old Nuri Shaalan in his aisled tent brought out a file of documents and asked which British pledge was to be believed. In his mood, upon my answer, lay the success or failure of Feisal. My advice, uttered with some agony of mind, was to trust the latest in date of the contradictions. This disingenuous answer promoted me, in six months, to be chief confidence-man. In Hejaz the Sherifs were everything, and I had allayed my conscience by telling Feisal how hollow his basis was. In Syria England was mighty and the Sherif very low. So I became the principal.

In revenge I vowed to make the Arab Revolt the engine of its own success, as well as handmaid to our Egyptian campaign: and vowed to lead it so madly in the final victory that expediency should counsel to the Powers a fair settlement of the Arabs' moral claims. This presumed my surviving the war, to win the later battle of the Council Chamber — immodest presumptions, which still balance in fulfilment.* Yet the issue of the fraud was beside the point.

Clearly I had no shadow of leave to engage the Arabs, unknowing, in a gamble of life and death. Inevitably and justly we should reap bitterness, a sorry fruit of heroic endeavour. So in resentment at my false place (did ever second lieutenant so lie abroad for his betters?) I

---

* 1919: but two years later Mr. Winston Churchill was entrusted by our harassed Cabinet with the settlement of the Middle East; and in a few weeks, at his conference in Cairo, he made straight all the tangle, finding solutions fulfilling (I think) our promises in letter and spirit (where humanly possible) without sacrificing any interest of our Empire or any interest of the peoples concerned. So we were quit of the war-time Eastern adventure, with clean hands, but three years too late to earn the gratitude which peoples, if not states, can pay.

undertook this long, dangerous ride, in which to see the more important of Feisal's secret friends, and to study key-positions of our future campaigns: but the results were incommensurate with the risks, and the act artistically unjustifiable, like the motive. I had whispered to myself 'Let me chance it, now, before we begin', seeing truly that this was the last chance, and that after a successful capture of Akaba I would never again possess myself freely, without association, in the security lurking for the obscure in their protective shadow.

Before me lay a vista of responsibility and command, which disgusted my thought-riddled nature. I felt mean, to fill the place of a man of action; for my standards of value were a wilful reaction against theirs, and I despised their happiness. Always my soul hungered for less than it had, since my senses, sluggish beyond the senses of most men, needed the immediacy of contact to achieve perception; they distinguished kinds only, not degrees.

When I returned it was June the sixteenth, and Nasir was still labouring in his tent. He and Auda had been seeing too much of one another for their good, and lately there had been a breach; but this was easily healed, and after a day the old chief was as much with us as ever, and as kind and difficult. We stood up always when he entered; not for his sheikhood, for sitting we received sheikhs of much older rank: but because he was Auda, and Auda was such a splendid thing to be. The old man loved it, and however much we might wrangle, everyone knew that really we were his friends.

We were now five weeks out from Wejh: we had spent nearly all the money we had brought with us: we had eaten all the Howeitat sheep: we had rested or replaced all our old camels: nothing hindered the start. The freshness of the adventure in hand consoled us for everything; and Auda, importing more mutton, gave a farewell feast, the greatest of the whole series, in his huge tent the eve before we started. Hundreds were present, and five fills of the great tray were eaten up in relay as fast as they were cooked and carried in.

Sunset came down, delightfully red, and after the feast the whole party lay round the outside coffee-hearth lingering under the stars, while Auda and others told us stories. In a pause I remarked casually that I had looked for Mohammed el Dheilan in his tent that afternoon, to thank him for the milch camel he had given me, but had not found him. Auda shouted for joy, till everybody looked at him; and then, in the silence which fell that they might learn the joke, he pointed to Mohammed sitting dismally beside the coffee mortar, and said in his huge voice:—

'Ho! Shall I tell why Mohammed for fifteen days has not slept in his tent?' Everybody chuckled with delight, and conversation stopped; all the crowd stretched out on the ground, chins in hands, prepared to take the good points of the story which they had heard perhaps twenty times. The women, Auda's three wives, Zaal's wife, and some of Mohammed's, who had been cooking, came across, straddling their bellies in the billowy walk which came of carrying burdens on their heads, till they were near the partition-curtain; and there they listened like the rest while Auda told at length how Mohammed had bought publicly in the bazaar at Wejh a costly string of pearls, and had not given it to any of his wives, and so they were all at odds, except in their common rejection of him.

The story was, of course, a pure invention — Auda's elvish humour heightened by the stimulus of Revolt — and the luckless Mohammed, who had dragged through the fortnight guesting casually with one or other of the tribesmen, called upon God for mercy, and upon me for witness that Auda lied. I cleared my throat solemnly. Auda asked for silence, and begged me to confirm his words.

I began with the introducing phrase of a formal tale: 'In the name of God the merciful, the loving-kind. We were six in Wejh. There were Auda, and Mohammed, and Zaal, Gasim el Shimt, Mufaddhi and the poor man (myself); and one night just before dawn, Auda said, " Let us make a raid against the market". And we said, "in the name of God". And we went; Auda in a white robe and a red head-cloth, and Kasim sandals of pieced leather; Mohammed in a silken tunic of "seven kings" and barefoot; Zaal ... I forget Zaal. Gasim wore cotton, and Mufaddhi was in silk of blue stripes with an embroidered head-cloth. Your servant was as your servant.'

My pause was still with astonishment. This was a close parody of Auda's epic style; and I mimicked also his wave of the hand, his round voice, and the rising and dropping tone which emphasized the points,

or what he thought were points, of his pointless stories. The Howeitat
sat silent as death, twisting their full bodies inside their sweat-stiffened
shirts for joy, and staring hungrily at Auda; for they all recognized the
original, and parody was a new art to them and to him. The coffee
man, Mufaddhi, a Shammar refugee from the guilt of blood, himself a
character, forgot to pile fresh thorns on his fire for fixity of listening to
the tale.

I told how we left the tents, with a list of the tents, and how we
walked down towards the village, describing every camel and horse
we saw, and all the passers-by, and the ridges, 'all bare of grazing for
by God that country was barren. And we marched: and after we had
marched the time of a smoked cigarette, we heard something, and
Auda stopped and said, "Lads, I hear something". And Mohammed
stopped and said, "Lads, I hear something". And Zaal, "By God, you
are right". And we stopped to listen, and there was nothing, and the
poor man said, "By God, I hear nothing". And Zaal said, "By God,
I hear nothing". And Mohammed said, "By God, I hear nothing".
And Auda said, "By God, you are right".

'And we marched and we marched, and the land was barren, and
we heard nothing. And on our right hand came a man, a negro, on a
donkey. The donkey was grey, with black ears, and one black foot,
and on its shoulder was a brand like this' (a scrabble in the air), 'and its
tail moved and its legs: Auda saw it, and said, "By God, a donkey".
And Mohammed said, "By the very God, a donkey and a slave". And
we marched. And there was a ridge, not a great ridge, but a ridge as
great as from the here to the what-do-you-call-it (lil biliyeh el hok) that
is yonder: and we marched to the ridge and it was barren. That land
is barren: barren: barren.

'And we marched: and beyond the what-do-you-call-it there was a
what-there-is as far as hereby from thence, and thereafter a ridge: and
we came to that ridge, and went up that ridge: it was barren, all that
land was barren: and as we came up that ridge, and were by the head of
that ridge, and came to the end of the head of that ridge, by God, by
my God, by very God, the sun rose upon us.'

It ended the session. Everyone had heard that sunrise twenty times,
in its immense bathos; an agony piled up of linked phrases, repeated

and repeated with breathless excitement by Auda to carry over for hours the thrill of a raiding story in which nothing happened; and the trivial rest of it was exaggerated the degree which made it like one of Auda's tales; and yet, also, the history of the walk to market at Wejh which many of us had taken. The tribe was in waves of laughter on the ground.

Auda laughed the loudest and longest, for he loved a jest upon himself; and the fatuousness of my epic had shown him his own sure mastery of descriptive action. He embraced Mohammed, and confessed the invention of the necklace. In gratitude Mohammed invited the camp to breakfast with him in his regained tent on the morrow, an hour before we started for the swoop on Akaba. We should have a sucking camel-calf boiled in sour milk by his wives: famous cooks, and a legendary dish!

Afterwards we sat by the wall of Nuri's manor, and saw the women take down the great tent, greater than Auda's, eight-bayed of twenty-four poles in all, longer and broader and loftier than any other in the tribe, and new, like the rest of Mohammed's goods. The Abu Tayi were rearranging their camp, for security when their fighting men marched away. Throughout the afternoon tents were coming in and being pitched by us. The oblong cloth was stretched flat upon the ground; the ropes at the end, in the sides, by the pole-gussets, strained out and tied to pegs. Then the housewife would insert the light poles one by one, under the cloth, and lever it up by them, until the whole was in place, pitched single-handed by the one weak woman, however rough the wind.

If it rained one row of poles was drawn in at the foot, so slanting the roof-cloth obliquely to the shower, and making it reasonably waterproof. In summer the Arab tent was less hot than our canvas tents, for the sun-heat was not absorbed in this loose woven fabric of hair and wool, with the air spaces and currents between its threads.

W E started an hour before noon. Nasir led us, riding his Ghazala — a camel vaulted and huge-ribbed as an antique ship; towering a good foot above the next of our animals, and yet perfectly proportioned, with a stride like an ostrich's — a lyrical beast, noblest and best bred of the Howeitat camels, a female of nine remembered dams. Auda was beside him, and I skirmished about their gravities on Naama, 'the hen-ostrich', a racing camel and my last purchase. Behind me rode my Ageyl, with Mohammed, the clumsy. Mohammed was now companioned by Ahmed, another peasant, who had been for six years living among the Howeitat by force of his thews and wits — a knowing eager ruffian.

Sixty feet of a rise took us out of Sirhan to the first terrace of the Ard el Suwan — a country of black flints upon marly limestone; not very solid, but hard enough in the tracks which the feet of passing centuries of camels had worn an inch or two into the surface. Our aim was Bair, a historic group of Ghassanid wells and ruins in the desert thirty or forty miles east of the Hejaz Railway. It lay some sixty miles ahead, and there we would camp a few days, while our scouts brought us flour from the hill villages above the Dead Sea. Our food from Wejh was nearly finished (except that Nasir still had some of the precious rice for great occasions), and we could not yet certainly forecast the date of our arrival in Akaba.

Our present party totalled more than five hundred strong; and the sight of this jolly mob of hardy, confident northerners chasing gazelle wildly over the face of the desert, took from us momentarily all sorry apprehension as to the issue of our enterprise. We felt it was a rice-night, and the chiefs of the Abu Tayi came to sup with us. Afterwards, with the embers of our coffee-fire pleasantly red between us against the cool of this upland north-country, we sat about on the carpets chatting discursively of this remote thing and that.

Nasir rolled over on his back, with my glasses, and began to study the stars, counting aloud first one group and then another; crying out with surprise at discovering little lights not noticed by his unaided eye. Auda set us on to talk of telescopes — of the great ones — and of how man in three hundred years had so far advanced from his first essay that now he built glasses as long as a tent, through which he counted thousands of unknown stars. 'And the stars — what are they?' We slipped into talk of suns beyond suns, sizes and distance beyond wit. 'What will now happen with this knowledge?' asked Mohammed. 'We shall set to, and many learned and some clever men together will make glasses as more powerful than ours, as ours than Galileo's; and yet more hundreds of astronomers will distinguish and reckon yet more thousands of now unseen stars, mapping them, and giving each one its name. When we see them all, there will be no night in heaven.'

'Why are the Westerners always wanting all?' provokingly said Auda. 'Behind our few stars we can see God, who is not behind your millions.' 'We want the world's end, Auda.' 'But that is God's,' complained Zaal, half angry. Mohammed would not have his subject turned. 'Are there men on these greater worlds?' he asked. 'God knows.' 'And has each the Prophet and heaven and hell?' Auda broke in on him. 'Lads, we know our districts, our camels, our women. The excess and the glory are to God. If the end of wisdom is to add star to star our foolishness is pleasing.' And then he spoke of money, and distracted their minds till they all buzzed at once. Afterwards he whispered to me that I must get him a worthy gift from Feisal when he won Akaba.

We marched at dawn, and in a hour topped the Wagf, the water-shed, and rode down its far side. The ridge was only a bank of chalk, flint-capped, a couple of hundred feet high. We were now in the hollow between the Snainirat on the south and, on the north, the three white heads of the Thlaithukhwat, a cluster of conical hills which shone brilliant as snow in the sunshine. Soon we entered Wadi Bair, and marched up and across it for hours. There had been a flood there in the spring, producing a rich growth of grasses between the scrubby bushes. It was green and pleasant to the eye and to our camels' hungry palates after the long hostility of the Sirhan.

Presently Auda told me he was riding ahead to Bair, and would I come? We went fast, and in two hours came upon the place suddenly,

K

under a knoll. Auda had hurried on to visit the tomb of his son Annad, who had been waylaid by five of his Motalga cousins in revenge for Abtan, their champion, slain by Annad in single combat. Auda told me how Annad had ridden at them, one against five, and had died as he should; but it left only little Mohammed between him and childlessness. He had brought me along to hear him greatly lament his dead.

However, as we rode down towards the graves, we were astonished to see smoke wreathing from the ground about the wells. We changed direction sharply, and warily approached the ruins. It seemed there was no one there; but the thick dung-cake round the well-brink was charred, and the well itself shattered at the top. The ground was torn and blackened as if by an explosion; and when we looked down the shaft we saw its steyning stripped and split, and many blocks thrown down the bore half choking it and the water in the bottom. I sniffed the air and thought the smell was dynamite.

Auda ran to the next well, in the bed of the valley below the graves; and that, too, was ragged about the head and choked with fallen stones. 'This,' said he, 'is Jazi work.' We walked across the valley to the third — the Beni Sakhr — well. It was only a crater of chalk. Zaal arrived, grave at sight of the disaster. We explored the ruined khan, in which were night-old traces of perhaps a hundred horse. There was a fourth well, north of the ruins in the open flat, and to it we went hopelessly, wondering what would become of us if Bair were all destroyed. To our joy it was uninjured.

This was a Jazi well, and its immunity gave strong colour to Auda's theory. We were disconcerted to find the Turks so ready, and began to fear that perhaps they had also raided El Jefer, east of Maan, the wells at which we planned to concentrate before we attacked. Their blocking would be a real embarrassment. Meanwhile, thanks to the fourth well, our situation, though uncomfortable, was not dangerous. Yet its water facilities were altogether insufficient for five hundred camels; so it became imperative to open the least damaged of the other wells — that in the ruins, about whose lip the turf smouldered. Auda and I went off with Nasir to look again at it.

An Ageyli brought us an empty case of Nobel's gelignite, evidently the explosive which the Turks had used. From scars in the ground it was clear that several charges had been fired simultaneously round the well-head, and in the shaft. Staring down it till our eyes were adjusted to its dark, we suddenly saw many niches cut in the shaft less than twenty feet below. Some were still tamped, and had wires hanging down.

Evidently there was a second series of charges, either inefficiently wired, or with a very long time-fuse. Hurriedly we unrolled our bucket-ropes, twined them together, and hung them freely down the middle of the well from a stout cross-pole, the sides being so tottery that the scrape of a rope might have dislodged their blocks. I then found that the charges were small, not above three pounds each, and had been wired in series with field telephone cable. But something had gone wrong. Either the Turks had scamped their job or their scouts had seen us coming before they had had time to re-connect.

So we soon had two fit wells, and a clear profit of thirty pounds of enemy gelignite. We determined to stay a week in this fortunate Bair. A third object — to discover the condition of the Jefer wells — was now added to our needs for food, and for news of the state of mind of the tribes between Maan and Akaba. We sent a man to Jefer. We prepared a little caravan of pack-camels with Howeitat brands and sent them across the line to Tafileh with three or four obscure clansmen — people who would never be suspected of association with us. They would buy all the flour they could and bring it back to us in five or six days' time.

As for the tribes about the Akaba road, we wanted their active help against the Turks to carry out the provisional plan we had made at Wejh. Our idea was to advance suddenly from El Jefer, to cross the railwayline and to crown the great pass — Nagb el Shtar — down which the road dipped from the Maan plateau to the red Guweira plain. To hold this pass we should have to capture Aba el Lissan, the large spring at its head, about sixteen miles from Maan; but the garrison was small, and we hoped to overrun it with a rush. We would then be astride the road, whose posts at the end of the week should fall from hunger; though probably before that the hill tribes, hearing of our successful beginning, would join us to wipe them out.

Crux of our plan was the attack on Aba el Lissan, lest the force in

Maan have time to sally out, relieve it, and drive us off the head of Shtar. If, as at present, they were only a battalion, they would hardly dare move; and should they let it fall while waiting for reinforcements to arrive, Akaba would surrender to us, and we should be based on the sea and have the advantageous gorge of Itm between us and the enemy. So our insurance for success was to keep Maan careless and weak, not suspecting our malevolent presence in the neighbourhood.

It was never easy for us to keep our movements secret, as we lived by preaching to the local people, and the unconvinced would tell the Turks. Our long march into Wadi Sirhan was known to the enemy, and the most civilian owl could not fail to see that the only fit objective was Akaba. The demolition of Bair (and Jefer, too, for we had it confirmed that the seven wells of Jefer were destroyed) showed that the Turks were to that extent on the alert.

However, there was no measuring the stupidity of the Turkish Army; a point which helped us now and again, and harmed us constantly, for we could not avoid despising them for it (Arabs being a race gifted with uncommon quickness of mind, and over-valuing it) and an army suffered when unable to yield honour to the enemy. For the moment the stupidity might be made use of; and so we had undertaken a prolonged campaign of deception, to convince them that our objective lay nearer to Damascus.

They were susceptible to pressure in that neighbourhood, for the railway from Damascus, north to Deraa and south to Amman, was the communication, not merely of Hejaz, but of Palestine; and if we attacked it we should do double damage. So, in my long trip round the north country, I had dropped hints of our near arrival in Jebel Druse; and I had been glad to let the notorious Nesib go up there, noisily, but with small resources. Nuri Shaalan had warned the Turks for us in the same sense; and Newcombe, down near Wejh, had contrived to lose official papers, including a plan (in which we were advance guard) for marching from Wejh, by Jefer and the Sirhan, to Tadmor, to attack Damascus and Aleppo. The Turks took the documents very seriously, and chained up an unfortunate garrison in Tadmor till the end of the war, much to our advantage.

CHAPTER L

IT seemed wise to make some concrete effort in the same direction during the week that we must spend in Bair, and Auda decided that Zaal should ride with me in command of a party to attack the line near Deraa. Zaal chose one hundred and ten men, individually, and we rode hard, in six-hour spells with one- or two-hour intervals, day and night. For me it was an eventful trip, for those reasons which made it dull to the Arabs; namely, that we were an ordinary tribal raiding party, riding on conventional lines, in the formation and after the pattern which generations of practice had proved efficient.

In the second afternoon we reached the railway just above Zerga, the Circassian village north of Amman. The hot sun and fast riding had tried our camels, and Zaal decided to water them at a ruined Roman village, the underground cisterns of which had been filled by the late rains. It lay within a mile of the railway, and we had to be circumspect, for the Circassians hated the Arabs, and would have been hostile had they seen us. Also there was a military post of two tents on a tall bridge just down the line. The Turks seemed active. Later we heard that a general's inspection was pending.

After the watering we rode another six miles, and in the early dark turned to Dhuleil bridge, which Zaal reported as a big one, good to destroy. The men and camels stayed on the high ground east of the railway to cover our retreat if anything untoward happened, while Zaal and I went down to the bridge to look it over. There were Turks two hundred yards beyond it, with many tents and cooking fires. We were puzzled to explain their strength, until we reached the bridge and found it being rebuilt; the spring flood had washed away four of its arches, and the line was temporarily laid on a deviation. One of the new arches was finished, another had the vault just turned, and the timber centring was set ready for a third.

Useless, of course, it was, bothering to destroy a bridge in such a state; so we drew off quietly (not to alarm the workmen), walking over loose stones which turned under our bare feet in a way imposing care if we would avoid risk of sprain. Once I put my foot on something moving, soft and cold, and stepped heavily, on chance it was a snake; but no harm followed. The brilliant stars cast about us a false light, not illumination, but rather a transparency of air lengthening slightly the shadow below each stone, and making a difficult greyness of the ground.

We decided to go further north, towards Minifir, where Zaal thought the land propitious for mining a train. A train would be better than a bridge, for our need was political, to make the Turks think that our main body was at Azrak in Sirhan, fifty miles away to the east. We came out on a flat plain, crossed by a very occasional shallow bed of fine shingle. Over this we were going easily when we heard a long rumble. We pricked ears, wondering: and there came out of the north a dancing plume of flame bent low by the wind of its speed. It seemed to light us, extending its fire-tagged curtain of smoke over our heads, so near were we to the railway; and we shrank back while the train rushed on. Two minutes' warning and I would have blown its locomotive into scrap.

Afterwards our march was quiet till the dawn, when we found ourselves riding up a narrow valley. At its head was a sharp turn to the left, into an amphitheatre of rock where the hill went up by step after step of broken cliff to a crest on which stood a massive cairn. Zaal said the railway was visible thence, and if this were true the place was an ideal ambush, for the camels could be herded without any guardians into the pit of excellent pasture.

I climbed at once to the cairn, the ruin of an Arab watch-tower of the Christian period, commanding a most gracious view of rich pastoral uplands beyond the line, which ran round the foot of our slope in a lazy curve, open to sight for perhaps five miles. Below on our left was the square box of the 'coffee-house', a railway halt, about which a few little soldiers were slouching peacefully. We lay alternately watching and sleeping, for many hours, during which a train ground slowly past up the stiff gradient. We made plans to descend upon the line that night, wherever seemed best for mining.

However, in mid-morning a dark mass approached from the northward. Eventually we made it out to be a force of perhaps one hundred and fifty mounted men, riding straight for our hill. It looked as though we had been reported; a quite possible thing, since all this area was grazed over by the sheep of the Belga tribes, whose shepherds, when they saw our stealthiness, would have taken us for robber-enemies and alarmed their tents.

Our position, admirable against the railway, was a death-trap in which to be caught by superior mobile forces: so we sent down the alarm, mounted and slipped across the valley of our entry, and over its eastern ridge into a small plain, where we could canter our animals. We made speed to low mounds on its further side, and got behind them before the enemy were in a position to see us.

There the terrain better suited our tactics and we waited for them; but they were at least imperfectly informed, for they rode past our old hiding-place and quickly away towards the south, leaving us puzzled. There were no Arabs among them — all were regulars — so we had not to fear being tracked, but here again it seemed as though the Turks were on the alert. This was according to my wish, and I was glad, but Zaal, on whom fell the military responsibility, was disquieted. He held a council with those others who knew the country, and eventually we remounted, and jogged off to another hill, rather north of our old one, but satisfactory enough. Particularly it happened to be free of tribal complications.

This was Minifir proper, a round-headed, grass-grown hill of two shoulders. The high neck between provided us, on its eastern face, a broad track perfectly covered from the north and south and west which afforded a safe retreat into the desert. At the top the neck was cupped, so that collected rain had made the soil rich, and the grazing sumptuous; but loosed camels required constant care, for if they wandered two hundred paces forward they became visible from the railway, a further four hundred yards down the western face of the hill.

On each side the shoulders pushed forward in spurs which the line passed in shallow cuttings. The excavated material had been thrown across the hollow in an embankment; through the centre of which a lofty culvert let the drainage of the little zigzag gully from the neck run down into a larger transverse valley bed beyond.

Northward the line curved away, hard uphill, to the wide level of the southern Hauran, spread out like a grey sky, and flecked with small dark clouds which were the dead basalt towns of Byzantine Syria. Southward was a cairn from which we could look down the railway for six miles or more.

The high land facing us to the west, the Belga, was spotted with black tent-villages of peasants in summer quarters. They could see us too, in our hill-cup, so we sent word who we were. Whereupon they kept silent till we had gone, and then were fervid and eloquent in proving that we fled eastward, to Azrak. When our messengers came back we had bread to eat — a luxury; since the dearth in Bair had reduced us to parched corn which, for lack of cooking-opportunity the men had been chewing raw. The trial was too steep for my teeth, so that I rode fasting.

Zaal and I buried that night on the culvert a great Garland mine, automatic-compound, to explode three charges in parallel by instantaneous fuse; and then lay down to sleep, sure that we would hear noises if a train came along in the dark and fired it. However, nothing happened, and at dawn I removed the detonators which (additional to the trigger action) had been laid on the metals. Afterwards we waited all day, fed and comfortable, cooled by a high wind which hissed like surf as it ruffled up the stiff-grassed hill.

For hours nothing came along: but at last there was a flutter among the Arabs, and Zaal, with the Hubsi and some of the more active men, dashed down towards the line. We heard two shots under us in the dead ground, and after half an hour the party reappeared, leading two ragged Turkish deserters from the mounted column of the day before. One had been badly wounded, while attempting to escape up the line; and in the afternoon he died, most miserable about himself and his fate. Exceptionally: for when death became certain most men felt the quietness of the grave waiting for them, and went to it not unwillingly. The other man was hurt also, a clean gunshot in the foot; but he was very feeble and collapsed when the wound grew painful with the cold. His thin body was so covered with bruises, tokens of army service and cause of his desertion, that he dared lie only on his face. We offered him the last of our bread and water and did what else we could for him: which was little.

Late in the afternoon came a thrill when the mule-mounted infantry reappeared, heading up-line towards us. They would pass below our ambush, and Zaal and the men were urgent to attack them on the sudden. We were one hundred, they little over two hundred. We had the upper ground, could hope to empty some of their saddles by our first volley, and then would camel-charge upon them. Camels, especially down a gentle slope, would overtake mules in a few strides, and their moving bulk would send spinning the lighter animals and their riders. Zaal gave me his word that no regular cavalry, let alone mere mounted infantry, could cope with tribal camels in a running fight. We should take not only the men, but their precious animals.

I asked him how many casualties we might incur. He guessed five or six, and then I decided to do nothing, to let them pass. We had one objective only, the capture of Akaba, and had come up here solely to make that easier by leading the Turks off on the false scent of thinking that we were at Azrak. To lose five or six men in such a demonstration, however profitable it proved financially, would be fatuous, or worse, because we might want our last rifle to take Akaba, the possession of which was vital to us. After Akaba had fallen we might waste men, if we felt callous; but not before.

I told Zaal, who was not content; while the furious Howeitat threatened to run off downhill at the Turks, willynilly. They wanted a booty of mules; and I, particularly, did not, for it would have diverted us. Commonly, tribes went to war to gain honour and wealth. The three noble spoils were arms, riding-animals, and clothes. If we took these two hundred mules, the proud men would throw up Akaba and drive them home by way of Azrak to their tents, to triumph before the women. As for prisoners, Nasir would not be grateful for two hundred useless mouths: so we should have to kill them; or let them go, revealing our numbers to the enemy.

We sat and gnashed our teeth at them and let them pass: a severe ordeal, from which we only just emerged with honour. Zaal did it. He was on his best behaviour, expecting tangible gratitude from me later; and glad, meanwhile, to show me his authority over the Beduin. They respected him as Auda's deputy, and as a famous fighter, and in one or two little mutinies he had shown a self-conscious mastery.

Now he was tested to the utmost. The Hubsi, Auda's cousin, a

K*

spirited youth, while the Turks were defiling innocently not three hundred yards from our itching rifle-muzzles, sprang to his feet and ran forward shouting to attract them, and compel a battle; but Zaal caught him in ten strides, threw him down and bludgeoned him savagely time and again till we feared lest the lad's now very different cries fulfil his former purpose.

It was sad to see a sound and pleasant little victory pass voluntarily out of our hands, and we were gloomy till evening came down and confirmed our sense that once more there would be no train. This was the final occasion, for thirst was hanging over us, and on the morrow the camels must be watered. So after nightfall we returned to the line, laid thirty charges of gelignite against the most-curved rails and fired them leisurely. The curved rails were chosen since the Turks would have to bring down new ones from Damascus. Actually, this took them three days; and then their construction train stepped on our mine (which we had left as hook behind the demolition's bait) and hurt its locomotive. Traffic ceased for three days while the line was picked over for traps.

For the moment of course, we could anticipate none of these good things. We did the destruction, returned sorrowfully to our camels, and were off soon after midnight. The prisoner was left behind on his hill-top, for he could neither walk nor ride, and we had no carriage for him. We feared he would starve to death where he lay: and, indeed, already he was very ill: so on a telegraph pole, felled across the rails by the damaged stretch, we put a letter in French and German, to give news of where he was, and that we had captured him wounded after a hard fight.

We hoped this might save him the penalties which the Turks inflicted on red-handed deserters, or from being shot if they thought he had been in collusion with us: but when we came back to Minifir six months later the picked bones of the two bodies were lying scattered on our old camping ground. We felt sorry always for the men of the Turkish Army. The officers, volunteer and professional, had caused the war by their ambition — almost by their existence — and we wished they could receive not merely their proportionate deserts, but all that the conscripts had to suffer through their fault.

CHAPTER LI

IN the night we lost our way among the stony ridges and valleys of Dhuleil, but kept moving until dawn, so that half an hour after sunrise, while the shadows were yet long across the green hollows, we had reached our former watering-place, Khau, whose ruins broke from the hill-top against Zerga like a scab. We were working hard at the two cisterns, watering our camels for the return march to Bair, when a young Circassian came in sight, driving three cows towards the rich green pasture of the ruins.

This would not do, so Zaal sent off his too-energetic offenders of the day previous to show their proper mettle by stalking him: and they brought him in, unharmed, but greatly frightened. Circassians were swaggering fellows, inordinate bullies in a clear road; but if firmly met they cracked; and so this lad was in a head-and-tail flux of terror offending our sense of respect. We drenched him with water till he recovered, and then in disposal set him to fight at daggers with a young Sherari, caught stealing on the march; but after a scratch the prisoner threw himself down weeping.

Now he was a nuisance, for if we left him he would give the alarm, and send the horsemen of his village out against us. If we tied him up in this remote place he would die of hunger or thirst; and, besides, we had not rope to spare. To kill him seemed unimaginative: not worthy of a hundred men. At last the Sherari boy said if we gave him scope he would settle his account and leave him living.

He looped his wrist to the saddle and trotted him off with us for the first hour, till he was dragging breathlessly. We were still near the railway, but four or five miles from Zerga. There he was stripped of presentable clothes, which fell, by point of honour, to his owner. The Sherari threw him on his face, picked up his feet, drew a dagger, and chopped him with it deeply across the soles. The Circassian howled with pain and terror, as if he thought he was being killed.

Odd as was the performance, it seemed effective, and more merciful than death. The cuts would make him travel to the railway on hands and knees, a journey of an hour; and his nakedness would keep him in the shadow of the rocks, till the sun was low. His gratitude was not coherent; but we rode away, across undulations very rich in grazing. The camels, with their heads down snatching plants and grass, moved uncomfortably for us cocked over the chute of their sloped necks; yet we must let them eat, since we were marching eighty miles a day, with halts to breathe only in the brief gloamings of dawn and sunset.

Soon after daylight we turned west, and dismounted, short of the railway among broken reefs of limestone, to creep carefully forward until Atwi station lay beneath us. Its two stone houses (the first only one hundred yards away) were in line, one obscuring the other. Men were singing in them without disquietude. Their day was beginning, and from the guard-room thin blue smoke curled into the air, while a soldier drove out a flock of young sheep to crop the rich meadow between the station and the valley.

This flock sealed the business, for after our horse-diet of dry corn we craved meat. The Arabs' teeth gritted as they counted ten, fifteen, twenty-five, twenty-seven. Zaal dropped into the valley bed where the line crossed a bridge, and with a party in file behind him, crept along till he faced the station across the meadow.

From our ridge we covered the station yard. We saw Zaal lean his rifle on the bank, shielding his head with infinite precaution behind grasses on the brink. He took slow aim at the coffee-sipping officers and officials in shaded chairs, outside the ticket office. As he pressed the trigger, the report overtook the crash of the bullet against the stone wall, while the fattest man bowed slowly in his chair and sank to the ground under the frozen stare of his fellows.

An instant later Zaal's men poured in their volleys, broke from the valley, and rushed forward: but the door of the northern house clanged to, and rifles began to speak from behind its steel window shutters. We replied, but soon saw our impotence, and ceased fire, as did the enemy. The Sherarat drove the guilty sheep eastward into the hills, where were the camels; everyone else ran down to join Zaal, who was busy about the nearer and undefended building.

Near the height of plundering came a pause and panic. The Arabs were such accustomed scouts that almost they felt danger before it came, sense taking precautions before mind was persuaded. Swinging down the line from the south was a trolley with four men, to whose ears the grinding wheels had deadened our shots. The Rualla section crept under a culvert three hundred yards up, while the rest of us crowded silently by the bridge.

The trolley rolled unsuspectingly over the ambush, who came out to line the bank behind, while we filed solemnly across the green in front. The Turks slowed in horror, jumped off, and ran into the rough: but our rifles cracked once more and they were dead. The trolley brought to our feet its load of copper wire and telegraph tools, with which we put 'earths' in the long-distance wire. Zaal fired our half of the station, whose petrol-splashed woodwork caught freely. The planks and cloth hangings twisted and jerked convulsively as the flames licked them up. Meanwhile the Ageyl were measuring out gelatine, and soon we lit their charges and destroyed a culvert, many rails, and furlongs of telegraph. With the roar of the first explosion our hundred knee-haltered camels rose smartly to their feet, and at each following burst hopped more madly on three legs till they shook off the rope-hitch about the fourth, and drove out every way like scattered starlings into the void. Chasing them and chasing the sheep took us three hours, for which graciously the Turks gave law, or some of us would have had to walk home.

We put a few miles between us and the railway before we sat down to our feast of mutton. We were short of knives, and, after killing the sheep in relay, had recourse to stray flints to cut them up. As men unaccustomed to such expedients, we used them in the eolithic spirit; and it came to me that if iron had been constantly rare we should have chipped our daily tools skilfully as palæoliths: whilst had we had no metal whatever, our art would have been lavished on perfect and polished stones. Our one hundred and ten men ate the best parts of twenty-four sheep at the sitting, while the camels browsed about, or ate what we left over; for the best riding-camels were taught to like cooked meat. When it was finished we mounted, and rode through the night towards Bair: which we entered without casualty, successful, well-fed, and enriched, at dawn.

CHAPTER LII

NASIR had done great work. A week's flour for us had come from Tafileh, to restore our freedom of movement. We might well take Akaba before we starved again. He had good letters from the Dhumaniyeh, the Darausha, and the Dhiabat, three Howeitat clans on Nagb el Shtar, the first difficult pass of the Maan-Akaba road. They were willing to help us, and if they struck soon and strongly at Aba el Lissan the great factor of surprise would probably mean success to their effort.

My hopefulness misled me into another mad ride, which miscarried. Yet the Turks did not take alarm. As my party rode in there came a messenger post-haste from Nuri Shaalan. He brought greetings, and Nuri's news that the Turks had called upon his son Nawaf, as guide hostage, to take four hundred cavalry from Deraa down the Sirhan in search of us. Nuri had sent his better-spared nephew Trad, who was conducting them by devious routes in which men and horses were suffering terribly from thirst. They were near Nebk, our old camping ground. The Turkish Government would believe us still in the Wadi till their cavalry returned. For Maan especially they had no anxiety since the engineers who had blown up Bair reported every source of water utterly destroyed, while the wells of Jefer had been dealt with a few days earlier.

It might be that Jefer really was denied to us; but we were not without hope that there, too, we should find the technical work of demolition ill-done by these pitiful Turks. Dhaif-Allah, a leading man of the Jazi Howeitat, one who came down to Wejh and swore allegiance, had been present in Jefer when the King's Well was fired by dynamite placed about its lip; and sent us secret word from Maan that he had heard the upper stones clap together and key over the mouth of the well. His conviction was that the shaft was intact, and the clearing of it a few hours' work. We hoped so; and rode away from Bair all in order, on June the twenty-eighth to find out.

Quickly we crossed the weird plain of Jefer. Next day by noon we were at the wells. They seemed most thoroughly destroyed; and the fear grew that we might find in them the first check to our scheme of operations, a scheme so much too elaborate that a check might be far reaching.

However, we went to the well — Auda's family property — of which Dhaif Allah had told us the tale, and began to sound about it. The ground rang hollow under our mallet, and we called for volunteers able to dig and build. Some of the Ageyl came forward, led by the Mirzugi, a capable camel boy of Nasir's. They started with the few tools we had. The rest of us formed a ring round the well-depression and watched them work, singing to them and promising rewards of gold when they had found the water.

It was a hot task in the full glare of the summer sun; for the Jefer plain was of hard mud, flat as the hand, blinding white with salt, and twenty miles across; but time pressed, because if we failed, we might have to ride fifty miles in the night to the next well. So we pushed the work by relays at speed through the midday heat, turning into labourers all our amenable fellows. It made easy digging, for the explosion which shifted the stones had loosened the soil.

As they dug and threw out the earth, the core of the well rose up like a tower of rough stones in the centre of the pit. Very carefully we began to take away the ruined head of the pile: difficult work, for the stones had become interlocked in their fall; but this was the better sign, and our spirits rose. Before sunset the workers shouted that there was no more packing-soil, that the interstices between the blocks were clear, and they heard the mud fragments which slipped through splashing many feet below.

Half an hour later came a rush and rumble of stones in the mouth, followed by a heavy splash and yells. We hurried down, and by the Mirzugi's torch saw the well yawning open, no longer a tube, but a deep bottle-shouldered pit, twenty feet across at the bottom, which was black with water and white in the middle with spray where the Ageyli who had been clearing when the key slipped was striking out lustily in the effort not to drown. Everybody laughed down the well at him, till at last Abdulla lowered him a noose of rope, and we drew him up, very wet and angry, but in no way damaged by his fall.

We rewarded the diggers, and feasted them on a weak camel, which had failed in the march to-day; and then all night we watered, while a squad of Ageyl, with a long chorus, steyned up to ground level an eight-foot throat of mud and stones. At dawn the earth was stamped in round this, and the well stood complete, as fit in appearance as ever. Only the water was not very much. We worked it the twenty-four hours without rest, and ran it to a cream; and still some of our camels were not satisfied.

From Jefer we took action. Riders went forward into the Dhumaniyeh tents to lead their promised attack against Fuweilah, the blockhouse which covered the head of the pass of Aba el Lissan. Our attack was planned for two days before the weekly caravan which, from Maan, replenished the client garrisons. Starvation would make reduction of these distant places easier, by impressing on them how hopelessly they were cut off from their friends.

We sat in Jefer meanwhile, waiting to hear the fortune of the attack. On its success or failure would depend the direction of our next march. The halt was not unpleasant, for our position had its comic side. We were within sight of Maan, during those minutes of the day in which the mirage did not make eyes and glasses useless; and yet we strolled about admiring our new well-lip in complete security, because the Turkish garrison believed water impossible here or at Bair, and were hugging the pleasant idea that we were now desperately engaged with their cavalry in Sirhan.

I hid under some bushes near the well for hours, against the heat, very lazy, pretending to be asleep, the wide silk sleeve of my pillow-arm drawn over my face as veil against the flies. Auda sat up and talked like a river, telling his best stories in great form. At last I reproved him with a smile, for talking too much and doing too little. He sucked his lips with pleasure of the work to come.

In the following dawn a tired horseman rode into our camp with news that the Dhumaniyeh had fired on the Fuweilah post the afternoon before as soon as our men had reached them. The surprise had not been quite complete; the Turks manned their dry stone breastworks and drove them off. The crestfallen Arabs drew back into cover and the enemy believing it only an ordinary tribal affray, had made a mounted sortie upon the nearest encampment.

One old man, six women and seven children were its only occupants. In their anger at finding nothing actively hostile or able-bodied, the troopers smashed up the camp and cut the throats of its helpless ones. The Dhumaniyeh on the hill-tops heard and saw nothing till it was too late; but then, in their fury, they dashed down across the return road of the murderers and cut them off almost to the last man. To complete their vengeance they assaulted the now weakly-garrisoned fort, carried it in the first fierceness of their rush, and took no prisoners.

We were ready saddled; and within ten minutes had loaded and marched for Ghadir el Haj, the first railway station south of Maan, on our direct road for Aba el Lissan. Simultaneously, we detached a small party to cross the railway just above Maan and create a diversion on that side. Especially they were to threaten the great herds of sick camels, casualties of the Palestine front, which the Turks pastured in the Shobek plains till once more fit for service.

We calculated that the news of their Fuweilah disaster would not have reached Maan till the morning, and that they could not drive in these camels (supposing our northern party missed them) and fit out a relief expedition, before nightfall; and if we were then attacking the line at Ghadir el Haj, they would probably divert the relief thither, and so let us move on Akaba unmolested.

With this hope we rode steadily through the flowing mirage till afternoon, when we descended on the line; and, having delivered a long stretch of it from guards and patrols, began on the many bridges of the captured section. The little garrison of Ghadir el Haj sallied out with the valour of ignorance against us, but the heat-haze blinded them, and we drove them off with loss.

They were on the telegraph, and would notify Maan, which beside, could not fail to hear the repeated thuds of our explosion. It was our aim to bring the enemy down upon us in the night; or rather down here, where they would find no people but many broken bridges, for we worked fast and did great damage. The drainage holes in the spandrils held from three to five pounds of gelatine each. We, firing our mines by short fuses, brought down the arch, shattered the pier, and stripped the side walls, in no more than six minutes' work. So we ruined ten bridges and many rails, and finished our explosive.

After dusk, when our departure could not be seen, we rode five miles westward of the line, to cover. There we made fires and baked bread. Our meal, however, was not cooked before three horsemen cantered up to report that a long column of new troops — infantry and guns — had just appeared at Aba el Lissan from Maan. The Dhumani-yeh, disorganized with victory, had had to abandon their ground without fighting. They were at Batra waiting for us. We had lost Aba el Lissan, the blockhouse, the pass, the command of the Akaba road: without a shot being fired.

We learned afterwards that this unwelcome and unwonted vigour on the part of the Turks was accident. A relief battalion had reached Maan that very day. The news of an Arab demonstration against Fuweilah arrived simultaneously; and the battalion, which happened to be formed up ready with its transport in the station yard, to march to barracks, was hurriedly strengthened by a section of pack artillery and some mounted men, and moved straight out as a punitive column to rescue the supposedly besieged post.

They had left Maan in mid-morning and marched gently along the motor road, the men sweating in the heat of this south country after their native Caucasian snows, and drinking thirstily of every spring. From Aba el Lissan they climbed uphill towards the old blockhouse, which was deserted except for the silent vultures flying above its walls in slow uneasy rings. The battalion commander feared lest the sight be too much for his young troops, and led them back to the roadside spring of Aba el Lissan, in its serpentine narrow valley, where they camped all night in peace about the water.

CHAPTER LIII

SUCH news shook us into quick life. We threw our baggage across our camels on the instant and set out over the rolling downs of this end of the tableland of Syria. Our hot bread was in our hands, and as we ate, there mingled with it the taste of the dust of our large force crossing the valley bottoms, and some taint of the strange keen smell of the wormwood which overgrew the slopes. In the breathless air of these evenings in the hills, after the long days of summer, everything struck very acutely on the senses: and when marching in a great column, as we were, the front camels kicked up the aromatic dust-laden branches of the shrubs, whose scent-particles rose into the air and hung in a long mist, making fragrant the road of those behind.

The slopes were clean with the sharpness of wormwood, and the hollows oppressive with the richness of their stronger, more luxuriant growths. Our night-passage might have been through a planted garden, and these varieties part of the unseen beauty of successive banks of flowers. The noises too were very clear. Auda broke out singing, away in front, and the men joined in from time to time, with the greatness, the catch at heart, of an army moving into battle.

We rode all night, and when dawn came were dismounting on the crest of the hills between Batra and Aba el Lissan, with a wonderful view westwards over the green and gold Guweira plain, and beyond it to the ruddy mountains hiding Akaba and the sea. Gasim abu Dumeik, head of the Dhumaniyeh, was waiting anxiously for us, surrounded by his hard-bitten tribesmen, their grey strained faces flecked with the blood of the fighting yesterday. There was a deep greeting for Auda and Nasir. We made hurried plans, and scattered to the work, knowing we could not go forward to Akaba with this battalion in possession of the pass. Unless we dislodged it, our two months' hazard and effort would fail before yielding even first-fruits.

Fortunately the poor handling of the enemy gave us an unearned advantage. They slept on, in the valley, while we crowned the hills in wide circle about them unobserved. We began to snipe them steadily in their positions under the slopes and rock-faces by the water, hoping to provoke them out and up the hill in a charge against us. Meanwhile, Zaal rode away with our horsemen and cut the Maan telegraph and telephone in the plain.

This went on all day. It was terribly hot — hotter than ever before I had felt it in Arabia — and the anxiety and constant moving made it hard for us. Some even of the tough tribesmen broke down under the cruelty of the sun, and crawled or had to be thrown under rocks to recover in their shade. We ran up and down to supply our lack of numbers by mobility, ever looking over the long ranges of hill for a new spot from which to counter this or that Turkish effort. The hill-sides were steep, and exhausted our breath, and the grasses twined like little hands about our ankles as we ran, and plucked us back. The sharp reefs of limestone which cropped out over the ridges tore our feet, and long before evening the more energetic men were leaving a rusty print upon the ground with every stride.

Our rifles grew so hot with sun and shooting that they seared our hands; and we had to be grudging of our rounds, considering every shot and spending great pains to make it sure. The rocks on which we flung ourselves for aim were burning, so that they scorched our breasts and arms, from which later the skin drew off in ragged sheets. The present smart made us thirst. Yet even water was rare with us; we could not afford men to fetch enough from Batra, and if all could not drink, it was better that none should.

We consoled ourselves with knowledge that the enemy's enclosed valley would be hotter than our open hills: also that they were Turks, men of white meat, little apt for warm weather. So we clung to them, and did not let them move or mass or sortie out against us cheaply. They could do nothing valid in return. We were no targets for their rifles, since we moved with speed, eccentrically. Also we were able to laugh at the little mountain guns which they fired up at us. The shells passed over our heads, to burst behind us in the air; and yet, of course, for all that they could see from their hollow place, fairly amongst us above the hostile summits of the hill.

Just after noon I had a heat-stroke, or so pretended, for I was dead weary of it all, and cared no longer how it went. So I crept into a hollow where there was a trickle of thick water in a muddy cup of the hills, to suck some moisture off its dirt through the filter of my sleeve. Nasir joined me, panting like a winded animal, with his cracked and bleeding lips shrunk apart in his distress: and old Auda appeared, striding powerfully, his eyes bloodshot and staring, his knotty face working with excitement.

He grinned with malice when he saw us lying there, spread out to find coolness under the bank, and croaked at me harshly, 'Well, how is it with the Howeitat? All talk and no work?' 'By God, indeed,' spat I back again, for I was angry with everyone and with myself, 'they shoot a lot and hit a little.' Auda almost pale with rage, and trembling, tore his head-cloth off and threw it on the ground beside me. Then he ran back up the hill like a madman, shouting to the men in his dreadful strained and rustling voice.

They came together to him, and after a moment scattered away downhill. I feared things were going wrong, and struggled to where he stood alone on the hill-top, glaring at the enemy: but all he would say to me was, 'Get your camel if you want to see the old man's work'. Nasir called for his camel and we mounted.

The Arabs passed before us into a little sunken place, which rose to a low crest; and we knew that the hill beyond went down in a facile slope to the main valley of Aba el Lissan, somewhat below the spring. All our four hundred camel men were here tightly collected, just out of sight of the enemy. We rode to their head, and asked the Shimt what it was and where the horsemen had gone.

He pointed over the ridge to the next valley above us, and said, 'With Auda there': and as he spoke yells and shots poured up in a sudden torrent from beyond the crest. We kicked our camels furiously to the edge, to see our fifty horsemen coming down the last slope into the main valley, like a run-away, at full gallop, shooting from the saddle. As we watched, two or three went down, but the rest thundered forward at marvellous speed, and the Turkish infantry, huddled together under the cliff ready to cut their desperate way out towards Maan, in the first dusk began to sway in and out, and finally broke before the rush, adding their flight to Auda's charge.

Nasir screamed at me, 'Come on', with his bloody mouth; and we plunged our camels madly over the hill, and down towards the head of the fleeing enemy. The slope was not too steep for a camel-gallop, but steep enough to make their pace terrific, and their course uncontrollable: yet the Arabs were able to extend to right and left and to shoot into the Turkish brown. The Turks had been too bound up in the terror of Auda's furious charge against their rear to notice us as we came over the eastward slope: so we also took them by surprise and in the flank; and a charge of ridden camels going nearly thirty miles an hour was irresistible.

My camel, the Sherari racer, Naama, stretched herself out, and hurled downhill with such might that we soon out-distanced the others. The Turks fired a few shots, but mostly only shrieked and turned to run: the bullets they did send at us were not very harmful, for it took much to bring a charging camel down in a dead heap.

I had got among the first of them, and was shooting, with a pistol of course, for only an expert could use a rifle from such plunging beasts; when suddenly my camel tripped and went down emptily upon her face, as though pole-axed. I was torn completely from the saddle, sailed grandly through the air for a great distance, and landed with a crash which seemed to drive all the power and feeling out of me. I lay there, passively waiting for the Turks to kill me, continuing to hum over the verses of a half-forgotten poem, whose rhythm something, perhaps the prolonged stride of the camel, had brought back to my memory as we leaped down the hill-side:

For Lord I was free of all Thy flowers, but I chose the world's sad roses.
And that is why my feet are torn and mine eyes are blind with sweat.

While another part of my mind thought what a squashed thing I should look when all that cataract of men and camels had poured over.

After a long time I finished my poem, and no Turks came, and no camel trod on me: a curtain seemed taken from my ears: there was a great noise in front. I sat up and saw the battle over, and our men driving together and cutting down the last remnants of the enemy. My camel's body had laid behind me like a rock and divided the charge into two streams; and in the back of its skull was the heavy bullet of the fifth shot I fired.

Mohammed brought Obeyd, my spare camel, and Nasir came back leading the Turkish commander, whom he had rescued, wounded, from Mohammed el Dheilan's wrath. The silly man had refused to surrender, and was trying to restore the day for his side with a pocket pistol. The Howeitat were very fierce, for the slaughter of their women on the day before had been a new and horrible side of warfare suddenly revealed to them. So there were only a hundred and sixty prisoners, many of them wounded; and three hundred dead and dying were scattered over the open valleys.

A few of the enemy got away, the gunners on their teams, and some mounted men and officers with their Jazi guides. Mohammed el Dheilan chased them for three miles into Mreigha, hurling insults as he rode, that they might know him and keep out of his way. The feud of Auda and his cousins had never applied to Mohammed, the political-minded, who showed friendship to all men of his tribe when he was alone to do so. Among the fugitives was Dhaif-Allah, who had done us the good turn about the King's Well at Jefer.

Auda came swinging up on foot, his eyes glazed over with the rapture of battle, and the words bubbling with incoherent speed from his mouth. 'Work, work, where are words, work, bullets, Abu Tayi' ... and he held up his shattered field-glasses, his pierced pistol-holster, and his leather sword-scabbard cut to ribbons. He had been the target of a volley which had killed his mare under him, but the six bullets through his clothes had left him scathless.

He told me later, in strict confidence, that thirteen years before he had bought an amulet Koran for one hundred and twenty pounds and had not since been wounded. Indeed, Death had avoided his face, and gone scurvily about killing brothers, sons and followers. The book was a Glasgow reproduction, costing eighteen pence; but Auda's deadliness did not let people laugh at his superstition.

He was wildly pleased with the fight, most of all because he had confounded me and shown what his tribe could do. Mohammed was wroth with us for a pair of fools, calling me worse than Auda, since I had insulted him by words like flung stones to provoke the folly which had nearly killed us all: though it had killed only two of us, one Rueili and one Sherari.

It was, of course, a pity to lose any one of our men, but time was of importance to us, and so imperative was the need of dominating Maan, to shock the little Turkish garrisons between us and the sea into sur-render, that I would have willingly lost much more than two. On occasions like this Death justified himself and was cheap.

I questioned the prisoners about themselves, and the troops in Maan; but the nerve crisis had been too severe for them. Some gaped at me and some gabbled, while others with helpless weepings, embraced my knees, protesting at every word from us that they were fellow Moslems and my brothers in the faith.

Finally I got angry and took one of them aside and was rough to him, shocking him by new pain into a half-understanding, when he answered well enough, and reassuringly, that their battalion was the only reinforcement, and it merely a reserve battalion; the two com-panies in Maan would not suffice to defend its perimeter.

This meant we could take it easily, and the Howeitat clamoured to be led there, lured by the dream of unmeasured loot, though what we had taken here was a rich prize. However, Nasir, and afterwards Auda, helped me stay them. We had no supports, no regulars, no guns, no base nearer than Wejh, no communications, no money even, for our gold was exhausted, and we were issuing our own notes, promises to pay 'when Akaba is taken', for daily expenses. Besides, a strategic scheme was not changed to follow up a tactical success. We must push to the coast, and re-open sea-contact with Suez.

Yet it would be good to alarm Maan further: so we sent mounted men to Mriegha and took it; and to Waheida and took it. News of this advance, of the loss of the camels on the Shobek road, of the demolition of El Haj, and of the massacre of their relieving battalion all came to Maan together, and caused a very proper panic. The military head-quarters wired for help, the civil authorities loaded their official archive into trucks, and left, hot-speed, for Damascus.

CHAPTER LIV

MEANWHILE our Arabs had plundered the Turks, their baggage train, and their camp; and soon after moonrise, Auda came to us and said that we must move. It angered Nasir and myself. To-night there was a dewy west wind blowing, and at Aba el Lissan's four thousand feet, after the heat and burning passion of the day, its damp chill struck very sharply on our wounds and bruises. The spring itself was a thread of silvery water in a runnel of pebbles across delightful turf, green and soft, on which we lay, wrapped in our cloaks, wondering if something to eat were worth preparing: for we were subject at the moment to the physical shame of success, a reaction of victory, when it became clear that nothing was worth doing, and that nothing worthy had been done.

Auda insisted. Partly it was superstition — he feared the newly-dead around us; partly lest the Turks return in force; partly lest other clans of the Howeitat take us, lying there broken and asleep. Some were his blood enemies; others might say they came to help our battle, and in the darkness thought we were Turks and fired blindly. So we roused ourselves, and jogged the sorry prisoners into line.

Most had to walk. Some twenty camels were dead or dying from wounds which they had got in the charge, and others were over weak to take a double burden. The rest were loaded with an Arab and a Turk; but some of the Turkish wounded were too hurt to hold themselves on pillion. In the end we had to leave about twenty on the thick grass beside the rivulet, where at least they would not die of thirst, though there was little hope of life or rescue for them.

Nasir set himself to beg blankets for these abandoned men, who were half-naked; and while the Arabs packed, I went off down the valley where the fight had been, to see if the dead had any clothing they could spare. But the Beduin had been beforehand with me, and had stripped them to the skin. Such was their point of honour.

To an Arab an essential part of the triumph of victory was to wear the clothes of an enemy: and next day we saw our force transformed (as to the upper half) into a Turkish force, each man in a soldier's tunic: for this was a battalion straight from home, very well found and dressed in new uniforms.

The dead men looked wonderfully beautiful. The night was shining gently down, softening them into new ivory. Turks were white-skinned on their clothed parts, much whiter than the Arabs; and these soldiers had been very young. Close round them lapped the dark wormwood, now heavy with dew, in which the ends of the moon-beams sparkled like sea-spray. The corpses seemed flung so pitifully on the ground, huddled anyhow in low heaps. Surely if straightened they would be comfortable at last. So I put them all in order, one by one, very wearied myself, and longing to be of these quiet ones, not of the restless, noisy, aching mob up the valley, quarrelling over the plunder, boasting of their speed and strength to endure God knew how many toils and pains of this sort; with death, whether we won or lost, waiting to end the history.

In the end our little army was ready, and wound slowly up the height and beyond into a hollow sheltered from the wind; and there, while the tired men slept, we dictated letters to the Sheikhs of the coastal Howeitat, telling them of the victory, that they might invite their nearest Turks, and hold them till we came. We had been kind to one of the captured officers, a policeman despised by his regular col-leagues, and him we persuaded to be our Turkish scribe to the com-mandants of Guweira, Kethera, and Hadra, the three posts between us and Akaba, telling them that if our blood was not hot we took prisoners, and that prompt surrender would ensure their good treat-ment and safe delivery to Egypt.

This lasted till dawn, and then Auda marshalled us for the road, and led us up the last mile of soft heath-clad valley between the rounded hills. It was intimate and homelike till the last green bank; when suddenly we realized it was the last, and beyond lay nothing but clear air. The lovely change this time checked me with amazement; and afterwards, however often we came, there was always a catch of eager-ness in the mind, a pricking forward of the camel and straightening up to see again over the crest into openness.

Shtar hill-side swooped away below us for hundreds and hundreds of feet, in curves like bastions, against which summer-morning clouds were breaking: and from its foot opened the new earth of the Guweira plain. Aba el Lissan's rounded limestone breasts were covered with soil and heath, green, well watered. Guweira was a map of pink sand, brushed over with streaks of watercourses, in a mantle of scrub: and, out of this, and bounding this, towered islands and cliffs of glowing sandstone, wind-scarped and rain-furrowed, tinted celestially by the early sun.

After days of travel on the plateau in prison valleys, to meet this brink of freedom was a rewarding vision, like a window in the wall of life. We walked down the whole zigzag pass of Shtar, to feel its excellence, for on our camels we rocked too much with sleep to dare see anything. At the bottom the animals found a matted thorn which gave their jaws pleasure; we in front made a halt, rolled on to sand soft as a couch, and incontinently slept.

Auda came. We pleaded that it was for mercy upon our broken prisoners. He replied that they alone would die of exhaustion if we rode, but if we dallied, both parties might die: for truly there was now little water and no food. However, we could not help it, and stopped that night short of Guweira, after only fifteen miles. At Guweira lay Sheikh ibn Jad, balancing his policy to come down with the stronger: and to-day we were the stronger, and the old fox was ours. He met us with honeyed speeches. The hundred and twenty Turks of the garrison were his prisoners; we agreed with him to carry them at his leisure and their ease to Akaba.

To-day was the fourth of July. Time pressed us, for we were hungry, and Akaba was still far ahead behind two defences. The nearer post, Kethira, stubbornly refused parley with our flags. Their cliff commanded the valley — a strong place which it might be costly to take. We assigned the honour, in irony, to ibn Jad and his unwearied men, advising him to try it after dark. He shrank, made difficulties, pleaded the full moon: but we cut hardly into this excuse, promising that to-night for a while there should be no moon. By my diary there was an eclipse. Duly it came, and the Arabs forced the post without loss, while the superstitious soldiers were firing rifles and clanging copper pots to rescue the threatened satellite.

Reassured we set out across the strandlike plain. Niazi Bey, the Turkish battalion commander, was Nasir's guest, to spare him the humiliation of Beduin contempt. Now he sidled up by me, and, his swollen eyelids and long nose betraying the moroseness of the man, began to complain that an Arab had insulted him with a gross Turkish word. I apologized, pointing out that it must have been learnt from the mouth of one of his Turkish fellow-governors. The Arab was repaying Cæsar.

Cæsar, not satisfied, pulled from his pocket a wizened hunch of bread to ask if it was fit breakfast for a Turkish officer. My heavenly twins, foraging in Guweira, had bought, found, or stolen a Turkish soldier's ration loaf; and we had quartered it. I said it was not breakfast but lunch and dinner, and perhaps to-morrow's meals as well. I, a staff officer of the British Army (not less well fed than the Turkish), had eaten mine with the relish of victory. It was defeat, not bread, which stuck in his gullet, and I begged him not to blame me for the issue of a battle imposed on both our honours.

The narrows of Wadi Itm increased in intricate ruggedness as we penetrated deeper. Below Kethira we found Turkish post after Turkish post, empty. Their men had been drawn in to Khadra, the entrenched position (at the mouth of Itm), which covered Akaba so well against a landing from the sea. Unfortunately for them the enemy had never imagined attack from the interior, and of all their great works not one trench or post faced inland. Our advance from so new a direction threw them into panic.

In the afternoon we were in contact with this main position, and heard from the local Arabs that the subsidiary posts about Akaba had been called in or reduced, so that only a last three hundred men barred us from the sea. We dismounted for a council, to hear that the enemy were resisting firmly in bomb-proof trenches with a new artesian well. Only it was rumoured that they had little food.

No more had we. It was a deadlock. Our council swayed this way and that. Arguments bickered between the prudent and the bold. Tempers were short and bodies restless in the incandescent gorge whose granite peaks radiated the sun in a myriad shimmering points of light, and into the depths of whose tortuous bed no wind could come to relieve the slow saturation of the air with heat.

Our numbers had swollen double. So thickly did the men crowd in the narrow space, and press about us, that we broke up our council twice or thrice, partly because it was not good that they should overhear us wrangling, partly because in the sweltering confinement our unwashed smells offended us. Through our heads the heavy pulses throbbed like clocks.

We sent the Turks summonses, first by white flag, and then by Turkish prisoners, but they shot at both. This inflamed our Beduin, and while we were yet deliberating a sudden wave of them burst up on to the rocks and sent a hail of bullets spattering against the enemy. Nasir ran out barefoot, to stop them, but after ten steps on the burning ground screeched for sandals; while I crouched in my atom of shadow, too wearied of these men (whose minds all wore my livery) to care who regulated their febrile impulses.

However, Nasir prevailed easily. Farraj and Daud had been ring-leaders. For correction they were set on scorching rocks till they should beg pardon. Daud yielded immediately; but Farraj, who, for all his soft form, was of whipcord and much the master-spirit of the two, laughed from his first rock, sat out the second sullenly, and gave way with a bad grace only when ordered to a third.

His stubbornness should have been stringently visited: but the only punishment, possible to our hands in this vagrant life was corporal, which had been tried upon the pair so often and so uselessly that I was sick of it. If confined this side of cruelty the surface pain seemed only to irritate their muscles into activities wilder than those for which they had been condemned. Their sins were elvish gaiety, the thought-lessness of unbalanced youth, the being happy when we were not; and for such follies to hurt them mercilessly like criminals till their self-control melted and their manhood was lost under the animal distress of their bodies, seemed to me degrading, almost an impiety towards two sunlit beings, on whom the shadow of the world had not yet fallen — the most gallant, the most enviable, I knew.

We had a third try to communicate with the Turks, by means of a little conscript, who said that he understood how to do it. He undressed and went down the valley in little more than boots. An hour later he proudly brought us a reply, very polite, saying that in two days, if help did not come from Maan, they would surrender.

Such folly (for we could not hold our men indefinitely) might mean the massacre of every Turk. I held no great brief for them, but it was better they be not killed, if only to spare us the pain of seeing it. Besides we might have suffered loss. Night operations in the staring moon would be nearly as exposed as day. Nor was this, like Aba el Lissan, an imperative battle.

We gave our little man a sovereign as earnest of reward, walked down close to the trenches with him, and sent in for an officer to speak with us. After some hesitation this was achieved, and we explained the situation on the road behind us; our growing forces; and our short control over their tempers. The upshot was that they promised to surrender at daylight. So we had another sleep (an event rare enough to chronicle) in spite of our thirst.

Next day at dawn fighting broke out on all sides, for hundreds more hill-men, again doubling our number, had come in the night; and, not knowing the arrangement, began shooting at the Turks, who defended themselves. Nasir went out, with ibn Dgheithir and his Ageyl marching in fours, down the open bed of the valley. Our men ceased fire. The Turks then stopped, for their rank and file had no more fight in them and no more food, and thought we were well supplied. So the surrender went off quietly after all.

As the Arabs rushed in to plunder I noticed an engineer in grey uniform, with red beard and puzzled blue eyes; and spoke to him in German. He was the well-borer, and knew no Turkish. Recent doings had amazed him, and he begged me to explain what we meant. I said that we were a rebellion of the Arabs against the Turks. This, it took him time to appreciate. He wanted to know who was our leader. I said the Sherif of Mecca. He supposed he would be sent to Mecca. I said rather to Egypt. He inquired the price of sugar, and when I replied, 'cheap and plentiful', he was glad.

The loss of his belongings he took philosophically, but was sorry for the well, which a little work would have finished as his monument. He showed me where it was, with the pump only half-built. By pulling on the sludge bucket we drew enough delicious clear water to quench our thirsts. Then we raced through a driving sand-storm down to Akaba, four miles further, and splashed into the sea on July the sixth, just two months after our setting out from Wejh.

BOOK V

MARKING TIME

Chapters LV to LXVIII

OUR *capture of Akaba closed the Hejaz war, and gave us the task of helping the British invade Syria. The Arabs working from Akaba became virtual right wing of Allenby's army in Sinai.*

To mark the changed relation Feisal, with his Army, was transferred to Allenby's command. Allenby now became responsible for his operations and equipment. Meanwhile we organized the Akaba area as an unassailable base, from which to hinder the Hejaz Railway.

ι

CHAPTER LV

THROUGH the whirling dust we perceived that Akaba was all a ruin. Repeated bombardments by French and English warships had degraded the place to its original rubbish. The poor houses stood about in a litter, dirty and contemptible, lacking entirely that dignity which the durability of their time-challenging bones conferred on ancient remains.

We wandered into the shadowed grove of palms, at the very break of the splashing waves, and there sat down to watch our men streaming past as lines of flushed vacant faces without message for us. For months Akaba had been the horizon of our minds, the goal: we had had no thought, we had refused thought of anything beside. Now, in achievement, we were a little despising the entities which had spent their extremest effort on an object whose attainment changed nothing radical either in mind or body.

In the blank light of victory we could scarcely identify ourselves. We spoke with surprise, sat emptily, fingered upon our white skirts; doubtful if we could understand or learn whom we were. Others' noise was a dreamlike unreality, a singing in ears drowned deep in water. Against the astonishment of this unasked-for continued life we did not know how to turn our gift to account. Especially for me was it hard, because though my sight was sharp, I never saw men's features: always I peered beyond, imagining for myself a spirit-reality of this or that: and to-day each man owned his desire so utterly that he was fulfilled in it, and became meaningless.

Hunger called us out of our trance. We had now seven hundred prisoners in addition to our own five hundred men and two thousand expectant allies. We had not any money (or, indeed, a market); and the last meal had been two days ago. In our riding-camels we possessed meat enough for six weeks, but it was poor diet, and a dear one, indulgence in which would bring future immobility upon us.

Green dates loaded the palms overhead. Their taste, raw, was nearly as nasty as the want they were to allay. Cooking left them still deplorable; so we and our prisoners sadly faced a dilemma of constant hunger, or of violent diurnal pains more proper to gluttony than to our expedient eating. The assiduous food-habit of a lifetime had trained the English body to the pitch of producing a punctual nervous excitation in the upper belly at the fixed hour of each meal: and we sometimes gave the honoured name of hunger to this sign that our gut had cubic space for more stuff. Arab hunger was the cry of a long-empty labouring body fainting with weakness. They lived on a fraction of our bulk-food and their systems made exhaustive use of what they got. A nomad army did not dung the earth richly with by-products.

Our forty-two officer prisoners were an intolerable nuisance. They were disgusted when they found how ill-provided we were: indeed they refused to believe it was not a fraud to annoy them, and plagued us for delicacies, as though Cairo lay hidden in our saddle-bags. To escape them Nasir and I slept. Always we tried to signalize each accomplished stage by this little extra peace; for in the desert we were only left alone by men and flies when lying on our backs, with a cloak to shield our faces, asleep or feigning sleep.

In the evening, our first reaction against success having passed off, we began to think how we should keep Akaba, having gained it. We settled that Auda should return to Guweira. He would there be covered by the descent of Shtar, and the Guweira sands. In fact, as safe as need be. But we would make him safer yet, in excess of precaution. We would put an outpost twenty miles to his north, in the impregnable rock-ruins of Nabathean Petra, and link them to him by a post at Delagha. Auda should also send men to Batra so that his Howeitat lie in a semi circle of four positions round the edge of the Maan highlands, covering every way towards Akaba.

These four positions existed independently. The enemy had swallowed Goltz' impertinent generalities about the interdependence of strong-posts. We looked to their delivering a spirited drive against one, and sitting afterwards in it dazed for an uncomfortable month, unable to advance for the threat of the remaining three, scratching their heads and wondering why the others did not fall.

Supper taught us the urgent need to send news over the one hundred and fifty miles to the British at Suez for a relief-ship. I decided to go across myself with a party of eight, mostly Howeitat, on the best camels in the force — one even was the famous Jedhah, the seven-year-old for whom the Nowasera had fought the beni Sakhr. As we rode round the bay we discussed the manner of our journey. If we went gently, sparing the animals, they might fail with hunger. If we rode hard they might break down with exhaustion or sore feet in mid-desert.

Finally we agreed to keep at a walk, however tempting the surface, for so many hours of the twenty-four as our endurance would allow. On such time-tests the man, especially if he were a foreigner, usually collapsed before the beast: in particular, I had ridden fifty miles a day for the last month, and was near my limit of strength. If I held out, we should reach Suez in fifty hours of a march; and, to preclude cooking-halts upon the road, we carried lumps of boiled camel and broiled dates in a rag behind our saddles.

We rode up the Sinai scarp by the pilgrims' granite-hewn road with its gradient of one in three and a half. The climb was severe, because hasty, and when we reached the crest before sunset both men and camels were trembling with fatigue. One camel we thence sent back as unfit for the trip: with the others we pushed out across the plain to some thorn-scrub, where they cropped for an hour.

Near midnight we reached Themed, the only wells on our route, in a clean valley-sweep below the deserted guard-house of the Sinai police. We let the camels breathe, gave them water and drank ourselves. Then forward again, plodding through a silence of night so intense that continually we turned round in the saddles at fancied noises away there by the cloak of stars. But the activity lay in ourselves, in the crackling of our passage through the undergrowth perfumed like ghost-flowers about us.

We marched into the very slow dawn. At sun-up we were far out in the plain through which sheaves of watercourses gathered towards Arish: and we stopped to give our camels a few minutes' mockery of pasture. Then again in the saddle till noon, and past noon, when behind the mirage rose the lonely ruins of Nekhl. These we left on our right. At sunset we halted for an hour.

Camels were sluggish, and ourselves utterly wearied; but Motlog, the one-eyed owner of Jedhah, called us to action. We remounted, and at a mechanical walk climbed the Mitla Hills. The moon came out and their tops, contoured in form-lines of limestone strata, shone as though crystalline with snow.

In the dawn we passed a melon field, sown by some adventurous Arab in this no-man's-land between the armies. We halted another of our precious hours, loosing the disgusted camels to search the sand-valleys for food while we cracked the unripe melons and cooled our chapped lips on their pithy flesh. Then again forward, in the heat of the new day; though the canal valley, constantly refreshed by breezes from the Gulf of Suez, was never too oppressive.

By midday we were through the dunes, after a happy switchback ride up and down their waves, and out on the flatter plain. Suez was to be guessed at, as the frise of indeterminate points mowing and bobbing in the mirage of the canal-hollow far in front.

We reached great trench-lines, with forts and barbed wire, roads and railways, falling to decay. We passed them without challenge. Our aim was the Shatt, a post opposite Suez on the Asiatic bank of the Canal, and we gained it at last near three in the afternoon, forty-nine hours out of Akaba. For a tribal raid this would have been fair time, and we were tired men before ever we started.

Shatt was in unusual disorder, without even a sentry to stop us, plague having appeared there two or three days before. So the old camps had been hurriedly cleared, left standing, while the troops bivouacked out in the clean desert. Of course we knew nothing of this, but hunted in the empty offices till we found a telephone. I rang up Suez headquarters and said I wanted to come across.

They regretted that it was not their business. The Inland Water Transport managed transit across the Canal, after their own methods. There was a sniff of implication that these methods were not those of the General Staff. Undaunted, for I was never a partisan of my nominal branch of the service, I rang up the office of the Water Board, and explained that I had just arrived in Shatt from the desert with urgent news for Headquarters. They were sorry, but had no free boats just then. They would be sure to send first thing in the morning, to carry me to the Quarantine Department: and rang off.

CHAPTER LVI

NOW I had been four months in Arabia continually on the move. In the last four weeks I had ridden fourteen hundred miles by camel, not sparing myself anything to advance the war; but I refused to spend a single superfluous night with my familiar vermin. I wanted a bath, and something with ice in it to drink: to change these clothes, all sticking to my saddle sores in filthiness: to eat something more tractable than green date and camel sinew. I got through again to the Inland Water Transport and talked like Chrysostom. It had no effect, so I became vivid. Then, once more, they cut me off. I was growing very vivid, when friendly northern accents from the military exchange floated down the line: 'It's no bluidy good, sir, talking to them fookin water boogers.'

This expressed the apparent truth; and the broad-spoken operator worked me through to the Embarkation Office. Here, Lyttleton, a major of the busiest, had added to his innumerable labours that of catching Red Sea warships one by one as they entered Suez roads and persuading them (how some loved it!) to pile high their decks with stores for Wejh or Yenbo. In this way he ran our thousands of bales and men, free, as a by-play in his routine; and found time as well to smile at the curious games of us curious folk.

He never failed us. As soon as he heard who and where I was, and what was not happening in the Inland Water Transport, the difficulty was over. His launch was ready: would be at the Shatt in half an hour. I was to come straight to his office: and not explain (till perhaps now after the war) that a common harbour launch had entered the sacred canal without permission of the Water Directorate. All fell out as he said. I sent my men and camels north to Kubri; where, by telephone from Suez, I would prepare them rations and shelter in the animal camp on the Asiatic shore. Later, of course, came their reward of hectic and astonishing days in Cairo.

Lyttleton saw my weariness and let me go at once to the hotel. Long ago it had seemed poor, but now was become splendid; and, after conquering its first hostile impression of me and my dress, it produced the hot baths and the cold drinks (six of them) and the dinner and bed of my dreams. A most willing intelligence officer, warned by spies of a disguised European in the Sinai Hotel, charged himself with the care of my men at Kubri and provided tickets and passes for me to Cairo next day.

The strenuous 'control' of civilian movement in the canal zone entertained a dull journey. A mixed body of Egyptian and British military police came round the train, interrogating us and scrutinizing our passes. It was proper to make war on permit-men, so I replied crisply in fluent English, 'Sherif of Mecca — Staff', to their Arabic inquiries. They were astonished. The sergeant begged my pardon: he had not expected to hear. I repeated that I was in the Staff uniform of the Sherif of Mecca. They looked at my bare feet, white silk robes and gold head-rope and dagger. Impossible! 'What army, sir?' 'Meccan.' 'Never heard of it: don't know the uniform.' 'Would you recognize a Montenegrin dragoon?'

This was a home-thrust. Any Allied troops in uniform might travel without pass. The police did not know all the allies, much less their uniforms. Mine might really be some rare army. They fell back into the corridor and watched me while they wired up the line. Just before Ismailia, a perspiring intelligence officer in wet khaki boarded the train to check my statements. As we had almost arrived I showed him the special pass with which the forethought of Suez had twice-armed my innocence. He was not pleased.

At Ismailia passengers for Cairo changed, to wait until the express from Port Said was due. In the other train shone an opulent saloon, from which descended Admiral Wemyss and Burmester and Neville, with a very large and superior general. A terrible tension grew along the platform as the party marched up and down it in weighty talk. Officers saluted once: twice: still they marched up and down. Three times was too much. Some withdrew to the fence and stood permanently to attention. These were the mean souls. Some fled: these were the contemptibles. Some turned to the bookstall and studied book-backs avidly: these were shy. Only one was blatant.

Burmester's eye caught my staring. He wondered who it was, for I was burned crimson and very haggard with travel. (Later I found my weight to be less than seven stone.) However, he answered; and I explained the history of our unannounced raid on Akaba. It excited him. I asked that the admiral send a storeship there at once. Burmester said the *Dufferin*, which came in that day, should load all the food in Suez, go straight to Akaba, and bring back the prisoners. (Splendid!) He would order it himself, not to interrupt the Admiral and Allenby.

'Allenby! what's he doing here?' cried I. 'Oh, he's in command now.' 'And Murray?' 'Gone home.' This was news of the biggest, importantly concerning me: and I climbed back and fell to wondering if this heavy, rubicund man was like ordinary generals, and if we should have trouble for six months teaching him. Murray and Belinda had begun so tiresomely that our thought those first days had been, not to defeat the enemy, but to make our own chiefs let us live. Only by time and performance had we converted Sir Archibald and his Chief of Staff who in their last months, wrote to the War Office commending the Arab venture, and especially Feisal in it. This was generous of them

and our secret triumph, for they were an odd pair in one chariot –
Murray all brains and claws, nervous, elastic, changeable; Lynden Bell
so solidly built up of layers of professional opinion, glued together after
Government testing and approval, and later trimmed and polished to
standard pitch.

At Cairo my sandalled feet slip-slapped up the quiet Savoy corridors
to Clayton, who habitually cut the lunch hour to cope with his thronging work. As I entered he glanced up from his desk with a muttered
'Mush fadi' (Anglo-Egyptian for 'engaged') but I spoke and got a
surprised welcome. In Suez the night before I had scribbled a short
report; so we had to talk only of what needed doing. Before the hour
ended, the Admiral rang up to say that the *Dufferin* was loading flour
for her emergency trip.

Clayton drew sixteen thousand pounds in gold and got an escort to
take it to Suez by the three o'clock train. This was urgent, that Nasir
might be able to meet his debts. The notes we had issued at Bair,
Jefer and Guweira were pencilled promises, on army telegraph forms,
to pay so much to bearer in Akaba. It was a great system, but no one
had dared issue notes before in Arabia, because the Beduins had neither
pockets in their shirts nor strong-rooms in their tents, and notes could
not be buried for safety. So there was an unconquerable prejudice
against them, and for our good name it was essential that they be early
redeemed.

Afterwards, in the hotel, I tried to find clothes less publicly exciting
than my Arab get-up; but the moths had corrupted all my former store,
and it was three days before I became normally ill-dressed.

Meanwhile I heard of Allenby's excellence, and of the last tragedy of
Murray, that second attack on Gaza, which London forced on one
too weak or too politic to resist; and how we went into it, everybody,
generals and staff-officers, even soldiers, convinced that we should
lose;

                                                    . Five
thousand eight hundred was the casualty bill. They said Allenby was
getting armies of fresh men, and hundreds of guns, and all would be
different.

L*

Before I was clothed the Commander-in-Chief sent for me, curiously. In my report, thinking of Saladin and Abu Obeida, I had stressed the strategic importance of the eastern tribes of Syria, and their proper use as a threat to the communications of Jerusalem. This jumped with his ambitions, and he wanted to weigh me.

It was a comic interview, for Allenby was physically large and confident, and morally so great that the comprehension of our littleness came slow to him. He sat in his chair looking at me — not straight, as his custom was, but sideways, puzzled. He was newly from France where for years he had been a tooth of the great machine grinding the enemy. He was full of Western ideas of gun power and weight — the worst training for our war — but, as a cavalryman, was already half persuaded to throw up the new school, in this different world of Asia, and accompany Dawnay and Chetwode along the worn road of manœuvre and movement; yet he was hardly prepared for anything so odd as myself — a little bare-footed silk-skirted man offering to hobble the enemy by his preaching if given stores and arms and a fund of two hundred thousand sovereigns to convince and control his converts.

Allenby could not make out how much was genuine performer and how much charlatan. The problem was working behind his eyes, and I left him unhelped to solve it. He did not ask many questions, nor talk much, but studied the map and listened to my unfolding of Eastern Syria and its inhabitants. At the end he put up his chin and said quite directly, 'Well, I will do for you what I can', and that ended it. I was not sure how far I had caught him; but we learned gradually that he meant exactly what he said; and that what General Allenby could do was enough for his very greediest servant.

CHAPTER LVII

UPON Clayton I opened myself completely. Akaba had been taken on my plan by my effort. The cost of it had fallen on my brains and nerves. There was much more I felt inclined to do, and capable of doing: — if he thought I had earned the right to be my own master. The Arabs said that each man believed his ticks to be gazelles: I did, fervently.

Clayton agreed they were spirited and profitable ticks; but objected that actual command could not be given to an officer junior to the rest. He suggested Joyce as commanding officer at Akaba: a notion which suited me perfectly. Joyce was a man in whom one could rest against the world: a serene, unchanging, comfortable spirit. His mind, like a pastoral landscape, had four corners to its view: cared-for, friendly, limited, displayed.

He had won golden opinions at Rabegh and Wejh, practising that very labour of building up an army and a base, which would be necessary at Akaba. Clayton-like, he was a good cartilage to set between opposing joints, but he had more laughter than Clayton, being broad and Irish and much over six feet in height. His nature was to be devoted to the nearest job without straining on his toes after longer horizons. Also, he was more patient than any recorded archangel, and only smiled that jolly smile of his whenever I came in with revolutionary schemes, and threw new ribbons of fancy about the neck of the wild thing he was slowly rearing.

The rest was easy. For supply officer we would have Goslett, the London business man who had made chaotic Wejh so prim. The aeroplanes could not yet be moved; but the armoured cars might come straight away, and a guard-ship if the Admiral was generous. We rang up Sir Rosslyn Wemyss, who was very generous: his flagship, the *Euryalus*, should sit there for the first few weeks.

Genius, this was, for in Arabia ships were esteemed by number of funnels, and the *Euryalus*, with four, was exceptional in ships. Her great reputation assured the mountains that we were indeed the winning side: and her huge crew, by the prompting of Everard Feilding for fun built us a good pier.

On the Arab side, I asked that the expensive and difficult Wejh be closed down, and Feisal come to Akaba with his full army. A sudden demand, it seemed to Cairo. So I went further, pointing out that the Yenbo-Medina sector also became a back-number; and advised the transfer to Akaba of the stores, money, and officers now devoted to Ali and Abdulla. This was ruled to be impossible. But my wish regarding Wejh was granted me in compromise.

Then I showed that Akaba was Allenby's right flank, only one hundred miles from his centre, but eight hundred miles from Mecca. As the Arabs prospered their work would be done more and more in the Palestine sphere. So it was logical that Feisal be transferred from the area of King Hussein to become an army commander of the Allied expedition of Egypt under Allenby.

This idea held difficulties. 'Would Feisal accept?' I had talked it over with him in Wejh months ago. 'The High Commissioner?' Feisal's army had been the largest and most distinguished of the Hejaz units: its future would not be dull. General Wingate had assumed full responsibility for the Arab Movement in its darkest moment, at great risk in reputation: dare we ask him to relinquish its advance-guard now on the very threshold of success?

Clayton, knowing Wingate very well, was not afraid to broach the idea to him: and Wingate replied promptly that if Allenby could make direct and large use of Feisal, it would be both his duty and his pleasure to give him up for the good of the show.

A third difficulty of the transfer might be King Hussein: an obstinate, narrow-minded, suspicious character, little likely to sacrifice a pet vanity for unity of control. His opposition would endanger the scheme: and I offered to go down to talk him over, calling on the way to get from Feisal such recommendations of the change as should fortify the powerful letters which Wingate was writing to the King. This was accepted. The *Dufferin*, on returning from Akaba, was detailed to take me to Jidda for the new mission.

She took two days to reach Wejh. Feisal, with Joyce, Newcombe, and all the army, was at Jeida, one hundred miles inland. Stent, who had succeeded Ross in command of the Arabian flight, sent me up by air; so we crossed comfortably at sixty miles an hour the hills learned toilsomely on camel-back.

Feisal was eager to hear the details of Akaba, and laughed at our prentice wars. We sat and made plans the whole night. He wrote to his father; ordered his camel corps to march upon Akaba forthwith; and made first arrangements towards getting Jaafar Pasha and his army ferried up in the long-suffering *Hardinge*.

At dawn they flew me back to Wejh, and, an hour after, the *Dufferin* was making for Jidda, where things became easy for me with Wilson's powerful help. To render Akaba, our most promising sector, strong, he sent up a shipload of reserve stores and ammunition, and offered us any of his officers. Wilson was of the Wingate school.

The King came down from Mecca and talked discursively. Wilson was the royal touchstone, by which to try doubtful courses. Thanks to him, the proposed transfer of Feisal to Allenby, was accepted at once, King Hussein taking the opportunity to stress his complete loyalty to our alliance. Then, changing his subject, as usual without obvious coherence, he began to expose his religious position, neither strong Shia nor strong Sunni, aiming rather at a simple pre-schism interpretation of the faith. In foreign politics he betrayed a mind as narrow as it had been broad in unworldly things; with much of that destructive tendency of little men to deny the honesty of opponents. I grasped something of the fixed jealousy which made the modern Feisal suspect in his father's court; and realized how easily mischief-makers could corrode the King.

While we played so interestingly at Jidda, two abrupt telegrams from Egypt shattered our peace. The first reported that the Howeitat were in treasonable correspondence with Maan. The second connected Auda with the plot. This dismayed us. Wilson had travelled with Auda, and formed the inevitable judgement of his perfect sincerity: yet Mohammed el Dheilan was capable of double play, and ibn Jad and his friends were still uncertain. We prepared to leave at once for Akaba. Treachery had not been taken into account when Nasir and I had built our plan for the town's defence.

Fortunately the *Hardinge* was in harbour for us. On the third afternoon we were in Akaba, where Nasir had no notion that anything was wrong. I told him only of my wish to greet Auda: he lent me a swift camel and a guide; and at dawn we found Auda and Mohammed and Zaal all in a tent at Guweira. They were confused when I dropped in on them, unheralded; but protested that all was well. We fed together as friends.

Others of the Howeitat came in, and there was gay talk about the war. I distributed the King's presents; and told them, to their laughter, that Nasir had got his month's leave to Mecca. The King, an enthusiast for the revolt, believed that his servants should work as manfully. So he would not allow visits to Mecca, and the poor men found continual military service heavy banishment from their wives. We had jested a hundred times that, if he took Akaba, Nasir would deserve a holiday; but he had not really believed in its coming until I gave him Hussein's letter the evening before. In gratitude he sold me Ghazala, the regal camel he won from the Howeitat. As her owner I became of new interest to the Abu Tayi.

After lunch, by pretence of sleep, I got rid of the visitors; and then abruptly asked Auda and Mohammed to walk with me to see the ruined fort and reservoir. When we were alone I touched on their present correspondence with the Turks. Auda began to laugh; Mohammed to look disgusted. At last they explained elaborately that Mohammed had taken Auda's seal and written to the Governor of Maan, offering to desert the Sherif's cause. The Turk had replied gladly, promising great rewards. Mohammed asked for something on account. Auda then heard of it, waited till the messenger with presents was on his way, caught him, robbed him to the skin: and was denying Mohammed a share of the spoils. A farcical story, and we laughed rightly over it: but there was more behind.

They were angry that no guns or troops had yet come to their support; and that no rewards had been given them for taking Akaba. They were anxious to know how I had learnt of their secret dealings, and how much more I knew. We were on a slippery ledge. I played on their fear by my unnecessary amusement, quoting in careless laughter, as if they were my own words, actual phrases of the letters they had exchanged. This created the impression desired.

Parenthetically I told them Feisal's entire army was coming up; and how Allenby was sending rifles, guns, high explosive, food and money to Akaba. Finally I suggested that Auda's present expenses in hospitality must be great; would it help if I advanced something of the great gift Feisal would make him, personally, when he arrived? Auda saw that the immediate moment would not be unprofitable: that Feisal would be highly profitable: and that the Turks would be always with him if other resources failed. So he agreed, in a very good temper, to accept my advance; and with it to keep the Howeitat well-fed and cheerful.

It was near sunset. Zaal had killed a sheep and we ate again in real amity. Afterwards I remounted, with Mufaddih (to draw Auda's allowance), and Abd el Rahman, a servant of Mohammed's who, so he whispered me, would receive any little thing I wished to send him separately. We rode all night towards Akaba, where I roused Nasir from sleep, to run over our last business. Then I paddled out in a derelict canoe from 'Euryalus jetty' to the *Hardinge* just as the first dawn crept down the western peaks.

I went below, bathed, and slept till mid-morning. When I came on deck the ship was rushing grandly down the narrow gulf under full steam for Egypt. My appearance caused a sensation, for they had not dreamed I could reach Guweira, assure myself, and get back in less than six or seven days, to catch a later steamer.

We rang up Cairo and announced that the situation at Guweira was thoroughly good, and no treachery abroad. This may have been hardly true; but since Egypt kept us alive by stinging herself, we must reduce impolitic truth to keep her confident and ourselves a legend. The crowd wanted book-heroes, and would not understand how more human old Auda was because, after battle and murder, his heart yearned towards the defeated enemy now subject, at his free choice, to be spared or killed: and therefore never so lovely.

CHAPTER LVIII

AGAIN there fell a pause in my work and again my thoughts built themselves up. Till Feisal and Jaafar and Joyce and the army came we could do little but think: yet that, for our own credit, was the essential process. So far our war had had but the one studied operation — the march on Akaba. Such haphazard playing with the men and movements of which we had assumed the leadership disgraced our minds. I vowed to know henceforward, before I moved, where I was going and by what roads.

At Wejh the Hejaz war was won: after Akaba it was ended. Feisal's army had cleared off its Arabian liabilities and now, under General Allenby the joint Commander-in-Chief, its role was to take part in the military deliverance of Syria.

The difference between Hejaz and Syria was the difference between the desert and the sown. The problem which faced us was one of character — the learning to become civil. Wadi Musa village was our first peasant recruit. Unless we became peasants too, the independence movement would get no further.

It was good for the Arab Revolt that so early in its growth this change imposed itself. We had been hopelessly labouring to plough waste lands; to make nationality grow in a place full of the certainty of God, that upas certainty which forbade all hope. Among the tribes our creed could be only like the desert grass — a beautiful swift seeming of spring; which, after a day's heat, fell dusty. Aims and ideas must be translated into tangibility by material expression. The desert men were too detached to express the one; too poor in goods, too remote from complexity, to carry the other. If we would prolong our life, we must win into the ornamented lands; to the villages where roofs or fields held men's eyes downward and near; and begin our campaign as we had begun that in Wadi Ais, by a study of the map, and a recollection of the nature of this our battleground of Syria.

Our feet were upon its southern boundary. To the east stretched the nomadic desert. To the west Syria was limited by the Mediterranean, from Gaza to Alexandretta. On the north the Turkish populations of Anatolia gave it an end. Within these limits the land was much parcelled up by natural divisions. Of them the first and greatest was longitudinal; the rugged spine of mountains which, from north to south, divided a coast strip from a wide inland plain. These areas had climatic differences so marked that they made two countries, two races almost, with their respective populations. The shore Syrians lived in different houses, fed and worked differently, used an Arabic differing by inflection and in tone from that of the inlanders. They spoke of the interior unwillingly, as of a wild land of blood and terror.

The inland plain was sub-divided geographically into strips by rivers. These valleys were the most stable and prosperous tillages of the country. Their inhabitants reflected them: contrasting, on the desert side, with the strange, shifting populations of the borderland, wavering eastward or westward with the season, living by their wits, wasted by drought and locusts, by Beduin raids; or, if these failed them, by their own incurable blood feuds.

Nature had so divided the country into zones. Man, elaborating nature, had given to her compartments an additional complexity. Each of these main north-and-south strip divisions was crossed and walled off artificially into communities at odds. We had to gather them into our hands for offensive action against the Turks. Feisal's opportunities and difficulties lay in these political complications of Syria which we mentally arranged in order, like a social map.

In the very north, furthest from us, the language-boundary followed, not inaptly, the coach road from Alexandretta to Aleppo, until it met the Baghdad Railway, up which it went to the Euphrates valley; but enclaves of Turkish speech lay to the south of this general line in the Turkoman villages north and south of Antioch, and in the Armenians who were sifted in among them.

Otherwise, a main component of the coast population was the community of Ansariya, those disciples of a cult of fertility, sheer pagan, anti-foreign, distrustful of Islam, drawn at moments towards Christians by common persecution. The sect, vital in itself, was clannish in feeling and politics. One Nosairi would not betray another, and would hardly not betray an unbeliever. Their villages lay in patches down the main hills to the Tripoli gap. They spoke Arabic, but had lived there since the beginning of Greek letters in Syria. Usually they stood aside from affairs, and left the Turkish Government alone in hope of reciprocity.

Mixed among the Ansariyeh were colonies of Syrian Christians; and in the bend of the Orontes had been some firm blocks of Armenians, inimical to Turkey. Inland, near Harim were Druses, Arabic in origin; and some Circassians from the Caucasus. These had their hand against all. North-east of them were Kurds, settlers of some generations back, who were marrying Arabs and adopting their politics. They hated native Christians most; and, after them, they hated Turks and Europeans.

Just beyond the Kurds existed a few Yezidis, Arabic-speaking, but in thought affected by the dualism of Iran, and prone to placate the spirit of evil. Christians, Mohammedans, and Jews, peoples who placed revelation before reason, united to spit upon Yezid. Inland of them stood Aleppo, a town of two hundred thousand people, an epitome of all Turkey's races and religions. Eastward of Aleppo, for sixty miles, were settled Arabs whose colour and manner became more and more tribal as they neared the fringe of cultivation where the semi-nomad ended and the Bedawi began.

A section across Syria from sea to desert, a degree further south, began in colonies of Moslem Circassians near the coast. In the new generation they spoke Arabic and were an ingenious race, but quarrelsome, much opposed by their Arab neighbours. Inland of them were Ismailiya. These Persian immigrants had turned Arab in the course of centuries, but revered among themselves one Mohammed, who in the flesh, was the Agha Khan. They believed him to be a great and wonderful sovereign, honouring the English with his friendship. They shunned Moslems, but feebly hid their beastly opinions under a veneer of orthodoxy.

Beyond them were the strange sights of villages of Christian tribal Arabs, under sheikhs. They seemed very sturdy Christians, quite unlike their snivelling brethren in the hills. They lived as the Sunni about them, dressed like them, and were on the best terms with them. East of the Christians lay semi-pastoral Moslem communities; and on the last edge of cultivation, some villages of Ismailia outcasts, in search of the peace men would not grant. Beyond were Beduin.

A third section through Syria, another degree lower, fell between Tripoli and Beyrout. First, near the coast, were Lebanon Christians; for the most part Maronites or Greeks. It was hard to disentangle the politics of the two Churches. Superficially, one should have been French and one Russian; but a part of the population, to earn a living, had been in the United States, and there developed an Anglo-Saxon vein, not the less vigorous, for being spurious. The Greek Church prided itself on being Old Syrian, autochthonous, of an intense localism which might ally it with Turkey rather than endure irretrievable domination by a Roman power.

The adherents of the two sects were at one in unmeasured slander, when they dared, of Mohammedans. Such verbal scorn seemed to salve their consciousness of inbred inferiority. Families of Moslems lived among them, identical in race and habit, except for a less mincing dialect, and less parade of emigration and its results.

On the higher slopes of the hills clustered settlements of Metawala, Shia Mohammedans from Persia generations ago. They were dirty, ignorant, surly and fanatical, refusing to eat or drink with infidels; holding the Sunni as bad as Christians; following only their own priests and notables. Strength of character was their virtue: a rare one in garrulous Syria. Over the hill-crest lay villages of Christian yeomen living in free peace with their Moslem neighbours as though they had never heard the grumbles of Lebanon. East of them were semi-nomad Arab peasantry; and then the open desert.

A fourth section, a degree southward, would have fallen near Acre, where the inhabitants, from the seashore, were first Sunni Arabs, then Druses, then Metawala. On the banks of the Jordan valley lived bitterly-suspicious colonies of Algerian refugees, facing villages of Jews. The Jews were of varied sorts. Some, Hebrew scholars of the traditionalist pattern, had developed a standard and style of living befitting the country: while the later comers, many of whom were German-inspired, had introduced strange manners, and strange crops, and European houses (erected out of charitable funds) into this land of Palestine, which seemed too small and too poor to repay in kind their efforts: but the land tolerated them. Galilee did not show the deep-seated antipathy to its Jewish colonists which was an unlovely feature of the neighbouring Judea.

Across the eastern plains (thick with Arabs) lay a labyrinth of crackled lava, the Leja, where the loose and broken men of Syria had foregathered for unnumbered generations. Their descendants lived there in lawless villages, secure from Turk and Beduin, and worked out their internecine feuds at leisure. South and south-west of them opened the Hauran, a huge fertile land; populous with warlike, self-reliant and prosperous Arab peasantry.

East of them were the Druses, heterodox Moslem followers of a mad and dead Sultan of Egypt. They hated Maronites with a bitter hatred; which, when encouraged by the Government and the fanatics of Damascus, found expression in great periodic killings. None the less the Druses were disliked by the Moslem Arabs and despised them in return. They were at feud with the Beduins, and preserved in their mountain a show of the chivalrous semi-feudalism of Lebanon in the days of their autonomous Emirs.

A fifth section in the latitude of Jerusalem would have begun with Germans and with German Jews, speaking German or German-Yiddish, more intractable even than the Jews of the Roman era, unable to endure contact with others not of their race, some of them farmers, most of them shopkeepers, the most foreign, uncharitable part of the whole population of Syria. Around them glowered their enemies, the sullen Palestine peasants, more stupid than the yeomen of North Syria, material as the Egyptians and bankrupt.

East of them lay the Jordan depth, inhabited by charred serfs; and across it group upon group of self-respecting village Christians who were, after their agricultural co-religionists of the Orontes valley, the least timid examples of our original faith in the country. Among them and east of them were tens of thousands of semi-nomad Arabs, holding the creed of the desert, living on the fear and bounty of their Christian neighbours. Down this debatable land the Ottoman Government had planted a line of Circassian immigrants from the Russian Caucasus. These held their ground only by the sword and the favour of the Turks, to whom they were, of necessity, devoted.

CHAPTER LIX

THE tale of Syria was not ended in this count of odd races and religions. Apart from the country-folk, the six great towns — Jerusalem, Beyrout, Damascus, Homs, Hama, and Aleppo — were entities, each with its character, direction, and opinion. The southernmost, Jerusalem, was a squalid town, which every Semitic religion had made holy. Christians and Mohammedans came there on pilgrimage to the shrines of its past, and some Jews looked to it for the political future of their race. These united forces of the past and the future were so strong that the city almost failed to have a present. Its people, with rare exceptions, were characterless as hotel servants, living on the crowd of visitors passing through. Ideals of Arab nationality were far from them, though familiarity with the differences of Christians at their moment of most poignant sentience had led the classes of Jerusalem to despise us all.

Beyrout was altogether new. It would have been bastard French in feeling as in language but for its Greek harbour and American college. Public opinion in it was that of the Christian merchants, fat men living by exchange; for Beyrout itself produced nothing. The next strongest component was the class of returned emigrants, happy on invested savings in the town of Syria which most resembled that Washington Avenue where they had made good. Beyrout was the door of Syria, a chromatic Levantine screen through which cheap or shop-soiled foreign influences entered: it represented Syria as much as Soho the Home Counties.

Yet Beyrout, because of its geographical position, because of its schools, and the freedom engendered by intercourse with foreigners, had contained before the war a nucleus of people, talking, writing, thinking like the doctrinaire Cyclopædists who paved the way for revolution in France. For their sake, and for its wealth, and its exceeding loud and ready voice, Beyrout was to be reckoned with.

Damascus, Homs, Hama and Aleppo were the four ancient cities in which native Syria took pride. They stretched like a chain along the fertile valleys between the desert and the hills. Because of their setting they turned their backs upon the sea and looked eastward. They were Arab, and knew themselves such. Of them, and of Syria, Damascus was the inevitable head; the seat of lay government; and the religious centre. Its sheikhs were leaders of opinion, more 'Meccan' than others elsewhere. Its fresh and turbulent citizens, always willing to strike, were as extreme in thought and word as in pleasure. The city boasted to move before any part of Syria. The Turks made it military head-quarters, just as certainly as the Arab Opposition, and Oppenheim, and Sheikh Shawish there established themselves. Damascus was a lode-star to which Arabs were naturally drawn: a capital which would not smoothly be subservient to any alien race.

Homs and Hama were twins disliking one another. All in them manufactured things: in Homs often cotton and wool, in Hama brocaded silks. Their industries were prosperous and increasing, their merchants quick to find new outlets, or to meet new tastes, in North Africa, the Balkans, Asia Minor, Arabia, Mesopotamia. They demon-strated the productive ability of Syria, unguided by foreigners, as Beyrout proved its skill in distribution. Yet while the prosperity of Beyrout made it Levantine, the prosperity of Homs and Hama re-inforced their localism; made them more firmly native, more jealously native. Almost it seemed as though familiarity with plant and power taught people that their fathers' manners were best.

Aleppo was a great city in Syria, but not of it, nor of Anatolia, nor of Mesopotamia. There the races, creeds, and tongues of the Ottoman Empire met and knew one another in a spirit of compromise. The clash of characteristics, which made its streets a kaleidoscope, imbued the Aleppine with a lewd thoughtfulness which corrected in him what was blatant in the Damascene. Aleppo had shared in all the civilizations which turned about it: the result seemed to be a lack of zest in its people's belief. Even so, they surpassed the rest of Syria. They fought and traded more; were more fanatical and vicious; and made most beautiful things: but all with a dearth of conviction which rendered barren their multitudinous strength.

It was typical of Aleppo that in it, while yet Mohammedan feeling ran high, more fellowship should rule between Christian and Mohammedan, Armenian, Arab, Turk, Kurd and Jew, than in perhaps any other great city of the Ottoman Empire, and that more friendliness, though little licence, should have been accorded to Europeans. Politically, the town stood aside altogether, save in Arab quarters which, like overgrown half-nomad villages scattered over with priceless mediæval mosques, extended east and south of the mural crown of its great citadel. The intensity of their self-sown patriotism tinged the bulk of the citizens outside them with a colour of local consciousness which was by so much less vivid than the Beyrout-acquired unanimity of Damascus.

All these peoples of Syria were open to us by the master-key of their common Arabic language. Their distinctions were political and religious: morally they differed only in the steady gradation from neurotic sensibility on the sea coast to reserve inland. They were quick-minded; admirers, but not seekers of truth; self-satisfied; not (like the Egyptians) helpless before abstract ideas, but unpractical; and so lazy in mind as to be habitually superficial. Their ideal was ease in which to busy themselves with others' affairs.

From childhood they were lawless, obeying their fathers only from physical fear; and their government later for much the same reason: yet few races had the respect of the upland Syrian for customary law. All of them wanted something new, for with their superficiality and lawlessness went a passion for politics, a science fatally easy for the Syrian to smatter, but too difficult for him to master. They were discontented always with what government they had; such being their intellectual pride; but few of them honestly thought out a working alternative, and fewer still agreed upon one.

In settled Syria there was no indigenous political entity larger than the village, in patriarchal Syria nothing more complex than the clan; and these units were informal and voluntary, devoid of sanction, with heads indicated from the entitled families only by the slow cementing of public opinion. All higher constitution was the imported bureau-system of the Turk, in practice either fairly good or very bad according to the frailty of the human instruments (generally gendarmes) through which, in the last resort, it worked.

The people, even the best-taught, showed a curious blindness to the unimportance of their country, and a misconception of the selfishness of great powers whose normal course was to consider their own interests before those of unarmed races. Some cried aloud for an Arab kingdom. These were usually Moslems; and the Catholic Christians would counter them by demanding European protection of a thelemic order, conferring privileges without obligation. Both proposals were, of course, far from the hearts of the national groups, who cried for autonomy for Syria, having a knowledge of what autonomy was, but not knowing Syria; for in Arabic there was no such name, nor any name for all the country any of them meant. The verbal poverty of their Rome-borrowed name indicated a political disintegration. Between town and town, village and village, family and family, creed and creed, existed intimate jealousies sedulously fostered by the Turks.

Time seemed to have proclaimed the impossibility of autonomous union for such a land. In history, Syria had been a corridor between sea and desert, joining Africa to Asia, Arabia to Europe. It had been a prize-ring, a vassal, of Anatolia, of Greece, of Rome, of Egypt, of Arabia, of Persia, of Mesopotamia. When given a momentary independence by the weakness of neighbours it had fiercely resolved into discordant northern, southern, eastern and western 'kingdoms' with the area at best of Yorkshire, at worst of Rutland; for if Syria was by nature a vassal country, it was also by habit a country of tireless agitation and incessant revolt.

The master-key of opinion lay in the common language: where also, lay the key of imagination. Moslems whose mother tongue was Arabic looked upon themselves for that reason as a chosen people. Their heritage of the Koran and classical literature held the Arabic-speaking peoples together. Patriotism, ordinarily of soil or race, was warped to a language.

A second buttress of a polity of Arab motive was the dim glory of the early Khalifate, whose memory endured among the people through centuries of Turkish misgovernment. The accident that these traditions savoured rather of the Arabian Nights than of sheer history maintained the Arab rank and file in their conviction that their past was more splendid than the present of the Ottoman Turk.

Yet we knew that these were dreams. Arab Government in Syria though buttressed on Arabic prejudices, would be as much 'imposed' as the Turkish Government, or a foreign protectorate, or the historic Caliphate. Syria remained a vividly coloured racial and religious mosaic. Any wide attempt after unity would make a patched and parcelled thing, ungrateful to a people whose instincts ever returned towards parochial home rule.

Our excuse for over-running expediency was War. Syria, ripe for spasmodic local revolt, might be seethed up into insurrection, if a new factor, offering to realize that centripetal nationalism of the Beyrout Cyclopædists, arose to restrain the jarring sects and classes. Novel the factor must be, to avoid raising a jealousy of itself: not foreign, since the conceit of Syria forbade.

Within our sight the only independent factor with acceptable groundwork and fighting adherents was a Sunni prince, like Feisal, pretending to revive the glories of Ommayad or Ayubid. He might momentarily combine the inland men until success came with its need to transfer their debauched enthusiasm to the service of ordered government. Then would come reaction; but only after victory; and for victory everything material and moral might be pawned.

There remained the technique and direction of the new revolts: but the direction a blind man could see. The critical centre of Syria in all ages had been the Yarmuk Valley, Hauran, and Deraa. When Hauran joined us our campaign would be well ended. The process should be to set up another ladder of tribes, comparable to that from Wejh to Akaba: only this time our ladder would be made of steps of Howeitat, Beni Sakhr, Sherarat, Rualla, and Serahin, to raise us three hundred miles to Azrak, the oasis nearest Hauran and Jebel Druse.

In character our operations of development for the final stroke should be like naval war, in mobility, ubiquity, independence of bases and communications, ignoring of ground features, of strategic areas, of fixed directions, of fixed points. 'He who commands the sea is at great liberty, and may take as much or as little of the war as he will.' And we commanded the desert. Camel raiding parties, self-contained like ships, might cruise confidently along the enemy's cultivation-frontier, sure of an unhindered retreat into their desert-element which the Turks could not explore.

Discrimination of what point of the enemy organism to disarrange would come to us with war practice. Our tactics should be tip and run: not pushes, but strokes. We should never try to improve an advantage. We should use the smallest force in the quickest time at the farthest place.

The necessary speed and range for distant war we would attain through the frugality of the desert men, and their efficiency on camels. The camel, that intricate, prodigious piece of nature, in expert hands yielded a remarkable return. On them we were independent of supply for six weeks, if each man had a half-bag of flour, forty-five pounds in weight, slung on his riding-saddle.

Of water we would not want to carry more than a pint each. The camels must drink, and there was no gain in making ourselves richer than our mounts. Some of us never drank between wells, but those were hardy men: most drank fully at each well, and carried a drink for an intermediate dry day. In summer the camels would do about two hundred and fifty miles after a watering; a three days' vigorous march. An easy stage was fifty miles: eighty was good: in an emergency we might do one hundred and ten miles in the twenty-four hours: twice the Ghazala, our greatest camel, did one hundred and forty-three alone with me. Wells were seldom a hundred miles apart, so the pint reserve was latitude enough.

Our six weeks' food gave us capacity for a thousand miles out and home. The endurance of our camels made it possible for us (for me, the camel-novice in the army, 'painful' would be the fitter word) to ride fifteen hundred miles in thirty days, without fear of starvation; because, even if we exceeded in time, each of us sat on two hundred pounds of potential meat, and the man made camel-less could double-bank another, riding two-up, in emergency.

The equipment of the raiding parties should aim at simplicity; with, nevertheless, a technical superiority over the Turks in the critical department. I sent to Egypt demands for great quantities of light automatic guns, Hotchkiss or Lewis, to be used as snipers' tools. The men we trained to them were kept deliberately ignorant of the mechanism, not to waste speed in action upon efforts at repair. Ours were battles of minutes, fought at eighteen miles an hour. If a gun jammed, the gunner must throw it aside and go in with his rifle.

Another distinguishing feature might be high explosives. We evolved special dynamite methods, and by the end of the war could demolish any quantity of track and bridges with economy and safety. Allenby was generous with explosive. It was only guns we never got until the last month — and the pity of it! In manœuvre war one long-range gun outweighed ninety-nine short.

The distribution of the raiding parties was unorthodox. We could not mix or combine tribes, because of their distrusts: nor could we use one in the territory of another. In compensation we aimed at the widest dissipation of force; and we added fluidity to speed by using one district on Monday, another on Tuesday, a third on Wednesday. Thus natural mobility was reinforced. In pursuit, our ranks refilled with fresh men at each new tribe, and maintained the pristine energy. In a real sense maximum disorder was our equilibrium.

The internal economy of our raiding parties achieved irregularity and extreme articulation. Our circumstances were not twice similar, so no system could fit them twice: and our diversity threw the enemy intelligence off the track. By identical battalions and divisions information built itself up, until a corps could be inferred on corpses from three companies. Our strengths depended upon whim.

We were serving a common ideal, without tribal emulation, and so could not hope for *esprit de corps*. Ordinary soldiers were made a caste either by great rewards in pay, dress and privilege: or by being cut off from life by contempt. We could not so knit man to man, for our tribesmen were in arms willingly. Many armies had been voluntarily enlisted: few served voluntarily. Any of our Arabs could go home without penalty whenever the conviction failed him: the only contract was honour.

Consequently we had no discipline in the sense in which it was restrictive, submergent of individuality, the Lowest Common De-nominator of men. In peace-armies discipline meant the hunt, not of an average but of an absolute; the hundred per cent standard in which the ninety-nine were played down to the level of the weakest man on parade. The aim was to render the unit a unit, the man a type; in order that their effort might be calculable, and the collective output even in grain and bulk. The deeper the discipline, the lower was the individual excellence; also the more sure the performance.

By this substitution of a sure job for a possible masterpiece, military science made a deliberate sacrifice of capacity in order to reduce the uncertain element, the bionomic factor, in enlisted humanity. Discipline's necessary accompaniment was compound or social war — that form in which the fighting man was the product of the multiplied exertions of a long hierarchy, from workshop to supply unit, which kept him active in the field.

The Arab war should react against this, and be simple and individual. Every enrolled man should serve in the line of battle and be self-contained there. The efficiency of our forces was the personal efficiency of the single man. It seemed to me that, in our articulated war, the sum yielded by single men would at least equal the product of a compound system of the same strength.

In practice we should not employ in the firing line the great numbers which a simple system put theoretically at our disposal, lest our attack (as contrasted with our threat) become too extended. The moral strain of isolated fighting made 'simple' war very hard upon the soldier, exacting from him special initiative, endurance, enthusiasm. Irregular war was far more intellectual than a bayonet charge, far more exhausting than service in the comfortable imitative obedience of an ordered army. Guerillas must be allowed liberal work room: in irregular war, of two men together, one was being wasted. Our ideal should be to make our battle a series of single combats, our ranks a happy alliance of agile commanders-in-chief.

CHAPTER LX

VESSELS steamed up the Gulf of Akaba. Feisal landed, and with him Jaafar, his staff, and Joyce, the fairy godmother. There came the armoured cars, Goslett, Egyptian labourers and thousands of troops. To repair the six weeks' peace, Falkenhayn had been down to advise the Turks, and his fine intelligence made them worthier our opposition. Maan was a special command, under Behjet, the old G.O.C. Sinai. He had six thousand infantry, a regiment of cavalry and mounted infantry, and had entrenched Maan till it was impregnable according to the standard of manœuvre war. A flight of aeroplanes operated daily thence. Great supply dumps had been collected.

By now the Turkish preparations were complete; they began to move, disclosing that their objective was Guweira, the best road for Akaba. Two thousand infantry pushed out to Aba el Lissan, and fortified it. Cavalry kept the outskirts, to contain a possible Arab counter-stroke from the Wadi Musa side.

This nervousness was our cue. We would play with them and provoke them to go for us in Wadi Musa, where the natural obstacles were so tremendous that the human defending factor might behave as badly as it liked, and yet hold the place against attack.

To bait the hook, the men of neighbouring Delagha were set busy. The Turks, full of spirit, put in a counter-stroke, and suffered sharply. We rubbed into the peasantry of Wadi Musa the rich booty now enjoyed by their rivals of Delagha. Maulud, the old war-horse, went up with his mule-mounted regiment, and quartered himself among the famous ruins of Petra. The encouraged Liathena, under their one-eyed sheikh, Khalil, began to foray out across the plateau, and to snap up by twos and threes Turkish riding or transport animals, together with the rifles of their occasional guards. This went on for weeks, while the irritated Turks grew hotter and hotter.

We could also prick the Turks into discomfort by asking General Salmond for his promised long-distance air raid on Maan. As it was difficult, Salmond had chosen Stent, with other tried pilots of Rabegh or Wejh, and told them to do their best. They had experience of forced landing on desert surfaces and could pick out an unknown destination across unmapped hills: Stent spoke Arabic perfectly. The flight had to be air-contained, but its commander was full of resource and display, like other bundles of nerves, who, to punish themselves, did outrageous things. On this occasion he ordered low flying, to make sure the aim; and profited by reaching Maan, and dropping thirty-two bombs in and about the unprepared station. Two bombs into the barracks killed thirty-five men and wounded fifty. Eight struck the engine-shed, heavily damaging the plant and stock. A bomb in the General's kitchen finished his cook and his breakfast. Four fell on the aerodrome. Despite the shrapnel our pilots and engines returned safely to their temporary landing ground at Kuntilla above Akaba.

That afternoon they patched the machines, and after dark slept under their wings. In the following dawn they were off once more, three of them this time, to Aba el Lissan, where the sight of the great camp had made Stent's mouth water. They bombed the horse lines and stampeded the animals, visited the tents and scattered the Turks. As on the day before, they flew low and were much hit, but not fatally. Long before noon they were back in Kuntilla.

Stent looked over the remaining petrol and bombs, and decided they were enough for one more effort. So he gave directions to everyone to look for the battery which had troubled them in the morning. They started in the midday heat. Their loads were so heavy they could get no height, and therefore came blundering over the crest behind Aba el Lissan, and down the valley at about three hundred feet. The Turks, always somnolent at noon, were taken completely by surprise. Thirty bombs were dropped: one silenced the battery, the others killed dozens of men and animals. Then the lightened machines soared up and home to El Arish. The Arabs rejoiced: the Turks were seriously alarmed. Behjet Pasha set his men to digging shelters, and when his aeroplanes had been repaired, he disposed them innocuously about the plateau for camp defence.

By air we had perturbed the Turks: by irritative raids we were luring them towards a wrong objective. Our third resource to ruin their offensive was to hinder the railway, whose need would make them split up the striking force on defensive duties. Accordingly we arranged many demolitions for mid-September.

I decided also to revive the old idea of mining a train. Something more vigorous and certain than automatic mines was indicated, and I had imagined a direct firing, by electricity, of a charge under the locomotive. The British sappers encouraged me to try, especially General Wright, the chief engineer in Egypt, whose experience took a sporting interest in my irregularities. He sent me the recommended tools: an exploder and some insulated cable. With them I went on board H.M.S. *Humber*, our new guard-ship, and introduced myself to Captain Snagge, in command.

Snagge was fortunate in his ship, which had been built for Brazil, and was much more comfortably furnished than British monitors; and we were doubly fortunate in him and in this, for he was the spirit of hospitality. His inquiring nature took interest in the shore, and saw the comic side even of our petty disasters. To tell him the story of a failure was to laugh at it, and always for a good story he gave me a hot bath, and tea with civilized trappings, free from every suspicion of blown sand. His kindness and help served us in lieu of visits to Egypt for repairs, and enabled us to hammer on against the Turks through month after month of feckless disappointment.

The exploder was in a formidable locked white box, very heavy. We split it open, found a ratchet handle, and pushed it down without harming the ship. The wire was heavy rubber-insulated cable. We cut it in half, fastened the ends to screw terminals on the box, and transmitted shocks to one another convincingly. It worked.

I fetched detonators. We stuffed the free ends of the cable into one and pumped the handle: nothing followed. We tried again and again ineffectually, grieving over it. At last Snagge rang his bell for the gunner warrant officer who knew all about circuits. He suggested special electric detonators. The ship carried six, and gave me three of them. We joined one up with our box, and when the handle was crashed down it popped off beautifully. So I felt that I knew all about it and turned to arrange the details of the raid.

Of targets, the most promising and easiest-reached seemed Mudowwara, a water station eighty miles south of Maan. A smashed train there would embarrass the enemy. For men, I would have the tried Howeitat; and, at the same time, the expedition would test the three Haurani peasants whom I had added to my personal followers. In view of the new importance of the Hauran, there was need for us to learn its dialect, the construction and jealousies of its clan-framework, and its names and roads. These three fellows, Rahail, Assaf and Hemeid, would teach me their home-affairs imperceptibly, as we rode on business, chatting.

To make sure of the arrested train required guns and machine-guns. For the first, why not trench-mortars? For the second, Lewis guns? Accordingly, Egypt chose two forceful sergeant-instructors from the Army School at Zeitun, to teach squads of Arabs in Akaba how to use such things. Snagge gave them quarters in his ship, since we had, as yet, no convenient English camp ashore.

Their names may have been Yells and Brooke, but became Lewis and Stokes after the jealously-loved tools. Lewis was an Australian, long, thin and sinuous, his supple body lounging in unmilitary curves. His hard face, arched eyebrows, and predatory nose set off the peculiarly Australian air of reckless willingness and capacity to do something very soon. Stokes was a stocky English yeoman, workmanlike and silent; always watching for an order to obey.

Lewis, full of suggestion, emerged bursting with delight at what had been well done whenever a thing happened. Stokes never offered opinion until after action, when he would stir his cap reflectively, and painstakingly recount the mistakes he must next time avoid. Both were admirable men. In a month, without common language or interpreter, they got on terms with their classes and taught them their weapons with reasonable precision. More was not required: for an empirical habit appeared to agree with the spirit of our haphazard raids better than complete scientific knowledge.

As we worked at the organization of the raid, our appetites rose. Mudowwara station sounded vulnerable. Three hundred men might rush it suddenly. That would be an achievement, for its deep well was the only one in the dry sector below Maan. Without its water, the train service across the gap would become uneconomic in load.